WEST ACADEMIC PUBL
EMERITUS ADVISORY ~~BOARD~~

JESSE H. CHOPER
Professor of Law and Dean Emeritus
University of California, Berkeley

YALE KAMISAR
Professor of Law Emeritus, University of San Diego
Professor of Law Emeritus, University of Michigan

MARY KAY KANE
Professor of Law, Chancellor and Dean Emeritus
University of California, Hastings College of the Law

LARRY D. KRAMER
President, William and Flora Hewlett Foundation

JAMES J. WHITE
Robert A. Sullivan Emeritus Professor of Law
University of Michigan

WEST ACADEMIC PUBLISHING'S
LAW SCHOOL ADVISORY BOARD

JOSHUA DRESSLER
Distinguished University Professor Emeritus
Michael E. Moritz College of Law, The Ohio State University

MEREDITH J. DUNCAN
Professor of Law
University of Houston Law Center

RENÉE McDONALD HUTCHINS
Dean and Joseph L. Rauh, Jr. Chair of Public Interest Law
University of the District of Columbia David A. Clarke School of Law

RENEE KNAKE JEFFERSON
Joanne and Larry Doherty Chair in Legal Ethics &
Professor of Law, University of Houston Law Center

ORIN S. KERR
Professor of Law
University of California, Berkeley

JONATHAN R. MACEY
Professor of Law,
Yale Law School

DEBORAH JONES MERRITT
Distinguished University Professor,
John Deaver Drinko/Baker & Hostetler Chair in Law
Michael E. Moritz College of Law, The Ohio State University

ARTHUR R. MILLER
University Professor, New York University
Formerly Bruce Bromley Professor of Law, Harvard University

GRANT S. NELSON
Professor of Law Emeritus, Pepperdine University
Professor of Law Emeritus, University of California, Los Angeles

A. BENJAMIN SPENCER
Dean & Chancellor Professor of Law
William & Mary Law School

CIVIL PROCEDURE

AN ACTIVE LEARNING APPROACH

Revised First Edition

■ ■ ■

Rory D. Bahadur

James R. Ahrens Chair in Tort Law
Washburn University School of Law

AMERICAN CASEBOOK SERIES®

The publisher is not engaged in rendering legal or other professional advice, and this publication is not a substitute for the advice of an attorney. If you require legal or other expert advice, you should seek the services of a competent attorney or other professional.

American Casebook Series is a trademark registered in the U.S. Patent and Trademark Office.

© 2021 LEG, Inc. d/b/a West Academic
© 2021 Revised First Edition LEG, Inc. d/b/a West Academic
    444 Cedar Street, Suite 700
    St. Paul, MN 55101
    1-877-888-1330

West, West Academic Publishing, and West Academic are trademarks of West Publishing Corporation, used under license.

Printed in the United States of America

ISBN: 978-1-63659-376-0

PREFACE

This casebook is structured and meant to be used differently than most casebooks. Every topic contains reading material exactly like most casebooks; however, all the reading material is followed by directed reading questions on the readings.

As far as you are concerned the major difference in the way this book should be used is as follows. You should not brief any of the cases. Instead you should read the cases etc. with the aim of the reading being to answer the directed reading questions which follow the reading material, and you should answer those questions BEFORE coming to class.

You should begin class with a typed/written answer to every directed reading question assigned for that class. You will not be able to fully answer all the questions, but you should type or write the answer that you attempted. It makes no difference if the answer is correct or not before class, but you must answer each question for the assigned reading before coming to class.

The questions are carefully designed to help you focus on the important elements of the reading and to make you more prepared for class than you normally would be, absent the directed reading approach. Your teacher will be teaching the material as if you have read the material and answered the assigned questions.

ACKNOWLEDGMENTS

When she was 42 years old my Jamaican grandmother was left without an income source and with 7 children to support. That woman got on an airplane to the United States and worked illegally for years as a maid and a geriatric nurse and sent money back to Jamaica to take care of her children. She became an American citizen pursuant to Ronald Reagan's immigration reform. Every one of her children became incredibly successful and kind people. One of those children was my mother.

My mother while at college in Jamaica, met a Trinidadian man of primarily Indian descent whose grandparents and great grandparents were indentured laborers brought to Trinidad to provide labor in the sugar cane fields after the end of slavery in the British Caribbean. I grew up in the country in Trinidad, surrounded by sugar cane fields and have vivid memories of living in a house with aunts and uncles and grandparents who were all indescribably important and influential.

Despite the often lack of running water it was truly the happiest nurturing environment anyone can imagine. To those Jamaican and Trinidadian extended families, I say thank you. You all instilled a work ethic in me and were/are an example that makes me ashamed to not work hard to this day. In fact, when I began law school it was one of my Jamaican aunts who opened her South Florida home to me while I attempted to get settled in a new city.

Two lessons from my childhood specifically are responsible for my love of teaching and the drive to constantly try to improve which led to this book. The first is my father repeatedly saying, "Don't do anything if you aren't going to try your hardest at it." The second is my mother, who was initially a high school chemistry teacher before becoming one of the most influential high school administrators in the Caribbean. If she felt the allotted time at school was inadequate, there were many Saturdays when we would wake up to find our living room occupied by her students, who she taught on countless weekends and afternoons. She never charged students for this extra teaching. She simply felt it was her responsibility to ensure they learned no matter when or where that learning occurred.

I also need to thank two of my colleagues at Washburn: James Concannon, who recently retired and who truly is a civil procedure encyclopedia; and Alex Glashausser, who is the smartest human being I know. Both Jim and Alex had been teaching civil procedure when I arrived at Washburn as a new civil procedure professor. They both went out of their way to provide a safe space for me to engage with them and learn the material even when it was patent I had no idea what I was doing. And they never ever felt the need to be hierarchical in our relationship, but always treated me as an equal, and by the time Jim retired, I would say we were an ego-free trio of civ pro dudes who truly listened to each other. When I discussed the proposed structure of the book with them, they both encouraged me to absolutely proceed.

This book is dedicated to all the above.

ACKNOWLEDGMENTS

SUMMARY OF CONTENTS

———

TABLE OF CONTENTS

TABLE OF CASES

The principal cases are in bold type.

TABLE OF U.S.C. SECTIONS

TABLE OF FEDERAL RULES OF CIVIL PROCEDURE

CIVIL PROCEDURE
AN ACTIVE LEARNING APPROACH

Revised First Edition

CHAPTER 1

THE ORIGIN AND IMPACT OF THE RULES

■ ■ ■

SIBBACH V. WILSON & CO., INC. (1941)

Supreme Court of the United States
312 U.S. 1

MR. JUSTICE ROBERTS delivered the opinion of the Court.

This case calls for decision as to the validity of Rules 35 and 37 of the Rules of Civil Procedure for District Courts of the United States.

In an action brought by the petitioner in the District Court for Northern Illinois to recover damages for bodily injuries, inflicted in Indiana, respondent answered denying the allegations of the complaint, and moved for an order requiring the petitioner to submit to a physical examination by one or more physicians appointed by the court to determine the nature and extent of her injuries. The court ordered that the petitioner submit to such an examination by a physician so appointed.

Compliance having been refused, the respondent obtained an order to show cause why the petitioner should not be punished for contempt. In response the petitioner challenged the authority of the court to order her to submit to the examination, asserting that the order was void. It appeared that the courts of Indiana, the state where the cause of action arose, hold such an order proper, whereas the courts of Illinois, the state in which the trial court sat, hold that such an order cannot be made.

The court adjudged the petitioner guilty of contempt, and directed that she be committed until she should obey the order for examination or otherwise should be legally discharged from custody. The petitioner appealed.

The Circuit Court of Appeals decided that Rule 35, which authorizes an order for a physical examination in such a case, is valid, and affirmed the judgment. The writ of certiorari was granted because of the importance of the question involved.

The Rules of Civil Procedure were promulgated under the authority of the Act of June 19, 1934, which is:

'Be it enacted * * * That the Supreme Court of the United States shall have the power to prescribe, by general rules, for the district courts of the United States and for the courts of the District of Columbia, the forms of process, writs, pleadings, and motions, and the practice and procedure in civil actions at law. Said rules shall neither abridge, enlarge, nor modify the substantive rights of any litigant. They shall take effect six months after their promulgation, and thereafter all laws in conflict therewith shall be of no further force or effect.

* * *

The text of the relevant portions of Rules 35 and 37 is:

'Rule 35. Physical And Mental Examination Of Persons

'(a) Order for Examination. In an action in which the mental or physical condition of a party is in controversy, the court in which the action is pending may order him to submit to a physical or mental examination by a physician. The order may be made only on motion for good cause shown and upon notice to the party to be examined and to all other parties and shall specify the time, place, manner, conditions, and scope of the examination and the person or persons by whom it is to be made.'

'Rule 37. Refusal To Make Discovery: Consequences

'(a) Refusal to Answer. * * *

'(b) Failure to Comply With Order.

'(1) Contempt. If a party or other witness refuses to be sworn or refuses to answer any question after being directed to do so by the court in the district in which the deposition is being taken, the refusal may be considered a contempt of that court.

'(2) Other Consequences. If any party * * * refuses to obey * * * an order made under Rule 35 requiring him to submit to a physical or mental examination, the court may make such orders in regard to the refusal as are just, and among others the following:

'(i) An order that * * * the physical or mental condition of the party * * * shall be taken to be established for the purposes of the action in accordance with the claim of the party obtaining the order;

'(ii) An order * * * prohibiting (the disobedient party) * * * from introducing evidence of physical or mental condition;

'(iii) An order striking out pleadings or parts thereof, or staying further proceedings until the order is obeyed, or dismissing the action or proceeding or any part thereof, or rendering a judgment by default against the disobedient party;

'(iv) An order striking out pleadings or orders or in addition thereto, an order directing the arrest of any party or agent of a party for disobeying any of such orders except an order to submit to a physical or mental examination.'

The contention of the petitioner, in final analysis, is that Rules 35 and 37 are not within the mandate of Congress to this court. This is the limit of permissible debate, since argument touching the broader questions of Congressional power and of the obligation of federal courts to apply the substantive law of a state is foreclosed.

Congress has undoubted power to regulate the practice and procedure of federal courts, and may exercise that power by delegating to this or other federal courts authority to make rules not inconsistent with the statutes or Constitution of the United States; but it has never essayed to declare the substantive state law, or to abolish or nullify a right recognized by the substantive law of the state where the cause of action arose, save where a right or duty is imposed in a field committed to Congress by the

Constitution. On the contrary it has enacted that the state law shall be the rule of decision in the federal courts.

Hence we conclude that the Act of June 19, 1934, was purposely restricted in its operation to matters of pleading and court practice and procedure. Its . . . provisos or caveats emphasize this restriction. [For example] the court shall not 'abridge, enlarge, nor modify the substantive rights', in the guise of regulating procedure.

* * *

Whatever may be said as to the effect of the Conformity Act while it remained in force, the rules, if they are within the authority granted by Congress, repeal that statute, and the District Court was not bound to follow the Illinois practice respecting an order for physical examination. On the other hand if the right to be exempt from such an order is one of substantive law, the Rules of Decision Act* required the District Court, though sitting in Illinois, to apply the law of Indiana, the state where the cause of action arose, and to order the examination. To avoid this dilemma the petitioner admits, and, we think, correctly, that Rules 35 and 37 are rules of procedure. She insists, nevertheless, that by the prohibition against abridging substantive rights, Congress has banned the rules here challenged. In order to reach this result she translates 'substantive' into 'important' or 'substantial' rights. And she urges that if a rule affects such a right, albeit the rule is one of procedure merely, its prescription is not within the statutory grant of power embodied in the Act of June 19, 1934. She contends that our decisions and recognized principles require us so to hold.

* * *

But if Rule 35 is within the authority granted, the federal legislature sanctioned it as controlling all district courts.

* * *

Finally, it is urged that Rules 35 and 37 work a major change of policy and that this was not intended by Congress. Apart from the fact already stated, that the policy of the states in this respect has not been uniform, it is to be noted that the authorization of a comprehensive system of court rules was a departure in policy, and that the new policy envisaged in the enabling act of 1934 was that the whole field of court procedure be regulated in the interest of speedy, fair and exact determination of the truth. The challenged rules comport with this policy. Moreover, in accordance with the Act, the rules were submitted to the Congress so that that body might examine them and veto their going into effect if contrary to the policy of the legislature.

The value of the reservation of the power to examine proposed rules, laws and regulations before they become effective is well understood by Congress. It is frequently, as here, employed to make sure that the action under the delegation squares with the Congressional purpose. Evidently the Congress felt the rule was within the ambit of the statute as no effort was made to eliminate it from the proposed body of rules, although this specific rule was attacked and defended before the committees of the two Houses . . . . That no adverse action was taken by Congress indicates, at least, that no

---

*   Now codified at 28 U.S.C. § 1652.

transgression of legislative policy was found. We conclude that the rules under attack are within the authority granted.

The District Court treated the refusal to comply with its order as a contempt and committed the petitioner therefor. Neither in the Circuit Court of Appeals nor here was this action assigned as error. We think, however, that in the light of the provisions of Rule 37 it was plain error of such a fundamental nature that we should notice it. Section (b)(2)(A)(iv) of Rule 37 exempts from punishment as for contempt the refusal to obey an order that a party submit to a physical or mental examination. The District Court was in error in going counter to this express exemption. The remedies available under the rule in such a case are those enumerated in Section (b)(2)(A)(i)–(ii) and (iii). For this error we reverse the judgment and remand the cause to the District Court for further proceedings in conformity to this opinion.

Reversed and remanded.

MR. JUSTICE FRANKFURTER (dissenting opinion omitted).

U.S. CONST. ARTICLE III § 1

The judicial power of the United States, shall be vested in one Supreme Court, and in such inferior courts as the Congress may from time to time ordain and establish . . . .

28 U.S.C. § 1331

The district courts shall have original jurisdiction of all civil actions arising under the Constitution, laws, or treaties of the United States.

28 U.S.C. § 1332

(a) The district courts shall have original jurisdiction of all civil actions where the matter in controversy exceeds the sum or value of $75,000, exclusive of interest and costs, and is between—

(1) citizens of different States; . . . .

28 U.S.C. § 2071

Rule-making power generally

(a) The Supreme Court and all courts established by Act of Congress may from time to time prescribe rules for the conduct of their business. Such rules shall be consistent with Acts of Congress and rules of practice and procedure prescribed under section 2072 of this title.

(b) Any rule prescribed by a court, other than the Supreme Court, under subsection (a) shall be prescribed only after giving appropriate public notice and an opportunity for comment. Such rule shall take effect upon the date specified by the prescribing court and shall have such effect on pending proceedings as the prescribing court may order.

(c)(1) A rule of a district court prescribed under subsection (a) shall remain in effect unless modified or abrogated by the judicial council of the relevant circuit.

(2) Any other rule prescribed by a court other than the Supreme Court under subsection (a) shall remain in effect unless modified or abrogated by the Judicial Conference.

(d) Copies of rules prescribed under subsection (a) by a district court shall be furnished to the judicial council, and copies of all rules prescribed by a court other than the Supreme Court under subsection (a) shall be furnished to the Director of the Administrative Office of the United States Courts and made available to the public.

(e) If the prescribing court determines that there is an immediate need for a rule, such court may proceed under this section without public notice and opportunity for comment, but such court shall promptly thereafter afford such notice and opportunity for comment.

(f) No rule may be prescribed by a district court other than under this section.

28 U.S.C. § 2072

Rules of procedure and evidence; power to prescribe

(a) The Supreme Court shall have the power to prescribe general rules of practice and procedure and rules of evidence for cases in the United States district courts (including proceedings before magistrate judges thereof) and courts of appeals.

(b) Such rules shall not abridge, enlarge or modify any substantive right. All laws in conflict with such rules shall be of no further force or effect after such rules have taken effect.

(c) Such rules may define when a ruling of a district court is final for the purposes of appeal under section 1291 of this title.

28 U.S.C. § 2073

Rules of Procedure and Evidence; method of prescribing

(a)(1) The Judicial Conference shall prescribe and publish the procedures for the consideration of proposed rules under this section.

(2) The Judicial Conference may authorize the appointment of committees to assist the Conference by recommending rules to be prescribed under sections 2072 and 2075 of this title. Each such committee shall consist of members of the bench and the professional bar, and trial and appellate judges.

(b) The Judicial Conference shall authorize the appointment of a standing committee on rules of practice, procedure, and evidence under subsection (a) of this section. Such standing committee shall review each recommendation of any other committees so appointed and recommend to the Judicial Conference rules of practice, procedure, and evidence and such changes in rules proposed by a committee appointed under subsection (a)(2) of this section as may be necessary to maintain consistency and otherwise promote the interest of justice.

(c)(1) Each meeting for the transaction of business under this chapter by any committee appointed under this section shall be open to the public, except when the committee so meeting, in open session and with a majority present, determines that it is in the public interest that all or part of the remainder of the meeting on that day shall be closed to the public, and states the reason for so closing the meeting. Minutes of each meeting for the transaction of business under this chapter shall be maintained by the committee and made available to the public, except that any portion of such minutes, relating to a closed meeting and made available to the public, may contain such deletions as may be necessary to avoid frustrating the purposes of closing the meeting.

(2) Any meeting for the transaction of business under this chapter, by a committee appointed under this section, shall be preceded by sufficient notice to enable all interested persons to attend.

(d) In making a recommendation under this section or under section 2072 or 2075, the body making that recommendation shall provide a proposed rule, an explanatory note on the rule, and a written report explaining the body's action, including any minority or other separate views.

(e) Failure to comply with this section does not invalidate a rule prescribed under section 2072 or 2075 of this title.

28 U.S.C. § 2074

Rules of procedure and evidence; submission to Congress; effective date

(a) The Supreme Court shall transmit to the Congress not later than May 1 of the year in which a rule prescribed under section 2072 is to become effective a copy of the proposed rule. Such rule shall take effect no earlier than December 1 of the year in which such rule is so transmitted unless otherwise provided by law. The Supreme Court may fix the extent such rule shall apply to proceedings then pending, except that the Supreme Court shall not require the application of such rule to further proceedings then pending to the extent that, in the opinion of the court in which such proceedings are pending, the application of such rule in such proceedings would not be feasible or would work injustice, in which event the former rule applies.

(b) Any such rule creating, abolishing, or modifying an evidentiary privilege shall have no force or effect unless approved by Act of Congress.

28 U.S.C. § 1652

The laws of the several states, except where the Constitution or treaties of the United States or Acts of Congress otherwise require or provide, shall be regarded as rules of decision in civil actions in the courts of the United States, in cases where they apply.

DIRECTED READING QUESTIONS

1. What generally do 28 U.S.C. §§ 2071–2074 permit the courts to do?

2. What are the federal district courts?

3. If you examine 28 U.S.C. § 2071 carefully, it uses the word "may," which is generally interpreted as giving permission. 28 U.S.C. § 2071 is a federal statute, and federal statutes are laws passed by the legislative branch or Congress. What in Article III might indicate that it is necessary for Congress to give the Supreme Court permission to create rules for the District Courts, even though the judiciary is a separate branch of government?

4. Describe the parallels between 28 U.S.C. §§ 2071–2074 and "the Act of June 19, 1934," referred to in the *Sibbach* case.

5. 28 U.S.C. §§ 1331 and 1332 are also federal statutes enacted by Congress which describe the categories of actions a federal district court may entertain. Do you understand now why Congress and not the Supreme Court determines what actions a federal district court may entertain?

6. Do you think the *Sibbach* case was a "1331 or 1332" case and why?

7. The Federal Rules of Civil Procedure became effective on September 16, 1938, and the *Sibbach* case was decided only three years after that date. In order to comprehend the impact of the rules and what the Court was struggling with, answer the following questions:

   a. In what state did the accident that is the subject of the suit occur?

   b. In what state was the suit filed?

   c. What substantive law would apply to the *Sibbach* case if the Federal Rules of Civil Procedure did not exist? Why would that particular substantive law apply?

   d. Did the Federal Rules of Civil Procedure render a change in the applicable substantive law? Could they?

   e. What procedural law would apply to the *Sibbach* case if the Federal Rules of Civil Procedure did not exist, and why would that particular procedural law apply?

   f. Did the Federal Rules of Civil Procedure render a change in the applicable procedural law?

8. Why, according to the *Sibbach* case, might lawyers be supportive of the Federal Rules of Civil Procedure?

9. The Plaintiff in *Sibbach* faces a dilemma because she will have to submit to a medical exam if she argues that the issue of whether a medical exam is permitted is substantive. But she will also have to submit to a medical exam if she argues that the issue of whether a medical exam is permitted is procedural. Explain the plaintiff's dilemma.

10. What does the plaintiff, therefore, try to argue about the impropriety of a medical exam?

11. The plaintiff successfully argues that the Federal Rules of Civil Procedure do not permit her to be held in contempt for refusing to submit to a Rule 35 medical examination. In support of this argument, she cites to FRCP 37(b)(2)(A)(vi). Turn to FRCP 37 in your rule books and find Rule 37(b)(2)(A)(vi). Why the discrepancy?

12. Please describe the "Rules Enabling" process provided for in 28 U.S.C. §§ 2071–2074.

CHAPTER 2

RULE READING TECHNIQUE AND ROADMAP OF A CIVIL ACTION

■ ■ ■

I.   RULE READING TECHNIQUE

The *Sibbach* case introduced us to Rules 35 and 37, or the "Physical and Mental Examinations" rule. Here are a few questions based on Rules 35 and 37. In order to answer them, you will need to read Rules 35 and 37 carefully.

DIRECTED READING QUESTIONS

In a federal district court sitting in diversity, Tracie sues Pat in negligence to recover bodily injuries caused when the car Pat was driving hit Tracie as Tracie was crossing the street. Tracie is claiming injuries to her legs and back and nothing else.

1.   Does Rule 35 allow an examination of Tracie's eyes?

2.   Tracie's friend Mac is expected to testify as an eye witness to the events leading to Tracie's injury. Pat has heard that Mac has been diagnosed and is currently receiving treatment for compulsive lying disorder. Does Rule 35 permit the court to order Mac to a mental examination as part of the discovery process?

3.   Assume Tracie's legs and back are examined by a doctor of Pat's choosing, pursuant to a Rule 35 order from the court.

    a.   Does Pat have to deliver to Tracie a copy of the examiner's report if Tracie requests a copy of it?

    b.   Assume that Pat delivers a copy of the examiner's report pursuant to Tracie's request. Is Pat entitled to reports of examinations of the same condition undertaken by other examiners which Tracie has in her possession after Pat requests them?

    c.   Assume that Pat furnished Tracie with a copy of the report of the Rule 35 examination ordered by the court without a request by Tracie for it. Is Pat entitled to reports of examinations undertaken by other examiners of the same condition which Tracie has in her possession?

    d.   Assume Pat refuses to deliver the report to Tracie on request from Tracie. May the court *sua sponte* order Pat to deliver the report?

    e.   If Pat still refuses to deliver the report after a court order, what may the court do? May Pat be held in contempt of court despite the *Sibbach* case?

II. ROADMAP OF A CIVIL ACTION

BAND'S REFUSE REMOVAL, INC. V. BOROUGH OF FAIR LAWN (1960)

Superior Court of New Jersey, Appellate Division
163 A.2d 465

The opinion of the court was delivered by

GOLDMANN, S.J.A.D.

Defendants Capasso appeal from a Law Division judgment declaring void Ab initio and setting aside their garbage removal contract with the Borough of Fair Lawn; declaring illegal and void Ab initio all payments made to them under the contract; setting aside as illegal and void Ab initio Fair Lawn ordinance No. 688, a supplement to the borough sanitary code; and awarding $303,052.62 in favor of the borough against them.

In February 1957 the Borough of Fair Lawn advertised for bids on a contract for the collection of garbage in town. After considering bids, the borough council voted unanimously to award the contract to the Capassos, the lowest qualifying bidder, at a base price of $18,260 per month. The contract was signed in May, the Capassos promptly began garbage collection and they continued to do so in a satisfactory manner through the trial and ensuing appeal.

In August 1957, the borough adopted ordinance 688, which required a permit to collect garbage and provided that only a person who held a contract with the town could be granted a permit. In effect, this meant that only the Capassos could collect garbage in Fair Lawn. Plaintiff Band's Refuse then had a contract to collect garbage from the Western Electric plant in town, so it applied for a permit. The borough denied the application pursuant to the ordinance.

On November 25, 1957, Band's Refuse filed a complaint alleging that ordinance 688 was arbitrary, discriminatory, unconstitutional, and ultra vires. It asked the court to declare the ordinance void and order the borough to renew its previous permit or issue a new one. Plaintiff sued the borough and a number of its officials, and all the defendants filed an answer alleging their action was proper since the contract had been awarded to the Capassos under proper competitive bidding as required by state statute. On motion, the Capassos themselves were allowed to intervene in the suit as defendants and filed an answer that was identical to the borough's. They also filed a counterclaim asking that the borough be restrained from issuing a permit to plaintiff during the term of their contract, restraining plaintiff from collecting garbage in the town and adjudging ordinance 688 and the contract valid.

Meanwhile, a grand jury investigation into garbage collection contracts in the county disclosed allegations of improprieties in the bidding of the Fair Lawn contract and led to indictments of numerous Fair Lawn officials. On May 15, 1958, plaintiff was allowed (over defendant's objections) to file an amended complaint which added a third count alleging that the Fair Lawn—Capasso contract was not the result of open competitive bidding but of "secret arrangements and understandings' which tainted the bidding with fraud. Both the municipal defendants and the Capassos filed answers denying fraud and claiming compliance with the bidding statutes.

At the same time the complaint was amended, the case was pretried by the trial judge who later presided at trial. Although the amendment expanded the issues involved, the pretrial order limited the fraud contentions to two discrete concerns. The trial was projected to take one day but it ended up taking 21 days.

* * *

The Capassos next contend that the judgment must be reversed because of the manner in which the trial judge conducted the proceedings. On the very first day of the trial, June 19, 1958, counsel for these defendants moved that the judge disqualify himself because his activities before trial demonstrated that he had prejudged the issues and exhibited a plan to use the litigation as a vehicle for a broad municipal investigation.

* * *

The trial judge then proceeded to appoint an Amicus curiae, whose duty it would be 'to present evidence, subpoena witnesses, examine all witnesses, and submit to the court briefs on the law and facts.'

Even a casual reading of the record, covering some 2,000 pages of printed appendix, reveals an extraordinary participation by the judge in the trial of the cause. He obviously had devoted much time in preparing for the questioning of witnesses and the offering of exhibits. This preparation on the part of the court extended to the issuance of subpoenas by the court itself and by its Amicus curiae, and the contacting of witnesses for their appearance. The trial judge secured files and documents from the prosecutor's office and sifted them in advance, in preparation of having such of them as he deemed relevant offered as exhibits.

At the hearings the judge called witnesses on his own motion or had the Amicus do so, and examined and cross-examined them at length. He offered exhibits he had called for. He ruled upon the propriety of his own questions and upon the admissibility of his own exhibits. On occasion he attacked the credibility of witnesses called by him.

In all, there were 32 witnesses who took the stand during the 21 trial days. Of these, the parties produced five; the trial judge, by his own subpoena, direction or arrangement, called 27. Of the latter, 24 were permitted to testify upon questioning by the court or Amicus curiae, and this over the objection of counsel for the Capassos that their names had not been supplied in answer to interrogatories.

Defendants Capasso do not question the right of a judge to interrogate a witness in order to qualify testimony or elicit additional information, or his right under special circumstances to summon a witness on his own initiative. Generally, a court's interrogation of witnesses, where not excessive, has been sustained. As was pointed out by our Supreme Court, the power to take an active part in the trial of a case must be exercised by the judge with the greatest restraint. "There is a point at which the judge may cross that find line that separates advocacy from impartiality. When that occurs there may be substantial prejudice to the rights of one of the litigants."

* * *

The power of a trial judge to call and examine witnesses is not unlimited. His conduct of a trial contrary to traditional rules and concepts which have been established for the protection of private rights constitutes a denial of due process. The limitations upon the activities and remarks of a trial judge have usually been considered within the frame of reference of a jury trial. However, the necessity of judicial self-restraint is no less important where the judge sits alone; if he participates to an unreasonable degree in the conduct of the trial, even to the point of assuming the role of an advocate, what he does may be just as prejudicial to a defendant's rights as if the case were tried to a jury.

It is our conclusion that the trial judge overstepped the permissible bounds of judicial inquiry in this case. In effect, he took on the role of advocate, his activities extending from investigation and preparation to the actual presentation of testimony and exhibits at the trial. He converted the action into what amounted to a municipal investigation. Cf. Canons of Judicial Ethics, Canon 15, dealing with a judge's interference in the conduct of a trial.

We agree with defendants Capasso that the trial court committed prejudicial error by producing a large number of witnesses and admitting their testimony in evidence.

* * *

The court, as noted, produced 27 witnesses on its own motion; 24 had not been named in the answer to interrogatories. Counsel for the Capassos had no advance notice of the identity of these witnesses and no opportunity to conduct adequate pretrial investigation. He made proper objection as each witness was called, but to no avail. The testimony they gave, as a reading of the trial judge's lengthy opinion and supplemental opinion will demonstrate, played an important part in the factual conclusions he reached.

* * *

It would seem anomalous to give a party protection from surprise witnesses when they are called by the opposition, but not when called by the court itself. The potential for harm is identical in either case. In addition, the testimony of the witnesses here called by the court brought entirely new issues into the case which were in no wise comprehended by the pretrial order. These issues found their way into the court's opinions and will be mentioned hereinafter.

* * *

The function of a trial judge is to serve litigants by determining their disputes and the issues implicated therein in accordance with applicable rules and law. Established procedures lie at the heart of due process and are as important to the attainment of ultimate justice as the factual merits of a cause. A judge may not initiate or inspire litigation and, by the same token, he may not expand a case before him by adding new issues which come to mind during the trial, without giving the parties affected a full and fair opportunity to meet those issues.

On September 11, 1958, the twelfth day of the trial, the recently substituted counsel for the borough and its officials applied for permission to change the position theretofore taken by them, as set forth in their original answer and amended answer and as repeated on a number of occasions during the preceding trial days. Up to that moment the borough and its officials had insisted that the ordinance and the contract were valid. These defendants were now allowed to file a second amended answer alleging fraud and the invalidity of the contract, and a cross-claim seeking recovery against the Capassos of all monies paid them under the contract. This change of position was permitted over the vigorous and extended objection of the Capassos' attorney. Counsel's request for adequate time to protect the interests of his client by investigation and discovery proceedings was promptly denied.

The Capassos insist that this sudden shift came as a shock and a surprise and amounted to a substantial deprivation of their fundamental rights. They quote from Grobart v. Society for Establishing Useful Manufactures, 2 N.J. 136, 149, 65 A.2d 833 (1949), where former Chief Justice Vanderbilt said:

'* * * It is not a mere matter of formal logic that leads the courts to insist that litigants shall not shift their position in Successive pleadings. * * * (S)hifting causes of action in successive pleading will completely block the purpose of all pleading, I.e., getting to an issue or issues where one party asserts the affirmative and the other the negative on a question or questions of law or of fact.'

* * *

If the Capasso contract was not in fact the result of Bona fide competitive bidding, it was important and proper from the point of view of the paramount public right and interest to allow the amended answer. However, fairness to defendants dictated that they be allowed a reasonable time for discovery and investigation, in order that the facts in support of their claim that the contract was valid might be developed and presented. They had up to that moment been dealing with a situation where the borough and its officials had stoutly affirmed the validity of the contract. The municipality had taken no steps to rescind the agreement, but had accepted scavenger service and made monthly payments thereunder even during the period of the hearings. Its position had been affirmed and reaffirmed, in its pleadings, in the pretrial order, and during the trial. Fundamental fairness required that the court allow the Capassos sufficient time to meet the radically new situation facing them. The denial of that opportunity was the denial of due process.

The judgment is reversed and the matter remanded for a full trial to determine the validity of the scavenger contract . . . .

Directed Reading Questions

4.   What happened in February 1957?

5.   What happened in August of 1957?

6.   What happened in November 1957?

7.   After the events in November 1957, what does Band's Refuse do?

8.   What is the significance of filing a complaint?

9.   What other rules touch on complaints?

10.   Does the filing of a complaint mean that the defendant has to respond?

11.   After being served with the complaint, what did the town do?

12.   What did the town do in their answer to the complaint, and why did they do what they did?

13. What rule instructs on when to file and serve an answer?

14. Rule 8(b)(1) provides what "a party must" do in responding to a pleading, but it does not mandate that the things which "must" be done in response be done in an answer. Does the prefatory language of Rule 12(b) permit another way to respond to a complaint, other than with an answer?

15. Capasso intervened as a defendant in this case. What does that mean?

16. After Capasso intervened as a defendant, what did Capasso do?

17. Draw a diagram of the lawsuit after Capasso intervenes as a defendant and responds.

18. How do you know a counterclaim is not a pleading? What is it, if not a pleading?

19. Can you think of an example where a counterclaim can be mistaken for a defense?

20. Which rule deals with counterclaims specifically?

21. Does Band's Refuse respond to the counterclaim?

22. What happens in May of 1958? What does Band's Refuse want to do as a result?

23. Which rule governs amendments of pleadings?

24. Does the language of the rule make it seem as though it is difficult or easy to amend a pleading?

25. What does "the case was pretried by the trial judge" mean?

26. Rule 16(c)(2) allows the judge to do most of what the judge did. Why then does the appellate court take issue with the judge's conduct?

27. Isn't the judge simply trying to find the truth?

28. Is discovering the truth the aim of civil litigation pursuant to the rules?

29. Examine Rules 12, 56, and 50 and see if you can explain the following, "Once a civil action is commenced there are three ways to end the civil action before a jury verdict and one way to negate the jury verdict."

CHAPTER 3

INTRODUCTION TO PLEADING

Rules 7–11

■ ■ ■

I. CONTEXTUALIZING RULES 7–11

Examine the complaint on the following pages, identify the rules that relate to each section of the complaint that is surrounded by a text box, and explain why each rule you identify is relevant.

I have done an example for you:

BOX 1:

BOX 2:

BOX 3: *10(a) & 7(a). Rule 10(a) mandates that each complaint has a caption and that each caption includes a Rule 7(a) designation. In this case the designation is "Complaint" as per 7(a)(1).*

BOX 4:

BOX 5:

BOX 6:

BOX 7:

BOX 8:

BOX 9:

<table>
<tr><td>IN THE UNITED STATES DISTRICT COURT
FOR THE SOUTHERN DISTRICT OF FLORIDA
CASE NO.</td><td>Box 1</td></tr>
</table>

JONATHAN D. SLOANE,
Plaintiff,

vs.

Box 2   CARNIVAL CORPORATION,
D/B/A CARNIVAL CRUISE LINES, INC.
Defendant.

_____/

<u>COMPLAINT</u>   Box 3

    COMES NOW, the Plaintiff, JONATHAN D. SLOANE by and through the undersigned counsel, and sues the Defendant, CARNIVAL CORPORATION, D/B/A CARNIVAL CRUISE LINES, INC. (hereinafter CARNIVAL), alleging as follows:

<u>GENERAL ALLEGATIONS</u>

1.   This action is an admiralty action where the matter in controversy exceeds the sum or value of $75,000, exclusive of interest and costs, and is between an American Corporate citizen and a citizen of New Zealand and falls within the class of actions allowed under 28 U.S.C. § 1332(a)(1)–(4) and Federal Jurisdiction is therefore proper under 28 U.S.C. § 1332 and 28 U.S.C. § 1333.

Box 4   Box 5

2. Plaintiff is entitled to, and demands a trial by jury pursuant to 28 U.S.C. § 1332.

3. At all times material hereto, Plaintiff, JONATHAN D. SLOANE, was a native of New Zealand.

4. At all times material hereto, Defendant, CARNIVAL, was a corporation authorized to do business in the State of Florida, and has by contract made itself subject to the jurisdiction of this Court.

5. At all times material hereto, CARNIVAL, owned and operated the cruise ship the Victory, sailing on or about December 15, 2002 from Miami, Florida to various foreign ports and returning to Miami on or about December 22, 2002.

6. On or about December 15, 2002, the Plaintiff, JONATHAN D. SLOANE, embarked on a cruise on the Victory as a fare paying passenger.

7. On or about December 18, 2002 JONATHAN SLOANE and his family were on deck ten (10) in the pool area watching his children use the water slide.

8. On or about that time JONATHAN SLOANE'S son slipped on a pool of water and fell in the area of the pool and in so doing wedged his hand between the pool's plexiglass barrier and lower border when he slipped.

9. JONATHAN SLOANE attempted to approach his son but violently slipped on the unreasonably slippery deck near the pool.

10. At the time JONATHAN SLOANE slipped and fell there were no warning signs that the deck was unreasonably and/or excessively slippery.

11. Defendant however was aware of the unreasonably and/or excessively slippery nature of the deck because Defendant had placed outdoor rugs on the majority of the deck surface, the purpose of which was to ensure that the deck did not become unreasonably and/or excessively slippery.

12. The area of the deck on which Defendant fell contained none of the blue rugs mentioned in the preceding paragraph.

13. Plaintiff JONATHAN SLOANE was examined by the ship's doctor and sent ashore in St. Martin for x-rays, which revealed a torn right patellar tendon.

14. Mr. Sloane was returned to the Victory with his right leg, from hip to ankle in a cast, and spent the majority of the rest of his cruise in a wheel chair in his cabin with his leg raised .

15. On or about December 22, 2002 Mr. Sloane was able to disembark the Victory and had to fly home to New Zealand under

the supervision of a nurse to administer blood thinning injections.

16. As a result, of his fall JONATHAN SLOANE suffered harm, including, without limitation, bodily injury and resulting pain and suffering, disability, mental anguish, loss of the capacity for the enjoyment of life, expense of hospitalization, medical and nursing care and treatment, loss of earnings, loss of ability to earn money and/or aggravation of a previously existing condition. One or more of the losses are permanent and/or continuing and Plaintiff will suffer the loss(es) in the future.

Box 6

NEGLIGENCE AGAINST CARNIVAL
on behalf of JONATHAN SLOANE

Box 7   Plaintiff realleges paragraphs one (1) through sixteen (16) above and further alleges as follows:

17. At all times material hereto, the Defendant, CARNIVAL, was responsible for the design, ownership, inspection, construction, maintenance and/or service of the deck on which JONATHAN SLOANE slipped and fell

18. At all times material hereto, the agents, employees, and/or independent contractors of the Defendant, CARNIVAL, owed a duty of reasonable care to the Plaintiff and all invitees, licensees, and/or other individuals lawfully upon the subject premises to provide a reasonably safe premise, and a duty to warn of existing dangerous conditions that it either knew or should have known about.

19. The Defendant, CARNIVAL, by and through its agents, employees, and/or independent contractors, breached the duties of reasonable care owed to the Plaintiff by committing one or more of the following acts and/or omissions:

(A) Negligent and careless failure to keep the pool deck area in a reasonably safe condition and to protect the Plaintiff from dangers of which the Defendant was aware of or reasonably should have been aware of;

(B) Negligent and careless failure to warn the Plaintiff of concealed dangers which are or should be known to the Defendant, CARNIVAL, and which were unknown to the Plaintiff and could not be discovered by him through the exercise of due care;

(C) Failure to conduct routine inspections of the pool deck area at reasonable intervals to determine whether the pool deck area was in a safe condition;

(D) Allowing a dangerous condition to exist on its premises specifically, by allowing the continued use of the pool deck area which was unreasonably dangerous, defective and unfit for the particular purpose for which it was designed, and constituted, in fact, a trap for those invitees attempting to walk upon the pool deck area;

(E) Negligently maintaining the subject pool deck area creating a dangerous condition;

(F) Negligently designing, installing, building, and/or constructing the subject pool deck area;

(G) Failing to follow proper codes, guidelines, regulations, industry standards, and/or construction standards in the design, installation, and/or constructing of the subject pool deck area;

(H) Failing to warn persons such as the Plaintiff of the dangerous condition that existed on the premises through the use of the pool deck area;

(I) Failing to instruct its employees and others as to the proper maintenance of the subject pool deck area, and to warn of the consequences of failing to maintain the subject pool deck area;

(J) Failing to correct a dangerous condition which existed through the use and operation of the pool deck area;

(K) Failing to properly hire and train its personnel in the maintenance of the subject pool deck area;

(L) Allowing a trap to exist on the premises for invitees such as the Plaintiff and other pedestrians walking on the pool deck area;

(M) Modifying or arranging for or allowing the modification of the pool deck area after its initial installation; and

(N) Failing to properly and adequately instruct its employees, agents, independent contractors, invitees, and/or owners of the Defendant in the safe manner in which to operate pool deck area.

(O) Failure to supervise and/or assist children and passengers in the pool deck area.

20. But for the above-mentioned breaches of duty JONATHAN SLOANE would not have been damaged as described more fully in paragraph 16.

21. As a direct and proximate cause of the Defendant's breaches of duty JONATHAN SLOANE was damaged as described more fully in paragraph 16.

22. CARNIVAL is vicariously liable for the negligence of employees, personnel, agents and/or apparent agents acting within the

scope of their employment with CARNIVAL and/or on the ship Victory.

WHEREFORE, the Plaintiff, JONATHAN D. SLOANE, <u>demands judgment</u> for damages against the Defendant, CARNIVAL, for a sum in excess of Seventy-Five Thousand Dollars ($75,000.00), exclusive of fees and costs plus all other awards, including but not limited to interest, and a trial by jury.

Box 8

Respectfully Submitted,   Box 9   Downs & Associates, P.A.   Rory D. Bahadur, Esq.   255 University Drive   Coral Gables, FL, 33134   Telephone No.: (305)-444-8226   rory.bahadur@dbwlaw.com   ———————————————   Rory Bahadur, Esq.   Florida Bar No.: 657344

DIRECTED READING QUESTIONS

1. Until 2015, the Federal Rules of Civil Procedure contained forms which practitioners could use as sample pleadings. According to the rules committee:

> the forms contained in the Appendix of Forms are sufficient to withstand attack under the rules under which they are drawn, and that the practitioner using them may rely on them to that extent. The circuit courts of appeals generally have upheld the use of the forms as promoting desirable simplicity and brevity of statement.

In 2015 the rules committee decided to do away with the appendix of forms but were careful to say that the forms continued to represent examples of pleadings that satisfied the Federal Rules.

> [the forms were adopted] when the Civil Rules were established in 1938 "to indicate, subject to the provisions of these rules, the simplicity and brevity of statement which the rules contemplate." The purpose of providing illustrations for the rules, although useful when the rules were adopted, has been fulfilled. Accordingly, recognizing that there are many excellent alternative sources for forms, including the website of the Administrative Office of the United States Courts, the websites of many district courts, and local law libraries that contain many commercially published forms, Rule 84 and the Appendix of Forms are no longer necessary and have been abrogated. The abrogation of Rule 84 does not alter existing pleading standards or otherwise change the requirements of Civil Rule 8.

The federal form for pleading negligence was initially Form #9, but it was renumbered as Form #11. Here is that form in its entirety:

Federal Rules of Civil Procedure: Form 11

COMPLAINT FOR NEGLIGENCE

1.   The plaintiff is [a citizen of State A] [a corporation incorporated under the laws of State A with its principal place of business in State A]. The defendant is [a citizen of State B] [a corporation incorporated under the laws of State B with its principal place of business in State B]. The amount in controversy, without interest and costs, exceeds the sum or value specified by 28 U.S.C. § 1332.

*   This action arises under [the United States Constitution; specify the article or amendment and the section] [a United States treaty; specify] [a federal statute, ___ U.S.C. § ___].*

*   This is a case of admiralty or maritime jurisdiction.*

2.   On, _____ at ___, the defendant negligently drove a motor vehicle against the plaintiff.

3.   As a result, the plaintiff was physically injured, lost wages or income, suffered physical and mental pain, and incurred medical expenses of $ <_____>.

*   Therefore, the plaintiff demands judgment against the defendant for $ <_____>, plus costs.*

Date:

_____

2.   Where in the complaint with the text boxes is the statement required by Rule 8(a)(2)?

3.   If paragraph 2 of Form 11 satisfies Rule 8(a)(2) then why does the Plaintiff in the complaint with the text boxes in the book go into so much more detail?

4.   Rule 8(b)(1) specifies that a party responding to a pleading "must" do two things. What must a party responding to a pleading do?

5.   Rule 8(b)(1) does not say that a party must respond to a pleading but only what a party must do if they respond. What rule provides consequences for not responding to a pleading?

6.   Even though Rule 8(b)(1) specifies what a response to a complaint must contain, does it mandate that those essential components be in a responsive pleading and does the prefatory language of Rule 12(b) provide an option for presenting certain defenses other than in a responsive pleading?

7.   What section of Rule 12 might a party responding to a complaint that does not satisfy Rule 8(a)(2) employ?

II. ALTERNATIVE AND INCONSISTENT PLEADING—*RULE 8(d)(2) & (3)*

McCORMICK v. KOPMANN (1959)
Appellate Court of Illinois, Third District
161 N.E. 2d 720

Lewis McCormick was killed when a truck operated by Defendant Kopmann collided with his automobile. McCormick's widow sued Kopmann and the Huls, owners of a tavern where McCormick had drunk beer before the accident. Count I, for damages under the Illinois Wrongful Death Act, alleged that Kopmann negligently drove his truck across the center line and collided with McCormick's automobile and that the said decedent was not driving negligently. Count IV, brought in the alternative to count I, sought damages under the Illinois Dram Shop Act. It alleged that the Huls sold alcoholic beverages to McCormick which rendered him intoxicated and that as a result of such intoxication he drove his vehicle in a negligent manner and caused a collision with Kopmann's truck.

Before trial, Kopmann moved to dismiss the complaint on the theory that the contradictions between Count I and Count IV were fatal. The trial court denied his motion. There was conflicting testimony at trial concerning whether McCormick or Kopmann had driven over the center line. There was also testimony that McCormick had drunk several beers at the Huls' tavern. The jury returned a verdict against Kopmann for $15,500 under Count I and for the Huls under Count IV.

Kopmann has appealed. His first contention is that the trial court erred in denying his pre-trial motion to dismiss the complaint. Kopmann is correct in asserting that the complaint contains inconsistent allegations. The allegation of Count I that McCormick was free from contributory negligence, cannot be reconciled with the allegation of Count IV that McCormick's intoxication was the proximate cause of his death.

Freedom from contributory negligence is a prerequisite to recovery under the Wrongful Death Act. If the **jury** had found that McCormick was intoxicated and that his intoxication caused the accident, it could not at the same time have found that McCormick was not contributorily negligent. Counts I and IV, therefore, are mutually exclusive; plaintiff may not recover upon both counts. It does not follow, however, that these counts may not be pleaded together.

[A]t the trial, Kopmann attempted to establish the truth of the allegations of Count IV that McCormick was intoxicated at the time of the collision and that his intoxication caused his death. He can hardly be heard now to say that before the trial, plaintiff should have known that these were not the facts. Here, either of two defendants may be liable to plaintiff, depending upon what the jury finds the facts to be. It has been aptly said that 'truth cannot be stated until known, and, for purposes of judicial administration, cannot be known until the trier of facts decides the fact issues. Plaintiff need not choose between the alternative counts. Such a requirement would, to a large extent, nullify the salutary purposes of alternative pleading.

DIRECTED READING QUESTIONS

8. Why is the Dram Shop Act (suit against a tavern for negligently serving someone too much to drink) claim inconsistent with the wrongful death claim (suit alleging someone's negligence; in this case, that the trucker's negligent driving caused death)?

9. What does the following statement from the case indicate that the jury found regarding the negligence of the plaintiff: "The jury returned a verdict against Kopmann for $15,500 under Count I and for the Huls under Count IV"?

10. What did Kopmann try to prove during trial but was unsuccessful at proving?

11. The case indicates that it is not possible for the **jury** (fact finder) to permit recovery under the Dram Shop Act and the wrongful death claim simultaneously, but it is perfectly fine to **plead** the claims simultaneously. What does the opinion indicate about the purpose of pleading as opposed to subsequent aspects of a civil action, such as discovery or fact finding and eventual resolution?

12. Does the concept of alternative pleading mean parties may allege even completely fabricated allegations in a pleading? For example, could the Plaintiff in the *McCormick* case have included a claim against the truck driver for conspiracy, and in support thereof alleged, "an alien spacecraft descended and a tractor beam pulled decedent's car into the path of the truck, the driver of which, conspired with the aliens to help them collect organs from research specimens?"

Help Angie out in as Many Ways as You Can

Angie is the defendant in a breach of contract case in federal court. These are the facts. Brent phoned his good buddy Angie up. He said, "Angie, I could really use your help to lift some debris out of my yard. Could you come over and give me a hand? If you do, I will cook you that lunch that I already owe you." Angie responded, "Sounds good. Let me think about it, and we'll see. It's possible I can come over on Sunday, and it will make me feel good to help you anyway." Angie never showed up, and three years later, Brent sued Angie for breach of a bilateral contract.

In his complaint, Brent includes all the stuff required by the rules governing pleading, such that the complaint satisfies the contract equivalent of Form 11. Assume that the statute of limitations on a contract claim in this jurisdiction is 2 years and, in her answer, Angie admits all the factual allegations of the complaint.

Here is some basic contract law:

A contract consists of an offer which must be definite, an acceptance of the offer, and an exchange of consideration. Moral obligations to perform are not valid consideration. Preexisting obligations are also not valid consideration.

A. What defenses might Angie raise at the pleading stage?

B. What is the difference between an *affirmative* defense found in Rule 8(c)(1) (e.g. statute of limitations) and a "regular" defense (e.g. Brett's request was not specific enough to be a valid offer)?

C. Why do we permit alternative pleading?

CHAPTER 4

RULE 11

■ ■ ■

ZUK V. EASTERN PENNSYLVANIA PSYCHIATRIC INSTITUTE OF THE MEDICAL COLLEGE OF PENNSYLVANIA (1996)

United States Courts of Appeal, Third Circuit
103 F.3d 294

This appeal brings into focus difficult questions relating to the evolving uses and purposes of Federal Rules of Civil Procedure (Fed.R.Civ.P.) Rule 11 sanctions . . . . The sanctions here stem from a suit filed in the United States District Court for the Eastern District of Pennsylvania by Benjamin Lipman, the appellant, in behalf of Dr. Gerald Zuk for copyright infringement against the Eastern Pennsylvania Psychiatric Institute (EPPI). The district court dismissed the action on a Rule 12(b)(6) motion filed by the defendant, and appellant and his client thereafter were subjected to joint and several liability in the sum of $15,000 for sanctions and defendant's counsel fees. Dr. Zuk settled his liability and Lipman appealed. We affirm in part and vacate in part.

I.

Dr. Zuk, a psychologist on the faculty EPPI, early in the 1970s had an EPPI technician film two of Dr. Zuk's family therapy sessions. As academic demand for the films developed, Zuk had EPPI duplicate the films and make them available for rental through their library. Zuk subsequently wrote a book which, among other things, contained transcripts of the therapy sessions. He registered the book in 1975 with the United States Copyright Office.

In 1980, upon a change in its ownership, EPPI furloughed Zuk. He thereupon requested that all copies of the films be returned to him; EPPI ignored the request. It would appear that EPPI continued to rent out the films for at least some time thereafter. For reasons which have not been made clear, after a long hiatus, Zuk renewed his attempts to recover the films in 1994. In 1995, appellant filed a suit in Zuk's behalf, alleging that EPPI was renting out the films and thereby infringed his copyright.

On June 19, 1995, EPPI moved for dismissal under Rule 12(b), and appellant filed a memorandum in opposition. While the motion was pending, EPPI mailed to Lipman a notice of its intention to move for sanctions under Rule 11[(c)(2)] on the grounds essentially that appellant had failed to conduct an inquiry into the facts reasonable under the circumstances and into the law. The district court entered an order granting the motion to dismiss. The court found that the copyright of the book afforded no protection to the films, that EPPI owned the copies of the films in its possession and that their use was not an infringement, and that in any event, Zuk's claims were barred by the statute of limitations.

On September 15, 1995 . . . [Defendant] filed a Rule 11 motion for sanctions, and appellant filed a memorandum in opposition. On November 1, the court entered an order to "show cause why Rule 11 sanctions should not be imposed for (a) filing the complaint, and failing to withdraw it; and (b) signing and filing each and every document presented." Appellant responded on December 1 with a declaration reiterating the facts of the case as he viewed them.

On February 1, 1996, the court, upon consideration of defendant's motion for attorney's fees and sanctions, ordered: "That plaintiff, Gerald Zuk, Ph.D., and plaintiff's counsel, Benjamin G. Lipman, Esq. are jointly and severally liable to the defendant for counsel fees in the sum of $15,000." We must ascertain the underpinnings for the Order. It appears that Dr. Zuk subsequently settled his liability with EPPI in the amount of $6,250, leaving appellant liable for $8,750. Appellant timely appealed.

* * *

A.

We note at the outset that we find no error in the district court's decision to impose sanctions pursuant to Fed.R.Civ.P. 11.[3] As noted above, we review a district court's decision to impose sanctions for abuse of discretion. An abuse of discretion in this context would occur if the court "based its ruling on an erroneous view of the law or a clearly erroneous assessment of the evidence."

Prior to a significant amendment in 1983, Rule 11 stated that an attorney might be subjected to disciplinary action only for a "wilful" violation of the rule. The Advisory Committee Notes to the 1983 amendment make clear that the wilfulness prerequisite has been deleted. Rather, the amended rule imposes a duty on counsel to make an inquiry into both the facts and the law which is "reasonable under the circumstances." This is a more stringent standard than the original good-faith formula, and it was expected that a greater range of circumstances would trigger its violation. The district court did not abuse its discretion in determining that appellant had not sufficiently investigated the facts of the case nor had he educated himself well enough as to copyright law. We therefore see no error in the court's decision to impose sanctions.

1. The Inquiry into The Facts

In dismissing the complaint, the court found that "[i]t . . . seems highly probable that plaintiff's claims are barred by the three-year statute of limitations." Later, in the Memorandum and Order imposing sanctions, the court noted that the "obvious" statute of limitations issue would have been resolved and no lawsuit filed, had appellant conducted an adequate investigation.

Dr. Zuk left EPPI in 1980, and it is undisputed that EPPI continued to rent out the films in question for some time thereafter. Appellant, however, had no evidence whatsoever, other than conjecture, to prove that the films were being rented in the three

---

[3] Appellant contended that he was not given the benefit of Rule 11's 21-day safe harbor, because the court dismissed the action before he had had the full opportunity to withdraw it. He thus claimed that sanctions were improper under Rule 11(c)(2) (upon motion by other party). EPPI maintained that the sanctions actually were imposed under Rule 11(c)(3) (on the court's initiative), which has no safe harbor provision. The court issued an order to show cause, which is required only under 11(c)(3), but stated that it was "in consideration of defendant's motion for sanctions." In its accompanying memorandum, the district court did not address this apparent inconsistency. At oral argument before this court, appellant acknowledged that he would not have withdrawn the complaint even if he had been given the full 21-day safe harbor. Thus, we need not address this contention.

years preceding the commencement of this action. The Advisory Committee Notes to the 1993 amendments to Rule 11 explain:

> "Tolerance of factual contentions in initial pleadings . . . when specifically identified as made on information and belief does not relieve litigants from the obligation to conduct an appropriate investigation into the facts that is reasonable under the circumstances; it is not a license to . . . make claims . . . without any factual basis or justification."

Appellant's assertions in . . . the complaint (in regard to EPPI's ongoing use of the films) are based purely upon Dr. Zuk's beliefs.[4] What little investigation appellant actually conducted did not reveal any information that the films were being rented out during the relevant period. Indeed, certain pre-filing correspondence with EPPI indicated that, pursuant to Dr. Zuk's earlier instructions, the library staff was cautioned not to rent any of Dr. Zuk's films. Nor are we persuaded by appellant's contention that further information would have been obtained during discovery. The Note cited above observes that discovery is not intended as a fishing expedition permitting the speculative pleading of a case first and then pursuing discovery to support it; the plaintiff must have some basis in fact for the action. The need for a reasonable investigation with respect to distribution of the film during the three-year period prior to the filing of the lawsuit is evident because of the long period allegedly spanned by the distribution.

2.   The Inquiry into the Law

Rule 11(b)(2) requires that all "claims, defenses, and other legal contentions [be] warranted by existing law or by a nonfrivolous argument for the extension, modification, or reversal of existing law or the establishment of new law." Appellant does not contend that any of the latter justifications apply, and so we must ascertain whether his legal arguments are "warranted by existing law." For reasons that follow, we conclude that they are not, and that sanctions therefore were within the sound discretion of the district court.

Appellant's legal research was faulty primarily in two particular areas: copyright law (pertaining to what the parties call the "registration issue") and the law of personal property (the "ownership issue"). Turning to the registration issue, appellant states that this was the first copyright case which he had handled, and points out that a practitioner has to begin somewhere. While we are sympathetic to this argument, its thrust is more toward the nature of the sanctions to be imposed rather than to the initial decision whether sanctions should be imposed. Regrettably, the reality of appellant's weak grasp of copyright law is that it caused him to pursue a course of conduct which was not warranted by existing law and compelled the defendant to expend time and money in needless litigation.

Appellant's primary contention is that by registering a copyright in his book, Dr. Zuk had somehow also protected the films reproduced in them. The logical progression is that because the book contained transcripts of the films, the words spoken in the films were protected, and thus so were the films. Although perhaps logical, this argument runs

---

[4]   EPPI emphasizes that while [the allegations regarding EPPI's ongoing use of the films] should have been pleaded on information and belief, they were instead phrased as "Dr. Zuk believes, and therefore avers, ..." In light of liberal federal pleading practice, we do not find this to be an important distinction.

contrary to copyright law. "The copyright in [a derivative] work . . . does not affect or enlarge the scope, duration, ownership, or subsistence of, any copyright protection in the preexisting material."

In all fairness to appellant, we should note that the cases and commentary interpreting this provision focus on derivative works which incorporate the preexisting work of a *different* author. Had appellant presented his argument as a matter of first impression, and argued for a new interpretation of the statute where the same individual authored both works, he might have stood upon a more solid footing. Instead, appellant's brief evidences what strikes us as a cursory reading of the copyright laws, and a strained analysis of [that law as interpreted by the courts].

* * *

B.

Having concluded that there is no error in the district court's decision to impose sanctions upon appellant under Rule 11, we turn now to the type and amount of sanctions imposed. We review the appropriateness of the sanctions imposed for abuse of discretion. As the courts have undergone experience with the application of Rule 11 sanctions, its scope has broadened and the emphasis of the Rule has changed.

According to *Wright & Miller:*

The 1993 revision . . . makes clear that the main purpose of Rule 11 is to deter, not to compensate. Accordingly, it changes the emphasis in the types of sanctions to be ordered. It envisions as the norm public interest remedies such as fines and reprimands, as opposed to the prior emphasis on private interest remedies. Thus, the Advisory Committee Notes state that any monetary penalty "should ordinarily be paid into the court" except "under unusual circumstances" when they should be given to the opposing party. Any sanction imposed should be calibrated to the least severe level necessary to serve the deterrent purpose of the Rule. In addition, the new Rule 11 contemplates greater use of nonmonetary sanctions, including reprimands, orders to undergo continuing education, and referrals to disciplinary authorities.

5A Charles Alan Wright & Arthur R. Miller, *Federal Practice & Procedure* § 1336 (2d ed. Supp. 1996).

This court has instructed the district courts that "[f]ee-shifting is but one of several methods of achieving the various goals of Rule 11," that they should "consider a wide range of alternative possible sanctions for violation of the rule," and that the "district court's choice of deterrent is appropriate when it is the *minimum* that will serve to *adequately* deter the undesirable behavior."

Thus, the district courts have been encouraged to consider mitigating factors in fashioning sanctions, most particularly the sanctioned party's ability to pay. Courts were also given examples of other factors they might consider, including whether the attorney has a history of this sort of behavior, the defendant's need for compensation, the degree of frivolousness, and the "willfulness" of the violation.

* * *

V.

To summarize, to the extent the Order of the district court dated February 1, 1996 imposed sanctions upon appellant pursuant to Fed.R.Civ.P. 11, it will be affirmed only as to the actual imposition of such sanctions. The Order will be vacated as to the type and amount of sanctions imposed . . . . The case will be remanded for further proceedings consistent with this opinion.

Each side to bear its own costs.

DIRECTED READING QUESTIONS

1. List the legally relevant facts for each time period below:

   a. The early 1970s

   b. 1975

   c. 1980

   d. 1994

   e. 1995

2. How does the school respond to the complaint?

3. When a motion is filed with the court and the parties are awaiting the court's decision on the motion, the motion is considered pending. What else did the defendant do while the motion was pending?

4. Does Rule 11 permit the motion to be filed with the court before serving it on the defendant?

5. On September 15, 1995, the defendants filed the Rule 11 motion that the defendant had previously served the plaintiff with. Did the court rule on the Rule 12(b)(6) motion before the Rule 11 motion was filed with the court? If yes, how did the court rule?

6. What happened on November 1, 1995?

7. Was the show cause order issued by the court appropriate here?

8. What happened on February 1, 1996?

9. What exactly are the bases asserted for sanctioning the plaintiff and attorney in the Rule 11 motion?

10. List each of the arguments against sanctions made by the attorney on appeal. Explain how the defendant responds to each argument and why or how the appellate court resolves each argument as it does.

Read Rule 11 carefully and justify your answers by citing to specific sections in the rule when answering the following questions.

11. After arguing for years about whether a contract was breached, Alpha decides to sue Beta. Before Alpha files the complaint against Beta, Alpha meets Beta in a public space and shows Beta the allegations in the complaint he plans to file. Beta tells Alpha, "Those allegations are all false and have no basis in fact or law and furthermore you are doing this just to harass me." Alpha smugly responds, "Yes. You are correct." Beta then states, "Dude, you are violating Rule 11(b)(1)–(3), and I will seek sanctions against you right

now." To which Alpha responds as he strides confidently away, "You can't. Not yet, anyway." Is Alpha correct?

12. As the litigation between Alpha and Beta progressed through discovery, Beta requested pursuant to Rule 34 that Alpha produce the contract which he claims is the basis of the breach of contract claim. Alpha responded by producing a totally and completely fabricated document which is not at all based in fact. What result if Beta moves for sanctions pursuant to Rule 11(b)(3) against Alpha, alleging that the "paper"/document Alpha produced contained false information unsupported by any evidence?

13. Reexamine the *Zuk* case. Would sanctions have been appropriate pursuant to Rule 11(b)(3), if the teacher first met and related the facts that formed the basis of the complaint against the school to the attorney a few hours before the apparent statute of limitations barred the action? In answering this question, please discuss the availability of sanctions against the attorney and the party separately and assume the teacher completely fabricated the facts he related to the attorney.

14. In which, if either, of the following two scenarios are the sanctions imposed appropriate?

Scenario 1	Scenario 2
Plaintiff's attorney filed a complaint containing wholly imagined factual allegations. Defendant answered the complaint and filed and served a motion for summary judgment. On the same day, Defendant served Plaintiff with a Rule 11 motion seeking sanctions. 3 months after the motion for summary judgment was filed, the court ruled in favor of the defendant on the SJ motion and the case was dismissed. The plaintiff had not yet withdrawn her complaint when the case was dismissed pursuant to summary judgment. The day after dismissal defendant filed the Rule 11 motion with the court and the court ruled on the defendant's Rule 11 motion, sanctioning both the plaintiff and the plaintiff's attorney by ordering them to pay $500.00 each into a legal aid charity.	Plaintiff's attorney filed a complaint containing wholly imagined factual allegations. Defendant answered the complaint and filed and served a motion for summary judgment. On the same day Defendant served Plaintiff with a Rule 11 motion seeking sanctions. The court ruled on the summary judgment motion and dismissed the case 11 days after the day both the summary judgment motion was filed and served, and the Rule 11 motion was served on the plaintiff. The day after dismissal defendant filed the Rule 11 motion with the court and the court ruled on the defendant's Rule 11 motion, sanctioning both the plaintiff and the plaintiff's attorney by ordering them to pay $500.00 each into a legal aid charity.

15. As you are walking into court to argue a summary judgment motion for one of your clients, a lawyer you knew from law school approaches you and gives you a complaint. He says the following to you.

    "I notice that your hearing is over at 9:40 a.m. At 10 a.m., I am scheduled to argue before another judge in the building why I should not be sanctioned for violating Rule 11(b)(2). The opposing party is arguing that the legal contentions in the complaint I just handed you are not warranted by existing law. Unfortunately, my child has some health issues which necessitate me leaving the building and heading to my kid's school immediately. Could you just fill in for me and do your best? You can't be sanctioned anyway because you did not sign the complaint. I'm the one who signed it, and you would just be arguing the motion for me."

If you argued the motion and the judge found the allegations in the complaint violated Rule 11(b)(2), could you be sanctioned even though you never signed the complaint?

16. May monetary sanctions be issued against an unrepresented party for violating Rule 11(b)?

CHAPTER 5

STATING A CLAIM

■ ■ ■

SWIERKIEWICZ V. SOREMA (2002)
Supreme Court of the United States
534 U.S. 506

Petitioner Akos Swierkiewicz is a native of Hungary, who at the time of his complaint was 53 years old. In April 1989, petitioner began working for respondent Sorema N. A., a reinsurance company headquartered in New York and principally owned and controlled by a French parent corporation. Petitioner was initially employed in the position of senior vice president and chief underwriting officer (CUO). Nearly six years later, François M. Chavel, respondent's Chief Executive Officer, demoted petitioner to a marketing and services position and transferred the bulk of his underwriting responsibilities to Nicholas Papadopoulo, a 32-year-old who, like Mr. Chavel, is a French national. About a year later, Mr. Chavel stated that he wanted to "energize" the underwriting department and appointed Mr. Papadopoulo as CUO. Petitioner claims that Mr. Papadopoulo had only one year of underwriting experience at the time he was promoted, and therefore was less experienced and less qualified to be CUO than he, since at that point he had 26 years of experience in the insurance industry.

Following his demotion, petitioner contends that he "was isolated by Mr. Chavel . . . excluded from business decisions and meetings and denied the opportunity to reach his true potential at SOREMA." Petitioner unsuccessfully attempted to meet with Mr. Chavel to discuss his discontent. Finally, in April 1997, petitioner sent a memo to Mr. Chavel outlining his grievances and requesting a severance package. Two weeks later, respondent's general counsel presented petitioner with two options: He could either resign without a severance package or be dismissed. Mr. Chavel fired petitioner after he refused to resign.

Petitioner filed a lawsuit alleging that he had been terminated on account of his national origin in violation of Title VII of the Civil Rights Act of 1964, and on account of his age in violation of the Age Discrimination in Employment Act of 1967 (ADEA). The United States District Court for the Southern District of New York dismissed petitioner's complaint because it found that he "ha[d] not adequately alleged a prima facie case, in that he ha[d] not adequately alleged circumstances that support an inference of discrimination." The United States Court of Appeals for the Second Circuit affirmed the dismissal, relying on its settled precedent, which requires a plaintiff in an employment discrimination complaint to allege facts constituting a prima facie case of discrimination under the framework set forth by this Court . . . . The Court of Appeals held that petitioner had failed to meet his burden because his allegations were "insufficient as a matter of law to raise an inference of discrimination." We granted certiorari, to resolve a split among the Courts of Appeals concerning the proper pleading standard for employment discrimination cases, and now reverse.

II

Applying Circuit precedent, the Court of Appeals required petitioner to plead a prima facie case of discrimination in order to survive respondent's motion to dismiss. In the Court of Appeals' view, petitioner was thus required to allege in his complaint: (1) membership in a protected group; (2) qualification for the job in question; (3) an adverse employment action; and (4) circumstances that support an inference of discrimination.

The prima facie case however, is an evidentiary standard, not a pleading requirement. [T]his Court [has previously] made clear that . . . that the prima facie case relates to the employee's burden of presenting evidence that raises an inference of discrimination. . . . We set forth the basic allocation of burdens and order of presentation of proof in a Title VII case alleging discriminatory treatment. First, the plaintiff has the burden of proving by the preponderance of the evidence a prima facie case of discrimination" ("This evidentiary relationship between the presumption created by a prima facie case and the consequential burden of production placed on the defendant is a traditional feature of the common law").

This Court has never indicated that the requirements for establishing a prima facie case . . . also apply to the pleading standard that plaintiffs must satisfy in order to survive a motion to dismiss. For instance, we have rejected the argument that a Title VII complaint requires greater "particularity," because this would "too narrowly constric[t] the role of the pleadings." Consequently, the ordinary rules for assessing the sufficiency of a complaint apply. ("When a federal court reviews the sufficiency of a complaint, before the reception of any evidence either by affidavit or admissions, its task is necessarily a limited one. The issue is not whether a plaintiff will ultimately prevail but whether the claimant is entitled to offer evidence to support the claims").

* * *

Furthermore, imposing the Court of Appeals' heightened pleading standard in employment discrimination cases conflicts with Federal Rule of Civil Procedure 8(a)(2), which provides that a complaint must include only "a short and plain statement of the claim showing that the pleader is entitled to relief." Such a statement must simply "give the defendant fair notice of what the plaintiff's claim is and the grounds upon which it rests." *Conley v. Gibson*, 355 U.S. 41, 47, 78 S.Ct. 99, 2 L.Ed.2d 80 (1957). This simplified notice pleading standard relies on liberal discovery rules and summary judgment motions to define disputed facts and issues and to dispose of unmeritorious claims. "The provisions for discovery are so flexible and the provisions for pretrial procedure and summary judgment so effective, that attempted surprise in federal practice is aborted very easily, synthetic issues detected, and the gravamen of the dispute brought frankly into the open for the inspection of the court." 5 C. Wright & A. Miller, Federal Practice and Procedure § 1202, p. 76 (2d ed. 1990).

Rule 8(a)'s simplified pleading standard applies to all civil actions, with limited exceptions. Rule 9(b), for example, provides for greater particularity in all averments of fraud or mistake.[3] This Court, however, has declined to extend such exceptions to other contexts. In *Leatherman* we stated: "[T]he Federal Rules do address in Rule 9(b) the

---

[3]   "In all averments of fraud or mistake, the circumstances constituting fraud or mistake shall be stated with particularity. Malice, intent, knowledge, and other condition of mind of a person may be averred generally."

question of the need for greater particularity in pleading certain actions, but do not include among the enumerated actions any reference to complaints alleging municipal liability under § 1983. *Expressio unius est exclusio alterius.*" [ ] Rule 9(b) makes no mention of municipal liability under . . . employment discrimination. Thus, complaints in these cases, as in most others, must satisfy only the simple requirements of Rule 8(a)[2].[4]

Other provisions of the Federal Rules of Civil Procedure are inextricably linked to Rule 8(a)'s simplified notice pleading standard. Rule 8(e)(1) states that "[n]o technical forms of pleading or motions are required," and Rule 8(f) provides that "[a]ll pleadings shall be so construed as to do substantial justice." Given the Federal Rules' simplified standard for pleading, "[a] court may dismiss a complaint only if it is clear that no relief could be granted under any set of facts that could be proved consistent with the allegations." If a pleading fails to specify the allegations in a manner that provides sufficient notice, a defendant can move for a more definite statement under Rule 12(e) before responding. Moreover, claims lacking merit may be dealt with through summary judgment under Rule 56. The liberal notice pleading of Rule 8(a) is the starting point of a simplified pleading system, which was adopted to focus litigation on the merits of a claim. See *Conley, supra,* at 48, 78 S.Ct. 99 ("The Federal Rules reject the approach that pleading is a game of skill in which one misstep by counsel may be decisive to the outcome and accept the principle that the purpose of pleading is to facilitate a proper decision on the merits").

Applying the relevant standard, petitioner's complaint easily satisfies the requirements of Rule 8(a) because it gives respondent fair notice of the basis for petitioner's claims. Petitioner alleged that he had been terminated on account of his national origin in violation of Title VII and on account of his age in violation of the ADEA. His complaint detailed the events leading to his termination, provided relevant dates, and included the ages and nationalities of at least some of the relevant persons involved with his termination. These allegations give respondent fair notice of what petitioner's claims are and the grounds upon which they rest. See *Conley, supra,* at 47, 78 S.Ct. 99. In addition, they state claims upon which relief could be granted under Title VII and the ADEA.

Respondent argues that allowing lawsuits based on conclusory allegations of discrimination to go forward will burden the courts and encourage disgruntled employees to bring unsubstantiated suits. Whatever the practical merits of this argument, the Federal Rules do not contain a heightened pleading standard for employment discrimination suits. A requirement of greater specificity for particular claims is a result that "must be obtained by the process of amending the Federal Rules, and not by judicial interpretation." Furthermore, Rule 8(a) establishes a pleading standard without regard to whether a claim will succeed on the merits. "Indeed it may appear on the face of the pleadings that a recovery is very remote and unlikely but that is not the test."

---

[4]   These requirements are exemplified by the Federal Rules of Civil Procedure Forms, which "are sufficient under the rules and are intended to indicate the simplicity and brevity of statement which the rules contemplate." For example, Form [11] sets forth a complaint for negligence in which plaintiff simply states in relevant part: "On June 1, 1936, in a public highway called Boylston Street in Boston, Massachusetts, defendant negligently drove a motor vehicle against plaintiff who was then crossing said highway."

For the foregoing reasons, we hold that an employment discrimination plaintiff need not plead a prima facie case of discrimination and that petitioner's complaint is sufficient to survive respondent's motion to dismiss. Accordingly, the judgment of the Court of Appeals is reversed, and the case is remanded for further proceedings consistent with this opinion.

It is so ordered.

————————

Federal Rules of Civil Procedure: Form 11

COMPLAINT FOR NEGLIGENCE

1.   The plaintiff is [a citizen of State A] [a corporation incorporated under the laws of State A with its principal place of business in State A]. The defendant is [a citizen of State B] [a corporation incorporated under the laws of State B with its principal place of business in State B]. The amount in controversy, without interest and costs, exceeds the sum or value specified by 28 U.S.C. § 1332.

This action arises under [the United States Constitution; specify the article or amendment and the section] [a United States treaty; specify] [a federal statute, ___U.S.C. § ___].

This is a case of admiralty or maritime jurisdiction.

2.   On, _____at ____, the defendant negligently drove a motor vehicle against the plaintiff.

3.   As a result, the plaintiff was physically injured, lost wages or income, suffered physical and mental pain, and incurred medical expenses of $ <_____>.

Therefore, the plaintiff demands judgment against the defendant for $ <_____>, plus costs.

Date:

————————————————————

DIRECTED READING QUESTIONS

1.   What are the essential facts of the *Swierkiewicz* case?

2.   What does the plaintiff allege in his lawsuit against the corporation?

3.   How does the corporation respond to the plaintiff's complaint?

4.   What is a *prima facie* case?

5.   What are the elements of a *prima facie* case for employment discrimination? Has the plaintiff alleged facts in support of each element?

6.   Why does the court conclude that a *prima facie* case should not be a requirement at the pleading stage?

7.   Explain how the court differentiates between the "simple" pleading standard in Rule 8(a)(2) which "applies to all civil actions, with limited exceptions" and the pleading standard found in Rule 9(b).

8.   Explain what the Court means by, "A requirement of greater specificity for particular claims is a result that 'must be obtained by the process of amending the Federal Rules, and not by judicial interpretation.'"

9. The Court reiterates, that the federal pleading standard under Rule 8(a)(2) is a liberal standard For example the opinion provides, "Furthermore, Rule 8(a) establishes a pleading standard without regard to whether a claim will succeed on the merits. 'Indeed it may appear on the face of the pleadings that a recovery is very remote and unlikely but that is not the test.'" The Court also seems to justify the liberal pleading standard by mentioning, "[m]oreover, claims lacking merit may be dealt with through summary judgment under Rule 56." Explain why the Court concludes liberal pleading standards are permissible given Rule 56.

10. Please make sure you understand that Form 11 referred to in footnote 4 of the opinion is included here just after the *Swierkiewicz* case.

11. The defendant "argues that allowing lawsuits based on conclusory allegations of discrimination to go forward will burden the courts and encourage disgruntled employees to bring unsubstantiated suits." How does the Court respond to this argument? How is the Court's response consistent with the rationale for permitting alternative pleading discussed in the *McCormick v. Kopmann* case?

12. What case does the *Swierkiewicz* Court primarily rely on as precedent to justify its decision?

13. Look at the language in Rule 8(a)(2) and understand that Form 11 is an example of how easy it is to satisfy the requirement that a pleading seeking relief must contain "a short and plain statement of the claim showing that the pleader is entitled to relief." Now look at the language of Rule 12(b)(6) and make sure it is clear that the defense of "failure to state a claim upon which relief can be granted" is essentially an assertion that the claimant failed to satisfy Rule 8(a)(2).

CONLEY V. GIBSON (1957)
Supreme Court of the United States
355 U.S. 41

MR. JUSTICE BLACK delivered the opinion of the Court.

Once again Negro employees are here under the Railway Labor Act asking that their collective bargaining agent be compelled to represent them fairly. In a series of cases . . . this Court has emphatically and repeatedly ruled that an exclusive bargaining agent under the Railway Labor Act is obligated to represent all employees in the bargaining unit fairly and without discrimination because of race and has held that the courts have power to protect employees against such invidious discrimination.

This class suit was brought in a Federal District Court in Texas by certain Negro members of the Brotherhood of Railway and Steamship Clerks, petitioners here, on behalf of themselves and other Negro employees similarly situated against the Brotherhood, its Local Union No. 28 and certain officers of both. In summary, the complaint made the following allegations relevant to our decision: Petitioners were employees of the Texas and New Orleans Railroad at its Houston Freight House. Local 28 of the Brotherhood was the designated bargaining agents under the Railway Labor Act for the bargaining unit to which petitioners belonged. A contract existed between the Union and the Railroad which gave the employees in the bargaining unit certain protection from discharge and loss of seniority. In May 1954, the Railroad purported to abolish 45 jobs held by petitioners or other Negroes all of whom were either discharged or demoted. In truth the 45 jobs were not abolished at all but instead filled by whites as the Negroes were ousted, except for a few instances where Negroes were rehired to fill their old jobs but with loss of seniority. Despite repeated pleas by petitioners, the Union, acting according to plan, did nothing to protect them against these discriminatory discharges and refused to give them protection comparable to that given white employees. The complaint then went on to allege that the Union had failed in general to represent Negro employees equally and in good faith. It charged that such discrimination constituted a violation of petitioners' right under the Railway Labor Act to fair representation from their bargaining agent. And it concluded by asking for relief in the nature of declaratory judgment, injunction and damages.

The respondents appeared and moved to dismiss the complaint [because] the complaint failed to state a claim upon which relief could be given. The District Court granted the motion to dismiss [and the Court of Appeals affirmed].

* * *

Turning to respondents' [argument], we hold . . . the complaint adequately set forth a claim upon which relief could be granted. In appraising the sufficiency of the complaint we follow, of course, the accepted rule that a complaint should not be dismissed for failure to state a claim unless it appears beyond doubt that the plaintiff can prove no set of facts in support of his claim which would entitle him to relief. Here, the complaint alleged, in part, that petitioners were discharged wrongfully by the Railroad and that the Union, acting according to plan, refused to protect their jobs as it did those of white employees or to help them with their grievances all because they were Negroes. If these allegations are proven there has been a manifest breach of the Union's statutory duty to represent fairly and without hostile discrimination all of the employees in the bargaining unit. This Court squarely held [previously] that discrimination in representation because of race is prohibited by the Railway Labor Act. The bargaining representative's duty not to draw 'irrelevant and invidious' distinctions among those it represents does not come to an abrupt end, as the respondents seem to contend, with the making of an agreement between union and employer. Collective bargaining is a continuing process. Among other things, it involves day-to-day adjustments in the contract and other working rules, resolution of new problems not covered by existing agreements, and the protection of employee rights already secured by contract. The bargaining representative can no more unfairly discriminate in carrying out these functions than it can in negotiating a collective agreement. A contract may be fair and impartial on its face yet administered in such a way, with the active or tacit consent of the union, as to be flagrantly discriminatory against some members of the bargaining unit.

* * *

The respondents also argue that the complaint failed to set forth specific facts to support its general allegations of discrimination and that its dismissal is therefore proper. The decisive answer to this is that the Federal Rules of Civil Procedure do not require a claimant to set out in detail the facts upon which he bases his claim. To the contrary, all the Rules require is 'a short and plain statement of the claim'[8] that will give the defendant fair notice of what the plaintiff's claim is and the grounds upon which it

---

[8]   See Rule 8(a)(2).

rests. The illustrative forms appended to the Rules plainly demonstrate this. Such simplified 'notice pleading' is made possible by the liberal opportunity for discovery and the other pretrial procedures established by the Rules to disclose more precisely the basis of both claim and defense and to define more narrowly the disputed facts and issues.[9] Following the simple guide of Rule 8(f) that 'all pleadings shall be so construed as to do substantial justice,' we have no doubt that petitioners' complaint adequately set forth a claim and gave the respondents fair notice of its basis. The Federal Rules reject the approach that pleading is a game of skill in which one misstep by counsel may be decisive to the outcome and accept the principle that the purpose of pleading is to facilitate a proper decision on the merits.

The judgment is reversed and the cause is remanded to the District Court for further proceedings not inconsistent with this opinion.

DIRECTED READING QUESTIONS

14. In *Conley,* why did the defendant argue the complaint failed to state a claim entitling the plaintiff to relief?

15. How did the Court respond to the defendant's argument?

16. Did the *Conley* complaint contain any facts?

17. What precisely does the *Conley* opinion say about the requirement of facts when attempting to state a claim pursuant to Rule 8(a)(2)?

18. How does *Conley* justify the liberal pleading standard of the Federal Rules of Civil Procedure?

19. Why is this liberal pleading standard considered a notice pleading standard?

BELL ATLANTIC CORP. v. TWOMBLY (2007)
Supreme Court of the United States
550 U.S. 544

JUSTICE SOUTER delivered the opinion of the Court.

Liability under § 1 of the Sherman Act, 15 U.S.C. § 1, requires a "contract, combination . . ., or conspiracy, in restraint of trade or commerce." The question in this putative class action is whether a § 1 complaint can survive a motion to dismiss when it alleges that major telecommunications providers engaged in certain parallel conduct unfavorable to competition, absent some factual context suggesting agreement, as distinct from identical, independent action. We hold that such a complaint should be dismissed.

The upshot of the 1984 divestiture of the American Telephone & Telegraph Company's (AT & T) local telephone business was a system of regional service monopolies (variously called "Regional Bell Operating Companies," "Baby Bells," or "Incumbent Local Exchange Carriers" (ILECs)), and a separate, competitive market for long-distance service from which the ILECs were excluded. More than a decade later, Congress

---

[9] See, e.g., Rule 12(e) (motion for a more definite statement); Rule 12(f) (motion to strike portions of the pleading); Rule 12(c) (motion for judgment on the pleadings); Rule 16 (pre-trial procedure and formulation of issue); Rules 26–37 (depositions and discovery); Rule 56 (motion for summary judgment): Rule 15 (right to amend).

withdrew approval of the ILECs' monopolies by enacting the Telecommunications Act of 1996 (1996 Act), 110 Stat. 56, which "fundamentally restructure[d] local telephone markets" and "subject[ed] [ILECs] to a host of duties intended to facilitate market entry." In recompense, the 1996 Act set conditions for authorizing ILECs to enter the long-distance market.

"Central to the [new] scheme [was each ILEC's] obligation . . . to share its network with competitors," which came to be known as "competitive local exchange carriers" (CLECs), A CLEC could make use of an ILEC's network in any of three ways: by (1) "purchas[ing] local telephone services at wholesale rates for resale to end users," (2) "leas[ing] elements of the [ILEC's] network 'on an unbundled basis,'" or (3) "interconnect[ing] its own facilities with the [ILEC's] network." Owing to the "considerable expense and effort" required to make unbundled network elements available to rivals at wholesale prices, the ILECs vigorously litigated the scope of the sharing obligation imposed by the 1996 Act, with the result that the Federal Communications Commission (FCC) three times revised its regulations to narrow the range of network elements to be shared with the CLECs.

Respondents William Twombly and Lawrence Marcus (hereinafter plaintiffs) represent a putative class consisting of all "subscribers of local telephone and/or high speed internet services . . . from February 8, 1996 to present." In this action against petitioners, a group of ILECs, plaintiffs seek treble damages and declaratory and injunctive relief for claimed violations of § 1 of the Sherman Act, which prohibits "[e]very contract, combination in the form of trust or otherwise, or conspiracy, in restraint of trade or commerce among the several States, or with foreign nations."

The complaint alleges that the ILECs conspired to restrain trade in two ways, each supposedly inflating charges for local telephone and high-speed Internet services. Plaintiffs say, first, that the ILECs "engaged in parallel conduct" in their respective service areas to inhibit the growth of upstart CLECs. Complaint ¶ 47. Their actions allegedly included making unfair agreements with the CLECs for access to ILEC networks, providing inferior connections to the networks, overcharging, and billing in ways designed to sabotage the CLECs' relations with their own customers. According to the complaint, the ILECs' "compelling common motivatio[n]" to thwart the CLECs' competitive efforts naturally led them to form a conspiracy; "[h]ad any one [ILEC] not sought to prevent CLECs . . . from competing effectively . . ., the resulting greater competitive inroads into that [ILEC's] territory would have revealed the degree to which competitive entry by CLECs would have been successful in the other territories in the absence of such conduct."

Second, the complaint charges agreements by the ILECs to refrain from competing against one another. These are to be inferred from the ILECs' common failure "meaningfully [to] pursu[e]" "attractive business opportunit[ies]" in contiguous markets where they possessed "substantial competitive advantages," [Complaint], ¶¶ 40–41, and from a statement of Richard Notebaert, chief executive officer (CEO) of the ILEC Qwest, that competing in the territory of another ILEC " 'might be a good way to turn a quick dollar but that doesn't make it right,' " [Complaint], ¶ 42.

The complaint couches its ultimate allegations this way:

"In the absence of any meaningful competition between the [ILECs] in one another's markets, and in light of the parallel course of conduct that each engaged in to prevent competition from CLECs within their respective local telephone and/or high speed internet services markets and the other facts and market circumstances alleged above, Plaintiffs allege upon information and belief that [the ILECs] have entered into a contract, combination or conspiracy to prevent competitive entry in their respective local telephone and/or high speed internet services markets and have agreed not to compete with one another and otherwise allocated customers and markets to one another." *Id.*, ¶ 51.[2]

The United States District Court for the Southern District of New York dismissed the complaint for failure to state a claim upon which relief can be granted. The District Court acknowledged that "plaintiffs may allege a conspiracy by citing instances of parallel business behavior that suggest an agreement," but emphasized that "while '[c]ircumstantial evidence of consciously parallel behavior may have made heavy inroads into the traditional judicial attitude toward conspiracy[, . . .] "conscious parallelism" has not yet read conspiracy out of the Sherman Act entirely.' " Thus, the District Court understood that allegations of parallel business conduct, taken alone, do not state a claim under § 1; plaintiffs must allege additional facts that "ten[d] to exclude independent self-interested conduct as an explanation for defendants' parallel behavior. The District Court found plaintiffs' allegations of parallel ILEC actions to discourage competition inadequate because "the behavior of each ILEC in resisting the incursion of CLECs is fully explained by the ILEC's own interests in defending its individual territory." As to the ILECs' supposed agreement against competing with each other, the District Court found that the complaint does not "alleg[e] facts . . . suggesting that refraining from competing in other territories as CLECs was contrary to [the ILECs'] apparent economic interests, and consequently [does] not rais[e] an inference that [the ILECs'] actions were the result of a conspiracy."

The Court of Appeals for the Second Circuit reversed, holding that the District Court tested the complaint by the wrong standard. It held that "plus factors are not *required* to be pleaded to permit an antitrust claim based on parallel conduct to survive dismissal." Although the Court of Appeals took the view that plaintiffs must plead facts that "include conspiracy among the realm of 'plausible' possibilities in order to survive a motion to dismiss," it then said that "to rule that allegations of parallel anticompetitive conduct fail to support a plausible conspiracy claim, a court would have to conclude that there is no set of facts that would permit a plaintiff to demonstrate that the particular parallelism asserted was the product of collusion rather than coincidence."

---

[2] In setting forth the grounds for § 1 relief, the complaint repeats these allegations in substantially similar language:

"Beginning at least as early as February 6, 1996, and continuing to the present, the exact dates being unknown to Plaintiffs, Defendants and their co-conspirators engaged in a contract, combination or conspiracy to prevent competitive entry in their respective local telephone and/or high speed internet services markets by, among other things, agreeing not to compete with one another and to stifle attempts by others to compete with them and otherwise allocating customers and markets to one another in violation of Section 1 of the Sherman Act." *Id.*, ¶ 64, App. 30–31.

We granted certiorari to address the proper standard for pleading an antitrust conspiracy through allegations of parallel conduct and now reverse.

[The Court proceeded to examine what evidence a plaintiff in a Sherman Act § 1 case would need to produce to survive a directed verdict.]

This case presents the antecedent question of what a plaintiff must plead in order to state a claim under § 1 of the Sherman Act. Federal Rule of Civil Procedure 8(a)(2) requires only "a short and plain statement of the claim showing that the pleader is entitled to relief," in order to "give the defendant fair notice of what the . . . claim is and the grounds upon which it rests," *Conley v. Gibson,* 355 U.S. 41, 47, 78 S.Ct. 99, 2 L.Ed.2d 80 (1957). While a complaint attacked by a Rule 12(b)(6) motion to dismiss does not need detailed factual allegations, a plaintiff's obligation to provide the "grounds" of his "entitle[ment] to relief" requires more than labels and conclusions, and a formulaic recitation of the elements of a cause of action will not do. [F]actual allegations must be enough to raise a right to relief above the speculative level. "[T]he pleading must contain something more . . . than . . . a statement of facts that merely creates a suspicion [of] a legally cognizable right of action"[3] on the assumption that all the allegations in the complaint are true (even if doubtful in fact).

In applying these general standards to a § 1 claim, we hold that stating such a claim requires a complaint with enough factual matter (taken as true) to suggest that an agreement was made. Asking for plausible grounds to infer an agreement does not impose a probability requirement at the pleading stage; it simply calls for enough fact to raise a reasonable expectation that discovery will reveal evidence of illegal agreement. And, of course, a well-pleaded complaint may proceed even if it strikes a savvy judge that actual proof of those facts is improbable, and "that a recovery is very remote and unlikely . . . ." Without more, parallel conduct does not suggest conspiracy, and a conclusory allegation of agreement at some unidentified point does not supply facts adequate to show illegality. Hence, when allegations of parallel conduct are set out in order to make a § 1 claim, they must be placed in a context that raises a suggestion of a preceding agreement, not merely parallel conduct that could just as well be independent action.

* * *

Thus, it is one thing to be cautious before dismissing an antitrust complaint in advance of discovery, but quite another to forget that proceeding to antitrust discovery can be expensive. As we indicated over 20 years ago "a district court must retain the power to insist upon some specificity in pleading before allowing a potentially massive factual controversy to proceed." "[T]he costs of modern federal antitrust litigation and the increasing caseload of the federal courts counsel against sending the parties into discovery when there is no reasonable likelihood that the plaintiffs can construct a claim from the events related in the complaint. That potential expense is obvious enough in the present case: plaintiffs represent a putative class of at least 90 percent of all subscribers to local telephone or high-speed Internet service in the continental United

---

[3]   The dissent greatly oversimplifies matters by suggesting that the Federal Rules somehow dispensed with the pleading of facts altogether. While, for most types of cases, the Federal Rules eliminated the cumbersome requirement that a claimant "set out *in detail* the facts upon which he bases his claim," *Conley v. Gibson,* 355 U.S. 41, 47 (1957), Rule 8(a)(2) still requires a "showing," rather than a blanket assertion, of entitlement to relief. Without some factual allegation in the complaint, it is hard to see how a claimant could satisfy the requirement of providing not only "fair notice" of the nature of the claim, but also "grounds" on which the claim rests.

States, in an action against America's largest telecommunications firms (with many thousands of employees generating reams and gigabytes of business records) for unspecified (if any) instances of antitrust violations that allegedly occurred over a period of seven years.

It is no answer to say that a claim just shy of a plausible entitlement to relief can, if groundless, be weeded out early in the discovery process through "careful case management," *post*, at 1975, given the common lament that the success of judicial supervision in checking discovery abuse has been on the modest side. And it is self-evident that the problem of discovery abuse cannot be solved by "careful scrutiny of evidence at the summary judgment stage," much less "lucid instructions to juries[.]" The threat of discovery expense will push cost-conscious defendants to settle even anemic cases before reaching those proceedings. Probably, then, it is only by taking care to require allegations that reach the level suggesting conspiracy that we can hope to avoid the potentially enormous expense of discovery in cases with no " 'reasonably founded hope that the [discovery] process will reveal relevant evidence' " to support a § 1 claim.

Plaintiffs do not, of course, dispute the requirement of plausibility and the need for something more than merely parallel behavior [but] their main argument against the plausibility standard at the pleading stage is its ostensible conflict with an early statement of ours construing Rule 8. Justice Black's opinion for the Court in *Conley v. Gibson* spoke not only of the need for fair notice of the grounds for entitlement to relief but of "the accepted rule that a complaint should not be dismissed for failure to state a claim unless it appears beyond doubt that the plaintiff can prove no set of facts in support of his claim which would entitle him to relief." This "no set of facts" language can be read in isolation as saying that any statement revealing the theory of the claim will suffice unless its factual impossibility may be shown from the face of the pleadings; and the Court of Appeals appears to have read *Conley* in some such way when formulating its understanding of the proper pleading standard.

* * *

We could go on, but there is no need to pile up further citations to show that *Conley's* "no set of facts" language has been questioned, criticized, and explained away long enough. To be fair to the *Conley* Court, the passage should be understood in light of the opinion's preceding summary of the complaint's concrete allegations, which the Court quite reasonably understood as amply stating a claim for relief. But the passage so often quoted fails to mention this understanding on the part of the Court, and after puzzling the profession for 50 years, this famous observation has earned its retirement. The phrase is best forgotten as an incomplete, negative gloss on an accepted pleading standard: once a claim has been stated adequately, it may be supported by showing any set of facts consistent with the allegations in the complaint. *Conley,* then, described the breadth of opportunity to prove what an adequate complaint claims, not the minimum standard of adequate pleading to govern a complaint's survival.

When we look for plausibility in this complaint, we agree with the District Court that plaintiffs' claim of conspiracy in restraint of trade comes up short. To begin with, the complaint leaves no doubt that plaintiffs rest their § 1 claim on descriptions of parallel conduct and not on any independent allegation of actual agreement among the ILECs. Although in form a few stray statements speak directly of agreement, on fair reading these are merely legal conclusions resting on the prior allegations. Thus, the complaint first takes account of the alleged "absence of any meaningful competition between [the ILECs] in one another's markets," "the parallel course of conduct that each [ILEC] engaged in to prevent competition from CLECs," "and the other facts and market circumstances alleged [earlier]"; "in light of" these, the complaint concludes "that [the ILECs] have entered into a contract, combination or conspiracy to prevent competitive entry into their ... markets and have agreed not to compete with one another." Complaint ¶ 51.[10]

* * *

Plaintiffs say that our analysis runs counter to *Swierkiewicz,* which held that "a complaint in an employment discrimination lawsuit [need] not contain specific facts establishing a prima facie case of discrimination . . . . They argue that just as the prima facie case is a "flexible evidentiary standard" that "should not be transposed into a rigid pleading standard for discrimination cases," "transpos[ing] 'plus factor' summary judgment analysis woodenly into a rigid Rule 12(b)(6) pleading standard . . . would be unwise." As the District Court correctly understood, however, "*Swierkiewicz* did not change the law of pleading, but simply re-emphasized . . . that the Second Circuit's use of a heightened pleading standard for Title VII cases was contrary to the Federal Rules' structure of liberal pleading requirements." Even though Swierkiewicz's pleadings "detailed the events leading to his termination, provided relevant dates, and included the ages and nationalities of at least some of the relevant persons involved with his termination," the Court of Appeals dismissed his complaint for failing to allege certain additional facts that Swierkiewicz would need at the trial stage to support his claim in the absence of direct evidence of discrimination. We reversed on the ground that the Court of Appeals had impermissibly applied what amounted to a heightened pleading requirement by insisting that Swierkiewicz allege "specific facts" beyond those necessary to state his claim and the grounds showing entitlement to relief.

Here, in contrast, we do not require heightened fact pleading of specifics, but only enough facts to state a claim to relief that is plausible on its face. Because the plaintiffs here have not nudged their claims across the line from conceivable to plausible, their complaint must be dismissed.

* * *

---

[10] If the complaint had not explained that the claim of agreement rested on the parallel conduct described, we doubt that the complaint's references to an agreement among the ILECs would have given the notice required by Rule 8. Apart from identifying a 7-year span in which the § 1 violations were supposed to have occurred (*i.e.,* "[b]eginning at least as early as February 6, 1996, and continuing to the present," *id.,* ¶ 64, App. 30), the pleadings mentioned no specific time, place, or person involved in the alleged conspiracies. This lack of notice contrasts sharply with the model form for pleading negligence, Form 9, which the dissent says exemplifies the kind of "bare allegation" that survives a motion to dismiss. *Post,* at 1977. Whereas the model form alleges that the defendant struck the plaintiff with his car while plaintiff was crossing a particular highway at a specified date and time, the complaint here furnishes no clue as to which of the four ILECs (much less which of their employees) supposedly agreed, or when and where the illicit agreement took place. A defendant wishing to prepare an answer in the simple fact pattern laid out in Form [11] would know what to answer; a defendant seeking to respond to plaintiffs' conclusory allegations in the § 1 context would have little idea where to begin.

The judgment of the Court of Appeals for the Second Circuit is reversed, and the case is remanded for further proceedings consistent with this opinion.

It is so ordered.

JUSTICE STEVENS, with whom JUSTICE GINSBURG joins . . . . dissenting.

Everything today's majority says would therefore make perfect sense if it were ruling on a Rule 56 motion for summary judgment and the evidence included nothing more than the Court has described. But it should go without saying in the wake of *Swierkiewicz* that a heightened production burden at the summary judgment stage does not translate into a heightened pleading burden at the complaint stage. The majority rejects the complaint in this case because—in light of the fact that the parallel conduct alleged is consistent with ordinary market behavior—the claimed conspiracy is "conceivable" but not "plausible."

I have my doubts about the majority's assessment of the plausibility of this alleged conspiracy. But even if the majority's speculation is correct, its "plausibility" standard is irreconcilable with Rule 8 and with our governing precedents.

DIRECTED READING QUESTIONS

20. Does the *Twombly* opinion assume that Form 11 remains valid even after the introduction of the plausibility standard?

21. Compare and explain how the *Twombly* opinion characterizes the allegations in the *Conley* complaint, the *Swierkiewicz* complaint, and Form 11, on the one hand, with the allegations in the *Twombly* complaint, on the other. As you do this, consider this excerpt from the defendant's motion to dismiss in the *Twombly* case:

> Plaintiffs **do not name any individual who is alleged to have agreed with any other individual**; they **do not indicate when any such agreement might have been reached** (only that it was "at least" more than seven years ago); they **do not suggest what form the agreement might have taken**, or even **whether such an agreement was express or merely tacit**; they **do not offer any mechanism for enforcement** of such an agreement; nor **do they even identify the corporate parties to the alleged agreement**. Without any such facts, plaintiffs cannot even meet the standard that they say should apply. The amended complaint here contains no such detail.

22. How do the *Twombly* and *Swierkiewicz* opinions differ in their view of discovery as a process which justifies a liberal pleading standard?

23. How does this Court modify the conceivability standard expressed in *Conley*?

24. Argue that the *Twombly* complaint failed the plausibility test because it did not contain enough information.

25. Argue that the *Twombly* complaint failed the plausibility test because it contained too much information.

26. The *Twombly* Court gives no weight to the allegation of conspiracy in assessing the sufficiency of the complaint because "conspiracy" is a legal conclusion. Yet the *Twombly*

Court approves of Form 11. Is "negligence" in Form 11 not also a legal conclusion? How do you explain this apparent discrepancy?

ASHCROFT V. IQBAL (2009)
Supreme Court of the United States
556 U.S. 662

JUSTICE KENNEDY delivered the opinion of the Court.

Javaid Iqbal (hereinafter respondent) is a citizen of Pakistan and a Muslim. In the wake of the September 11, 2001, terrorist attacks he was arrested in the United States on criminal charges and detained by federal officials. Respondent claims he was deprived of various constitutional protections while in federal custody. To redress the alleged deprivations, respondent filed a complaint against numerous federal officials, including John Ashcroft, the former Attorney General of the United States, and Robert Mueller, the Director of the Federal Bureau of Investigation (FBI). Ashcroft and Mueller are the petitioners in the case now before us. As to these two petitioners, the complaint alleges that they adopted an unconstitutional policy that subjected respondent to harsh conditions of confinement on account of his race, religion, or national origin.

In the District Court petitioners . . . moved to dismiss the suit, contending the complaint was not sufficient to state a claim against them. The District Court denied the motion to dismiss, concluding the complaint was sufficient to state a claim despite petitioners' official status at the times in question. Petitioners brought an interlocutory appeal in the Court of Appeals for the Second Circuit. The court, without discussion, assumed it had jurisdiction over the order denying the motion to dismiss; and it affirmed the District Court's decision.

Respondent's account of his prison ordeal could, if proved, demonstrate unconstitutional misconduct by some governmental actors. But the allegations and pleadings with respect to these actors are not before us here. This case instead turns on a narrower question: Did respondent, as the plaintiff in the District Court, plead factual matter that, if taken as true, states a claim that petitioners deprived him of his clearly established constitutional rights. We hold respondent's pleadings are insufficient.

I

Following the 2001 attacks, the FBI and other entities within the Department of Justice began an investigation of vast reach to identify the assailants and prevent them from attacking anew. The FBI dedicated more than 4,000 special agents and 3,000 support personnel to the endeavor. By September 18 "the FBI had received more than 96,000 tips or potential leads from the public."

* * *

In the ensuing months the FBI questioned more than 1,000 people with suspected links to the attacks in particular or to terrorism in general. Of those individuals, some 762 were held on immigration charges; and a 184-member subset of that group was deemed to be "of 'high interest' " to the investigation. The high-interest detainees were held under restrictive conditions designed to prevent them from communicating with the general prison population or the outside world.

Respondent was one of the detainees. According to his complaint, in November 2001 agents of the FBI and Immigration and Naturalization Service arrested him on charges of fraud in relation to identification documents and conspiracy to defraud the United States. Pending trial for those crimes, respondent was housed at the Metropolitan Detention Center (MDC) in Brooklyn, New York. Respondent was designated a person "of high interest" to the September 11 investigation and in January 2002 was placed in a section of the MDC known as the Administrative Maximum Special Housing Unit ADMAX SHU). As the facility's name indicates, the ADMAX SHU incorporates the maximum security conditions allowable under Federal Bureau of Prisons regulations. *Ibid.* ADMAX SHU detainees were kept in lockdown 23 hours a day, spending the remaining hour outside their cells in handcuffs and leg irons accompanied by a four-officer escort.

Respondent pleaded guilty to the criminal charges, served a term of imprisonment, and was removed to his native Pakistan. He then filed a *Bivens* action in the United States District Court for the Eastern District of New York against 34 current and former federal officials and 19 "John Doe" federal corrections officers. The defendants range from the correctional officers who had day-to-day contact with respondent during the term of his confinement, to the wardens of the MDC facility, all the way to petitioners—officials who were at the highest level of the federal law enforcement hierarchy.

The 21-cause-of-action complaint does not challenge respondent's arrest or his confinement in the MDC's general prison population. Rather, it concentrates on his treatment while confined to the ADMAX SHU. The complaint sets forth various claims against defendants who are not before us. For instance, the complaint alleges that respondent's jailors "kicked him in the stomach, punched him in the face, and dragged him across" his cell without justification, subjected him to serial strip and body-cavity searches when he posed no safety risk to himself or others, and refused to let him and other Muslims pray because there would be "[n]o prayers for terrorists."

The allegations against petitioners are the only ones relevant here. The complaint contends that petitioners designated respondent a person of high interest on account of his race, religion, or national origin, in contravention of the First and Fifth Amendments to the Constitution. The complaint alleges that "the [FBI], under the direction of Defendant MUELLER, arrested and detained thousands of Arab Muslim men . . . as part of its investigation of the events of September 11." It further alleges that "[t]he policy of holding post-September-11th detainees in highly restrictive conditions of confinement until they were 'cleared' by the FBI was approved by Defendants ASHCROFT and MUELLER in discussions in the weeks after September 11, 2001." Lastly, the complaint posits that petitioners "each knew of, condoned, and willfully and maliciously agreed to subject" respondent to harsh conditions of confinement "as a matter of policy, solely on account of [his] religion, race, and/or national origin and for no legitimate penological interest." The pleading names Ashcroft as the "principal architect" of the policy, and identifies Mueller as "instrumental in [its] adoption, promulgation, and implementation."

Petitioners moved to dismiss the complaint for failure to state sufficient allegations to show their own involvement in clearly established unconstitutional conduct. The District Court denied their motion. Accepting all of the allegations in respondent's complaint as true, the court held that "it cannot be said that there [is] no set of facts on which [respondent] would be entitled to relief as against" petitioners. Invoking the collateral-order doctrine petitioners filed an interlocutory appeal in the United States Court of Appeals for the Second Circuit. While that appeal was pending, this Court decided *Bell Atlantic Corp. v. Twombly* (2007), which discussed the standard for evaluating whether a complaint is sufficient to survive a motion to dismiss.

The Court of Appeals considered *Twombly's* applicability to this case. Acknowledging that *Twombly* retired the *Conley* no-set-of-facts test relied upon by the District Court, the Court of Appeals' opinion discussed at length how to apply this Court's "standard for assessing the adequacy of pleadings." It concluded that *Twombly* called for a "flexible 'plausibility standard,' which obliges a pleader to amplify a claim with some factual allegations in those contexts where such amplification is needed to render the claim *plausible*." The court found that petitioners' appeal did not present one of "those contexts" requiring amplification. As a consequence, it held respondent's pleading adequate to allege petitioners' personal involvement in discriminatory decisions which, if true, violated clearly established constitutional law.

* * *

We granted certiorari, 554 U.S. ___, 128 S.Ct. 2931, 171 L.Ed.2d 863 (2008), and now reverse.

IV

A

We turn to respondent's complaint. Under Federal Rule of Civil Procedure 8(a)(2), a pleading must contain a "short and plain statement of the claim showing that the pleader is entitled to relief." As the Court held in *Twombly,* the pleading standard Rule 8 announces does not require "detailed factual allegations," but it demands more than an unadorned, the-defendant-unlawfully-harmed-me accusation. A pleading that offers "labels and conclusions" or "a formulaic recitation of the elements of a cause of action will not do." Nor does a complaint suffice if it tenders "naked assertion[s]" devoid of "further factual enhancement."

To survive a motion to dismiss, a complaint must contain sufficient factual matter, accepted as true, to "state a claim to relief that is plausible on its face." A claim has facial plausibility when the plaintiff pleads factual content that allows the court to draw the reasonable inference that the defendant is liable for the misconduct alleged. The plausibility standard is not akin to a "probability requirement," but it asks for more than a sheer possibility that a defendant has acted unlawfully. Where a complaint pleads facts that are "merely consistent with" a defendant's liability, it "stops short of the line between possibility and plausibility of 'entitlement to relief.' "

Two working principles underlie our decision in *Twombly*. First, the tenet that a court must accept as true all of the allegations contained in a complaint is inapplicable to legal conclusions. Threadbare recitals of the elements of a cause of action, supported by mere conclusory statements, do not suffice. . . . Rule 8 marks a notable and generous departure from the hypertechnical, code-pleading regime of a prior era, but it does not unlock the doors of discovery for a plaintiff armed with nothing more than conclusions. Second, only a complaint that states a plausible claim for relief survives a motion to dismiss. Determining whether a complaint states a plausible claim for relief will, as the Court of Appeals observed, be a context-specific task that requires the reviewing court to draw on its judicial experience and common sense. But where the well-pleaded facts do not permit the court to infer more than the mere possibility of misconduct, the complaint has alleged—but it has not "show[n]"—"that the pleader is entitled to relief." Fed. Rule Civ. Proc. 8(a)(2).

In keeping with these principles a court considering a motion to dismiss can choose to begin by identifying pleadings that, because they are no more than conclusions, are not entitled to the assumption of truth. While legal conclusions can provide the framework of a complaint, they must be supported by factual allegations. When there are well-pleaded factual allegations, a court should assume their veracity and then determine whether they plausibly give rise to an entitlement to relief.

Our decision in *Twombly* illustrates the two-pronged approach. There, we considered the sufficiency of a complaint alleging that incumbent telecommunications providers had entered an agreement not to compete and to forestall competitive entry, in violation of the Sherman Act. Recognizing that § 1 enjoins only anticompetitive conduct "effected by a contract, combination, or conspiracy," the plaintiffs in *Twombly* flatly pleaded that the defendants "ha[d] entered into a contract, combination or conspiracy to prevent competitive entry . . . and ha[d] agreed not to compete with one another." The complaint also alleged that the defendants' "parallel course of conduct . . . to prevent competition" and inflate prices was indicative of the unlawful agreement alleged.

The Court held the plaintiffs' complaint deficient under Rule 8. In doing so it first noted that the plaintiffs' assertion of an unlawful agreement was a " 'legal conclusion' " and, as such, was not entitled to the assumption of truth. Had the Court simply credited the allegation of a conspiracy, the plaintiffs would have stated a claim for relief and been entitled to proceed perforce. The Court next addressed the "nub" of the plaintiffs' complaint—the well-pleaded, nonconclusory factual allegation of parallel behavior—to determine whether it gave rise to a "plausible suggestion of conspiracy." Acknowledging that parallel conduct was consistent with an unlawful agreement, the Court nevertheless concluded that it did not plausibly suggest an illicit accord because it was not only compatible with, but indeed was more likely explained by, lawful, unchoreographed free-market behavior. Because the well-pleaded fact of parallel conduct, accepted as true, did not plausibly suggest an unlawful agreement, the Court held the plaintiffs' complaint must be dismissed.

B

Under *Twombly* 's construction of Rule 8, we conclude that respondent's complaint has not "nudged [his] claims" of invidious discrimination "across the line from conceivable to plausible."

We begin our analysis by identifying the allegations in the complaint that are not entitled to the assumption of truth. Respondent pleads that petitioners "knew of, condoned, and willfully and maliciously agreed to subject [him]" to harsh conditions of confinement "as a matter of policy, solely on account of [his] religion, race, and/or national origin and for no legitimate penological interest." The complaint alleges that Ashcroft was the "principal architect" of this invidious policy, and that Mueller was "instrumental" in adopting and executing it. These bare assertions, much like the pleading of conspiracy in *Twombly,* amount to nothing more than a "formulaic recitation of the elements" of a constitutional discrimination claim, namely, that petitioners adopted a policy " 'because of,' not merely 'in spite of,' its adverse effects upon an identifiable group," As such, the allegations are conclusory and not entitled to be assumed true. *Twombly.* To be clear, we do not reject these bald allegations on the ground that they are unrealistic or nonsensical. We do not so characterize them any more than the Court in *Twombly* rejected the plaintiffs' express allegation of a " 'contract, combination or conspiracy to prevent competitive entry,' " because it thought that claim too chimerical to be maintained. It is the conclusory nature of respondent's allegations, rather than their extravagantly fanciful nature, that disentitles them to the presumption of truth.

We next consider the factual allegations in respondent's complaint to determine if they plausibly suggest an entitlement to relief. The complaint alleges that "the [FBI], under the direction of Defendant MUELLER, arrested and detained thousands of Arab Muslim men . . . as part of its investigation of the events of September 11." It further claims that "[t]he policy of holding post-September-11th detainees in highly restrictive conditions of confinement until they were 'cleared' by the FBI was approved by Defendants ASHCROFT and MUELLER in discussions in the weeks after September 11, 2001." Taken as true, these allegations are consistent with petitioners' purposefully designating detainees "of high interest" because of their race, religion, or national origin. But given more likely explanations, they do not plausibly establish this purpose.

The September 11 attacks were perpetrated by 19 Arab Muslim hijackers who counted themselves members in good standing of al Qaeda, an Islamic fundamentalist group. Al Qaeda was headed by another Arab Muslim—Osama bin Laden—and composed in large part of his Arab Muslim disciples. It should come as no surprise that a legitimate policy directing law enforcement to arrest and detain individuals because of their suspected link to the attacks would produce a disparate, incidental impact on Arab Muslims, even though the purpose of the policy was to target neither Arabs nor Muslims. On the facts respondent alleges the arrests Mueller oversaw were likely lawful and justified by his nondiscriminatory intent to detain aliens who were illegally present in the United States and who had potential connections to those who committed terrorist acts. As between that "obvious alternative explanation" for the arrests, *Twombly,* and the purposeful, invidious discrimination respondent asks us to infer, discrimination is not a plausible conclusion.

But even if the complaint's well-pleaded facts give rise to a plausible inference that respondent's arrest was the result of unconstitutional discrimination, that inference alone would not entitle respondent to relief. It is important to recall that respondent's complaint challenges neither the constitutionality of his arrest nor his initial detention in the MDC. Respondent's constitutional claims against petitioners rest solely on their ostensible "policy of holding post-September-11th detainees" in the ADMAX SHU once they were categorized as "of high interest." To prevail on that theory, the complaint must contain facts plausibly showing that petitioners purposefully adopted a policy of classifying post-September-11 detainees as "of high interest" because of their race, religion, or national origin.

This the complaint fails to do. Though respondent alleges that various other defendants, who are not before us, may have labeled him a person "of high interest" for impermissible reasons, his only factual allegation against petitioners accuses them of adopting a policy approving "restrictive conditions of confinement" for post-September-11 detainees until they were " 'cleared' by the FBI." *Ibid.* Accepting the truth of that allegation, the complaint does not show, or even intimate, that petitioners purposefully housed detainees in the ADMAX SHU due to their race, religion, or national origin. All it plausibly suggests is that the Nation's top law enforcement officers, in the aftermath of a devastating terrorist attack, sought to keep suspected terrorists in the most secure conditions available until the suspects could be cleared of terrorist activity. Respondent does not argue, nor can he, that such a motive would violate petitioners' constitutional obligations. He would need to allege more by way of factual content to "nudg[e]" his claim of purposeful discrimination "across the line from conceivable to plausible." *Twombly.*

To be sure, respondent can attempt to draw certain contrasts between the pleadings the Court considered in *Twombly* and the pleadings at issue here. In *Twombly,* the complaint alleged general wrongdoing that extended over a period of years, whereas here the complaint alleges discrete wrongs—for instance, beatings—by lower level Government actors. The allegations here, if true, and if condoned by petitioners, could be the basis for some inference of wrongful intent on petitioners' part. Despite these distinctions, respondent's pleadings do not suffice to state a claim. Unlike in *Twombly,* where the doctrine of *respondeat superior* could bind the corporate defendant, here, as we have noted, petitioners cannot be held liable unless they themselves acted on account of a constitutionally protected characteristic. Yet respondent's complaint does not contain any factual allegation sufficient to plausibly suggest petitioners' discriminatory state of mind. His pleadings thus do not meet the standard necessary to comply with Rule 8.

It is important to note, however, that we express no opinion concerning the sufficiency of respondent's complaint against the defendants who are not before us. Respondent's account of his prison ordeal alleges serious official misconduct that we need not address here. Our decision is limited to the determination that respondent's complaint does not entitle him to relief from petitioners.

C

Respondent offers three arguments that bear on our disposition of his case, but none is persuasive.

1

Respondent first says that our decision in *Twombly* should be limited to pleadings made in the context of an antitrust dispute. This argument is not supported by *Twombly* and is incompatible with the Federal Rules of Civil Procedure. Though *Twombly* determined the sufficiency of a complaint sounding in antitrust, the decision was based on our interpretation and application of Rule 8. That Rule in turn governs the pleading standard "in all civil actions and proceedings in the United States district courts." Fed. Rule Civ. Proc. 1. Our decision in *Twombly* expounded the pleading standard for "all civil actions," and it applies to antitrust and discrimination suits alike.

2

Respondent next implies that our construction of Rule 8 should be tempered where, as here, the Court of Appeals has "instructed the district court to cabin discovery in such a way as to preserve" petitioners' defense of qualified immunity "as much as possible in anticipation of a summary judgment motion." We have held, however, that the question presented by a motion to dismiss a complaint for insufficient pleadings does not turn on the controls placed upon the discovery process. *Twombly.* ("It is no answer to say that a claim just shy of a plausible entitlement to relief can, if groundless, be weeded out early in the discovery process through careful case management given the common lament that the success of judicial supervision in checking discovery abuse has been on the modest side."

Our rejection of the careful-case-management approach is especially important in suits where Government-official defendants are entitled to assert the defense of qualified immunity. The basic thrust of the qualified-immunity doctrine is to free officials from the concerns of litigation, including "avoidance of disruptive discovery." There are serious and legitimate reasons for this.

If a Government official is to devote time to his or her duties, and to the formulation of sound and responsible policies, it is counterproductive to require the substantial diversion that is attendant to participating in litigation and making informed decisions as to how it should proceed. Litigation, though necessary to ensure that officials comply with the law, exacts heavy costs in terms of efficiency and expenditure of valuable time and resources that might otherwise be directed to the proper execution of the work of the Government. The costs of diversion are only magnified when Government officials are charged with responding to, as Judge Cabranes aptly put it, "a national and international security emergency unprecedented in the history of the American Republic."

It is no answer to these concerns to say that discovery for petitioners can be deferred while pretrial proceedings continue for other defendants. It is quite likely that, when discovery as to the other parties proceeds, it would prove necessary for petitioners and their counsel to participate in the process to ensure the case does not develop in a misleading or slanted way that causes prejudice to their position. Even if petitioners are not yet themselves subject to discovery orders, then, they would not be free from the burdens of discovery.

We decline respondent's invitation to relax the pleading requirements on the ground that the Court of Appeals promises petitioners minimally intrusive discovery. That promise provides especially cold comfort in this pleading context, where we are impelled to give real content to the concept of qualified immunity for high-level officials who must be neither deterred nor detracted from the vigorous performance of their duties. Because respondent's complaint is deficient under Rule 8, he is not entitled to discovery, cabined or otherwise.

3

Respondent finally maintains that the Federal Rules expressly allow him to allege petitioners' discriminatory intent "generally," which he equates with a conclusory allegation. It follows, respondent says, that his complaint is sufficiently well pleaded because it claims that petitioners discriminated against him "on account of [his] religion, race, and/or national origin and for no legitimate penological interest." Were we required to accept this allegation as true, respondent's complaint would survive petitioners' motion to dismiss. But the Federal Rules do not require courts to credit a complaint's conclusory statements without reference to its factual context.

It is true that Rule 9(b) requires particularity when pleading "fraud or mistake," while allowing "[m]alice, intent, knowledge, and other conditions of a person's mind [to] be alleged generally." But "generally" is a relative term. In the context of Rule 9, it is to be compared to the particularity requirement applicable to fraud or mistake. Rule 9 merely excuses a party from pleading discriminatory intent under an elevated pleading standard. It does not give him license to evade the less rigid—though still operative—strictures of Rule 8. . . . And Rule 8 does not empower respondent to plead the bare elements of his cause of action, affix the label "general allegation," and expect his complaint to survive a motion to dismiss.

V

We hold that respondent's complaint fails to plead sufficient facts to state a claim for purposeful and unlawful discrimination against petitioners. The Court of Appeals should decide in the first instance whether to remand to the District Court so that respondent can seek leave to amend his deficient complaint.

The judgment of the Court of Appeals is reversed, and the case is remanded for further proceedings consistent with this opinion.

It is so ordered.

DIRECTED READING QUESTIONS

27. Summarize the facts of the *Iqbal* case and identify the claims in the complaint and the allegations in support of those claims.

28. Why do Mueller and Ashcroft assert the complaint fails to state a claim upon which relief can be granted?

29. Explain the district court's decision to deny the defendant's motion to dismiss.

30. Explain the Appellate Court's decision to deny the defendant's motion to dismiss.

31. What broad rules regarding the sufficiency of a claim does the Supreme Court articulate?

32. Describe the three-step plausibility analysis the *Iqbal* Court announces. How does the *Iqbal* Court explain the result in *Twombly*?

33. Can you reconcile prong 3 of the analysis with the Court's statement that plausibility is distinct from probability?

34. According to *Iqbal*, what mechanism should the judge employ to determine relative likelihoods at the pleading stage? Does this give the judge too much control over litigation outcomes?

35. How can the plaintiff, charged with the duty to perform an inquiry reasonable under the circumstances, not be violating Rule 11 if an impartial, non-investigating judge can conclude at the pleading stage that there is a more likely explanation for the facts than the theory of relief asserted by the plaintiff? Note that this conclusion is made with enough certainty to deny the plaintiff discovery.

36. Describe the analytical sequence involved in the Court's conclusion that the *Iqbal* complaint was not plausible.

37. Explain how the following are legal conclusions rather than factual assertions:

  a.   Willfully

  b.   Maliciously

  c.   Knowledge

38. What is a *Bivens* claim? How does this impact the Court's evaluation of the Plaintiff's argument that the factual specificity of the *Iqbal* complaint makes it more akin to the *Conley* and *Swierkiewicz* complaints and unlike the *Twombly* complaint?

39. What three arguments not related to *Bivens* litigation does the Plaintiff make, and how does the Court rule on these arguments?

40. Would the *Conley* and *Swierkiewicz* complaints be plausible under the *Iqbal* plausibility standard?

41. Can you tell the difference between the standard required for an 8(a)(2) claim and a 9(b) claim now given the Supreme Court's requirement that the facts alleged give rise to a "reasonable inference" that the theory of relief asserted explains the facts alleged?

42. Did *Iqbal* change the pleading standard? Consider the following:

Statements from the *Swierkiewicz* Motion to Dismiss describing the heightened pleading standard adopted by the District And Appellate Courts, which the Supreme Court Claimed it was Without Power to Implement by Judicial Interpretation	Statements from the *Iqbal* opinion which the Supreme Court announces as not a heightened pleading standard
In order to survive a motion to dismiss "a plaintiff must specifically allege the events claimed to constitute intentional discrimination as well as circumstances giving rise to a plausible inference' of discrimination.*	To survive a motion to dismiss, a complaint must contain sufficient factual matter, accepted as true, to "state a claim to relief that is plausible on its face. . . .†
Bare assertions of discrimination without more, are insufficient to state a claim for discrimination." Conclusory pleading allegations "fails to satisfy the minimum pleading requirements applicable to claims arising under Title VII.‡	Threadbare recitals of the elements of a cause of action, supported by mere conclusory statements, do not suffice.§

---

*   Swierkiewicz Motion to Dismiss at ¶ 8.
†   Iqbal, 556 U.S. at 1949.
‡   Swierkiewicz Mot. To Dismiss ¶ 10.
§   Iqbal, 556 U.S. at 1949.

Plaintiff alleging [national origin] discrimination must do more than recite conclusory assertions . . . In this action plaintiff does not allege any facts that would connect her national origin with her termination, such that the Court could plausibly infer discriminatory intent.*	First, the tenet that a court must accept a complaint's allegations as true is inapplicable to threadbare recitals of a cause of action's elements, supported by mere conclusory statements. The Rule does call for sufficient factual matter, accepted as true, to "state a claim to relief that is plausible on its face.†

---

*   Swierkiewicz Motion to Dismiss at ¶ 10.

†   Iqbal, 556 U.S. at 1949.

CHAPTER 6

RESPONDING TO A PLEADING SEEKING RELIEF

■ ■ ■

I. SERVICE OF PROCESS

DIRECTED READING QUESTIONS

1. Relate the requirements of Rule 4(a) to the summons form included on the next pages.

2. Review Rule 4 and explain how "Service of Process" puts the defendant on notice of the claim against him.

3. Examine the Return of Service affidavit, required by Rule 4(*l*), on the second page of the summons below and explain how this is relevant to the time periods in Rule 12(a)(1)(A).

AO 440 (Rev. 06/12) Summons in a Civil Action

UNITED STATES DISTRICT COURT
for the
_____ District of _____

_____)))) *Plaintiff(s)*) v.))) _____) *Defendant(s)*)	Civil Action No.

SUMMONS IN A CIVIL ACTION

To: (Defendant's name and address)

A lawsuit has been filed against you.

Within 21 days after service of this summons on you (not counting the day you received it)—or 60 days if you are the United States or a United States agency, or an officer or employee of the United States described in Fed. R. Civ. P. 12(a)(2) or (3)—you must serve on the plaintiff an answer to the attached complaint or a motion under Rule 12 of the Federal Rules of Civil Procedure. The answer or motion must be served on the plaintiff or plaintiff's attorney, whose name and address are:

If you fail to respond, judgment by default will be entered against you for the relief demanded in the complaint. You also must file your answer or motion with the court.

CLERK OF COURT

Date: _____

_____
Signature of Clerk or Deputy Clerk

AO 440 (Rev. 06/12) Summons in a Civil Action (Page 2)

RETURN OF SERVICE	
Service of the Summons and complaint was made by me	DATE
NAME OF SERVER (PRINT)	TITLE
Check one box below to indicate appropriate method of service	

☐   Served personally upon the third-party defendant. Place where served: _____
_____
_____
_____

☐   Left copies thereof at the defendant's dwelling house or usual place of abode with a person of suitable age and discretion
Name of person with whom the summons was left: _____
_____

☐   Returned unexecuted: _____
_____
_____

☐   Other (specify): _____
_____

STATEMENT OF SERVICE FEES		
TRAVEL:	SERVICES	TOTAL

DECLARATION OF SERVER
I declare under penalty of perjury under the laws of the United States of America that the foregoing information contained in the Return of Service and Statement of Service Fees is true and correct.

Executed on   _____   _____
               Date   *Signature of Server*

                                               _____
                                               Address of Server

II. BROAD CONTEXTUALIZATION

DIRECTED READING QUESTIONS

4. In answering these questions assume the complaint contains enough facts to survive the *Iqbal* standard. Alpha sues Beta, and Alpha's complaint alleges the following:

    I.   Beta owed Alpha a duty.

    II.   Beta breached that duty.

    III. Beta's breach of duty was the cause in fact and proximate cause of the harm to Alpha.

    IV.   The harm Alpha suffered is harm to person or property and therefore cognizable in a negligence cause of action.

    a.   How should Beta respond to the complaint if Beta knows all the allegations in the complaint are true?

    b.   How should Beta respond to the complaint in a pure comparative negligence jurisdiction if Beta is uncertain whether she owed Alpha a duty, but she believes Alpha's negligent driving contributed to Alpha's harm and also caused some harm to Beta?

    c.   How should Alpha respond to Beta's answer if Beta answers the complaint by admitting all the allegations in Alpha's complaint but asserts the following immaterial matters as defenses: Alpha is incapable of running three miles and Alpha is ugly?

III. NOT RESPONDING—DEFAULT AND DEFAULT JUDGMENT

SHEPARD CLAIMS SERVICE, INC. V. WILLIAM DARRAH AND ASSOCIATES (1986)

United States Court of Appeals, Sixth Circuit
796 F.2d 190

LIVELY, CHIEF JUDGE.

A panel of this court entered an order granting an interlocutory appeal from the district court's denial of a motion to set aside an entry of default. Having considered the briefs and oral argument of counsel together with the record on appeal, the court concludes that it must vacate the district court order and remand for further proceedings.

I.

A fairly full statement of facts is required. On August 21, 1984 Shepard Claims Services, Inc. (Shepard) filed this contract action in the district court against William Darrah & Associates (Darrah), with jurisdiction based on diversity of citizenship. The complaint alleged essentially that Darrah, a South Carolina-based insurance broker, failed to pay Shepard, a Michigan independent claims adjuster, for services rendered. Following some difficulty in service by mail, service in person was carried out on February 7, 1985.

On February 22, 1985 defendant Darrah's attorney's secretary secured by telephone an extension of time for filing an answer. A confirmation letter from defense counsel, drafted and signed by the secretary with the vacationing counsel's permission, stated: "This letter will confirm my secretary's conversation with your secretary of February 22, 1985, to the effect that you have granted my office *45 days from February 22, 1985,* to answer the Complaint in the above captioned cause of action against my client, Will Darrah."

By April 10 defendant had filed no answer, so plaintiff Shepard requested that the clerk enter Darrah's default. On April 19 Darrah filed a "Notice of Retention," following on April 26 with an answer and then on April 29 with a notice of affirmative defenses, a counterclaim, interrogatories and a request for production of documents. On May 1 defendant filed a response to plaintiff's motion for default judgment (which had not been filed as of that time) and a motion to set aside entry of default pursuant to Rule 55(c), Fed.R.Civ.P. On May 8 plaintiff filed its motion for default judgment and response to defendant's motion to set aside entry of default. Along with the motion to set aside entry of default defendant filed two affidavits, from defense counsel and his secretary, in which they stated their understanding of the extension to run 45 days in addition to the normal period of 30 days under Rule 4(e), Fed.R.Civ.P., rather than from February 22. Under this interpretation the answer would have been due on April 23. The confirming letter, according to the secretary, "contained a misstatement" of what she believed was the arrangement and what she informed her employer. Defense counsel did not review the confirming letter upon his return and apparently did not examine the file until the day he filed his "appearance." Defense counsel insists that he did not learn of the April 10 entry of default until April 29, by letter from opposing counsel.

The district court held a hearing on pending motions on May 28, after which the court denied defendant's motion to set aside entry of default. In its order the district court found that defendant's attorney engaged in culpable conduct when he permitted his secretary to make arrangements for the extension and then failed to review the secretary's letter upon returning from vacation.

The district court denied the defendant's motion for reconsideration and certified the case for an interlocutory appeal pursuant to 28 U.S.C. § 1292(b) upon finding that "a substantial basis exists for a difference of opinion on the question of setting aside the default in this matter, and that an immediate appeal may materially advance the termination of this litigation."

II.

A.

In *United Coin Meter Co. v. Seaboard Coastline R.R.,* this court considered a set of circumstances quite similar to those recorded in the present case. After the parties were unable to go forward with a scheduled hearing on the defendant's motion to dismiss, opposing counsel agreed to a 20-day period for the defendant to file an answer. Plaintiff's counsel construed the agreement as running from April 28, while defendant's counsel believed the time ran from May 5. When no answer was filed by April 28, plaintiff's counsel caused a default to be entered by the clerk. The only matter in dispute was the date from which the 20-day period was to run.

Following a hearing the district court found no "excusable neglect" on the part of the defendant. The court also concluded that the affidavits of the defendant failed to establish the existence of a meritorious defense. The district court refused to set aside the default and entered a default judgment for the full amount sought in the complaint. A hearing was held on the defendant's motion for reconsideration. The district court denied reconsideration, finding that there was no "good cause" for setting aside entry of default or the default judgment.

This court reversed the district court in *United Coin,* finding that the criteria controlling the court's decision on a Rule 55(c) motion had not been satisfied. In agreement with other courts, we concluded that three factors determine the outcome of such a motion:

1. Whether the plaintiff will be prejudiced;

2. Whether the defendant has a meritorious defense; and

3. Whether culpable conduct of the defendant led to the default.

In *United Coin* the plaintiff did not claim prejudice and this court found that the defendant had established a meritorious defense, one "good at law" without reference to the likelihood of success. The decisive issue was whether the default resulted from the defendant's "culpable conduct." In determining that the third requirement had not been met, we repeatedly stated that the defendant's conduct had not been "willful."

B.

The present case differs from *United Coin* in at least one material respect. In *United Coin,* a default judgment was entered, whereas this interlocutory appeal was taken before entry of judgment. If the only issue relates to entry of default, Rule 55(c), Fed.R.Civ.P., provides the standard—"good cause shown." After entry of a default judgment, the court may set the judgment aside "in accordance with Rule 60(b)," which lists several grounds for relief from judgment. Despite this difference the district court and the parties in the present case recognized *United Coin* as the controlling decision. However, the district court found the *United Coin* opinion "ambiguous as to the precise definition of culpable conduct."

On appeal Darrah argues that *United Coin* is not ambiguous, that it clearly adopted the "willful conduct" definition by citing with approval cases from other circuits that equated culpable conduct with willfulness. The sole reference to negligence in the *United Coin* opinion is contained in a discussion of the standards applicable to a Rule 60(b) motion, under which "excusable neglect" is a ground for relief. Darrah asserts that nothing in the opinion indicates that the "good cause" standard of Rule 55(c) is satisfied by a showing of counsel's negligence.

Shepard contends that the district court correctly found that counsel for the defendant was the "designer" of the agreement for additional time to plead, and that his failure to comply with the agreed limitations was "culpable negligence." Shepard argues that the failure of Darrah and its counsel to abide by the time limits they "designed" could properly be found willful, and therefore culpable, conduct.

III.

Rule 55(c) leaves to the discretion of the trial judge the decision whether to set aside an entry of default. However, a strong preference for trials on the merits in federal courts has led to the adoption of a somewhat modified standard of review where defaults are involved. In *United Coin* we wrote:

> Trials on the merits are favored in federal courts and a "glaring abuse" of discretion is not required for reversal of a court's refusal to relieve a party of the harsh sanction of default. The Fifth Circuit came to a similar conclusion [recognizing] . . . that such a standard does not vest the trial court with completely unfettered discretion. . . . [W]hen the grant of a default judgment precludes consideration of the merits of a case, "even a slight abuse [of discretion] may justify reversal."

Since entry of default is just the first procedural step on the road to obtaining a default judgment, the same policy of favoring trials on the merits applies whether considering a motion under Rule 55(c) or Rule 60(b). In practice a somewhat more lenient standard is applied to Rule 55(c) motions where there has only been an entry of default than to Rule 60(b) motions where judgment has been entered. As the court stated in *Chrysler Credit Corp. v. Macino,* 710 F.2d 363, 368 (7th Cir.1983), "Although the elements for relief under Rule 55(c) and Rule 60(b) are substantially the same, the standards are applied more stringently when considering a motion to vacate a default judgment under Rule 60(b)." "Before considering whether the district court properly refused to set aside the default judgment in the case at bar, we note that there is a distinction between the appropriate standard for setting aside a *default* and that appropriate for setting aside a *default judgment*."

Once a defendant fails to file a responsive answer, he is in *default,* and an entry of *default* may be made by either the clerk or the judge. A *default judgment* can be entered by a clerk only if a claim is liquidated or, if a claim is unliquidated, by the judge after a hearing on damages. A *default* can be set aside under rule 55(c) for "good cause shown," but a default that has become final as a *judgment* can be set aside only under the stricter rule 60(b) standards for setting aside final, appealable orders.

IV.

In a different setting the district judge's orders in the present case might not constitute an abuse of discretion. However, we must consider the fact that the plaintiff suffered no prejudice by reason of the tardy pleadings and the defendant did present a meritorious defense in its answer. These findings of the district court are clearly supported by the record. All three factors must be considered in ruling on a motion to set aside entry of default. However, when the first two factors militate in favor of setting aside the entry, it is an abuse of discretion for a district court to deny a Rule 55(c) motion in the absence of a willful failure of the moving party to appear and plead.

The conduct of Darrah's counsel, Mark Shreve, was careless and inexcusable. Nevertheless, it is not necessary that conduct be excusable to qualify for relief under the "good cause" standard of Rule 55(c). We agree [that] "When the issue is one of whether to set aside an entry of default so that the "good cause" standard of Rule 55(c) is applicable, it is not absolutely necessary that the neglect or oversight offered as reason for the delay in filing a responsive pleading be excusable."

The district court stated that defense counsel's conduct, "if not intentional, is certainly 'culpable conduct'." In making this finding the district court apparently relied on the negligence of the defendant's lawyer in not reviewing the work of his secretary.

To be treated as culpable, the conduct of a defendant must display either an intent to thwart judicial proceedings or a reckless disregard for the effect of its conduct on those proceedings. As in *United Coin,* the delay in the present case resulted from a dispute over the date from which an agreed extension was to run. Darrah's attorney filed an entry of appearance and an answer shortly after learning that default had been entered on the basis of Shepard's interpretation of the agreement. The delay was not lengthy and there was no pattern of disregard for court orders or rules. Under these circumstances the strong policy in favor of deciding cases on their merits outweighs any inconvenience to the court or Shepard resulting from the relatively short delay in answering. We agree with the summary of court holdings in 6 Moore's Federal Practice ¶ 55.01[2]:

> Where the defaulting party and counsel have not shown disrespect for the court, or have given evidence of respect for the court's process by their haste in acting to set aside the default, the courts have been inclined towards leniency. . . . Clearly, however, the court may refuse to set aside a default, where the defaulting party has no meritorious defense, where the default is due to willfulness or bad faith, or where the defendant offers no excuse at all for the default.

We do not believe it appropriate to attempt a precise definition of "culpable conduct." Where the party in default satisfies the first two requirements for relief and moves promptly to set aside the default before a judgment is entered, the district court should grant the motion if the party offers a credible explanation for the delay that does not exhibit disregard for the judicial proceedings.

A default judgment deprives the client of his day in court, and should not be used as a vehicle for disciplining attorneys. Although Shepard has made unverified claims that Darrah encouraged its attorney's conduct, there is no basis in the record for finding that the present case involved a deliberate attempt by Darrah to delay the proceedings. Although a party who chooses an attorney takes the risk of suffering from the attorney's incompetence, we do not believe that this record exhibits circumstances in which a client should suffer the ultimate sanction of losing his case without any consideration of the merits because of his attorney's neglect and inattention.

We can understand and sympathize with the reaction of the district court to Shreve's conduct and his explanations or excuses. The "Notice of Retention" indicated that someone in Shreve's office recognized that the time for pleading might be near, or past. Yet another week went by before Shreve filed his answer. The secretary's affidavit ascribed the misunderstanding to a "misstatement" in the letter that the affiant herself wrote. The misunderstanding could have been cured if Shreve had examined the correspondence upon his return from vacation and contacted Shepard's attorney for confirmation.

Despite this evidence of inattention and disarray in defense counsel's office, the fact remains that Shepard suffered no prejudice and Darrah would be deprived of an opportunity to present its defense at a trial if the default were not set aside.

Our disposition of the case does not preclude the district court from assessing or determining some appropriate penalty or sanction against the defendant or his counsel for the delay occasioned by the careless and inexcusable conduct of defendant's counsel herein discussed.

The judgment of the district court is reversed, and the cause is remanded for further proceedings. No costs are allowed.

DIRECTED READING QUESTIONS

5.   When did service of process occur?

6.   How many days did the defendant have to respond after service before the parties modified the time?

7.   What happened on February 22, 1985?

8.   Explain the difference between the plaintiff's and the defendant's interpretation of the agreement regarding an extension of time.

9.   What Rule provides for the entry of default by the clerk? Does the clerk have a choice if the request for a default is properly supported?

10. What is a docket?

11. What does plead or otherwise defend mean?

12. Examine Rules 37(b)(2)(A)(vi) and 41(b) and note what general principles these two rules and Rule 55 might reflect.

13. Why does the defense attorney file a Notice of Retention on April 19, a full 10 days after the entry of default? What is a Notice of Retention? *Hints: The opinion provides, "entry of default is just the first procedural step on the road to obtaining a default judgment . . . ." The defendant was served with a notice of hearing on May 1.*

14. What is the difference between the *United Coin* case and the present case? Is the appellate court's reliance on *United Coin* consistent with the language of Rule 55(c)?

15. What three factors does this court analyze to determine whether a default should be set aside and how does the court analyze them?

16. What is the purpose of default? Why does this court imply default is a disfavored procedural mechanism?

IV. RESPONDING WITH A RULE 12 MOTION

DIRECTED READING QUESTIONS

17. Why are Rules 12(b), 12(e), and 12(f) motions considered pre-answer motions?

18. Use the internet to research and explain briefly, in your own words, exactly what a party is asserting when he/she asserts each of the seven defenses listed in Rule 12(b).

19. Alpha sues Beta for intentional infliction of emotional distress. Within the 21-day period mandated by Rule 12(a)(1)(A)(i), Beta files a pre-answer motion asserting the defense of improper venue. The motion is denied. Carefully review Rule 12(g) and 12(h) and explain whether, after the denial of the motion, Beta may file a subsequent pre-answer motion:

   a. Asserting the defense of lack of personal jurisdiction

   b. Asserting the defense of insufficient process

   c. Asserting the defense of insufficient service of process

   d. Seeking a motion for a more definite statement

   e. Asserting the defense of failure to state a claim upon which relief could be granted

   f. Asserting the defense of lack of subject matter jurisdiction

   g. Asserting the defense of failure to join a party under Rule 19

20. Same facts as above, except that after the denial of the motion Beta responds to being served by filing and serving an answer to Alpha's complaint. Which of the seven defenses listed in Rule 12(b) may Beta include in his answer? Justify your answer by citing to language in Rule 12.

21. Same facts as above, except that Beta responds to being served by filing a motion for a more definite statement. The court grants the motion, and Alpha provides a more definite statement. Does Rule 12(g)(2) prevent Beta from filing another pre-answer motion asserting the defenses of failure to state a claim upon which relief may be granted?

22. Explain the precise language in Rule 12 which mandates the outcomes in the following scenarios.

   • SCENARIO 1:

      o Alpha sues Beta for intentional infliction of emotional distress. Beta files a motion asserting only the defense of insufficient service of process in response to the complaint. The motion is denied. Beta has waived the defenses in Rule 12(b)(2)–(4).

   • SCENARIO 2:

      o Alpha sues Beta for intentional infliction of emotional distress. Beta files a motion asserting the defense of improper venue. The motion is denied. Beta may not make another pre-answer motion asserting any of the defenses in Rule 12(b)(2)–(7) or the objections listed in Rule 12(e) and 12(f).

   • SCENARIO 3:

      o Alpha sues Beta for intentional infliction of emotional distress. Beta files a motion asserting the defense of improper venue. The motion is denied. Beta may not make another pre-answer motion asserting any of the defenses in Rule 12(b)(2)–(7) or the objections listed in Rule 12(e) and 12(f). However, Beta may subsequently raise the defenses listed in Rule 12(b)(6) and 12(b)(7) in one of the following three ways: in any pleading allowed or ordered under Rule 7(a); by a motion under Rule 12(c); or at trial.

- SCENARIO 4:
  - o   Alpha sues Beta for intentional infliction of emotional distress. Beta does not file a motion in response to the complaint, but instead files a responsive pleading which asserts only the defense of lack of personal jurisdiction. Beta has waived the defenses listed in Rule 12(b)(3)–(5).

23. Alpha sues Beta for intentional infliction of emotional distress. Beta responds to the complaint by filing a motion asserting the defense of improper venue. The motion is denied. Beta subsequently answers the complaint and admits everything in Alpha's complaint, including Alpha's allegation that the incident that forms the basis of the allegation occurred ten years ago.

    a.   If the statute of limitations is three years, explain how Beta may subsequently MOVE for dismissal on the basis of failure to state a claim upon which relief could be granted.

    b.   Would Beta have been permitted to MOVE for dismissal on the basis of failure to state a claim upon which relief could be granted before filing his answer but after the motion asserting improper venue was denied?

    c.   After the denial of the motion, would Beta have been able to answer the complaint and assert the defense of failure to state a claim in the answer, even though it was not included in his initial motion?

24. According to Rule 4(c)(1), proper service mandates that "[a] summons must be served with a copy of the complaint." Assume that a defendant is served with a summons, but the process server neglects to also provide a copy of the complaint. Which defense, Rule 12(b)(4) or 12(b)(5), is the precise defense addressing this scenario?

25. Rule 12(a)(4)(B) explains what the non-movant must do after the court grants a motion for a more definite statement. Why is the motion for a more definite statement the only Rule 12 motion with specific instructions about what must occur if the motion is granted?

26. Alpha files and serves a complaint against Beta. The complaint is unintelligible, and as a result, Beta's only response is a motion for a more definite statement. The motion is granted. Alpha serves a more definite statement, which is intelligible. Beta then responds by filing a subsequent motion. According to Rule 12(g)(2), which of the seven defenses listed in Rule 12(b) may not be included in this motion?

V. THE ANSWER AND COUNTERCLAIMS

Here is an answer to the complaint you were provided in Chapter 3.

IN THE UNITED STATES DISTRICT COURT
FOR THE SOUTHERN DISTRICT OF FLORIDA
CASE NO.

JONATHAN D. SLOANE,
           Plaintiff,

vs.

CARNIVAL CORPORATION,
D/B/A CARNIVAL CRUISE LINES, INC.
           Defendant.

_____/

ANSWER

COMES NOW, the Defendant, CARNIVAL CORPORATION, D/B/A CARNIVAL CRUISE LINES INC. (hereinafter CARNIVAL), by and through the undersigned counsel, and files this answer to the Plaintiff, JONATHAN D. SLOANE's complaint alleging as follows:

GENERAL ALLEGATIONS

1. Denied as to amount in controversy. Admitted as to everything else.

2. Admitted.

3. Admitted.

4. Admitted.

5. Admitted.

6. Admitted.

7. Admitted.

8. Admitted.

9. Denied as to unreasonably slippery nature of the deck. Unknown and therefore denied as to violence of slip.

10. Denied.

11. Admitted that outdoor rugs were placed on deck 10. Denied as to the conclusion regarding majority and purpose of rugs.

12. Unknown and therefore denied.

13. Admitted.

14. Admitted.

15. Admitted.

16. Denied.

COUNT I—NEGLIGENCE AGAINST CARNIVAL
on behalf of JONATHAN SLOANE

17. Admitted.

18. Admitted.

19. Denied:

    (A) Denied;

    (B) Denied;

    (C) Denied;

    (D) Denied;

    (E) Denied;

    (F) Denied;

    (G) Denied;

    (H) Denied;

    (I) Denied;

    (J) Denied;

    (K) Denied;

    (L) Denied;

    (M) Denied;

    (N) Denied.

    (O) Denied.

20. Denied.

21. Denied.

22. Admitted.

AFFIRMATIVE DEFENSES

23. Contributory Negligence. Sloane was intoxicated at the time he fell, and this was the cause in fact and proximate cause of his injury.

24. Assumption of Risk. Sloane unreasonably and voluntarily chose to extricate his son instead of calling a crew member qualified and trained to perform the extrication.

25. Waiver. By purchasing the ticket for the cruise which contained a waiver of the passenger's rights regarding litigation, Sloane waived his right to seek judicial redress for any injuries he may have incurred aboard the vessel Victory.

WHEREFORE, the Defendant, CARNIVAL, demands judgment against, the Plaintiff, JONATHAN D. SLOANE plus all other awards this court deems appropriate.

CERTIFICATE OF SERVICE

I HEREBY CERTIFY that a true and correct copy of the foregoing was sent via U.S. mail and facsimile on the _____ day of _____, 2004, to: Rory D. Bahadur, Esq., Downs & Associates, P.A., 255 University Drive, Coral Gables, FL 33134.

> Respectfully Submitted,
>
> Attorneys for Defendant
> 1234 Sunset Ocean Drive
> Miami, FL, 33810
> Telephone No.: (305)-625-9108
> MaryTime@deweycheatum&howe
>
> _____
>
> Mary Time, Esq.
> Florida Bar No.: 0000000

DIRECTED READING QUESTIONS

27. Make sure you can identify how this answer satisfies the requirements of Rule 8(b)(1)(A) and 8(b)(1)(B).

28. What else should the defendant include in their answer if they contend that the plaintiff slipped (as described in the complaint from Chapter 3) because the plaintiff was negligent, and the plaintiff's fall caused significant damage to the deck of the ship?

29. Is a counterclaim a pleading?

30. Is a crossclaim a pleading?

31. What is the difference between a counterclaim and a crossclaim? In answering this question, consider the following fact pattern. Plaintiff is struck by employee who was driving employer's vehicle negligently during the course and scope of employment. Plaintiff sues employee in negligence and employer in vicarious liability, then the following happens in the sequence listed:

    a. Employer realizes that plaintiff was also driving negligently, and that plaintiff's negligence caused damage to employer's vehicle. Employer files a claim for negligence against the plaintiff;

    b. Employer decides to also file a claim against employee in the event employer is found to be vicariously liable;

    c. Employee is also hurt in the accident but feels that it was employer's negligence in training employee that caused the crash and the harm to employee. As a result, employee files a claim against employer seeking to recover for the harm the employer's negligent training caused employee.

32. Rule 13(a)(1) states that "a [responsive] pleading *must state* as a counterclaim" any claim the pleader has which satisfies the conditions in Rule 13(a)(1)(A). What is the consequence of not stating such a claim as a counterclaim? Does this explain why such a claim is considered compulsory?

WIGGLESWORTH V. TEAMSTERS LOCAL UNION NO. 592 (1975)
United States District Court for the Eastern District of Virginia
68 F.R.D. 609

WARRINER, DISTRICT JUDGE.

Plaintiff Welford Wigglesworth, Jr., a member of Teamsters Local Union No. 592, has filed a complaint under the Labor Management Reporting Disclosures Act, 'Act,' alleging that the union and its president have violated certain of his rights as protected by the Act. Specifically, the complaint avers that during meetings of defendant Local No. 592 held on 8 September 1974 and 13 October 1974, plaintiff was prevented from exercising his right to freedom of speech, and was denied his request to have the union membership informed of their rights as required by the Act.

In addition to denying generally the allegations in the complaint, defendants asserted a counterclaim alleging the following: On 3 December 1974, the day on which the complaint was filed, plaintiff called a press conference at which he accused the union of being dominated by the 'Mafia' and that a certain past local union election had been 'fixed.' Defendants claim that these remarks constituted libel and slander . . . .

The matter is now before the Court on plaintiff's motion to dismiss the counterclaim, *inter alia*, for lack of subject matter jurisdiction. There is no diversity of citizenship between the parties, and jurisdiction is founded solely on [28 U.S.C. § 1331].

Defendants' initial contention is that the motion to dismiss for lack of subject matter jurisdiction is untimely and should therefore be denied. However, Rule 12(h)(3), Fed.R.Civ.P. plainly states that challenges to the Court's subject matter jurisdiction may be raised at any time, and the cases have consistently so held. Therefore, the defendants' claim of untimeliness is without merit.

Defendants' counterclaim was filed pursuant to Rule 13, Fed.R.Civ.P. which distinguishes between 'compulsory' and 'permissive' counterclaims. If the defendants' claim arises out of the transaction or occurrence that is the subject matter of the opposing party's claim, then, if certain other requisites not here pertinent, are met, it is compulsory. By definition, compulsory claims are '[need] no independent basis of [f]ederal jurisdiction is required.' Alternatively, if the counterclaim is unconnected with the transaction out of which the primary claim arose, it is permissive, and independent jurisdictional grounds are required.

The threshold question to be decided is whether defendants' counterclaims arise out of the same transaction or occurrence that is the subject matter of the plaintiff's claim. If so, then the counterclaims are compulsory, and are properly before the Court. Thus, the definition of 'transaction or occurrence' is critical to this determination.

There is a substantial body of law which liberally defines the test of compulsoriness as requiring that there be not so much 'an absolute identity of factual backgrounds for the two claims, but only a logical relationship between them.' In *Moore v. New York Cotton Exchange*, the Supreme Court explained that "[t]ransaction' is a word of flexible meaning. It may comprehend a series of many occurrences, depending not so much upon the immediateness of their connection as upon their logical relationship.'

Defendants maintain that under this liberal test, their counterclaims meet the criteria set forth for compulsoriness, and therefore are properly within the Court's ancillary jurisdiction. We must disagree.

The gravamen of plaintiff's claim is that he was denied his right to free speech and expression at certain past union meetings. Thus, the claim arises solely from the alleged wrongful conduct on the part of the union at the specific union meetings in question. Determination of the validity of that claim is limited to ascertaining whether the challenged union meetings were conducted in conformity with the mandates of the Act. However, defendants' counterclaim for libel and slander is predicated on events which are in no wise part of the transactions or occurrences which gave rise to plaintiff's claim. This aspect of the counterclaim is grounded on words allegedly spoken by plaintiff many months after the union meetings in question. There is no indication that the alleged remarks at the press conference on 3 December 1974 had any relationship, logical or otherwise, to the events which transpired at certain past union meetings.

* * *

After an extensive analysis of the various standards which have been employed to ascertain the nature of a counterclaim, Court[s have] base[d] [their] determination on whether the same evidence would support or refute the opposing claims. If the same evidence would substantially dispose of the issues raised by the opposing claims, then the counterclaims were compulsory; if not, then they were permissive.

Applying [this] standard to the facts of this case, [the] conclusion seems inescapable. The evidence necessary for the union to prevail on its libel and slander claims is not relevant to plaintiff's case. Alternatively, the proof of violations by the union under the L.M.R.D.A. varies substantially from that necessary to recover for libel and slander. Similarly, proof of plaintiff's willful abuse of process with resulting damage to the union is quite distinct from that necessary to establish an infringement of plaintiff's rights under the federal statute.

There being no connection between the events giving rise to the counterclaims asserted by defendants, and the transaction or occurrence upon which plaintiff's claim is based, the Court holds that the counterclaims are permissive. Noting that such claims are between non-diverse parties, and are grounded solely in state law, the Court observes that they are without independent jurisdictional support, and must therefore be dismissed, unless falling within an exception to the jurisdictional requirement.

* * *

Accordingly, plaintiff's motion to dismiss the counterclaims will be granted.

DIRECTED READING QUESTIONS

33. Please identify the claim made by the union member (plaintiff) in his complaint. Explain why subject matter jurisdiction exists for this claim.

34. What claim is asserted as a counterclaim in the union's (defendant) answer? What are the elements of these claims?

35. Is the claim asserted by the defendant in the counterclaim a state law or federal law claim? What is the basis of subject matter jurisdiction for the claim in the counterclaim?

36. Examine 28 U.S.C. § 1367(a). Explain how § 1367(a) might provide a federal court subject matter jurisdiction over a claim for which there is not ordinarily a jurisdictional basis if that claim is related enough to a claim for which subject matter jurisdiction exists.

37. Based on your answer in question 35, explain why it is important to classify the libel/slander claims as compulsory counterclaims.

38. Did the court conclude that the defendant's counterclaims were compulsory?

39. Identify the test that the court employed to determine whether the counterclaims were compulsory and explain how the court so concluded.

40. What is the justification for the compulsory counterclaim rule?

41. Would the question of whether the counterclaim was compulsory be any closer if the plaintiff's complaint alleged that the reason his free speech rights were violated on September 8 and October 13, 1974 was because on those dates, the union prevented him from saying exactly what he said at his December 3 press conference?

42. Answer the following hypothetical and explain your answer.

On September 2, 2014, Alpha was driving his car down the single lane Pacific Coast Highway after a particularly stressful day. Proceeding in the opposite direction was an intoxicated driver named Beta. Beta's intoxication along with Alpha's distracted driving led to a head on collision. It just so happened that Charlie, a foreign tourist who was a pedestrian, suffered injuries because immediately after the collision both cars collided with him. Alpha and Beta were also injured in the crash.

Alpha sued Beta, alleging negligence per se because Beta's blood alcohol level was above the statutory limit at the time of the crash. Since Alpha and Beta were from different states and the amount in controversy exclusive of interests and costs was greater than $75,000, the action was commenced in federal district court pursuant to diversity jurisdiction.

At the time Beta was served with Alpha's complaint, Charlie and Beta had already settled without litigation. Charlie planned to sue Alpha at a later date, perhaps after the resolution of Alpha's action against Beta.

Alpha filed his complaint and served Beta on May 1, 2016. Beta contacted an attorney the day after service, and Beta's attorney filed a notice of appearance the day after that. Beta's attorney then left for vacation and returned 19 days after service was effectuated on Beta. He then filed a Rule 12(e) motion for a more definite statement. The motion was granted on September 4, 2016, and Alpha filed and served a more definite complaint which Beta answered. Beta's answer contained a counterclaim for common law negligence against Alpha. In her counterclaim, Beta is seeking unspecified damages for pain, suffering, and medical bills.

Alpha then moved to dismiss the counterclaim for failure to state a claim because the 2-year statute of limitations on Beta's negligence claim had run.

Charlie was in no hurry to file his action against Alpha because he knew that the statute of limitations for a negligence claim by a foreigner against a citizen of the United States was 8 years.

a.   Should Alpha's motion to dismiss Beta's counterclaim be granted?

b. Assuming Alpha prevails in his suit against Beta, does Rule 13(a) bar Charlie's planned claim against Alpha because both claims arose "out of the same transaction or occurrence?"

VI. VOLUNTARY DISMISSAL

DIRECTED READING QUESTIONS

43. Why should there be limits on a plaintiff's ability to file a claim against a defendant then voluntarily dismiss the claim, only to refile the claim and dismiss it again, in a recurring fashion?

44. Revisit the Brent v Angie for Breach of Contract hypothetical after question 12 in Chapter 3. May Brent file a notice of voluntary dismissal before Angie responds to the suit?

45. Assume the first time Brent sued Angie for breach of contract was in state court and Angie removed the action to federal court. May Brent file a notice of voluntary dismissal after removal without a court order?

46. Assume Brent sues and serves Angie for the first time for breach of contract in an action in federal court. May Brent file a notice of voluntary dismissal without a court order after Angie files and serves a Rule 12(b)(6) motion to dismiss?

47. Assume Brent sues and serves Angie for the first time for breach of contract in an action in federal court. May Brent file a notice of voluntary dismissal without a court order after Angie files and serves a Rule 12(b)(6) motion to dismiss and attaches a document titled "Non Contractual Arrangement Between Brent and Angie" to the motion and asks the court to examine the document in support of her motion because it will prove their arrangement was not a contract?

48. Assume Brent first filed the breach of contract suit Against Angie in federal court. He then voluntarily dismissed the action before Angie responded. Brent then refiled the identical action in state court and then voluntarily dismissed the action once again. Does this second dismissal operate as an adjudication on the merits as per the second sentence of Rule 41(a)(1)(B)?

49. If a Plaintiff who sues and serves Defendant for the first time for breach of contract files a notice of voluntary dismissal under Rule 41(a)(1)(A)(i), is the dismissal with prejudice?

50. Plaintiff sues Defendant in state court, and then Plaintiff dismisses the suit. Two months later, Plaintiff sues the same Defendant on the identical cause of action in federal court. Plaintiff and Defendant then get together and sign a stipulation of voluntary dismissal.

    a. Do the parties need a court order for voluntary dismissal to be effective?

    b. Is the action considered to be a dismissal with prejudice?

    c. If the second dismissal was via a notice of dismissal rather than a stipulation, is the dismissal an adjudication on the merits?

51. Plaintiff sues Defendant in state court, and then Plaintiff dismisses the suit. Two months later, Plaintiff sues the same Defendant on the identical cause of action in federal court. Defendant files and serves an answer. Is a court order required for dismissal on Plaintiff's request?

52. Riegfried and Soy are suing Cavid Dopperfield for copyright infringement in the United States District Court for the District of Nevada. Originally, Riegfried and Soy filed the suit in Nevada state court thinking they would have more luck with the jury. They then filed a notice of dismissal in the Nevada state court because Cavid Dopperfield did nothing else but serve them with the state equivalent of a Rule 11 motion, basically letting them know that copyright suits are properly brought only in federal court and not state court. Riegfried and Soy then sued their attorney, who represented them in the state court action, for malpractice. The recovery from the malpractice suit was large enough for them to hire the huge Vegas law firm of Dewey, Cheatum and How to represent them in the current copyright infringement suit now in federal court. Cavid Dopperfield files and serves an answer containing a counterclaim. Immediately after this, Riegfried and Soy realize they cannot win the copyright infringement suit and seek to voluntarily dismiss the copyright suit. Which of the following is true?

   a.   If Dopperfield's counterclaim cannot remain pending for independent adjudication, Riegfried and Soy must obtain a court order to voluntarily dismiss the copyright claim.

   b.   Because Riegfried and Soy previously dismissed the state action based on the same claim, the dismissal of the federal copyright claim must be considered an adjudication on the merits.

   c.   Even if Dopperfield's counterclaim cannot remain pending for independent adjudication, Riegfried and Soy may still obtain voluntary dismissal without a court order.

   d.   Riegfried and Soy may voluntarily dismiss the suit by filing a notice of dismissal of their suit and the counterclaim.

VII. AMENDMENTS

KRUPSKI V. COSTA CROCIERE S. P. A. (2010)
Supreme Court of the United States
560 U.S. 538

Rule 15(c) of the Federal Rules of Civil Procedure governs when an amended pleading "relates back" to the date of a timely filed original pleading and is thus itself timely even though it was filed outside an applicable statute of limitations. Where an amended pleading changes a party or a party's name, the Rule requires, among other things, that "the party to be brought in by amendment . . . knew or should have known that the action would have been brought against it, but for a mistake concerning the proper party's identity." Rule 15(c)(1)(C). In this case, the Court of Appeals held that Rule 15(c) was not satisfied because the plaintiff knew or should have known of the proper defendant before filing her original complaint. The court also held that relation back was not appropriate because the plaintiff had unduly delayed in seeking to amend. We hold that relation back under Rule 15(c)(1)(C) depends on what the party to be added knew or should have known, not on the amending party's knowledge or its timeliness in seeking to amend the pleading. Accordingly, we reverse the judgment of the Court of Appeals.

I

On February 21, 2007, petitioner, Wanda Krupski, tripped over a cable and fractured her femur while she was on board the cruise ship Costa Magica. Upon her return home, she acquired counsel and began the process of seeking compensation for her injuries. Krupski's passenger ticket—which explained that it was the sole contract between each passenger and the carrier, included a variety of requirements for obtaining damages for an injury suffered on board one of the carrier's ships. The ticket identified the carrier as

> Costa Crociere S. p. A., an Italian corporation, and all Vessels and other ships owned, chartered, operated, marketed or provided by Costa Crociere, S. p. A., and all officers, staff members, crew members, independent contractors, medical providers, concessionaires, pilots, suppliers, agents and assigns onboard said Vessels, and the manufacturers of said Vessels and all their component parts.

The ticket required an injured party to submit "written notice of the claim with full particulars . . . to the carrier or its duly authorized agent within 185 days after the date of injury." The ticket further required any lawsuit to be "filed within one year after the date of injury" and to be "served upon the carrier within 120 days after filing." For cases arising from voyages departing from or returning to a United States port in which the amount in controversy exceeded $75,000, the ticket designated the United States District Court for the Southern District of Florida in Broward County, Florida, as the exclusive forum for a lawsuit. The ticket extended the "defenses, limitations and exceptions . . . that may be invoked by the CARRIER" to "all persons who may act on behalf of the CARRIER or on whose behalf the CARRIER may act," including "the CARRIER's parents, subsidiaries, affiliates, successors, assigns, representatives, agents, employees, servants, concessionaires and contractors" as well as "Costa Cruise Lines N. V.," identified as the "sales and marketing agent for the CARRIER and the issuer of this Passage Ticket Contract." The front of the ticket listed Costa Cruise Lines' address in Florida and stated that an entity called "Costa Cruises" was "the first cruise company in the world" to obtain a certain certification of quality.

On July 2, 2007, Krupski's counsel notified Costa Cruise Lines of Krupski's claims. On July 9, 2007, the claims administrator for Costa Cruise requested additional information from Krupski "[i]n order to facilitate our future attempts to achieve a pre-litigation settlement." The parties were unable to reach a settlement, however, and on February 1, 2008—three weeks before the 1-year limitations period expired—Krupski filed a negligence action against Costa Cruise, invoking the diversity jurisdiction of the Federal District Court for the Southern District of Florida. The complaint alleged that Costa Cruise "owned, operated, managed, supervised and controlled" the ship on which Krupski had injured herself; that Costa Cruise had extended to its passengers an invitation to enter onto the ship; and that Costa Cruise owed Krupski a duty of care, which it breached by failing to take steps that would have prevented her accident. The complaint further stated that venue was proper under the passenger ticket's forum selection clause and averred that, by July 2007 notice of her claims, Krupski had complied with the ticket's presuit requirements. Krupski served Costa Cruise on February 4, 2008.

Over the next several months—after the limitations period had expired—Costa Cruise brought Costa Crociere's existence to Krupski's attention three times. First, on February 25, 2008, Costa Cruise filed its answer, asserting that it was not the proper defendant, as it was merely the North American sales and marketing agent for Costa Crociere, which was the actual carrier and vessel operator. Second, on March 20, 2008, Costa Cruise listed Costa Crociere as an interested party in its corporate disclosure statement. Finally, on May 6, 2008, Costa Cruise moved for summary judgment, again stating that Costa Crociere was the proper defendant.

On June 13, 2008, Krupski responded to Costa Cruise's motion for summary judgment, arguing for limited discovery to determine whether Costa Cruise should be dismissed. According to Krupski, the following sources of information led her to believe Costa Cruise was the responsible party: The travel documents prominently identified Costa Cruise and gave its Florida address; Costa Cruise's Web site listed Costa Cruise in Florida as the United States office for the Italian company Costa Crociere; and the Web site of the Florida Department of State listed Costa Cruise as the only "Costa" company registered to do business in that State. Krupski also observed that Costa Cruise's claims administrator had responded to her claims notification without indicating that Costa Cruise was not a responsible party. With her response, Krupski simultaneously moved to amend her complaint to add Costa Crociere as a defendant.

On July 2, 2008, after oral argument, the District Court denied Costa Cruise's motion for summary judgment without prejudice and granted Krupski leave to amend, ordering that Krupski effect proper service on Costa Crociere by September 16, 2008. Complying with the court's deadline, Krupski filed an amended complaint on July 11, 2008, and served Costa Crociere on August 21, 2008. On that same date, the District Court issued an order dismissing Costa Cruise from the case pursuant to the parties' joint stipulation, Krupski apparently having concluded that Costa Cruise was correct that it bore no responsibility for her injuries.

Shortly thereafter, Costa Crociere—represented by the same counsel who had represented Costa Cruise,—moved to dismiss, contending that the amended complaint did not relate back under Rule 15(c) and was therefore untimely. The District Court agreed. Rule 15(c), the court explained, imposes three requirements before an amended complaint against a newly named defendant can relate back to the original complaint. First, the claim against the newly named defendant must have arisen "out of the conduct, transaction, or occurrence set out—or attempted to be set out—in the original pleading." Fed. Rules Civ. Proc. 15(c)(1)(B), (C). Second, "within the period provided by Rule 4(m) for serving the summons and complaint" (which is ordinarily 120 days* from when the complaint is filed, see Rule 4(m)), the newly named defendant must have "received such notice of the action that it will not prejudiced in defending on the merits." Rule 15(c)(1)(C)(i). Finally, the plaintiff must show that, within the Rule 4(m) period, the newly named defendant "knew or should have known that the action would have been brought against it, but for a mistake concerning the proper party's identity." Rule 15(c)(1)(C)(ii).

The first two conditions posed no problem, the court explained: The claim against Costa Crociere clearly involved the same occurrence as the original claim against Costa

---

*   Rule 4(m) has since been amended and the relevant time period is now 90 days.

Cruise, and Costa Crociere had constructive notice of the action and had not shown that any unfair prejudice would result from relation back. But the court found the third condition fatal to Krupski's attempt to relate back, concluding that Krupski had not made a mistake concerning the identity of the proper party. Relying on Eleventh Circuit precedent, the court explained that the word "mistake" should not be construed to encompass a deliberate decision not to sue a party whose identity the plaintiff knew before the statute of limitations had run. Because Costa Cruise informed Krupski that Costa Crociere was the proper defendant in its answer, corporate disclosure statement, and motion for summary judgment, and yet Krupski delayed for months in moving to amend and then in filing an amended complaint, the court concluded that Krupski knew of the proper defendant and made no mistake.

The Eleventh Circuit affirmed in an unpublished *per curiam* opinion. Rather than relying on the information contained in Costa Cruise's filings, all of which were made after the statute of limitations had expired, as evidence that Krupski did not make a mistake, the Court of Appeals noted that the relevant information was located within Krupski's passenger ticket, which she had furnished to her counsel well before the end of the limitations period. Because the ticket clearly identified Costa Crociere as the carrier, the court stated, Krupski either knew or should have known of Costa Crociere's identity as a potential party. It was therefore appropriate to treat Krupski as having chosen to sue one potential party over another.

* * *

We granted certiorari to resolve tension among the Circuits over the breadth of Rule 15(c)(1)(C)(ii), and we now reverse.

II

Under the Federal Rules of Civil Procedure, an amendment to a pleading relates back to the date of the original pleading when:

"(A) the law that provides the applicable statute of limitations allows relation back;

"(B) the amendment asserts a claim or defense that arose out of the conduct, transaction, or occurrence set out—or attempted to be set out—in the original pleading; or

"(C) the amendment changes the party or the naming of the party against whom a claim is asserted, if Rule 15(c)(1)(B) is satisfied and if, within the period provided by Rule 4(m) for serving the summons and complaint, the party to be brought in by amendment:

"(i) received such notice of the action that it will not be prejudiced in defending on the merits; and

"(ii) knew or should have known that the action would have been brought against it, but for a mistake concerning the proper party's identity." Rule 15(c)(1).

In our view, neither of the Court of Appeals' reasons for denying relation back under Rule 15(c)(1)(C)(ii) finds support in the text of the Rule. We consider each reason in turn.

A

The Court of Appeals first decided that Krupski either knew or should have known of the proper party's identity and thus determined that she had made a deliberate choice instead of a mistake in not naming Costa Crociere as a party in her original pleading. By focusing on Krupski's knowledge, the Court of Appeals chose the wrong starting point. The question under Rule 15(c)(1)(C)(ii) is not whether Krupski knew or should have known the identity of Costa Crociere as the proper defendant, but whether Costa Crociere knew or should have known that it would have been named as a defendant but for an error. Rule 15(c)(1)(C)(ii) asks what the prospective *defendant* knew or should have known during the Rule 4(m) period, not what the *plaintiff* knew or should have known at the time of filing her original complaint.

Information in the plaintiff's possession is relevant only if it bears on the defendant's understanding of whether the plaintiff made a mistake regarding the proper party's identity. For purposes of that inquiry, it would be error to conflate knowledge of a party's existence with the absence of mistake. A mistake is "[a]n error, misconception, or misunderstanding; an erroneous belief." Black's Law Dictionary 1092 (9th ed.2009); see also Webster's Third New International Dictionary 1446 (2002) (defining "mistake" as "a misunderstanding of the meaning or implication of something"; "a wrong action or statement proceeding from faulty judgment, inadequate knowledge, or inattention"; "an erroneous belief"; or "a state of mind not in accordance with the facts"). That a plaintiff knows of a party's existence does not preclude her from making a mistake with respect to that party's identity. A plaintiff may know that a prospective defendant—call him party A—exists, while erroneously believing him to have the status of party B. Similarly, a plaintiff may know generally what party A does while misunderstanding the roles that party A and party B played in the "conduct, transaction, or occurrence" giving rise to her claim. If the plaintiff sues party B instead of party A under these circumstances, she has made a "mistake concerning the proper party's identity" notwithstanding her knowledge of the existence of both parties. The only question under Rule 15(c)(1)(C)(ii), then, is whether party A knew or should have known that, absent some mistake, the action would have been brought against him.

Respondent urges that the key issue under Rule 15(c)(1)(C)(ii) is whether the plaintiff made a deliberate choice to sue one party over another. We agree that making a deliberate choice to sue one party instead of another while fully understanding the factual and legal differences between the two parties is the antithesis of making a mistake concerning the proper party's identity. We disagree, however, with respondent's position that any time a plaintiff is aware of the existence of two parties and chooses to sue the wrong one, the proper defendant could reasonably believe that the plaintiff made no mistake. The reasonableness of the mistake is not itself at issue. As noted, a plaintiff might know that the prospective defendant exists but nonetheless harbor a misunderstanding about his status or role in the events giving rise to the claim at issue, and she may mistakenly choose to sue a different defendant based on that misimpression. That kind of deliberate but mistaken choice does not foreclose a finding that Rule 15(c)(1)(C)(ii) has been satisfied.

This reading is consistent with the purpose of relation back: to balance the interests of the defendant protected by the statute of limitations with the preference expressed in the Federal Rules of Civil Procedure in general, and Rule 15 in particular, for resolving disputes on their merits. A prospective defendant who legitimately believed that the limitations period had passed without any attempt to sue him has a strong interest in repose. But repose would be a windfall for a prospective defendant who understood, or who should have understood, that he escaped suit during the limitations period only because the plaintiff misunderstood a crucial fact about his identity. Because a plaintiff's knowledge of the existence of a party does not foreclose the possibility that she has made a mistake of identity about which that party should have been aware, such knowledge does not support that party's interest in repose.

* * *

B

* * *

Moreover, the Rule mandates relation back once the Rule's requirements are satisfied; it does not leave the decision whether to grant relation back to the district court's equitable discretion. See Rule 15(c)(1) ("An amendment . . . *relates back* . . . when" the three listed requirements are met (emphasis added)).

The mandatory nature of the inquiry for relation back under Rule 15(c) is particularly striking in contrast to the inquiry under Rule 15(a), which sets forth the circumstances in which a party may amend its pleading before trial. By its terms, Rule 15(a) gives discretion to the district court in deciding whether to grant a motion to amend a pleading to add a party or a claim. Following an initial period after filing a pleading during which a party may amend once "as a matter of course," "a party may amend its pleading only with the opposing party's written consent or the court's leave," which the court "should freely give . . . when justice so requires." Rules 15(a)(1)–(2). We have previously explained that a court may consider a movant's "undue delay" or "dilatory motive" in deciding whether to grant leave to amend under Rule 15(a). As the contrast between Rule 15(a) and Rule 15(c) makes clear, however, the speed with which a plaintiff moves to amend her complaint or files an amended complaint after obtaining leave to do so has no bearing on whether the amended complaint relates back.

* * *

As we have explained, the question under Rule 15(c)(1)(C)(ii) is what the prospective defendant reasonably should have understood about the plaintiff's intent in filing the original complaint against the first defendant. To the extent the plaintiff's postfiling conduct informs the prospective defendant's understanding of whether the plaintiff initially made a "mistake concerning the proper party's identity," a court may consider the conduct . . . .

C

Applying these principles to the facts of this case, we think it clear that the courts below erred in denying relation back under Rule 15(c)(1)(C)(ii). The District Court held that Costa Crociere had "constructive notice" of Krupski's complaint within the Rule 4(m) period. Costa Crociere has not challenged this finding. Because the complaint made clear that Krupski meant to sue the company that "owned, operated, managed, supervised and controlled" the ship on which she was injured, and also indicated (mistakenly) that Costa

Cruise performed those roles. Costa Crociere should have known, within the Rule 4(m) period, that it was not named as a defendant in that complaint only because of Krupski's misunderstanding about which "Costa" entity was in charge of the ship—clearly a "mistake concerning the proper party's identity."

* * *

Respondent also argues that Krupski's failure to move to amend her complaint during the Rule 4(m) period shows that she made no mistake in that period. But as discussed, any delay on Krupski's part is relevant only to the extent it may have informed Costa Crociere's understanding during the Rule 4(m) period of whether she made a mistake originally. Krupski's failure to add Costa Crociere during the Rule 4(m) period is not sufficient to make reasonable any belief that she had made a deliberate and informed decision not to sue Costa Crociere in the first instance. Nothing in Krupski's conduct during the Rule 4(m) period suggests that she failed to name Costa Crociere because of anything other than a mistake.

It is also worth noting that Costa Cruise and Costa Crociere are related corporate entities with very similar names; "crociera" even means "cruise" in Italian. This interrelationship and similarity heighten the expectation that Costa Crociere should suspect a mistake has been made when Costa Cruise is named in a complaint that actually describes Costa Crociere's activities . . . . In addition, Costa Crociere's own actions contributed to passenger confusion over "the proper party" for a lawsuit. The front of the ticket advertises that "Costa Cruises" has achieved a certification of quality without clarifying whether "Costa Cruises" is Costa Cruise Lines, Costa Crociere, or some other related "Costa" company. Indeed, Costa Crociere is evidently aware that the difference between Costa Cruise and Costa Crociere can be confusing for cruise ship passengers. See, *e.g., Suppa v. Costa Crociere, S. p. A.,* No. 07–60526–CIV, 2007 WL 4287508, *1 (S.D.Fla., Dec. 4, 2007) (denying Costa Crociere's motion to dismiss the amended complaint where the original complaint had named Costa Cruise as a defendant after "find[ing] it simply inconceivable that Defendant Costa Crociere was not on notice . . . that . . . but for the mistake in the original Complaint, Costa Crociere was the appropriate party to be named in the action").

In light of these facts, Costa Crociere should have known that Krupski's failure to name it as a defendant in her original complaint was due to a mistake concerning the proper party's identity. We therefore reverse the judgment of the Court of Appeals for the Eleventh Circuit and remand the case for further proceedings consistent with this opinion.

It is so ordered.

DIRECTED READING QUESTIONS

53. What does Rule 4(m) require a party to do?

54. According to Rule 15(c)(1)(C), exactly what must occur "within the period provided by Rule 4(m)," in order for a pleading to relate back when the pleading changes the name of the party whom the pleading is asserting a claim against?

55. When is it important that an amendment to a pleading "relate back"?

56. What happened on February 21, 2007?

57. What did the ticket require an injured passenger to do?

58. Who does the ticket identify as the carrier?

59. Who does the ticket identify as the sales and marketing agent for the carrier?

60. What happened on July 2 and July 9, 2007?

61. What happened on February 1, 2008, "three weeks before the 1-year statute of limitations expired"?

62. What is the source of the 1-year statute of limitations?

63. What happened on February 4, 2008?

64. When, in relation to the expiration of the statute of limitations, did Costa Cruise bring Costa Crociere's existence to the attention of the plaintiff?

65. What happened on each of the following dates: February 25, 2008, March 20, 2008 and May 6, 2008?

66. Describe the sequence of events that occurred between June 13 and August 21, 2008?

67. What happened "shortly thereafter" August 21, 2008?

68. Explain the ruling of the district court, which the appellate court affirmed.

69. How does the Supreme Court explain the error made by the lower courts?

70. According to the Supreme Court, how can a deliberate decision ever be considered a mistake?

71. How does the Supreme Court's ruling reflect a balancing of the interests protected by the statute of limitations and the interests protected by Rule 15?

72. Does the Supreme Court differentiate between the discretion afforded a district court regarding its decision about whether to grant leave to amend under Rule 15(a) and whether an amendment relates back under Rule 15(c)?

73. Does Rule 15 require the new party named in the amended complaint to be served within the period provided by Rule 4(m)? What does your answer indicate about the formality of the "notice" required in Rule 15(c)(1)(C)(i)?

74. Suppose that in *Costa* a Florida statute stated, "In any civil action, process may issue against an assumed defendant. If the plaintiff subsequently discovers the assumed defendant is not the proper party, it may file an amended complaint substituting the correct defendant for the assumed defendant, and the amended complaint relates back to the date of the original complaint." What section of Rule 15 should plaintiff rely on in seeking to amend?

CHAPTER 7

DISCOVERY

Rules 26–37 and 45

■ ■ ■

DIRECTED READING QUESTIONS

1. Examine the Complaint provided to you in Chapter 3 and the Answer to that Complaint provided to you in Chapter 6. Using the Answer, write an "A" at the end of every allegation in the Complaint that was admitted in the Answer and a "D" at the end of every allegation in the Complaint that was denied in the Answer.

2. Explain how the complaint and answer taken together help frame the scope of discovery. Based on your comparison of the Complaint and Answer in question 1 above, list three things for which no discovery is needed and think of three examples of information you would need if you were the plaintiff and three examples of information you would need if you were the defendant during discovery.

I. RULE 26—CONTEXTUALIZATION

Rule 26 is a difficult rule for students to understand. It is detailed, nuanced, and expansive and is often a challenge to contextualize. If we think of the discovery devices as the soldiers in the information retrieval war, then Rule 26 is the command center setting the parameters for the operation of the discovery devices. The following exercise is designed to help you contextualize the contents of Rule 26 and to force you to read the rule as carefully as it needs to be read.

Instructions

Fill in the blanks on the following pages with the statements from the "Table of Statements." Of course, the statements are jumbled. Please write in the statements which complete the missing portions of the worksheet in the appropriate place in the worksheet. Each statement may only be used only once.

Every disclosure under Rule 26(a)(1) or (a)(3) and every discovery request must be _____ _____.

There are _____ basic forms of disclosure. These are _____ _____ _____ must be supplemented as per Rule ____.

When a civil action is initiated the first thing a party should do in terms of disclosure requirements is read rule _____ to determine whether or not this is an action requiring initial disclosure. If this is not an action exempt from initial disclosure, then the party must initially disclose the following pursuant to Rule _____ _____ _____

_____
_____

These initial disclosures are typically made _____
_____. However, if a party is joined to the action after the Rule 26(f) conference then disclosure must be made within _____
_____. According to Rule 26(a)(1)(E), no party can delay making these disclosures because it is unhappy with another party's disclosure or lack thereof or that it is not yet prepared enough to disclose fully.

The second type of disclosure mentioned by the rule is _____ as per Rule 26(a)(2). Expert disclosure must occur at least _____, but if the expert testimony is being used solely to rebut another party's expert, then disclosure _____
_____. Expert disclosure consists of typically a written report _____ and _____ by the witness and it must contain a _____
_____
_____
_____
_____
_____
_____
_____.

The third type of disclosure mentioned in Rule 26(a)(3) is the _____. These disclosures must occur _____ and they basically consist of _____
_____. As in Rule 26(a)(1)(A)(i), (ii) evidence used _____ need not be disclosed as per Rule _____. After pretrial disclosure occurs a party objecting to the use of a deposition or the inclusion of an exhibit disclosed as per the pretrial disclosure rules has _____ to object or all objections are waived except those under _____
_____.

While disclosure is done without a request the next stage of retrieving information necessary to the resolution of the action is called discovery. Discovery is a process by which the parties seek the information from each other or persons by using the devices and tools in rules, _____
_____. Failure to follow discovery requirements may lead to sanctions as outlined in Rule __.

The scope of discovery is broad, and information properly sought is not limited to information that would be admissible at trial. Instead discovery _____
_____
_____
_____. Like disclosure and as per Rule _____
_____
_____.

A party may withhold information it _____. And it may also withhold _____
_____ as specified in Rule 26(b)(3). The classification of information as such is subject to a challenge by the requesting party, however. In order to properly withhold the information the party who is claiming it

is not required to disclose, must as per Rule _____
_____
_____
_____
_____.

Of course, if a party accidentally produces in discovery something it believes it did not have to, based on the privilege or work product doctrines, then the procedures described in Rule _____ _____ MAY protect the party who believes it accidentally produced the materials.

In addition to privilege or work product, other limits on the scope of discovery also apply. On motion or on its own the court may limit discovery if _____
_____
_____
_____
_____
_____
_____. These limits are found in Rule 26(b)(2)(C)(i)−(iii). The federal decisions related to the Rule 26(b)(2)(C)(i)−(iii) limits are described as _____ because they deliberately leave room for discretionary interpretation by the trial judge.

In addition to the above there is a separate, "namby pamby"* rule which relates to _____
_____ and reads a little like a ping pong game.

A party seeking to get another party to respond to discovery previously propounded on that unresponsive party may file _____ with the court. A party seeking to not respond to a discovery request may file a motion for a _____ under Rule _____.

TABLE OF STATEMENTS

the discovery sought is unreasonably cumulative or duplicative, or can be obtained from some other source that is more convenient, less burdensome, or less expensive; (ii) the party seeking discovery has had ample opportunity to obtain the information by discovery in the action; or (iii) is outside the scope permitted by Rule 26(b)(1)
protective order
27−36 and 45
believes is privileged
documents and tangible things prepared in anticipation of litigation (work product rule)
is proper if it seeks information regarding any nonprivileged matter that is relevant to any party's claim or defense and proportional to the needs of the case, considering the importance of the issues at stake in the action, the amount in controversy, the parties' relative access to relevant information, the parties' resources, the importance of the discovery in resolving the issues, and whether the burden or expense of the proposed discovery outweighs its likely benefit.
37

---

*　Defined by the American heritage Dictionary (4th edition) as lacking vigor or decisiveness.

26(c)
26(b)(5)(B)
30 days before trial
26(d)(1), a party may not seek discovery from any source before the parties have conferred as required by 26(f), except in a proceeding exempt from disclosure or as authorized by these rules.
Federal Rules of Evidence 402 and 403
26(b)(5)(A)(i), (ii): expressly make the claim; and (ii) describe the nature of the documents, communications, or tangible things not produced or disclosed—and do so in a manner that, without revealing information itself privileged or protected, will enable other parties to assess the claim
pretrial disclosure
a motion to compel
prepared
26(a)(3)(A)
(i) a complete statement of all opinions the witness will express and the basis and reasons for them; (ii) the facts or data considered by the witness in forming them; (iii) any exhibits that will be used to summarize or support them; (iv) the witness's qualifications, including a list of all publications authored in the previous 10 years; (v) a list of all other cases in which, during the previous 4 years, the witness testified as an expert at trial or by deposition; and (vi) a statement of the compensation to be paid for the study and testimony in the case
an updated witness list, a designation of those witnesses expected to testify live and those who will likely testify by deposition or by transcript, and an exhibit list
signed
discovery of Electronically Stored Information
expert disclosure
30 days of service or joinder as per Rule 26(a)(1)(D)
solely for impeachment
within 14 days after the Rule 26(f) conference, but before the Rule 16(b) scheduling order is issued according to Rule 26(a)(1)(C).
26(a)(1)(B)
90 days before trial generally
must be made w/in 30 days of the expert disclosure of the party who may be rebutted
initial disclosure, disclosure of expert testimony and pretrial disclosures. All forms of disclosure, responses to interrogatories, requests for production or requests for admissions
debatable
26(a)(1)(A)(i)–(iv): Witness lists except for witnesses used solely for impeachment, all docs, ESI and tangible things the party has in its control, custody or possession except those used solely for impeachment, materials the party relied on in computing the claimed damage award amount that are not privileged, any insurance agreements whereby an insurer would be liable for satisfying the judgment

26(e)
three
signed by at least one attorney of record or by the party.
14 days

II. RULE 26—CAREFUL READING

DIRECTED READING QUESTIONS

3.   What is the difference between disclosure and discovery?

4.   Is it true that if the action is not one of those exempted from disclosure in Rule 26(a)(1)(B) then the party's must make all required disclosures under Rule 26(a)?

5.   Is it true that if the action is one of the actions listed as exempt in Rule 26(a)(1)(B) the parties need not make any of the required disclosures in Rule 26(a)?

6.   Apart from timing, what is the difference between the information required to be disclosed in Rule 26(a)(1)(A)(i) and 26(a)(3)(A)(i)?

7.   What happens if you try to call witnesses or enter exhibits at trial which you failed to disclose pursuant to Rule 26(a) or in your pretrial disclosures?

8.   If you fail to disclose a witness or information pursuant to Rule 26(a) and then discover that you should have disclosed them, what provision of Rule 26 allows you to supplement your disclosure?

9.   Is it true or false that, according to Rule 5(d)(1), no disclosure or discovery is to be filed with the court unless it is to be used in the proceeding or the court orders it?

10. Is it true or false that if a proceeding is exempt from initial disclosure under Rule 26(a)(1)(B), then it is likewise exempt from the requirement of a discovery conference?

11. Rule 26(b)(2)(B) has specific language about discovery of a certain type of information. What kind of information does this specific language refer to and why is there specific language about it?

12. If a party objects to the production of ESI because of undue burden or cost, does the court have to consider other portions of the rule besides 26(b)(2)(B), in determining whether good cause for production nevertheless exists?

13. Plaintiff sues defendant in United States District Court for the District of Kansas. One of the witnesses is being deposed by remote means in Miami, Florida. The United States District Court for the Southern District of Florida is therefore the court for the district where the deposition is being taken. If the lawyer for the deponent wants to move for a protective order, which court must she ask to issue the protective order?

14. Before filing a motion for a protective order, what must the party asking for the protective order do?

15. Must the parties use the discovery devices in the order in which they are listed in the Rules?

16. What is the "discovery equivalent" of Rule 11?

17. If a person or party is served with an unsigned discovery response, what must that person or party do?

III. EXPERT WITNESS DISCLOSURE/DISCOVERY

Expert witnesses are often intimidating and very persuasive to lay people, especially juries. They know more about the particular subject matter that they are testifying about than most attorneys. The discovery rules therefore have specific provisions which allow attorneys to question the expert in order to be able to effectively rebut the expert's assertions. For example, Rule 26(a)(2) and 26(b)(4).

Please watch the following actual video of an expert deposition. Observe how the attorney's questioning in deposition impacts the persuasiveness and apparent competence of the expert. The discovery rules allow us to get past the façade of a powerfully convincing expert and to even the playing field between the attorney and the expert.

https://www.youtube.com/watch?v=y2X52rS-ZLE.

DIRECTED READING QUESTIONS

18. Are the following true or false?

    a.   Rule 26(a)(2) governs both expert witnesses and the experts described in 26(b)(4)(D).

    b.   All expert witnesses need to submit a written report.

19. What is the difference between a Rule 26(a)(2)(B) expert and a Rule 26(a)(2)(C) expert? Give an example of each.

20. Are the following true or false?

    a.   Rule 26(b)(4)(A) governs both expert witnesses and experts who are employed as non-testifying experts.

    b.   Rule 26(b)(4)(A) applies only to experts who have to submit a written report.

    c.   Rule 26(b)(4)(B) applies both to experts who have to submit a written report and those who do not.

21. Explain the role of the expert referred to in Rule 26(b)(4)(D) and explain the similarity of Rule 26(b)(3)(A)(ii) and 26(b)(4)(D)(ii).

IV. THE DISCOVERY DEVICES—*RULES 26–37 AND 45*

DIRECTED READING QUESTIONS

Please state whether the following statements are true or false or provide answers to the questions asked. Please support your response by citing to specific language within the discovery rules.

22. In an adversarial system such as ours, absent a formal discovery request, a party need not ever provide any information to an opposing party in a lawsuit.

23. Under the rules of discovery, an opposing party *may* have a right to depose certain experts who are not expected to testify at trial.

24. Rule 11 does not apply to discovery or disclosure.

25. There is no disclosure or discovery "equivalent" of Rule 11.

26. A court *may* strike a discovery paper if it is not signed.

27. All experts retained by a party need to be disclosed to the opposing party, and the opposing party has a right to depose them.

28. As part of initial disclosure, a party must disclose the name of each individual likely to have discoverable information.

29. All disclosures and discovery requests must be filed promptly after service with the court.

30. A party may never seek discovery from any source until after the parties have conferred as per Rule 26(f).

31. Alpha sued Beta for violation of a federal statute. After Beta's attempt to resolve the matter via a Rule 12 motion failed, Beta, who is the only named defendant, answered and denied almost every allegation in Alpha's complaint. The parties proceeded to discovery. Alpha is interested in information a witness Charlie might have.

    a. Do the discovery rules permit Alpha to compel Charlie to attend a deposition?

    b. Do the discovery rules permit Alpha to compel Charlie to provide answers to interrogatories?

    c. Do the discovery rules permit Alpha to compel Charlie to produce documents or tangible things?

    d. Do the discovery rules permit Alpha to compel Charlie to admit the truth of any matters?

32. Only the CEO of a corporate party may answer interrogatories served on the corporation to the extent of her personal knowledge only.

33. Answers to interrogatories can be used at trial to the extent permitted by the Federal Rules of Evidence.

34. Depositions of an unavailable witness may be used for any purpose as permitted by the Federal Rules of Evidence.

35. An admission in response to a request for admission conclusively establishes the admitted matter.

36. None of the discovery devices require leave of court.

37. In an action styled *A vs. B*, can A or B be sanctioned for failing to produce another person in their custody or under their legal control to submit to a physical or mental examination, after the court orders an examination of the person?

38. Even though a party or person may be subjected to a Rule 35 examination, a Rule 35 order can only issue against a party.

39. An action styled *A vs. B* is pending in the U.S. District Court for the District of Kansas. B wants to depose C, who is a Miami, Florida resident. Can B do this via telephone?

40. An action styled *A vs. B* is pending in the U.S. District Court for the District of Kansas. B wants to depose C, who is a Miami, Florida resident. C refuses to agree to be deposed by B. Can the U.S. District Court for the District of Kansas issue a valid subpoena, if B wants to depose C via telephone while C is in Miami?

41. A response to a request for admission in one action may be used against the party in another proceeding.

42. Apart from the names of the discovery devices, there is no difference between a deposition upon written questions and interrogatories.

43. A deposition within the United States can never be taken before a person, unless that person is an officer authorized to administer oaths by federal law or the law of the place where the deposition is taken or the person is appointed by the court where the action is pending to administer oaths and take testimony.

44. In a matter styled *A vs. B*, can A be liable in attorneys' fees to B if B showed up for a deposition noticed by A of a nonparty witness, who failed to show up because A failed to serve a subpoena on the nonparty witness?

45. The parties may agree to extend the time for discovery.

46. A plans to sue B soon in a federal district court. A has heard there is a person who might have discoverable information but is ailing and might die any day now. A does not know what the information the person has is. May A depose the person pursuant to Rule 27?

47. A sues corporation B. A *properly* notices B's deposition. B designates someone as required by Rule 30(b)(6). The designated person is wholly unaware of the answers to any of the questions asked. May A move for sanctions?

48. A sues B. During A's deposition of a witness C, C's attorney objects to a question on the grounds of relevance. Is it proper for C's attorney to instruct C not to answer a question because it seeks the discovery of irrelevant information?

V.   SCOPE OF DISCOVERY—*RULE 26*

DAVIS V. ROSS (1985)
United States District Court for the Southern District of New York
107 F.R.D. 326

ROBERT L. CARTER, DISTRICT JUDGE.

Plaintiff Gail Davis has instituted this defamation action, seeking one million dollars in compensatory damages and one million dollars in punitive damages, based on an October 11, 1983 letter written and disseminated by defendant Diana Ross . . . . [The letter stated "that plaintiff and others were no longer in the defendant's employment and that, if defendant 'let an employee go, it's because either their work or their personal habits are not acceptable to me,' and that she did not recommend those people."] The case is currently before the court on the parties' cross-motions to compel discovery.

Davis seeks discovery of three sets of data. First, she wishes to obtain information concerning Ross' net worth and annual income. Davis argues that this material is discoverable because evidence of a defendant's wealth is relevant in an action for punitive damages.

The New York courts have recognized, however, that a plaintiff's interest in proving the amount of the defendant's wealth must be balanced against the defendant's right to privacy and general desire not to divulge his or her financial status—especially since plausible claims for punitive damages can easily be made in many actions. Consequently, the rule in New York is that "evidence of defendant's wealth [can] not be brought out upon trial unless and until the jury [brings] in a special verdict that plaintiff is entitled to punitive damages against defendant." Discovery of defendant's net wealth will become necessary only in the event plaintiff obtains such a special verdict.

Davis argues that the rule of *Rupert v. Sellers* should not govern this case because she entered into a confidentiality order which, she says, should eliminate any concern for privacy on defendant's part. Defendant responds, quite rightly, that the existence of a confidentiality order does not undermine the rationale of *Rupert v. Sellers.* Ross should not be compelled to disclose private facts to *anyone*—even to someone who has agreed to keep the information confidential—until it is found that plaintiff is entitled to punitive damages. As a federal court sitting in New York, we are required to follow and apply [New York Law]. The motion to compel discovery of Ross' wealth and income is denied.

Plaintiff's second discovery request is for documents reflecting billings by the law firm of Loeb & Loeb and/or John Frankenheimer (a partner in the firm) to Ross and to entities in which she has an interest, and for the records reflecting payment of such bills. Plaintiff argues that this material is discoverable because the defendant has stated that Frankenheimer will be an important witness; therefore, plaintiff asserts, the amount of fees Ross paid Frankenheimer would be relevant to the issue of Frankenheimer's bias and credibility.

Plaintiff is entitled to probe for bias by inquiring into the existence and nature of the relationship between Frankenheimer and Ross. Specifically, plaintiff may discover what, if any, fee arrangements and retainer agreements were entered into between the two. However, the amount of fees earned, without more, is not probative of a witness' bias. Even where a witness' entire livelihood derives from employment by the party for whom he testifies, courts have declined to infer bias from the mere fact of employment. In this case, the court is especially reluctant to pry into the details of the attorney-client relationship or to order burdensome discovery. Consequently, plaintiff's motion to compel discovery of legal fees is denied.

Plaintiff's third request is to discover the names of other employees who have complained about defendant, and the nature of their complaints. Plaintiff's argument for discoverability rests on the Second Circuit's interpretation of the allegedly libelous letter in question. In the letter, Ross stated that Davis no longer worked for her, and then wrote: "If I let an employee go, it is because their work or their personal habits are not acceptable to me. I do not recommend these people." According to the Court of Appeals, the statement, "I do not recommend these people," tends to objectify Ross' evaluation of Davis, and implies that others would also find Davis' work or personal habits unacceptable.

Plaintiff argues that the truth of this statement—that Davis' work or personal habits are objectively unacceptable—will be at issue. Consequently, plaintiff asserts, the material sought is discoverable because "[i]f in fact it was defendant's personality that was a problem and not plaintiff's the jury would be entitled to conclude that there was nothing objectionable about plaintiff's work or personal habits and that defendant is liable for defamation." (Plaintiff's letter dated July 3, 1985, at 9).

The logic of plaintiff's argument is tenuous. Whether Ross is a "good" or "bad" employer, popular or unpopular with employees, is not probative of whether Davis' personal or work habits were objectively satisfactory. Even if other employees *have* complained about Ross, that would not affect a jury's assessment of Davis' personal or work habits one way or the other. The issue in this case is whether Ross libeled Davis, and the material plaintiff seeks to discover does not bear on that.

Plaintiff also argues that the information is discoverable because it bears on Ross' credibility (Plaintiff's letter dated July 3, 1985, at 9). The court simply does not see the connection between Ross' reputation as an employer and her capacity for truth-telling. In short, the information sought by plaintiff is irrelevant to any material issue, and is not calculated to lead to any admissible evidence. Consequently, plaintiff's motion is denied.

* * *

IT IS SO ORDERED.

DIRECTED READING QUESTIONS

49. Please describe the lawsuit that is at issue in this opinion.

50. Is the cause of action a state law or federal law cause of action? What is the basis of the federal court's subject matter jurisdiction?

51. What discovery is the plaintiff seeking?

52. What is the broad standard (hint: see Rule 26(b)(1)) a party must consider when propounding discovery requests?

53. How does the plaintiff argue that the information on net worth is relevant?

54. Explain why the court denies the plaintiff's request regarding net worth. Do you agree with the court?

55. The plaintiff's second discovery request asks for information about how much the defendant paid a law firm that employs the defendant's witness as a partner. Please explain why the court denied this discovery request and why you agree or disagree with the court's decision.

56. The plaintiff's final discovery request seeks, "the names of other employees who have complained about the defendant and the nature of their complaints." Please explain why the plaintiff argues that this information is relevant and why the court disagrees with the plaintiff.

57. Articulate another objection to the plaintiff's final discovery request based on the language in Rule 26(b)(2)(C).

VI. EXEMPTIONS FROM DISCOVERY— *ATTORNEY CLIENT AND WORK PRODUCT*

HICKMAN V. TAYLOR (1947)

Supreme Court of the United States
329 U.S. 495

[This is the decision that established the work product doctrine.]

In our opinion, neither Rule 26 nor any other rule dealing with discovery contemplates production under such circumstances. That is not because the subject matter is privileged or irrelevant, as those concepts are used in these rules. Here is simply an attempt, without purported necessity or justification, to secure written statements, private memoranda and personal recollections prepared or formed by an adverse party's counsel in the course of his legal duties. As such, it falls outside the arena of discovery and contravenes the public policy underlying the orderly prosecution and defense of legal claims. Not even the most liberal of discovery theories can justify unwarranted inquiries into the files and the mental impressions of an attorney.

Historically, a lawyer is an officer of the court and is bound to work for the advancement of justice while faithfully protecting the rightful interests of his clients. In performing his various duties, however, it is essential that a lawyer work with a certain degree of privacy, free from unnecessary intrusion by opposing parties and their counsel. Proper preparation of a client's case demands that he assemble information, sift what he considers to be the relevant from the irrelevant facts, prepare his legal theories and plan his strategy without undue and needless interference. That is the historical and the necessary way in which lawyers act within the framework of our system of jurisprudence to promote justice and to protect their clients' interests. This work is reflected, of course, in interviews, statements, memoranda, correspondence, briefs, mental impressions, personal beliefs, and countless other tangible and intangible ways—aptly though roughly termed by the Circuit Court of Appeals in this case as the 'Work product of the lawyer.' Were such materials open to opposing counsel on mere demand, much of what is now put down in writing would remain unwritten. An attorney's thoughts, heretofore inviolate would not be his own. Inefficiency, unfairness and sharp practices would inevitably develop in the giving of legal advice and in the preparation of cases for trial. The effect on the legal profession would be demoralizing. And the interests of the clients and the cause of justice would be poorly served.

IN RE HUMAN TISSUE PRODUCTS LIABILITY LITIGATION (2008)

United States District Court for the District of New Jersey
255 F.R.D. 151

When a case is based on federal diversity jurisdiction, courts are to decide issues of attorney-client privilege based on state law. [In federal question cases issues of attorney client privilege are based on federal law.]

* * *

The attorney-client privilege protects confidential communications between a client and an attorney made in the course of a professional relationship [and] "The communication itself must be primarily or predominantly of a legal character." The attorney-client privilege is limited to communications—not underlying facts.

Unlike the attorney client privilege, the work product privilege is governed, even in diversity cases, by a uniform federal standard. The federal work-product doctrine is set forth in Federal Rule of Civil Procedure 26(b)(3), which provides:

[(3) *Trial Preparation: Materials.*

(A) *Documents and Tangible Things.* Ordinarily, a party may not discover documents and tangible things that are prepared in anticipation of litigation or for trial by or for another party or its representative (including the other party's attorney, consultant, surety, indemnitor, insurer, or agent). But, subject to Rule 26(b)(4), those materials may be discovered if:

(i)   they are otherwise discoverable under Rule 26(b)(1); and

(ii) the party shows that it has substantial need for the materials to prepare its case and cannot, without undue hardship, obtain their substantial equivalent by other means.

(B) *Protection Against Disclosure.* If the court orders discovery of those materials, it must protect against disclosure of the mental impressions, conclusions, opinions, or legal theories of a party's attorney or other representative concerning the litigation.]

DIRECTED READING QUESTIONS

58. What are the differences, including purpose, between the attorney client privilege and the work product protection? How many potential variants of each exist in the federal courts?

59. Give an example of:

a.   Something protected by the work product doctrine but not by the attorney client privilege.

b.   Something protected by the attorney client privilege but not by the work product doctrine.

c.   Something protected by both the attorney client privilege and the work product doctrine.

60. Must a court order the disclosure of material that would otherwise be protected under the attorney client privilege, when the party seeking the information demonstrates convincingly that the requirements of Rule 26(b)(3)(A)(i)–(ii) are met?

61. Alpha was injured while operating a shredder manufactured by Beta. Alpha properly commenced an action against Beta in the appropriate U.S. district court. Prior to trial, Alpha sought discovery of a report which had given to Beta by Charlie, who is a claims investigator for Beta. Charlie had inspected the machine and investigated the accident right after it happened because Beta, on the advice of his attorney, felt litigation was imminent and the report would bring him up to speed on any potential defenses

available. Charlie died the day after submitting his report, and during Charlie's funeral, the shredder was destroyed by an accidental fire.

    a.   Assume Charlie is not qualified as an expert. Should Alpha's request be granted?

    b.   Assume that Beta's attorney wrote handwritten notes related to the litigation on the only remaining copy of the report. Specifically, Beta's attorney highlighted, circled, and underlined various sections of the report and made detailed comments accordingly. The comments included for example:

        i.   "This shows that under state law we will have problems with the duty prong of negligence. See *Holt v. Garrish* and *Boyle v. Klein*."

        ii.   "This shows that no matter what they say, we will win on proximate cause— dispositive to ask client about the redundancy of safety procedures."

62.   Uiara was a Brazilian Jiu-Jitsu blackbelt. She taught classes in Manhattan, New York for years. Her clients adored her because of her excellent teaching ability and her unique techniques to transition from full guard to leg lock submission attempts. She journaled every single class with every student immediately after the class. She did this because she wanted to note what went well and what didn't in the lesson and to think about ways to improve her teaching based on these notes. One of her students, Carl, seemed to have a particularly difficult time understanding the fundamentals of Brazilian Jiu-Jitsu, and he especially struggled with the hip and shoulder position transitions necessary to escape the full mount. After about three months of lessons, he became frustrated and quit. Three years after he quit, he filed a lawsuit against Uiara alleging that she defrauded him because she charged him for lessons, and he alleged she was not qualified to teach. During discovery in the lawsuit, Carl asked for a copy of Uiara's journal notes from his classes. Uiara objected and claimed the journal notes were protected by the work-product privilege. Is Uiara correct?

63.   Attorney represents defendant client in a breach of contract case. Attorney, as part of his representation, asks client to write a summary of all the events that occurred. In the summary written by the client, the client lists his actions in detail, including what he stated to the opposing party at all times during the transaction.

    a.   Is the client's statement subject to discovery? Why or why not?

    b.   If you conclude that the statement itself is not subject to discovery, how might the opposing party obtain some of the information contained in the statement?

64.   Explain how the attorney client privilege and the work product doctrine affect the discoverability of otherwise relevant information.

VII. ELECTRONIC DISCOVERY CONSIDERATIONS

DIRECTED READING QUESTIONS

65.   Before the advent of electronically stored information ("ESI"), what exactly would an attorney do when they received a request for production from opposing counsel?

66.   Where is potentially relevant ESI located?

67.   A plaintiff sues a truck driver and his employer, a trucking company, in federal court, alleging that the trucker caused an accident by driving negligently and injuring the

plaintiff. The complaint further alleged that, at the time of the accident, the trucker's negligence was due to fatigue because the trucker was driving for longer hours and with less rest than federal regulations mandated. The attorneys representing plaintiff and defendant were experienced trial attorneys, but they were uncomfortable with "new-fangled" electronic discovery. As a result, they both stipulated that they would not seek electronic discovery. Instead they agreed to rely only on the paper logbooks that the truck driver completed and not on the GPS tracking devices mandated by federal regulations. The paper logs of the truck driver indicated that he did not drive more than he was supposed to, and the defendant moved for dismissal. The judge insisted that the attorneys examine the ESI. Contrary to the paper logs, the ESI indicated that the trucker had exceeded the federal mandates for driving time and had less rest than federal law requires. Are these two attorneys competent to practice law in this century?

68. How is digital information different than paper information?

69. Give an example of an issue related to "form of production" that might arise under Rule 34 which is unique to electronic discovery.

70. The complex and detailed issues related to electronic discovery are beyond the scope of this casebook. But for a more detailed discussion of how electronic discovery is challenging the adversarial justice system and the cost sharing model of discovery, *see* Rory Bahadur, *Electronic Discovery, Informational Privacy, Facebook and Utopian Civil Justice*, 79 MISS. L.J. 317 (2009).

VIII.   DISCOVERY SANCTIONS—*RULES 26–37*

DIRECTED READING QUESTIONS

71. Rule 37 is referenced in Rules 26–36 five different times. Find and explain each of the five references.

72. Alpha sues Beta in federal court for negligence. Beta answers, raising his defenses but does not include a counterclaim against Alpha in his answer. Beta also denies the allegations in Alpha's complaint with the exception of the subject matter jurisdiction, venue, and personal jurisdiction allegations. Because the proceeding was not one exempt from initial discovery, the parties were required to develop a proposed discovery plan as per Rule 26(f)(1). Beta refuses to participate in framing a discovery plan. What, if any, sanctions are available against Beta? Is a motion required for sanctions? How much discretion does the court have in determining the nature of any sanctions if sanctions are available?

73. Same facts as question 72, but the parties manage to frame a discovery plan. Beta asks Alpha in an interrogatory to list all the facts that Alpha relies on in his assertion that Beta breached a duty owed to Alpha. Alpha thinks the question is "ridiculous" and just an attempt on Beta's part to bury him in documents. Alpha therefore objects to the discovery request based on Rule 26(b)(2)(C)(ii), even though Alpha knows Beta did not have ample opportunity to obtain the information. Basically, Alpha simply objected because he wanted to harass Beta. What, if any, sanctions are available against Alpha? Is a motion required for sanctions? How much discretion does the court have in determining the nature of any sanctions if sanctions are available?

74. Pursuant to Rule 30(b)(1), Alpha properly gives notice to Beta of Beta's deposition. Consider the following scenarios. What, if any, sanctions are available? Is a motion

required for sanctions? How much discretion does the court have in determining the nature of any sanctions if sanctions are available if:

a. Alpha decides not to show up for Beta's deposition?

b. Alpha shows up, but Beta decides he simply has better things to do than attend his deposition and does not show up for the deposition described in the notice?

75. In an action styled *Alpha vs. Beta* to recover damages to Charlie, a person in Alpha's control, the court orders Alpha to produce Charlie for a Rule 35 medical examination. Charlie refuses to attend the medical examination. May Charlie be sanctioned for failing to attend the medical examination?

76. Explain how Rule 37(a) and (b) are similar to Rule 11.

77. In the action *Alpha vs. Beta*, Alpha refuses to provide Beta with certain documents in response to Beta's request for production. Beta responds by filing a motion to compel Alpha to produce the documents before he attempts to resolve the matter with Alpha. How should the court rule on Beta's motion?

78. In the action *Alpha vs. Beta*, Beta files an appropriately certified motion to compel production of certain documents that Alpha refuses to produce pursuant to Beta's request for production. The court rules in Beta's favor and orders Alpha to produce the documents within thirty days. What, if any, sanctions are available? Is a motion required for sanctions? How much discretion does the court have in determining the nature of any sanctions, if sanctions are available?

79. Would your answer be any different if Alpha had produced the documents after being served with the motion but before the court heard the arguments on the motion to compel?

80. Alpha decides to ignore the court, and after thirty days, Alpha still does not produce the documents. What, if any, sanctions are available? Is a motion required for sanctions? How much discretion does the court have in determining the nature of any sanctions, if sanctions are available?

81. Assume the court ruled against Beta and denied Beta's motion to compel. What, if any, sanctions are available? Is a motion required for sanctions? How much discretion does the court have in determining the nature of any sanctions, if sanctions are available?

82. Answer the following hypothetical.

Mike sued Molly in federal court for harm caused to him when Molly's car crashed into Mike as he was crossing the street. His complaint satisfied Rule 8(a)(1) and 8(a)(3), and in order to satisfy Rule 8(a)(2) Mike pled as follows:

1. On *January 14, 2011*, at *5019 SW 16th Street in the City of Chicago in the State of Illinois*, the defendant negligently drove a motor vehicle against the plaintiff.

2. As a result, the plaintiff was physically injured, lost wages or income, suffered physical and mental pain, and incurred medical expenses of $10,000,000.00.

Mike was rushed to the emergency room ("ER") after the incident alleged in the complaint, and his initial treating doctor was Dr. Michelle Palin. After initial ER stabilization, he was admitted to the hospital, and several surgeries were performed on his lower arm to address complications with injuries suffered when Molly's car struck him.

After surgery, Mike was treated with heparin, which is a medication that prevents premature clotting in blood vessels typically associated with surgery. However, when Mike was treated with the heparin, he immediately suffered severe clotting in small arteries in his brain. Mike suffered a series of permanently disabling strokes as a result of the rapid onset clots.

After the abnormal clotting was discovered, Mike had his choice of vascular specialists from which to receive the necessary further treatment. He chose Dr. Nancy Boehner for a number of reasons, including the fact that Dr. Boehner was one of a few recognized experts on clotting disorders. Mike's brother who is his attorney also encouraged Mike to choose Dr. Boehner because she had a very authoritative persona and if it became necessary, she would be able to convince a jury with testimony.

Dr. Boehner discovered that Mike suffered from a rare condition called heparin induced thrombocytopenia which was previously undiagnosed. People suffering from this rare disease develop massive clots in response to heparin treatment instead of experiencing a decline in clot formation as is typical in heparin therapy. Dr. Boehner was able to prevent the formation of any more clots by treating Mike with a variety of anticoagulant drugs.

Molly initially moved for dismissal pursuant to Rule 12(b)(6) arguing that Mike's complaint was not plausible. After reviewing Rule 84, the district court reluctantly denied Molly's motion. Molly then answered Mike's complaint denying allegation 1 to the extent that it alleged she was negligent but admitting that her car struck Mike on the date and at the time and place alleged. She claimed she was without knowledge as to allegation 2.

During disclosure, Mike identified Dr. Boehner as one of his testifying experts but failed to provide any report required by Rule 26(a)(2)(B)(i)–(vi). Instead, Mike simply disclosed that Dr. Boehner was going to testify at trial regarding the fact that Mike suffered from heparin induced thrombocytopenia and that it caused the clots. Mike and his lawyer were ecstatic that an expert such as Dr. Boehner was available to testify on their behalf. They were, however, very disappointed that Dr. Boehner charged $600 per hour for expert deposition testimony and $850 per hour for expert trial testimony. Despite the high fees, Mike decided to use Dr. Boehner to testify because she was such a believable and authoritative witness.

Later, during discovery, Molly propounded an interrogatory to Mike which asked him to: "Please explain how you calculated the value of the damage award you seek." In response to the interrogatory and after further discovery, it became evident that Mike was suing Molly for all the harm he suffered including the strokes and the associated permanent disability under an eggshell plaintiff theory. The Illinois eggshell plaintiff rule which applied in this diversity case states that a defendant takes a plaintiff as she finds him, and the defendant is liable for all harm caused to the plaintiff whether or not the harm was foreseeable.

Twenty-nine days after the scheduled close of all discovery, Molly now moves for partial summary judgment using the rationale of *Celotex* and cites the testimony of her expert that it was not heparin induced thrombocytopenia but rather Mike's obesity that was responsible for the abnormal clotting observed. She argues further that, because the clotting was caused by his obesity, a previously undiagnosed condition did not cause the harm and as a result, the eggshell plaintiff rule cannot apply. The parties stipulate for the purposes of the motion that Molly's argument regarding the inapplicability of the eggshell rule if Mike's obesity is the cause of his clotting is correct. She therefore seeks summary judgment on all claims for harm other than those occasioned by the collision itself. In response, Mike produces an affidavit from Dr. Boehner which states, in relevant part, as follows:

1. My name is Nancy Boehner.

2. I am a board certified expert in vascular diseases.

3. I am internationally acclaimed as a leading expert on Heparin Induced Thrombocytopenia.

4. I have personal knowledge of what I will testify on because I treated the Plaintiff after the defendant's car collided with him.

5. I will testify as follows:

    a. The plaintiff suffered severe clots after surgery upon exposure to therapeutic levels of heparin.

    b. Such clotting is considered medically atypical.

    c. In my opinion the plaintiff suffers from Heparin Induced Thrombocytopenia, and this condition was responsible for the clots observed and the associated permanent neurological impairment suffered by the plaintiff.

Molly's lawyer argues that, under the rationale of *Celotex*, Mike has not met his burden of production necessary to stave off summary judgment in her favor because Dr. Boehner's affidavit cannot be used to support Mike's response to Molly's motion for summary judgment. Please **explain** whether Molly's lawyer is or is not correct.

CHAPTER 8

SUMMARY JUDGMENT

■ ■ ■

I. GENERAL CONSIDERATIONS

DIRECTED READING QUESTIONS

1. According to Rule 56(a), a movant is entitled to summary judgment when the movant demonstrates two things. What are those two things?

2. The second of those things is showing that the movant is "entitled to judgment as a matter of law." What is judgment as a matter of law?

3. A sues B for breach of contract. A's complaint contains a perfectly stated claim for breach of contract. A bases this claim on a document ("the document"), which was supposedly signed by A and B on a certain date. The document however expressly states, "This Document is Not a Contract."

    a. Notwithstanding the availability of other defenses, how should a court respond to B's Rule 12(b)(6) motion to dismiss A's "perfectly stated claim?"

    b. What result, according to Rule 12(d), if B attaches the document to B's motion to dismiss and the court does not exclude the document?

    c. What do the differences in your answer to (a) and (b) teach about the general differences between a motion to dismiss and a motion for summary judgment?

4. What do Rule 56(b) and 56(c) imply about when a summary judgment motion is typically ripe or appropriate?

5. May a party delay a summary judgment motion by demonstrating specific reasons why it needs more time to defend a motion for summary judgment?

6. Is it permissible to move for summary judgment when the only document filed in an action is a complaint? Consider the following hypothetical complaints in this regard:

    i. On [*date*], in Topeka, Kansas, the Pope, after getting stoned while attending a pro-choice rally on a secret trip from the Vatican to attend a Kansas City Royals game, negligently drove a motor vehicle against plaintiff Sarah Palin while she was tooling around town with her best friends, Michelle Obama and Hillary Clinton. As a result, plaintiff was physically injured, lost wages or income, suffered physical and mental pain, and incurred medical expenses of $_____.*

    ii. On [*date*], in Topeka, Kansas, Superhero emerged from the comic book that plaintiff was reading and battered plaintiff. As a result, plaintiff was physically injured, lost

---

*   These examples involving the Pope are not meant to offend anyone by suggesting in any way that the Pope would or could engage in these activities. To the contrary, the use of such an implausible scenario is designed to reiterate the significance of the implausibility standard, to contrast it with the old *Conley* standard, and to illustrate the strategic litigation choices involved when deciding between a motion for summary judgment and a motion to dismiss pursuant to Rule 12(b)(6). Neither should these purely satirical teaching examples be viewed as any expression of my views on the customs and beliefs of Catholicism or any other major religion.

wages or income, suffered physical and mental pain, and incurred medical expenses of $_____.

7. What is the difference between when a party's case has been dismissed pursuant to summary judgment and when a party's claim is dismissed pursuant to a motion to dismiss for failure to state a claim?

8. What is the result of a court denying a motion for summary judgment?

9. What is the difference between a final summary judgment and a partial summary judgment?

II. MATERIALITY, ENTITLEMENT TO JUDGMENT AS A MATTER OF LAW AND CREDIBILITY

ANDERSON V. LIBERTY LOBBY, INC. (1986)
Supreme Court of the United States
477 U.S. 242

As to materiality, the substantive law will identify which facts are material. Only disputes over facts that might affect the outcome of the suit under the governing law will properly preclude the entry of summary judgment. Factual disputes that are irrelevant or unnecessary will not be counted. See generally. This materiality inquiry is independent of and separate from the question of the incorporation of the evidentiary standard into the summary judgment determination. That is, while the materiality determination rests on the substantive law, it is the substantive law's identification of which facts are critical and which facts are irrelevant that governs. Any proof or evidentiary requirements imposed by the substantive law are not germane to this inquiry, since materiality is only a criterion for categorizing factual disputes in their relation to the legal elements of the claim and not a criterion for evaluating the evidentiary underpinnings of those disputes.

More important for present purposes, summary judgment will not lie if the dispute about a material fact is "genuine," that is, if the evidence is such that a reasonable jury could return a verdict for the nonmoving party. In *First National Bank of Arizona v. Cities Service Co.,* we affirmed a grant of summary judgment for an antitrust defendant where the issue was whether there was a genuine factual dispute as to the existence of a conspiracy. We noted Rule 56[c]'s* provision that a party opposing a properly supported motion for summary judgment " 'may not rest upon the mere allegations or denials of his pleading, but . . . must set forth specific facts showing that there is a genuine issue for trial.' " We observed further that

> "[i]t is true that the issue of material fact required by Rule 56[a] to be present to entitle a party to proceed to trial is not required to be resolved conclusively in favor of the party asserting its existence; rather, all that is required is that sufficient evidence supporting the claimed factual dispute be shown to require a jury or judge to resolve the parties' differing versions of the truth at trial."

---

* The language of Rule 56 and the relevant sections have been amended since 1986. The editor has inserted the current sections of the rule wherever the rule is cited in this opinion.

We went on to hold that, in the face of the defendant's properly supported motion for summary judgment, the plaintiff could not rest on his allegations of a conspiracy to get to a jury without "any significant probative evidence tending to support the complaint."

Again, in *Adickes v. S.H. Kress & Co.,* the Court emphasized that the availability of summary judgment turned on whether a proper jury question was presented. There, one of the issues was whether there was a conspiracy between private persons and law enforcement officers. The District Court granted summary judgment for the defendants, stating that there was no evidence from which reasonably minded jurors might draw an inference of conspiracy. We reversed, pointing out that the moving parties' submissions had not foreclosed the possibility of the existence of certain facts from which "it would be open to a jury . . . to infer from the circumstances" that there had been a meeting of the minds.

Our prior decisions may not have uniformly recited the same language in describing genuine factual issues under Rule 56, but it is clear enough from our recent cases that at the summary judgment stage the judge's function is not himself to weigh the evidence and determine the truth of the matter but to determine whether there is a genuine issue for trial. [T]here is no issue for trial unless there is sufficient evidence favoring the nonmoving party for a jury to return a verdict for that party.

And, as we noted above, Rule 56[a] provides that the trial judge shall then grant summary judgment if there is no genuine issue as to any material fact and if the moving party is entitled to judgment as a matter of law. There is no requirement that the trial judge make findings of fact. The inquiry performed is the threshold inquiry of determining whether there is the need for a trial—whether, in other words, there are any genuine factual issues that properly can be resolved only by a finder of fact because they may reasonably be resolved in favor of either party.

Petitioners suggest, and we agree, that this standard mirrors the standard for a directed verdict under Federal Rule of Civil Procedure 50(a), which is that the trial judge must direct a verdict if, under the governing law, there can be but one reasonable conclusion as to the verdict. If reasonable minds could differ as to the import of the evidence, however, a verdict should not be directed. As the Court long ago said and has several times repeated:

> "Nor are judges any longer required to submit a question to a jury merely because some evidence has been introduced by the party having the burden of proof, unless the evidence be of such a character that it would warrant the jury in finding a verdict in favor of that party. Formerly it was held that if there was what is called a *scintilla* of evidence in support of a case the judge was bound to leave it to the jury, but recent decisions of high authority have established a more reasonable rule, that in every case, before the evidence is left to the jury, there is a preliminary question for the judge, not whether there is literally no evidence, but whether there is any upon which a jury could properly proceed to find a verdict for the party producing it, upon whom the *onus* of proof is imposed."

* * *

Because the Court of Appeals did not apply the correct standard in reviewing the District Court's grant of summary judgment, we vacate its decision and remand the case for further proceedings consistent with this opinion.

It is so ordered.

CELOTEX V. CATRETT (1986)
Supreme Court of the United States
477 U.S. 317

[Widow sues corporation in negligence alleging that her husband was killed by exposure to asbestos. The defendant moved for summary judgment claiming that plaintiff failed in discovery to produce any evidence that its product was the proximate cause of the injuries.]

* * *

Under Rule 56,* summary judgment is proper "if the pleadings, depositions, answers to interrogatories, and admissions on file, together with the affidavits, if any, show that there is no genuine issue as to any material fact and that the moving party is entitled to a judgment as a matter of law." In our view, the plain language of Rule 56 mandates the entry of summary judgment, after adequate time for discovery and upon motion, against a party who fails to make a showing sufficient to establish the existence of an element essential to that party's case, and on which that party will bear the burden of proof at trial. In such a situation, there can be "no genuine issue as to any material fact," since a complete failure of proof concerning an essential element of the nonmoving party's case necessarily renders all other facts immaterial. The moving party is "entitled to a judgment as a matter of law" because the nonmoving party has failed to make a sufficient showing on an essential element of her case with respect to which she has the burden of proof. "[T]h[e] standard [for granting summary judgment] mirrors the standard for a directed verdict under Federal Rule of Civil Procedure 50(a) . . . ." *Anderson v. Liberty Lobby, Inc.* (1986).

* * *

The Federal Rules of Civil Procedure have for almost 50 years authorized motions for summary judgment upon proper showings of the lack of a genuine, triable issue of material fact. Summary judgment procedure is properly regarded not as a disfavored procedural shortcut, but rather as an integral part of the Federal Rules as a whole, which are designed "to secure the just, speedy and inexpensive determination of every action." Before the shift to "notice pleading" accomplished by the Federal Rules, motions to dismiss a complaint or to strike a defense were the principal tools by which factually insufficient claims or defenses could be isolated and prevented from going to trial with the attendant unwarranted consumption of public and private resources. But with the advent of "notice pleading," the motion to dismiss seldom fulfills this function anymore, and its place has been taken by the motion for summary judgment. Rule 56 must be construed with due regard not only for the rights of persons asserting claims and

---

* Because of the difference in language and structure of Rule 56 since 1986 when this opinion was published the editor has removed references to specific sections of the Rule in the opinion which no longer correspond to the language cited.

defenses that are adequately based in fact to have those claims and defenses tried to a jury, but also for the rights of persons opposing such claims and defenses to demonstrate in the manner provided by the Rule, prior to trial, that the claims and defenses have no factual basis.

The judgment of the Court of Appeals is accordingly reversed, and the case is remanded for further proceedings consistent with this opinion.

DIRECTED READING QUESTIONS

10. The burden of proof in a civil trial is divided into the burden of persuasion and the burden of production. The burden of persuasion is relevant to whether a party has put on enough evidence to convince a jury in a civil trial. For example, a civil plaintiff must put on enough evidence to persuade a jury that the plaintiff is entitled to relief by a preponderance of the evidence or is more likely than not entitled to relief. If the jury in a civil trial concludes that the plaintiff's entitlement to relief is just as likely as the plaintiff's lack of entitlement to relief, then the defendant wins. However, judgment as a matter of law and hence summary judgment (because the second prong of summary judgment is entitlement to judgment as a matter of law) are concerned with burdens of production which are also called burdens of going forward. Read Rule 50(a) and the two case excerpts above carefully and articulate what the burden of production is and distinguish it from the burden of persuasion.

11. Please explain how the defendant in *Celotex* proved that there was "no genuine dispute as to any material fact and the movant [was] entitled to judgment as a matter of law."

III. CREDIBILITY AND DETERMINING IF THE BURDEN OF PERSUASION IS MET

ARNSTEIN V. PORTER (1946)
United States Court of Appeals, Second Circuit
154 F.2d 464

The principal question on this appeal is whether the lower court, under Rule 56, properly deprived plaintiff of a trial of his copyright infringement action. The answer depends on whether 'there is the slightest doubt as to the facts. In applying that standard here, it is important to avoid confusing two separate elements essential to a plaintiff's case in such a suit: (a) that defendant copied from plaintiff's copyrighted work and (b) that the copying (assuming it to be proved) went to far as to constitute improper appropriation.

As to the first—copying—the evidence may consist (a) of defendant's admission that he copied or (b) of circumstantial evidence—usually evidence of access—from which the trier of the facts may reasonably infer copying.

* * *

After listening to the compositions as played in the phonograph recordings submitted by defendant, we find similarities; but we hold that unquestionably, standing alone, they do not compel the conclusion, or permit the inference, that defendant copied. The similarities, however, are sufficient so that, if there is enough evidence of access to permit the case to go to the jury, the jury may properly infer that the similarities did not result from coincidence.

Summary judgment was, then, proper if indubitably defendant did not have access to plaintiff's compositions. Plainly that presents an issue of fact. On that issue, the district judge, who heard no oral testimony, had before him the depositions of plaintiff and defendant. The judge characterized plaintiff's story as 'fantastic'; and, in the light of the references in his opinion to defendant's deposition, the judge obviously accepted defendant's denial of access and copying. Although part of plaintiff's testimony on deposition (as to 'stooges' and the like) does seem 'fantastic,' yet plaintiff's credibility, even as to those improbabilities, should be left to the jury. If evidence is 'of a kind that greatly taxes the credulity of the judge, he can say so, or, if he totally disbelieves it, he may announce that fact, leaving the jury free to believe it or not.' If, said Winslow, J., 'evidence is to be always disbelieved because the story told seems remarkable or impossible, then a party whose rights depend on the proof of some facts out of the usual course of events will always be denied justice simply because his story is improbable.' We should not overlook the shrewd proverbial admonition that sometimes truth is stranger than fiction.

But even if we were to disregard the improbable aspects of plaintiff's story, there remain parts by no means 'fantastic.' On the record now before us, more than a million copies of one of his compositions were sold; copies of others were sold in smaller quantities or distributed to radio stations or band leaders or publishers, or the pieces were publicly performed. If, after hearing both parties testify, the jury disbelieves defendant's denials, it can, from such facts, reasonably infer access. It follows that, as credibility is unavoidably involved, a genuine issue of material fact presents itself. With credibility a vital factor, plaintiff is entitled to a trial where the jury can observe the witnesses while testifying. Plaintiff must not be deprived of the invaluable privilege of cross-examining the defendant—the 'crucial test of credibility'—in the presence of the jury. Plaintiff, or a lawyer on his behalf, on such examination may elicit damaging admissions from defendant; more important, plaintiff may persuade the jury, observing defendant's manner when testifying, that defendant is unworthy of belief.

To be sure, plaintiff examined defendant on deposition. But the right to use depositions for discovery, or for limited purposes at a trial, of course does not mean that they are to supplant the right to call and examine the adverse party, if he is available, before the jury. For the demeanor of witnesses is recognized as a highly useful, even if not an infallible, method of ascertaining the truth and accuracy of their narratives. As we have said, 'a deposition has always been, and still is, treated as a substitute, a second-best, not to be used when the original is at hand' for it deprives 'of the advantage of having the witness before the jury.' It has been said that as 'the appearance and manner of the witness' is often 'a complete antidote' to what he testifies, 'we cannot very well overestimate the importance of having the witness examined and cross-examined in presence of the court and jury.' Judge Lumpkin remarked that 'the oral testimony of the witness, in the presence of the Court and Jury, is much better evidence than his deposition can be * * *' Coxe, J., noted that 'a witness may convince all who hear him testify that he is disingenuous and untruthful, and yet his testimony, when read, may convey a most favorable impression.' As a deposition 'cannot give the look or manner of the witness: his hesitation, his doubts, his variations of language, his confidence or precipitancy, his calmness or consideration;' it 'is * * * or it may be, the dead body of the evidence, without its spirit * * *' 'It is sometimes difficult and impossible to get so full, explicit, and perspicuous a statement of facts from the witness through a deposition as it is by his examination before court and jury.' 'The right of a party, therefore, to have a witness subjected to the personal view of the jury, is a valuable right, of which he should not be deprived * * * except by necessity. And that necessity ceases whenever the witness is within the power of the court, and may be produced upon the trial.'

Modified in part; otherwise reversed and remanded.

CLARK, CIRCUIT JUDGE (dissenting).

* * *

Since the legal issue seems thus clear to me, I am loath to believe that my colleagues will uphold a final judgment of plagiarism on a record such as this. The present holding is therefore one of those procedural mountains which develop where it is thought that justice must be temporarily sacrificed, lest a mistaken precedent be set at large. The conclusion that the precedent would be mistaken appears to rest on two premises: a belief in the efficacy of the jury to settle issues of plagiarism, and a dislike of the rule established by the Supreme Court as to summary judgments. Now, as to the first, I am not one to condemn jury trials, since I think it has a place among other quite finite methods of fact-finding. But * * * surely we cannot now say that a verdict should not be directed . . . .

The second premise—dislike of the summary-judgment rule—I find difficult to appraise or understand. Seemingly the procedure is not to be generally favored, but with certain exceptions, the extent of which is unclear. And perhaps it is not to be employed at all in plagiarism cases. Since, however, the clear-cut provisions of F.R. 56 conspicuously do not contain either a restriction on the kinds of actions to which it is applicable (unlike most state summary procedures) or any presumption against its use, it is necessary to refashion the rule . . . . That is a novel method of amending rules of procedure. It subverts the plans and hopes of the profession for careful, informed study leading to the adoption and to the amendment of simple rules which shall be uniform throughout the country . . . .

In fact, however, cases, texts, and articles without dissent accept and approve the summary judgment as an integral and useful part of the procedural system envisaged by the rules . . . . It is, indeed, more necessary in the system of simple pleading now enforced in the federal courts; for under older procedures, useless and unnecessary trials could be avoided, in theory at least, by the then existing demurrer and motion practice. But that stressed pleading forms, rather than the merits, while summary judgment and its popular correlative, pre-trial procedure, F.R. 16, go directly to the merits. One unfortunate consequence of eliminating summary procedure is that it affords support for the plea of return to the old demurrer, which, however clumsily, did get rid of some of the cases which did not deserve a protracted and expensive trial. Of course it is error to deny trial when there is a genuine dispute of facts; but it is just as much error—perhaps more in cases of hardship, or where impetus is given to strike suits—to deny or postpone judgment where the ultimate legal result is clearly indicated.

DYER V. MacDOUGALL (1952)
United States Court of Appeals, Second Circuit
201 F.2d 265

L. HAND, CIRCUIT JUDGE.

This case comes up on appeal by the plaintiff from a judgment summarily dismissing the third and fourth counts of a complaint for libel and slander . . . . We may start with the amended complaint, which was filed on November 24, 1950. It was in four counts, of which the first alleged that the defendant, Albert E. MacDougall, had said of the plaintiff at a directors' meeting of the 'Queensboro Corporation': 'You are stabbing me in the back.' The second count alleged that MacDougall had written a letter to one, Dorothy Russell Hope, the plaintiff's wife's sister, containing the words: 'He'—the plaintiff—'has made false statements to my clients in Philadelphia,' and 'He has presented bills for work he has not done.' The third count alleged that MacDougall had said to a lawyer, named Almirall, that a letter sent out by the plaintiff to the shareholders of the 'Queensboro Corporation' was 'a blackmailing letter.' The fourth count alleged that MacDougall's wife, as MacDougall's agent, had said to Mrs. Hope that the plaintiff had 'written and sent out a blackmailing letter.' On December 26, 1950, the defendants, before answer, moved for judgment summarily dismissing the second, third and fourth counts, supporting their motion by affidavits of MacDougall, MacDougall's wife, and Almirall, and by a deposition of Mrs. Hope, which the plaintiff himself had already taken. Each of the defendants unequivocally denied the utterance of the slanders attributed to him or her; and Almirall and Mrs. Hope denied that he or she had heard the slanders uttered. On his part the plaintiff replied with several affidavits of his own, the contents of all of which would, however, be inadmissible as evidence at a trial upon the issue of utterance. On January 24, 1951, the defendants filed an unverified answer denying the defamatory utterances, and on the same day they brought on their motion for hearing before Judge Kennedy. He offered the plaintiff an opportunity to take depositions of Mr. and Mrs. MacDougall and of Almirall, and a second deposition of Mrs. Hope; and by consent the case was then adjourned to allow the plaintiff to take the depositions. However, towards the end of October 1951, he told the court that he did not wish to do so, and on December 28, 1951 (the defendants having meanwhile withdrawn their motion as to the second count), the judge decided the defendants' motion by summarily dismissing the third and fourth counts on the ground that upon the trial the plaintiff would have no evidence to offer in support of the slanders except the testimony of witnesses, all of whom would deny their utterance.

* * *

The question is whether, in view of the defendants' affidavits and Mrs. Hope's deposition, there was any 'genuine issue' under Rule 56[a] as to the utterance of the slanders. The defendants had the burden of proving that there was no such issue; on the other hand, at a trial the plaintiff would have the burden of proving the utterances; and therefore, if the defendants on the motion succeeded in proving that the plaintiff would not have enough evidence to go to the jury on the issue, the judgment was right. As the plaintiff has refused to avail himself of the privilege under Rule 56[d] of examining by deposition the witnesses whom the defendants proposed to call at the trial, we must assume that what they said in their affidavits they would have repeated in their depositions; and that what they would have said in their depositions, they would say at a trial, with one possible exception, the consideration of which we will postpone for the time being. With that reserve we will therefore first discuss the judgment on the assumption that the record before us contains all the testimony that would appear at a trial in support of the slanders.

* * *

[I]f the cause went to trial, the plaintiff would have no witnesses by whom he could prove the slanders alleged in the third and fourth counts, except the two defendants, Almirall and Mrs. Hope; and they would all deny that the slanders had been uttered. On such a showing how could he escape a directed verdict? It is true that the carriage, behavior, bearing, manner and appearance of a witness—in short, his 'demeanor'—is a part of the evidence. The words used are by no means all that we rely on in making up our minds about the truth of a question that arises in our ordinary affairs, and it is abundantly settled that a jury is as little confined to them as we are. They may, and indeed they should, take into consideration the whole nexus of sense impressions which they get from a witness. This we have again and again declared, and have rested our affirmance of findings of fact of a judge, or of a jury, on the hypothesis that this part of the evidence may have turned the scale.[1] Moreover, such evidence may satisfy the tribunal, not only that the witness' testimony is not true, but that the truth is the opposite of his story; for the denial of one, who has a motive to deny, may be uttered with such hesitation, discomfort, arrogance or defiance, as to give assurance that he is fabricating, and that, if he is, there is no alternative but to assume the truth of what he denies.

Nevertheless, although it is therefore true that in strict theory a party having the affirmative might succeed in convincing a jury of the truth of his allegations in spite of the fact that all the witnesses denied them, we think it plain that a verdict would nevertheless have to be directed against him. This is owing to the fact that otherwise in such cases there could not be an effective appeal from the judge's disposition of a motion for a directed verdict. He, who has seen and heard the 'demeanor' evidence, may have been right or wrong in thinking that it gave rational support to a verdict; yet, since that evidence has disappeared, it will be impossible for an appellate court to say which he was. Thus, he would become the final arbiter in all cases where the evidence of witnesses present in court might be determinative. We need not say that in setting aside a verdict the judge has not a broader discretion that in directing one; for we have before us only the equivalent of a direction. It may be argued that such a ruling may deprive a party of a possibly rational verdict, and indeed that is theoretically true, although the occasions must be to the last degree rare in which the chance so denied is more than fanciful. Nevertheless we do not hesitate to set against the chance so lost, the protection of a review of the judge's decision.

There remains the second point which we reserved for separate discussion: i.e. whether by an examination in open court the plaintiff might extract from the four witnesses admissions which he would not have got on the depositions that he refused. Although this is also at best a tenuous possibility, we need not say that there could never be situations in which it might justify denying summary judgment. It might appear for

---

[1] *Arnstein v. Porter.*

example that upon a deposition a witness had been recalcitrant, or crafty, or defiant, or evasive, so that the immediate presence of a judge in a court-room was likely to make him tell more. That would be another matter; and it might be enough. But the plaintiff is in no position to invoke such a possibility for he has refused to try out these witnesses upon deposition, where he might discover whether there was any basis for supposing that awe of a judge was necessary to make them more amenable. A priori we will not assume that that is true. The course of procedural reform has all indeed been towards bringing witnesses before the tribunal when it is possible; but that is not so much because more testimony can be got out of them as because only so can the 'demeanor' evidence be brought before the tribunal.

Judgment affirmed.

DIRECTED READING QUESTIONS

12. Where does the "evidence" typically needed for summary judgment come from?

13. What are the basic facts of *Arnstein*? What is the cause of action?

14. What are the two elements of the cause of action in *Arnstein*?

15. What are the two ways that a plaintiff can prove the first of the two elements required in *Arnstein*?

16. What does the court "unquestionably" hold?

17. What does *Arnstein* tell you about the role of credibility in a summary judgment decision? How might you use a credibility argument to stave off a motion for summary judgment against your client?

18. What are the basic facts of the *Dyer* case?

19. What happened in *Dyer* on December 26, 1950?

20. How did the defendants support their motion for summary judgment? What did the documents used to support the defendant's motion for summary judgment state?

21. How did the plaintiff respond to the defendants' motion for summary judgment? What section of Rule 56 permits the defendant to object to the materials that the plaintiff used to support his response to the motion?

22. What happened on January 24, 1951?

23. How does the judge respond to the defendant's actions on January 24, 1951? What did the judge's response permit the plaintiff to do?

24. On October 31, 1951, the case indicates that the plaintiff did not take the judge's offer. Why do you think the plaintiff did not take the judge up on the offer?

25. Explain why in *Arnstein* summary judgment was denied, but in *Dyer* summary judgment was appropriate given the language in both cases highlighted below.

Arnstein	*Dyer*
"If, after hearing both parties testify, the jury disbelieves defendant's denials, it can, from such facts, reasonably infer access. It follows that, as credibility is	"It is true that the carriage, behavior, bearing, manner and appearance of a witness—in short, his 'demeanor'—is a part of the evidence. The words used are

unavoidably involved, a genuine issue of material fact presents itself. With credibility a vital factor, plaintiff is entitled to a trial where the jury can observe the witnesses while testifying. Plaintiff must not be deprived of the invaluable privilege of cross-examining the defendant—the 'crucial test of credibility'—in the presence of the jury. Plaintiff, or a lawyer on his behalf, on such examination may elicit damaging admissions from defendant; more important, plaintiff may persuade the jury, observing defendant's manner when testifying, that defendant is unworthy of belief."	by no means all that we rely on in making up our minds about the truth of a question that arises in our ordinary affairs, and it is abundantly settled that a jury is as little confined to them as we are. They may, and indeed they should, take into consideration the whole nexus of sense impressions which they get from a witness. This we have again and again declared, and have rested our affirmance of findings of fact of a judge, or of a jury, on the hypothesis that this part of the evidence may have turned the scale.[1] Moreover, such evidence may satisfy the tribunal, not only that the witness' testimony is not true, but that the truth is the opposite of his story; for the denial of one, who has a motive to deny, may be uttered with such hesitation, discomfort, arrogance or defiance, as to give assurance that he is fabricating, and that, if he is, there is no alternative but to assume the truth of what he denies. Nevertheless, although it is therefore true that in strict theory a party having the affirmative might succeed in convincing a jury of the truth of his allegations in spite of the fact that all the witnesses denied them, we think it plain that a verdict would nevertheless have to be directed against him."

26. How does the rationale of the *Arnstein* case in the table above relate to the difference between giving testimony at a deposition and doing so in a courtroom during trial?

27. How does the difference between the majority and dissent in *Arnstein* remind us that the central question for judgment as a matter of law (the second prong of summary judgment) is whether the non-movant has enough evidence in support of their position, rather than just any evidence?

28. Imagine you are sitting alone in your office and the opposing party sends you a motion for summary judgment against your client. How might you respond to a motion for summary judgment? Think of practical solutions instead of theoretical responses here.

29. Create a hypothetical to illustrate a factual dispute which is not material.

30. Create a hypothetical where the movant's entitlement to judgment as a matter of law renders all factual disputes immaterial.

---

[1]   *Arnstein v. Porter.*

31. Create an example of where there are no factual disputes, but the movant is not entitled to judgment as a matter of law.

CHAPTER 9

JUDGMENT AS A MATTER OF LAW

■ ■ ■

I. CONTEXTUALIZING JUDGMENT AS A MATTER OF LAW

DIRECTED READING QUESTIONS

1. Points for you to note:

    a. You already know that the second prong of summary judgment is entitlement to "Judgment as a Matter of Law," so we have already discussed much of this topic.

    b. The older case law describes:

        i. a Rule 50(a) motion for judgment as a matter of law as a motion for a directed verdict;

        ii. a Rule 50(b) renewed motion for judgment as a matter of law as a motion for judgment notwithstanding the verdict or "JNOV."

2. What does the term JNOV (the old name for a Rule 50(b) motion) and the bolded title of Rule 50(b) tell you about when this motion is made?

3. What does Rule 50(a)(2) tell you about the timing of a Rule 50(a) motion?

4. Read Rule 50(a) and 50(b) carefully. Does this rule only apply in jury trials?

5. What is the typical sequence of a jury trial? *You can google this.*

6. What does the "fully heard" requirement of Rule 50(a) tell you about when the motion is typically considered to be timely?

7. Read Rule 50(b) carefully and see if you can glean whether the filing of a Rule 50(b) motion requires the filing of a Rule 50(a) motion. Is the Rule 50(b) motion merely a "renewed" motion of the same Rule 50(a) motion previously made?

8. What relief does Rule 50(b) encourage a movant to alternatively or jointly seek when filing a Rule 50(b) motion? Explain why the rule would encourage this alternative or joint relief.

9. According to Rule 50(c), what must a court do when it grants a renewed motion for judgment as a matter of law?

10. Do the following fill-in-the-blank worksheet and see if you can glean the difference between a motion for judgment as a matter of law and a motion for a new trial.

Rule 50/Rule 59

Please fill in the blanks using each statement contained in the Table of Statements only once to complete the Rule 50/Rule 59 review sheet. This will be hard but fight through it.

A court may properly grant a rule 50 motion, _____
_____
_____.

In contrast, a court may properly grant a Rule 59 motion _____
_____. The standard for granting a Rule 59 motion therefore seems less restrictive than the standard for the granting a Rule 50 motion. A new trial may be granted where the jury verdict is against _____
_____. Interestingly then, a Rule 59 motion allows a court to review the _____ of the evidence as opposed to a Rule 50 motion. A new trial may also be granted for a reason which seems to mirror the language of 60(b)(2) or when _____ exists, and the movant can show that:

    1.   It existed at the time of trial but was not discovered until after trial;

    2.   Due diligence could not have discovered it;

    3.   It is material and admissible; and

    4.   If it had been considered the result would have been different.

In fact, Rule 60(b)(2) functionally, if not literally, extends the time for the filing of this type of motion despite the strictures of Rule _____.

However, it is important to note that a Rule 60 motion does not affect the _____
_____ whereas a motion under Rule 59, for example a Rule 59(e) motion to alter or amend the judgment, does.

Another reason for granting a new trial would be _____. In order to prevail on this type of Rule 59 motion, the movant must demonstrate:

    1.   An error in the selection process such as a lie told during voir dire which prevented a proper for cause challenge; and

    2.   The error was not harmless.

Additionally, a court may grant a new trial when the verdict is _____. However, it is important to note that a court could grant the new trial in this situation solely on the issue of _____
_____ since the language of Rule 59(a)(1) allows a new trial on "all or some of the _____
_____." The granting of a new trial on this basis is complicated by a procedure known as _____
_____, in which the court will conditionally deny the new trial and ask the party who was awarded the excessive verdict to accept _____ in lieu of the granting of a motion for a new trial. If the party agrees with the court's offer and accepts reduced damages in lieu of a new trial, then it waives its right to _____ the issue of damages. If the party does not accept the court's offer of reduced damages, then a _____, and no appeal is possible until another judgment is entered.

On the opposite end of the spectrum, the court may order a new trial if it thinks the verdict is ____
_____. Unlike the immediately preceding situation, if the court grants a new trial for this

reason, it cannot offer an _____ of the award in lieu of a new trial but must _____ the motion for new trial.

A trial court's ruling on a motion for a new trial is reviewed for _____,
while a trial court's ruling on a motion for judgment as a matter of law is reviewed _____.
This stricter standard of review for the ruling on a judgment as a matter of law is likely because granting a Rule 59 motion is thought not to offend the _____
_____ as much as granting a Rule 50 motion.

It is also important to note that appeals are always from judgments, except in the rare situations when an _____ appeal is allowed. As a result, the appeals we read about in our casebooks are appeals from judgments and not, in the strictest sense, appeals from denials of Rule 50 or Rule 59 motions.

For example, the proper appeal from a denial of a Rule 59 motion _____
_____
_____.   During   this
appeal from the _____, you can argue the propriety of the denial of the motion.

Similarly, when contesting the denial of a Rule 50(b) motion at trial, what you are actually appealing is the _____
_____. Interestingly though, some courts say in order to preserve the issue of _____
_____ for appeal, a Rule 50(b) motion must be made at trial.

TABLE OF STATEMENTS

when the court finds that a reasonable jury would not have a legally sufficient evidentiary basis to find for the party on that issue
finality of the judgment
verdict which the court leaves undisturbed when it enters judgment
weight
grant
damages
new trial is mandatory
is the appeal of the judgment that the court let stand in the trial for which no new trial now takes place because of the denial of the new trial motion
abuse of discretion
for any reason for which a new trial has heretofore been granted in an action at law or in federal court
6(b)(2)
excessive
juror misconduct
reduced damages
issues
appeal

upward modification	
de novo	
judgment itself	
insufficiency of evidence	
newly discovered evidence	
inadequate	
Seventh Amendment right to jury trial	
remittitur	
interlocutory	
the clear weight of the evidence	

11. Aaron visited Dr. Smith for a toothache. After examining him, she reached into a drawer, removed a tube, and administered an analgesic cream from the tube to the painful tooth. A little while later on the drive home, Aaron noticed the pain had not subsided. A little further along on the drive home, Aaron passed out from a sudden increase in pain and crashed his car into a pole and suffered injuries. Aaron sued Dr. Smith for negligence and pursuant to Rule 39(a) demanded a federal trial by jury in his complaint. At trial, Aaron's expert witness, Dr. Molar, gave really insightful testimony that left the jury with a lot to chew on. He testified that his examination of Aaron indicated that Aaron's tooth had rapidly disintegrated and the rapid disintegration was the cause of the acute pain that caused the crash. Further, in his expert opinion, he opined that Dr. Smith had accidentally administered a corrosive chemical used in extractions instead of an analgesic cream to Aaron's tooth. Additionally, he testified that it was customary for dentists to keep both analgesics and the corrosive cream in the same drawer and because both substances were manufactured by the same company, their packaging material was remarkably similar and, as a result, both substances were easily mistaken. When Dr. Smith testified, she denied using a corrosive cream instead of an analgesic but she did admit that Dr. Molar was correct in that "it was customary for dentists to keep both analgesics and the corrosive cream in the same drawer and because both substances were manufactured by the same company, their packaging material was remarkably similar and, as a result, both substances were easily mistaken." She further testified that she did in fact keep both chemicals in the same drawer, but that she did not confuse the substances. She also opined that the sudden disintegration of Aaron's tooth was due to a genetic condition. Dr. Molar then further testified that the disintegration of the tooth was more rapid and acute than occurs when the cause is a genetic predisposition.

    a. If Aaron moves for a Rule 50(a) judgment as a matter of law:

        i. His motion should be granted because Dr. Smith testified that she kept both the analgesic and the corrosive agent in the same drawer.

        ii. His motion should be granted because of Dr. Molar's testimony.

        iii. His motion should be denied.

        iv. None of the above.

b. Assume that Dr. Smith moved for a Rule 50(a) judgment as a matter of law, and that the motion was granted. Aaron then appealed. The court of appeals should:

  i.   Reverse the judgment and order a new trial.

  ii. Reverse the judgment and direct that judgment be entered for Aaron.

  iii. Affirm the judgment.

  iv. None of the above.

c. Assume that neither party moved for a Rule 50(a) judgment as a matter of law. The case went to the jury, which returned a verdict for Aaron. Dr. Smith then moved pursuant to Rule 50(b) for judgment as a matter of law. The trial judge granted Dr. Smith's Rule 50(b) motion. Aaron then appealed the Rule 50(b) motion granted by the trial court. The court of appeals should:

  i.   Reverse the judgment since a Rule 50(b) motion can only be properly made if it is joined with a Rule 59 motion.

  ii. Affirm the judgment.

  iii. Affirm the judgment since the standard of review when reviewing the granting of a Rule 50(b) motion is abuse of discretion.

  iv. Reverse the judgment and reinstate the verdict for Aaron.

II. THE MECHANICS OF THE RULE 50 MOTIONS

DIRECTED READING QUESTIONS

12. Plaintiff sues Defendant and the jury returns a verdict for Plaintiff. Defendant properly moves for post-verdict judgment as a matter of law under Rule 50(b) and joins a motion for a new trial under Rule 59 as permitted by Rule 50(b).

  a. What are the court's options in ruling on the renewed motion?

  b. Assume the court grants the Defendant's motion for judgment as a matter of law. What can the Plaintiff do?

  c. Assume the court grants the Defendant's motion for judgment as a matter of law. What happens to the judgment if the Plaintiff elects to move for a new trial, and the court grants Plaintiff's Rule 50(d) motion for a new trial?

  d. Assume the court grants the Defendant's motion for judgment as a matter of law. What happens if the Plaintiff elects to move for a new trial, and the court denies Plaintiff's motion for a new trial?

13. Plaintiff sues Defendant and the jury returns a verdict for Plaintiff. Defendant properly moves for post-verdict judgment as a matter of law under Rule 50(b) and joins a motion for a new trial under Rule 59 as permitted by Rule 50(b).

  a. Assume the court grants the Defendant's motion for judgment as a matter of law. What else must the court do?

  b. Is this mandatory ruling effective in any way before the appellate court gets involved?

c.   Assume that the Defendant's renewed motion for judgment as a matter of law is denied and the Defendant appeals the judgment subsequently entered on the verdict for the Plaintiff. May the Plaintiff raise the issue of its entitlement to a new trial on appeal?

14. On Monday, Plaintiff wins a jury verdict. On that same day, the court enters it in the civil docket as per Rule 79(a)(2)(C) but fails to set out the judgment in a separate document. How many days does the Defendant have to file a Rule 59 or Rule 50(b) motion, assuming there are no legal holidays involved and the clerk's office remains accessible?

15. Plaintiff wins on a special verdict or a general verdict with interrogatories. May the clerk properly enter judgment without the court's approval?

16. A train jumps its tracks at a railroad crossing and crashes into a car. The driver of the car is severely injured and sues the railroad company in negligence. At trial, the sole issues contested were:

a.   whether the train tracks were negligently maintained;

b.   whether the engineer was adequately trained;

c.   whether the train was travelling at the recommended speed;

d.   whether the train was negligently maintained; and

e.   whether the crossing signals were in proper working order.

At the end of the trial, the judge submits the case to the jury and asks them to return a verdict. He also asks the jury a series of written questions which he submits to them along with the verdict form and the jury instructions and instructs them to answer these questions. The jury returns a verdict finding the defendant liable to the plaintiff for $15 million dollars. They answered the written questions submitted with the jury instructions and verdict form as follows:

JUDGE'S QUESTIONS	JURY'S ANSWERS
Were the train tracks negligently maintained?	No.
Was the engineer adequately trained?	Yes.
Was the train travelling at the recommended speed?	Yes.
Was the train negligently maintained?	No.
Were the crossing signals in proper working order?	Yes.

What are the judge's options?

17. In a negligence case, the judge asks the jury to render a verdict. In addition to the jury instructions and the verdict form, the judge submits the following interrogatories to the jury.

a.   Did the defendant owe the plaintiff a duty of care? The jury answers no.

b.   Did the defendant breach the duty of care owed to the plaintiff? The jury answers yes.

c.   Did the defendant's breach of duty cause the harm to the plaintiff? The jury answers yes.

d. Did the defendant experience harm to its person or property? The jury answers yes.

The jury also returns a damage award in its verdict for the plaintiff. What are the judge's options?

CHAPTER 10

JOINDER

■ ■ ■

I. RULE 14, THIRD-PARTY PRACTICE

DIRECTED READING QUESTIONS

1. While driving, plaintiff's car was struck by a truck driven by a delivery truck driver who at the time of the accident was delivering packages in the course and scope of his employment with the corporation, Deliveryex, Inc. Plaintiff sued Deliveryex, Inc. under a vicarious liability theory to recover for the harm caused to Plaintiff's car in the accident. Diagram each of the following scenarios.

   a. Diagram the original lawsuit.

   b. Deliveryex then impleads Driver, alleging that if Deliveryex is liable for the harm that Driver's negligence caused, then Driver will be required to compensate Deliveryex for what it paid to Plaintiff.

   c. Driver realizes that part of the reason he was driving negligently is because Deliveryex was negligent in the training it provided him. As a result, he decides that he is not responsible for all the harm caused Plaintiff, and so he seeks to reduce how much he would have to pay Deliveryex if Deliveryex is found liable. Additionally, driver suffered harm in the accident and seeks to recover from Deliveryex the proportion of the harm attributable to Deliveryex's negligent training.

   d. Driver realizes that plaintiff was also negligent, and Driver raises as a defense that some of the plaintiff's harm was caused by Plaintiff's own negligence. Driver seeks to recover from Plaintiff the harm caused to Driver in the accident which is attributable to Plaintiff's negligence.

   e. Plaintiff then realizes that she should also sue driver directly.

   f. Finally, Driver realizes that a pedestrian was shining a laser light directly into driver's eyes when the accident occurred and Driver seeks to recover from pedestrian any damages caused to Plaintiff because of pedestrian shining the laser.

   g. Plaintiff realizes that part of the reason she was driving negligently is because passenger, who was in her car, was deliberately and intermittently blocking plaintiff's view and distracting plaintiff despite plaintiff's protests. Plaintiff realizes that if she is liable to Driver, Passenger should be responsible for some of the harm.

II. INTRODUCTION TO RULE 18, JOINDER OF CLAIMS

DIRECTED READING QUESTIONS

2.   A sues B for violation of a federal statute in federal court. A decides to join a state law claim that A has against B for conversion because B stole A's bicycle. Does Rule 18 permit A to join the claim for conversion with the claim for violation of a federal statute in one federal court action?

3.   Assume Rule 18 allowed the joinder of the conversion claim and the federal statutory claims in question 2. Does it make any difference in terms of the federal court's ability to hear the conversion claim if the conversion claim and the statutory claim are derived from a common nucleus of operative fact or if they are unrelated? TO BE ANSWERED ONLY AFTER YOU DO SUPPLEMENTAL JURISDICTION.

III. INTRODUCTION TO RULE 20, JOINDER OF PARTIES

DIRECTED READING QUESTIONS

4.   Consider the following actions and come up with a hypothetical where Rule 20 would allow the action.

    a. $Plaintiff_1$ + $Plaintiff_2$ + $Plaintiff_3$ v. Defendant

    b.   Plaintiff v. $Defendant_1$ + $Defendant_2$ + $Defendant_3$

5.   There are more complicated issues relating to joinder, not covered in this chapter, that we will revisit after we have completed subject matter jurisdiction. But for now, revisit Rule 13(a)(1)(A) and Rule 15(c)(1)(B) and look ahead to 28 U.S.C. § 1367(a). See if you can articulate anything that these two rules and the statute have in common with Rule 20.

IV. RULE 19, COMPULSORY JOINDER OF PARTIES

DIRECTED READING QUESTIONS

6.   Examine Rule 12(b)(7) and Rule 12(h)(2) carefully. Be clear that you understand that failure to join someone "under Rule 19" is a defense and can result in dismissal. The rest of this chapter will examine when the failure to join someone under Rule 19 mandates dismissal and when it does not.

JANNEY MONTGOMERY SCOTT, INC. v. SHEPARD NILES, INC. (1993)

United States Third Circuit Court of Appeals
11 F.3d 399

HUTCHINSON, CIRCUIT JUDGE.

    Appellant, Janney Montgomery Scott, Inc. ("Janney"), appeals an order of the United States District Court for the Eastern District of Pennsylvania granting appellee, Shepard Niles, Inc.'s ("Shepard Niles") motion for . . . failure to join an indispensable party in Janney's breach of contract action. The person whose non-joinder resulted in dismissal is Shepard Niles' parent corporation, The Underwood Group, Ltd. ("Underwood"), a citizen of Pennsylvania. In doing so, the district court had to make an initial determination that Underwood, Shepard Niles' parent, was a necessary party* under Rule 19(a) before it could hold that Underwood was an indispensable party† under Rule 19(b) whose non-joinder required dismissal because joinder would deprive the district court of diversity jurisdiction. Initially, the district court had subject matter jurisdiction in diversity because Janney is a citizen of Pennsylvania and Shepard Niles is a citizen of New York.

In Shepard Niles' motion to dismiss for failure to join Underwood, it stated that Underwood, its parent and the sole signatory to the contract Janney sued on, was both necessary and indispensable to Janney's action under Rule 19. The question before us is whether the district court could give complete relief to the parties before it without prejudice to them or the absent person, Underwood, in a breach of contract action against only one of the two co-obligors that might be liable to Janney, the obligee on the contract. If the relief Janney requests does not prejudice the absent co-obligor, Underwood, or subject either Janney or Shepard Niles to a threat of duplicative or inconsistent judgments, Underwood is not a necessary party under Rule 19(a).

If Underwood is not a necessary party under Rule 19(a), we need not reach the question whether it is indispensable under Rule 19(b). In this case, we have concluded that Underwood will not be prejudiced and neither Janney nor Shepard Niles will be subjected to duplicative or inconsistent judgments. Therefore, we hold that Underwood is not a necessary party under Rule 19(a). Accordingly, we will reverse the district court's order granting Shepard Niles' motion to dismiss without reaching the question whether Underwood is indispensable under Rule 19(b).

I.   *Factual & Procedural History*

Janney is an investment banking corporation organized under Pennsylvania law with its principal place of business in Philadelphia, Pennsylvania. Underwood is a closely-held Pennsylvania corporation with its principal place of business in Pennsylvania; Shepard Niles is incorporated under New York law, with its principal place of business in New York.

On January 12, 1990, Janney and Underwood executed an Investment Banking Agreement ("Agreement"). In it, Janney agreed to serve as an advisor to Underwood and its subsidiaries, including Shepard Niles, and to assist them in obtaining private placement financing to refinance Shepard Niles' debt obligations.

The agreement stated "Janney Montgomery Scott Inc. [sic] ("JMS") is delighted to serve as the exclusive investment banking advisor for The Underwood Group, Ltd. *and subsidiaries* ("Underwood" or the "Company") in connection with the proposed Private Placement financing." *Id.* (emphasis added). Under the Agreement, Janney agreed to introduce Underwood to potential sources for the financing Shepard Niles wanted to obtain and to provide substantial ongoing support in securing such financing.

* * *

---

*   The heading of Rule 19(a) is now "Persons Required to Be Joined if Feasible." Formerly a person who was required to be joined if feasible was known in the rule and the case law as a necessary party.

†   Previously a party was deemed indispensable under 19(b) when it was decided that the action could not proceed without that person being joined as a party and it wasn't feasible to join the party.

In February 1990, when Janney's efforts had yet to show concrete results, Underwood entered into negotiations with Unibank PLC [a Danish Company] . . . . By the fall of 1990, Unibank . . . had [obtained financing for Shepard Niles]. Janney did not introduce either of these two companies to Underwood and its subsidiaries, but Janney does allege that it provided substantial advice and support to Underwood and Shepard Niles throughout the negotiations. It contends that under the Agreement this advice and support entitle it to a contingent fee which it seeks to recover from Shepard Niles in this action and from Underwood in the related state action that Janney filed in [Philadelphia State Court on October 4, 1990] against Underwood . . . . In addition, on October 23, 1991, after some discovery in the state action, Janney filed an action in [federal] court against Unibank for tortious interference with contract.

On February 7, 1992, in the federal action against Unibank for tortious interference with contract, Janney filed a motion to amend its complaint to add Shepard Niles as a defendant. The district court denied it. Thereafter, on March 17, 1992, Janney filed the present breach of contract action against Shepard Niles [in federal court]. Shepard Niles responded with a Federal Rule of Civil Procedure 12(b)(6) motion to dismiss . . . . The district court denied this motion. After the pleadings in the district court had closed and discovery was nearly completed, Shepard Niles filed its Rule 12(c) motion for judgment on the pleadings for failure to join Underwood as an indispensable party. On January 4, 1993, the district court granted Shepard Niles' Rule 12(c) motion . . . . Janney has timely appealed the order granting Shepard Niles' Rule 12(c) motion for judgment on the pleadings and dismissing of the breach of contract action for non-joinder.

* * *

III. *Rule 19 Analysis*

Federal Rule of Civil Procedure 19 determines when joinder of a particular party is compulsory. A court must first determine whether a party should be joined if "feasible" under Rule 19(a). If the party should be joined but joinder is not feasible because it would destroy diversity, the court must then determine whether the absent party is "indispensable" under Rule 19(b). If the party is indispensable, the action therefore cannot go forward. Thus, we must first determine whether Underwood, as a co-obligor to the Agreement, is a so-called "necessary" party who must be joined under Rule 19(a) if joinder is feasible. If we decide that the district court erred in its conclusion that Underwood was, in this sense, a "necessary" party under Rule 19(a), we need not reach or decide whether the district court abused its discretion when it held that Underwood was an "indispensable" party under Rule 19(b).

Rule 19(a) defines the parties who are "necessary" in the sense that their joinder is compulsory "if feasible." It states, in pertinent part:

A person . . . shall be joined as a party in the action if (1)[A] in the person's absence complete relief cannot be accorded among those already parties, or [B the person claims an interest relating to the subject of the action and is so situated that the disposition of the action in the person's absence may (i) as a practical matter impair or impede the person's ability to protect that interest or (ii) leave any of the persons already parties subject to a substantial risk of incurring double, multiple, or otherwise inconsistent obligations by reason of the claimed interest.

Clauses [a](1)[A] and [B] of Rule 19(a) are phrased in the disjunctive and should be so treated. Thus, any party whose absence results in any of the problems identified in either subsections (a)(1)[A] or (a)[1][B] is a party whose joinder is compulsory if feasible. In other words, a holding that joinder is compulsory under Rule 19(a) is a necessary predicate to a district court's discretionary determination under Rule 19(b) that the case must be dismissed because joinder of the party is not feasible and the party is indispensable to the just resolution of the controversy.

A.   *Rule 19(a)(1)[A]*

Under Rule 19(a), we ask first whether complete relief can be accorded to the parties to the action in the absence of the unjoined party. Fed.R.Civ.P. 19(a)(1)[A]. A Rule 19(a)(1)[A] inquiry is limited to whether the district court can grant complete relief to the persons already parties to the action. The effect a decision may have on the absent party is not material. Here, the district court concluded that complete relief could be afforded Janney and Shepard Niles in the absence of Underwood. Shepard Niles does not seriously dispute this conclusion. For the following reasons, we agree with the district court on this point.

In applying Rule 19(a)(1)[A] to this case, the specific question before us is whether a court can grant complete relief in a breach of contract action to the parties before it when only one of two co-obligors has been joined as a defendant. The answer to this specific question depends on the law of contracts concerning the joint and several liability of persons who are co-promisors or co-obligors on one agreement . . . . In Pennsylvania, whether liability on a contract is joint or joint and several seems to be treated as a question of construction or interpretation, not as a rule of law.

[T]he Agreement in question can be construed or interpreted as a contract imposing joint and several liability on its co-obligors, Shepard Niles and Underwood, complete relief may be granted in a suit against only one of them.

* * *

Therefore, because the Agreement can be construed to impose joint and several liability, Underwood is not a necessary party under subsection (a)(1), and we must affirm the district court's holding that complete relief could be granted between Shepard Niles and Janney without Underwood's presence.

B.   *Rule 19(a)(1)[B]*

Though Underwood was not a party that had to be joined under Rule 19(a)(1)[A] because complete relief could be granted the parties already present, the district court concluded Underwood's joinder was compulsory under both Rule 19(a)[1][B](i) and 19(a)[1][B](ii). Unlike subsection (a)(1)[A], subsection (a)(2) requires a court to take into consideration the effect that resolution of the dispute among the parties before it may have on an absent party.

1.   *Rule 19(a)[1][B](i)*

Subsection (a)[1][B](i) requires a court to decide whether determination of the rights of the parties before it would impair or impede an absent party's ability to protect its interest in the subject matter of the litigation. Shepard Niles argues that the district court correctly held Underwood is a necessary party because any decision in the federal action in Janney's favor would be a persuasive precedent against Underwood in the ongoing state action. The district court agreed and held that "as a practical matter, the disposition of this action in Underwood's absence [would] impair or impede Underwood's ability to protect its interest."

According to the district court, it was likely that any decision reached in the federal action would affect the pending state court action [because of the collateral estoppel or res judicata effect of the judgment on Underwood.

* * *

[However] Underwood would not be bound [because of] the general rule res judicata or collateral estoppel] applies only to persons who were either parties to the prior action or shared the same interest as the parties who were present in the prior action and [Underwood is not a party in this action, so it will not be bound by the judgment.]

2.   *Rule 19(a)[1][B](ii)*

We have yet to consider the effect of Rule 19(a)[1][B](ii) on the non-joinder of Underwood. It requires us to decide whether continuation of this action in the absence of Underwood would expose Shepard Niles to the "substantial risk of incurring double, multiple, or otherwise inconsistent obligations by reason of the claimed interest."

* * *

It is, of course, possible, as the district court concluded, that if Shepard Niles is held liable in the federal action, it "may ultimately be responsible for the entire claim if Underwood is found not liable in the State Court Action." This is not, however, the double liability that Rule 19(a)[1][B](ii) refers to [but simply the single liability Shepard Niles is responsible for under the doctrine of joint and several liability].

* * *

IV.   *Conclusion*

Underwood's joinder is not necessary under Rule 19(a)(1)[A] because the district court can give complete relief to Janney and Shepard Niles in their action. Rule 19(a)[1][B](i) is not triggered by the mere possibility that continuation of this federal case could have some effect on later litigation between Janney and Underwood . . . . Nor will continuation of this action in Underwood's absence expose Shepard Niles to . . . double liability under Rule 19(a)[1][B](ii). Therefore, we conclude that the district court erred when it held that Underwood was a party who had to be joined under Rule 19(a) if its joinder were feasible. That conclusion makes it unnecessary for us to decide whether the district court abused its discretion when it decided that Underwood was an indispensable party under Rule 19(b).

The district court's determination that Underwood is a necessary party will be reversed and the case will be remanded for further proceedings consistent with this opinion.

DIRECTED READING QUESTIONS

7.   Examine Rule 12(b)(7) carefully. What does it suggest about Rule 19?

8.   Very carefully map out the procedural posture for this case paying particular attention to what happened on:

    a.   January 12, 1990

    b.   February 1990

    c.   Fall 1990

    d.   October 4, 1990

    e.   October 23, 1991

    f.   February 7, 1992

    g.   March 1992

    h.   January 4, 1993

9.   VERY CAREFULLY, try to articulate exactly why Shepard Niles is arguing the action should be dismissed. Remember a Rule 12(b)(7) motion to dismiss because of failure to join a party under Rule 19 is an assertion by the moving party that a certain person who is not currently joined as a party needs to be joined as a party or the court must dismiss the action because that unjoined person is so important to the action that the action cannot proceed without them.

10. What is the analytical sequence for determining whether the non-joinder of someone as a party requires dismissal of the action pursuant to Rule 19? Read the opinion and Rule 19 carefully.

11. Please explain how a Rule 12(b)(7) motion can be denied either after a Rule 19(a) analysis or a Rule 19(b) analysis, but that the granting of a Rule 12(b)(7) motion can only occur after a Rule 19(b) analysis.

12. What did the district court conclude about Underwood under Rule 19? Explain how those conclusions resulted in dismissal.

13. At the appellate level, Shepard Niles makes three arguments about why the appellate court should find that Underwood is a party that is required to be joined if feasible under Rule 19(a). The appellate court ultimately concludes that Underwood is not a party that is required to be joined if feasible under Rule 19(a) and so denies the Rule 12(b)(7) motion.

    a.   Explain the argument based on Rule 19(a)(1)(A) that Shepard Niles makes and why the appellate court disagrees.

    b.   Explain the argument based on Rule 19(a)(1)(B)(i) that Shepard Niles makes and why the appellate court disagrees.

    c.   Explain the argument based on Rule 19(a)(1)(B)(ii) that Shepard Niles makes and why the appellate court disagrees.

14. Batman sues Robin for damages pursuant to the federal inefficacy statute which states, "A superhero may sue another person with whom he operates as a dynamic duo for inefficacy if that person does nothing but say silly things." Robin is served and responds by filing and serving a motion raising the defense of Rule 12(b)(7) because Cat Woman was not joined as a defendant. Which of the following are incorrect?

I.   In ruling on the motion, the court must decide what action is necessary if joinder is not feasible.

II. In ruling on the motion, the court must decide the extent to which a judgment rendered in Cat Woman's absence might prejudice Cat Woman or the existing parties.

III. In ruling on the motion, the court must consider whether Cat Woman is subject to service of process.

IV. In ruling on the motion, the court must consider whether in Cat Woman's absence the court cannot accord complete relief among the existing parties.

V.   In ruling on the motion, the court must consider whether Cat Woman's joinder will deprive the court of subject matter jurisdiction.

VI. In ruling on the motion, the court must consider whether to order the joinder of Cat Woman.

   a.   II only

   b.   I and II only

   c.   All except I

   d.   All

CHAPTER 11

SUBJECT MATTER JURISDICTION

Constitutional and Statutory Limits on the Power of the Inferior Federal Courts

■ ■ ■

I. THE REQUIREMENT OF BOTH A CONSTITUTIONAL AND STATUTORY JURISDICTIONAL GRANT

DIRECTED READING QUESTIONS

1. Examine Article III, § 1 of the Constitution and explain what the "inferior Courts" are.

2. Examine Article III, § 2 of the Constitution carefully and answer whether the Constitution provides for subject matter jurisdiction over the following cases or controversies.

    a. A citizen of Kansas sues a citizen of Missouri for harm caused by actions which constitute breach of contract under Kansas law.

    b. A citizen of Kansas sues a citizen of Kansas for harm caused by actions which constitute breach of contract under Kansas law.

    c. A citizen of Kansas sues a citizen of Kansas for harm caused by defendant's actions which violate Title VII of the Civil Rights Act of 1964.

    d. A seafarer employed on a ship sues the owner of the ship for harm caused by the shipowner's violation of a maritime safety statute.

3. Where is the first place you need to look to see whether a federal district court has subject matter jurisdiction over a case or controversy?

SHELDON V. SILL (1850)
Supreme Court of the United States
49 U.S. 441

MR. JUSTICE GRIER delivered the opinion of the court.

The only question which it will be necessary to notice in this case is, whether the Circuit Court had jurisdiction.

Sill, the complainant below, a citizen of New York, filed his bill in the Circuit Court of the United States for Michigan, against Sheldon, claiming to recover the amount of a bond and mortgage, which had been assigned to him by Hastings, the President of the Bank of Michigan.

Sheldon, in his answer, among other things, pleaded that 'the bond and mortgage in controversy, having been originally given by a citizen of Michigan to another citizen of the same state, and the complainant being assignee of them, the Circuit Court had no jurisdiction.'

The eleventh section of the Judiciary Act, which defines the jurisdiction of the Circuit Courts, restrains them from taking 'cognizance of any suit to recover the contents of any promissory note or other chose in action, in favor of an assignee, unless a suit might have been prosecuted in such court to recover the contents, if no assignment had been made, except in cases of foreign bills of exchange.'

The third article of the Constitution declares that 'the judicial power of the United States shall be vested in one Supreme Court, and such inferior courts as the Congress may, from time to time, ordain and establish.' The second section of the same article enumerates the cases and controversies of which the judicial power shall have cognizance, and, among others, it specifies 'controversies between citizens of different states.'

It has been alleged, that this restriction of the Judiciary Act, with regard to assignees of choses in action, is in conflict with this provision of the Constitution, and therefore void.

It must be admitted, that if the Constitution had ordained and established the inferior courts, and distributed to them their respective powers, they could not be restricted or divested by Congress. But as it has made no such distribution, one of two consequences must result,—either that each inferior court created by Congress must exercise all the judicial powers not given to the Supreme Court, or that Congress, having the power to establish the courts, must define their respective jurisdictions. The first of these inferences has never been asserted, and could not be defended with any show of reason, and if not, the latter would seem to follow as a necessary consequence. And it would seem to follow, also, that, having a right to prescribe, Congress may withhold from any court of its creation jurisdiction of any of the enumerated controversies. Courts created by statute can have no jurisdiction but such as the statute confers. No one of them can assert a just claim to jurisdiction exclusively conferred on another, or withheld from all.

The Constitution has defined the limits of the judicial power of the United States, but has not prescribed how much of it shall be exercised by the Circuit Court; consequently, the statute which does prescribe the limits of their jurisdiction, cannot be in conflict with the Constitution, unless it confers powers not enumerated therein.

Such has been the doctrine held by this court since its first establishment. To enumerate all the cases in which it has been either directly advanced or tacitly assumed would be tedious and unnecessary.

[I]t was contended, [other cases] in this case, that, as it was a controversy between citizens of different states, the Constitution gave the plaintiff a right to sue in the Circuit Court, notwithstanding he was an assignee within the restriction of the eleventh section of the Judiciary Act. But the court said,—'The political truth is, that the disposal of the judicial power (except in a few specified instances) belongs to Congress; and Congress is not bound to enlarge the jurisdiction of the Federal courts to every subject, in every form which the Constitution might warrant.' This decision was made in 1799; since that time, the same doctrine has been frequently asserted by this court . . . .

The complainant in this case is the purchaser and assignee of a sum of money, a debt, a chose in action, not of a tract of land. He seeks to recover by this action a debt assigned to him. He is therefore the 'assignee of a chose in action,' within the letter and spirit of the act of Congress under consideration, and cannot support this action in the Circuit Court of the United States, where his assignor could not.

The judgment of the Circuit Court must therefore be reversed, for want of jurisdiction.

Order.

This cause came on to be heard on the transcript of the record from the Circuit Court of the United States for the District of Michigan, and was argued by counsel. On consideration whereof, it is now here ordered and decreed by this court, that this cause be, and the same is hereby, reversed, for the want of jurisdiction in that court, and that this cause be, and the same is hereby, remanded to the said Circuit Court, with directions to dismiss the bill of complaint for the want of jurisdiction.

THE JUDICIARY ACT OF 1789

SEC. 11. And be it further enacted, That the circuit courts shall have original cognizance, concurrent with the courts of the several States, of all suits of a civil nature at common law or in equity, where the matter in dispute exceeds, exclusive of costs, the sum or value of five hundred dollars, and the United States are plaintiffs, or petitioners; or an alien is a party, or the suit is between a citizen of the State where the suit is brought, and a citizen of another State. And shall have exclusive cognizance of all crimes and offences cognizable under the authority of the United States, except where this act otherwise provides, or the laws of the United States shall otherwise direct, and concurrent jurisdiction with the district courts of the crimes and offences cognizable therein. But no person shall be arrested in one district for trial in another, in any civil action before a circuit or district court. And no civil suit shall be brought before either of said courts against an inhabitant of the United States, by any original process in any other district than that whereof he is an inhabitant, or in which he shall be found at the time of serving the writ, *nor shall any district or circuit court have cognizance of any suit to recover the contents of any promissory note or other chose in action in favour of an assignee, unless a suit might have been prosecuted in such court to recover the said contents if no assignment had been made, except in cases of foreign bills of exchange.* And the circuit courts shall also have appellate jurisdiction from the district courts under the regulations and restrictions herein after provided.

DIRECTED READING QUESTIONS

4.   Today, the circuit courts in the federal system are the appellate courts. Why was the circuit court actually the trial court in *Sheldon v. Sill?*

5.   Where is the plaintiff in *Sheldon v. Sill* from?

6.   Where is the defendant in *Sheldon v. Sill* from?

7.   Please describe IN DETAIL, the events which gave rise to the suit in *Sheldon v. Sill.*

8. Why does the Supreme Court conclude that there is no subject matter jurisdiction? What does this conclusion mean is the second place that you need to look to see whether a federal court has subject matter jurisdiction?

9. Review the materials we did for the *Sibbach* case and see if you can articulate why, in addition to a constitutional grant of jurisdiction, we also need a congressional grant of jurisdiction before a federal district court has subject matter jurisdiction.

10. Does *Sheldon v. Sill* answer the question of whether Congress is obligated to give the inferior federal courts the full extent of the jurisdiction provided for in the Constitution?

11. Can Congress give the federal district courts more jurisdiction than the Constitution describes in Article III?

12. According to *Sheldon v. Sill*, can Congress restrict the jurisdiction of the Supreme Court?

13. Here is the Judiciary Act of 1875.

The Judiciary Act of 1875

> Be it enacted by the Senate and House of Representatives of the United States of America in Congress assembled, That the circuit courts of the United States shall have original cognizance, concurrent with the courts of the several States, of all suits of a civil nature at common law or in equity, where the matter in dispute exceeds, exclusive of costs, the sum or value of five hundred dollars, and arising under the Constitution or laws of the United States, or treaties made, or which shall be made, under their authority . . . .

You were provided with the Judiciary act of 1789 when we discussed *Sheldon v. Sill*. Read both acts carefully and determine whether there is subject matter jurisdiction for the each of the following actions. Note the Judiciary Act of 1875 did not replace the Judiciary Act of 1789, but just established an additional basis for subject matter jurisdiction.

a. Before 1875 Michigan citizen sues Kansas citizen in federal court in Michigan, alleging that Kansas citizen violated the "laws of the United States" and caused the Michigan citizen harm in excess of $500

b. Before 1875 Michigan citizen 1 sues Michigan citizen 2 in federal court in Michigan, alleging that Michigan Citizen 2 violated the "laws of the United States," and caused Michigan citizen 1 harm in excess of $500.

c. After 1875 Michigan citizen sues Kansas citizen in federal court in Michigan, alleging that Kansas citizen violated the "laws of the United States" and caused the Michigan citizen harm in excess of $500.

d. After 1875 Michigan citizen 1 sues Michigan citizen 2 in federal court in Michigan, alleging that Michigan Citizen 2 violated the "laws of the United States" and caused Michigan citizen 1 harm in excess of $500.

14. Below is the text of Article III containing various constitutional grants of subject matter jurisdiction. Below the text of Article III are three boxes which contain congressional grants of jurisdiction (statutes). Circle the language in the constitutional text and draw an arrow to the box which represents the congressional grant (statute) of subject matter jurisdiction derived from the constitutional text.

Article III

The judicial power shall extend to all cases, in law and equity, arising under this Constitution, the laws of the United States, and treaties made, or which shall be made, under their authority;—to all cases affecting ambassadors, other public ministers and consuls;—to all cases of admiralty and maritime jurisdiction;—to controversies to which the United States shall be a party;—to controversies between two or more states;—between a state and citizens of another state;—between citizens of different states;—between citizens of the same state claiming lands under grants of different states, and between a state, or the citizens thereof, and foreign states, citizens or subjects.

28 U.S.C. § 1333 The district courts shall have original jurisdiction, exclusive of the courts of the States, of: (1) Any civil case of admiralty or maritime jurisdiction, saving to suitors in all cases all other remedies to which they are otherwise entitled. **28 U.S.C. § 1331** The district courts shall have original jurisdiction of all civil actions arising under the Constitution, laws, or treaties of the United States.	**28 U.S.C. § 1332** (a) The district courts shall have original jurisdiction of all civil actions where the matter in controversy exceeds the sum or value of $75,000, exclusive of interest and costs, and is between— (1) citizens of different States; (2) citizens of a State and citizens or subjects of a foreign state; (3) citizens of different States and in which citizens or subjects of a foreign state are additional parties; and (4) a foreign state, defined in section 1603(a) of this title, as plaintiff and citizens of a State or of different States.

II. INTRODUCTORY CONTEXTUALIZATION OF THE DIFFERENCE BETWEEN SUBJECT MATTER JURISDICTION AND PERSONAL JURISDICTION

The United States district courts are the trial courts of the federal court system. Within limits set by Congress and the Constitution, the district courts have jurisdiction to hear nearly all categories of federal cases, including both civil and criminal matters. Every day hundreds of people across the nation are selected for jury duty and help decide some of these cases.

There are 94 federal judicial districts, including at least one district in each state, the District of Columbia, and Puerto Rico. Three territories of the United States—the Virgin Islands, Guam, and the Northern Mariana Islands—have district courts that hear federal cases, including bankruptcy cases.

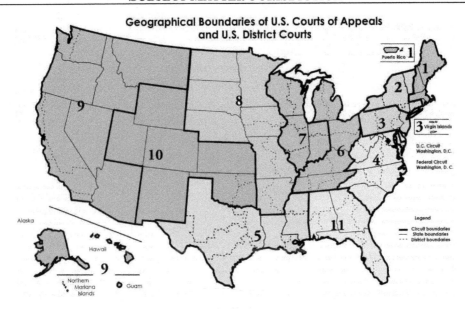

Geographical Boundaries of U.S. Courts of Appeals and U.S. District Courts

DIRECTED READING QUESTIONS

15. What do you notice about the boundaries of the 11 federal appellate circuits and the boundaries of the district courts?

16. What is the difference between Oklahoma and Kansas on this map? See also the map on the following page.

17. Suppose a citizen in Texas County, Oklahoma wants to sue another citizen of Texas County, Oklahoma in federal court for violation of a federal statute which occurred in Texas County, Oklahoma. Is the only court with subject matter jurisdiction the United States District Court for the Western District of Oklahoma?

MAP OF OKLAHOMA'S FEDERAL JUDICIAL DISTRICTS

18. Suppose our plaintiff moves from Texas County, Oklahoma to Hawaii after the defendant violated the federal statute, and then plaintiff files suit in the United States District Court for the District of Hawaii.

    a.   Does the federal district court in Hawaii have subject matter jurisdiction?

    b.   How do you feel about the Hawaii court being the court where the trial will take place?

    c.   Suppose, however, that the Texas County defendant, when she gets notice of the suit in Hawaii, decides that Hawaii is a cool place and she does not mind being sued there. *May* the Hawaii court hear the case?

    d.   Can you now see the difference between Rule 12(b)(1) and Rule 12(b)(2)?

19. Would there be federal subject matter jurisdiction if the Texas County, Oklahoma plaintiff sued the Texas County, Oklahoma defendant for violation of state law?

20. Same facts as question 19. However, both Oklahomans think it is acceptable to go to federal court. Does subject matter jurisdiction exist? How does your answer reiterate the rule that while personal jurisdiction is waivable, subject matter jurisdiction is not?

21. If there is no federal subject matter jurisdiction for the case in question 19, where may the case be heard?

III. DIVERSITY JURISDICTION

A. FUNDAMENTALS OF DIVERSITY JURISDICTION

DIRECTED READING QUESTIONS

22. What are the lessons of *Sheldon v. Sill?*

23. Compare the language in Article III, § 2 and 28 U.S.C. § 1332(a)–(c) which represent the constitutional and statutory grants of diversity jurisdiction. Is the language identical? If not, what is the difference?

Article III, § 2	28 U.S.C. § 1332(a)–(c)
Provides jurisdiction for controversies between:	Provides jurisdiction ONLY where the amount in controversy is more than $75,000, exclusive of interests and costs, and the controversy is between:
<ul><li>2 or more states;</li><li>a state and citizens of another state;*</li><li>citizens of different states;</li><li>citizens of the same state claiming lands under grants of different states;</li><li>a state or the citizens thereof and</li></ul>	(a) (1) citizens of different States; (2) citizens of a State and citizens or subjects of a foreign state, except that the district courts shall not have original jurisdiction under this subsection of an action between citizens of a State and citizens or

---

    * This jurisdictional grant is severely restricted by the Eleventh Amendment. This is just for your information, but you will explore this in more detail if you take a Federal Courts class.

○ foreign states; ○ foreign citizens or subjects	subjects of a foreign state who are lawfully admitted for permanent residence in the United States and are domiciled in the same State; (3) Citizens of different States and in which citizens or subjects of a foreign state are additional parties; and (4) A foreign state as defined in FSIA as the plaintiff and citizens of a State or of different States (b) The court may impose costs on a plaintiff who ends up receiving less than $75,000 (c) Corporation Section For the purposes of this section and section 1441 of this title— (1) a corporation shall be deemed to be a citizen of every State and foreign state by which it has been incorporated AND of the State or foreign state where it has its principal place of business

24. Why have this type of jurisdiction, which is typically called diversity or alienage jurisdiction?

25. You will notice that in 28 U.S.C. § 1332, the word "state" contains either an upper case "S" or a lower case "s." I have bolded the upper case "S"s wherever they are found in the statute. What is the significance of the upper and lower case "S" in the word state in the statute?

26. Is there subject matter jurisdiction over the following suit: Massachusetts citizen v. Vermont citizen and Massachusetts citizen? Remember there are two places we must check to determine whether a federal trial court has subject matter jurisdiction. Congress can give less than the subject matter jurisdiction provided for in the Constitution. Note also that in 1806, the Supreme Court held, regarding the diversity jurisdiction statute, "[i]f there be two or more joint plaintiffs, and two or more joint defendants, each of the plaintiffs must be capable of suing each of the defendants, in the courts of the United States, in order to support the jurisdiction." *Strawbridge v. Curtiss*. Articulate what is meant by the following phrase: "the Constitution only requires minimum diversity, but the statutory grant of diversity jurisdiction requires complete diversity."

MAS V. PERRY (1974)

United States Court of Appeal, Fifth Circuit
489 F.2d 1396

AINSWORTH, CIRCUIT JUDGE:

This case presents questions pertaining to federal diversity jurisdiction under 28 U.S.C. § 1332, which, pursuant to article III, section II of the Constitution, provides for original jurisdiction in federal district courts of all civil actions that are between, inter alia, citizens of different States or citizens of a State and citizens of foreign states and in which the amount in controversy is more than $10,000.

Appellees Jean Paul Mas, a citizen of France, and Judy Mas were married at her home in Jackson, Mississippi. Prior to their marriage, Mr. and Mrs. Mas were graduate assistants, pursuing coursework as well as performing teaching duties, for approximately nine months and one year, respectively, at Louisiana State University in Baton Rouge, Louisiana. Shortly after their marriage, they returned to Baton Rouge to resume their duties as graduate assistants at LSU. They remained in Baton Rouge for approximately two more years, after which they moved to Park Ridge, Illinois. At the time of the trial in this case, it was their intention to return to Baton Rouge while Mr. Mas finished his studies for the degree of Doctor of Philosophy. Mr. and Mrs. Mas were undecided as to where they would reside after that.

Upon their return to Baton Rouge after their marriage, appellees rented an apartment from appellant Oliver H. Perry, a citizen of Louisiana. This appeal arises from a final judgment entered on a jury verdict awarding $5,000 to Mr. Mas and $15,000 to Mrs. Mas for damages incurred by them as a result of the discovery that their bedroom and bathroom contained 'two-way' mirrors and that they had been watched through them by the appellant during three of the first four months of their marriage.

At the close of the appellees' case at trial, appellant made an oral motion to dismiss for lack of jurisdiction. The motion was denied by the district court. Before this Court, appellant challenges the final judgment below solely on jurisdictional grounds, contending that appellees failed to prove diversity of citizenship among the parties and that the requisite jurisdictional amount is lacking with respect to Mr. Mas. Finding no merit to these contentions, we affirm. Under section 1332(a)(2), the federal judicial power extends to the claim of Mr. Mas, a citizen of France, against the appellant, a citizen of Louisiana. Since we conclude that Mrs. Mas is a citizen of Mississippi for diversity purposes, the district court also properly had jurisdiction under section 1332(a)(1) of her claim.

It has long been the general rule that complete diversity of parties is required in order that diversity jurisdiction obtain; that is, no party on one side may be a citizen of the same State as any party on the other side. *Strawbridge v. Curtiss.* This determination of one's State Citizenship for diversity purposes is controlled by federal law, not by the law of any State. As is the case in other areas of federal jurisdiction, the diverse citizenship among adverse parties must be present at the time the complaint is filed. Jurisdiction is unaffected by subsequent changes in the citizenship of the parties. The burden of pleading the diverse citizenship is upon the party invoking federal jurisdiction, and if the diversity jurisdiction is properly challenged, that party also bears the burden of proof.

To be a citizen of a State within the meaning of section 1332, a natural person must be both a citizen of the United States, and a domiciliary of that State. For diversity purposes, citizenship means domicile; mere residence in the State is not sufficient.

A person's domicile is the place of 'his true, fixed, and permanent home and principal establishment, and to which he has the intention of returning whenever he is absent therefrom . . . .' A change of domicile may be effected only by a combination of two elements: (a) taking up residence in a different domicile with (b) the intention to remain there.

It is clear that at the time of her marriage, Mrs. Mas was a domiciliary of the State of Mississippi. While it is generally the case that the domicile of the wife—and, consequently, her State citizenship for purposes of diversity jurisdiction—is deemed to be that of her husband, we find no precedent for extending this concept to the situation here, in which the husband is a citizen of a foreign state but resides in the United States. Indeed, such a fiction would work absurd results on the facts before us. If Mr. Mas were considered a domiciliary of France—as he would be since he had lived in Louisiana as a student-teaching assistant prior to filing this suit, then Mrs. Mas would also be deemed a domiciliary, and thus, fictionally at least, a citizen of France. She would not be a citizen of any State and could not sue in a federal court on that basis; nor could she invoke the alienage jurisdiction to bring her claim in federal court, since she is not an alien. On the other hand, if Mrs. Mas's domicile were Louisiana, she would become a Louisiana citizen for diversity purposes and could not bring suit with her husband against appellant, also a Louisiana citizen, on the basis of diversity jurisdiction. These are curious results under a rule arising from the theoretical identity of person and interest of the married couple.

An American woman is not deemed to have lost her United States citizenship solely by reason of her marriage to an alien. Similarly, we conclude that for diversity purposes a woman does not have her domicile or State Citizenship changed solely by reason of her marriage to an alien.

Mrs. Mas's Mississippi domicile was disturbed neither by her year in Louisiana prior to her marriage nor as a result of the time she and her husband spent at LSU after their marriage, since for both periods she was a graduate assistant at LSU. Though she testified that after her marriage she had no intention of returning to her parents' home in Mississippi, Mrs. Mas did not effect a change of domicile since she and Mr. Mas were in Louisiana only as students and lacked the requisite intention to remain there. Until she acquires a new domicile, she remains a domiciliary, and thus a citizen, of Mississippi.[2]

Appellant also contends that Mr. Mas's claim should have been dismissed for failure to establish the requisite jurisdictional amount for diversity cases of more than $10,000.

---

[2] The original complaint in this case was filed within several days of Mr. and Mrs. Mas's realization that they had been watched through the mirrors, quite some time before they moved to Park Ridge, Illinois. Because the district court's jurisdiction is not affected by actions of the parties subsequent to the commencement of the suit, see C. Wright, Federal Courts 93 (1970), page 1400 supra, the testimony concerning Mr. and Mrs. Mas's moves after that time is not determinative of the issue of diverse citizenship, though it is of interest insofar as it supports their lack of intent to remain permanently in Louisiana.

In their complaint Mr. and Mrs. Mas alleged that they had each been damaged in the amount of $100,000. As we have noted, Mr. Mas ultimately recovered $5,000.

It is well settled that the amount in controversy is determined by the amount claimed by the plaintiff in good faith. Federal jurisdiction is not lost because a judgment of less than the jurisdictional amount is awarded. That Mr. Mas recovered only $5,000 is, therefore, not compelling. As the Supreme Court stated in: "The sum claimed by the plaintiff controls if the claim is apparently made in good faith." It must appear to a legal certainty that the claim is really for less than the jurisdictional amount to justify dismissal. The inability of the plaintiff to recover an amount adequate to give the court jurisdiction does not show his bad faith or oust the jurisdiction . . . .

His good faith in choosing the federal forum is open to challenge not only by resort to the face of his complaint, but by the facts disclosed at trial, and if from either source it is clear that his claim never could have amounted to the sum necessary to give jurisdiction there is no injustice in dismissing the suit.

Having heard the evidence presented at the trial, the district court concluded that the appellees properly met the requirements of section 1332 with respect to jurisdictional amount. Upon examination of the record in this case, we are also satisfied that the requisite amount was in controversy.

Thus the power of the federal district court to entertain the claims of appellees in this case stands on two separate legs of diversity jurisdiction: a claim by an alien against a State citizen; and an action between citizens of different States . . . .

Affirmed.

DIRECTED READING QUESTIONS

27. The first paragraph of the case indicates that for 28 U.S.C. § 1332, the amount in controversy requirement is $10,000. Is this a typo?

28. Please carefully read the following language from the case and explain the landlord's contentions on appeal relating to subject matter jurisdiction.

Appellees Jean Paul Mas, a citizen of France, and Judy Mas were married at her home in Jackson, Mississippi. Prior to their marriage, Mr. and Mrs. Mas were graduate assistants, pursuing coursework as well as performing teaching duties, for approximately nine months and one year, respectively, at Louisiana State University in Baton Rouge, Louisiana. Shortly after their marriage, they returned to Baton Rouge to resume their duties as graduate assistants at LSU. They remained in Baton Rouge for approximately two more years, after which they moved to Park Ridge, Illinois. At the time of the trial in this case, it was their intention to return to Baton Rouge While Mr. Mas finished his studies for the degree of Doctor of Philosophy. Mr. and Mrs. Mas were undecided as to where they would reside after that.

Upon their return to Baton Rouge after their marriage, appellees rented an apartment from appellant Oliver H. Perry, a citizen of Louisiana. This appeal arises from a final judgment entered on a jury verdict awarding $5,000 to Mr. Mas and $15,000 to Mrs. Mas for damages incurred by them as a result of the discovery that their bedroom and bathroom contained 'two-way' mirrors and that they had been watched through them by the appellant during three of the first four months of their marriage.

29. How did the court conclude that Mrs. Mas was a citizen of Mississippi, even though she had no intention of returning to Mississippi?

30. How did the court conclude that the amount in controversy requirement was satisfied for Mr. Mas, even though he only recovered $5,000 and the amount in controversy was $10,000?

31. Please explain what the court considers "absurd results" and how those absurd results would come about.

32. In the statute, CITIZENSHIP = DOMICILE

    Note the following:

    a. State of Domicile is the most recent state where person has

        i. Resided, with

        ii. The intent to remain indefinitely, which can be framed as the stay is open-ended or the person has no plans to leave after a certain date or event.

            i. Evidence of practical affairs can help prove intent but is not dispositive.

    b. Until the two criteria above are met in a new state, residence remains in the old domicile. This is true even if the person has no plans to return to the old domicile.

    c. Domicile is determined at the time the complaint is filed.

    d. Domicile at birth is domicile unless it changes.

33. What is the "possibility rule" for amount in controversy?

B. MECHANICS OF THE DIVERSITY JURISDICTION STATUTE

DIRECTED READING QUESTIONS

For questions 34–41, assume the amount in controversy requirement is met, and explain which of the following suits satisfy the diversity requirement of 28 U.S.C. § 1332.

34. A green card holder domiciled in Texas sues a Texas citizen.

35. A green card holder domiciled in Texas sues another green card holder domiciled in Texas.

36. A green card holder domiciled in Texas sues another green card holder domiciled in Kansas.

37. Three people, a Delaware citizen, an alien, and a Texas citizen, sue two people, an alien and a Massachusetts citizen.

38. A Delaware resident who is an alien sues two people: an alien and a Massachusetts citizen.

39. A foreigner is in the U.S. on a work visa. She owns houses in both Texas and Delaware and spends equal time in each state working for a nationwide corporation. Her car is registered in Texas, she has a Texas driver's license, and she lists Texas as her address for ninety percent of her bills and mail. She sues a citizen of Delaware.

40. A corporation incorporated in France with its principal place of business in New Jersey sues two other corporations: one is a corporation incorporated in France with its principal place of business in France, and the other is incorporated in Delaware with its principal place of business in Massachusetts.

41. Same facts as the previous question, except that the foreign corporate defendant is incorporated in China and has its principal place of business in Maine.

42. How do we determine a corporation's "principal place of business"?

43. Is there jurisdiction pursuant to 28 U.S.C. § 1332 for a suit by an alien corporation suing a partnership organized in Delaware with some partners who are aliens?

IV. FEDERAL QUESTION JURISDICTION

A. THE WELL PLEADED COMPLAINT RULE

DIRECTED READING QUESTIONS

44. The Act of 1875 was the first general or broad statutory grant of jurisdiction to the inferior federal courts of "arising under" jurisdiction. The current incarnation of the Act of 1875 is 28 U.S.C. § 1331. Where were claims arising under federal law typically adjudicated between the time of the Constitution's ratification in 1788 and the passing of the Act of 1875?

OSBORN V. BANK OF THE UNITED STATES (1824)
Supreme Court of the United States
22 U.S. 738

[Before the "Act of 1875" conferred broad arising under jurisdiction on the inferior federal courts, there were a few federal statutes that purported to grant arising under jurisdiction in narrow and specific situations. For example, soon after ratification of the Constitution, the brand-new United States federal government began setting up federal banks or banks of the United States. Naturally because the federal, United States of America is physically nothing more than the landmasses occupied by the states and territories, these federal banks, once established, were located within the borders of certain states.

The federal banks were incorporated pursuant to a federal statute. The incorporation statute, provided in part, that the Bank "shall be 'made able and capable in law,' 'to sue and be used, plead and be impleaded, answer and be answered, defend and be defended, in all State Courts having competent jurisdiction, and in any [trial] Court of the United States.''*]

In 1819, shortly after its incorporation, the United States Bank located in Ohio filed suit in federal court seeking an injunction to prevent the state auditor from collecting certain dues that entities doing business in Ohio had to pay the state. The bank argued that it was exempt from having to pay those state fees. The federal trial court agreed,

---

*   This paragraph was added by the editor and creates context for the *Osborn* case.

and the state of Ohio appealed to the United States Supreme Court] contest[ing] the jurisdiction of the federal Court on two grounds:

1st. That the act of Congress has not given it.

2d. That, under the Constitution, Congress cannot give it.

The first part of the objection depends entirely on the language of the act. The words are, that the Bank shall be 'made able and capable in law,' 'to sue and be used, plead and be impleaded, answer and be answered, defend and be defended, in all State Courts having competent jurisdiction, and in any [trial] Court of the United States.'

* * *

The act of incorporation, then, confers jurisdiction on the [trial] Courts of the United States, if Congress can confer it.

We will now consider the constitutionality of the clause in the act of incorporation, which authorizes the Bank to sue in the federal Courts.

* * *

The 2d article [of the Constitution] vests the whole executive power in the President; and the 3d article declares, 'that the judicial power shall extend to all cases in law and equity arising under this constitution, the laws of the United States, and treaties made, or which shall be made, under their authority.'

This clause enables the judicial department to receive jurisdiction to the full extent of the constitution, laws, and treaties of the United States, when any question respecting them shall assume such a form that the judicial power is capable of acting on it. That power is capable of acting only when the subject is submitted to it by a party who asserts his rights in the form prescribed by law. It then becomes a case, and the constitution declares, that the judicial power shall extend to all cases arising under the constitution, laws, and treaties of the United States.

[This] suit, is a case, and the question is, whether it arises under a law of the United States?

The appellants contend, that it does not, because several questions may arise in it, which depend on [state] law, not on any act of Congress.

* * *

We ask, then, if it can be sufficient to exclude this jurisdiction, that the case involves questions depending on [state law]?

* * *

We think, then, that when a question to which the judicial power of the Union is extended by the constitution, forms an ingredient of the [case], it is in the power of Congress to give the [trial] Courts jurisdiction of that cause, although other questions of fact or of law may be involved in it.

Affirmed.

LOUISVILLE & NASHVILLE R. CO. V. MOTTLEY (1908)

Supreme Court of the United States
211 U.S. 149

Statement by MR. JUSTICE MOODY:

The appellees (husband and wife), being residents and citizens of Kentucky, brought this suit in equity in the circuit court of the United States for the western district of Kentucky against the appellant, a railroad company and a citizen of the same state. The object of the suit was to compel the specific performance of the following contract:

> The Louisville & Nashville Railroad Company, in consideration that E. L. Mottley and wife, Annie E. Mottley, have this day released company from all damages or claims for damages for injuries received by them on the 7th of September, 1871, in consequence of a collision of trains on the railroad of said company at Randolph's Station, Jefferson County, Kentucky, hereby agrees to issue free passes on said railroad and branches now existing or to exist, to said E. L. & Annie E. Mottley for the remainder of the present year, and thereafter to renew said passes annually during the lives of said Mottley and wife or either of them.

The bill alleged that in September, 1871, plaintiffs, while passengers upon the defendant railroad, were injured by the defendant's negligence, and released their respective claims for damages in consideration of the agreement for transportation during their lives, expressed in the contract. It is alleged that the contract was performed by the defendant up to January 1, 1907, when the defendant declined to renew the passes. The bill then alleges that the refusal to comply with the contract was based solely upon that part of the act of Congress of June 29, 1906, which forbids the giving of free passes or free transportation. The bill further alleges . . . that the act of Congress referred to does not prohibit the giving of passes under the circumstances of this case . . . . The defendant demurred to the bill. The judge of the circuit court overruled the demurrer, entered a decree for the relief prayed for, and the defendant appealed directly to this court.

MR. JUSTICE MOODY, after making the foregoing statement, delivered the opinion of the court:

The question[ ] of law [ ] raised by the demurrer to the bill, w[as] brought here by appeal, and ha[s] been argued before us. [It is], whether that part of the act of Congress of June 29, 1906, which forbids the giving of free passes or the collection of any different compensation for transportation of passengers than that specified in the tariff filed, makes it unlawful to perform a contract for transportation of persons who, in good faith, before the passage of the act, had accepted such contract in satisfaction of a valid cause of action against the railroad . . . . We do not deem it necessary, however, to consider [this question], because, in our opinion, the court below was without jurisdiction of the cause. Neither party has questioned that jurisdiction, but it is the duty of this court to see to it that the jurisdiction of the circuit court, which is defined and limited by statute, is not exceeded. This duty we have frequently performed of our own motion.

There was no diversity of citizenship, and it is not and cannot be suggested that there was any ground of jurisdiction, except that the case was a 'suit . . . arising under the Constitution or laws of the United States.' It is the settled interpretation of these words, as used in this statute, conferring jurisdiction, that a suit arises under the Constitution and laws of the United States only when the plaintiff's statement of his own cause of action shows that it is based upon those laws or that Constitution. It is not enough that the plaintiff alleges some anticipated defense to his cause of action, and asserts that the defense is invalidated by some provision of the Constitution of the United States. Although such allegations show that very likely, in the course of the litigation, a question under the Constitution would arise, they do not show that the suit, that is, the plaintiff's original cause of action, arises under the Constitution.

* * *

'A suggestion of one party, that the other will or may set up a claim under the Constitution or laws of the United States, does not make the suit one arising under that Constitution or those laws.' Again, in *Boston & M. Consol. Copper & S. Min. Co. v. Montana Ore Purchasing Co.*, the plaintiff brought suit in the circuit court of the United States for the conversion of copper ore and for an injunction against its continuance. The plaintiff then alleged, for the purpose of showing jurisdiction, in substance, that the defendant would set up in defense certain laws of the United States. The cause was held to be beyond the jurisdiction of the circuit court, the court saying, by Mr. Justice Peckham

> 'It would be wholly unnecessary and improper, in order to prove complainant's cause of action, to go into any matters of defense which the defendants might possibly set up, and then attempt to reply to such defense, and thus, if possible, to show that a Federal question might or probably would arise in the course of the trial of the case. To allege such defense and then make an answer to it before the defendant has the opportunity to itself plead or prove its own defense is inconsistent with any known rule of pleading, so far as we are aware, and is improper.

> 'The rule is a reasonable and just one that the complainant in the first instance shall be confined to a statement of its cause of action, leaving to the defendant to set up in his answer what his defense is, and, if anything more than a denial of complainant's cause of action, imposing upon the defendant the burden of proving such defense.

> 'Conforming itself to that rule, the complainant would not, in the assertion or proof of its cause of action, bring up a single Federal question. The presentation of its cause of action would not show that it was one arising under the Constitution or laws of the United States.

> 'The only way in which it might be claimed that a Federal question was presented would be in the complainant's statement of what the defense of defendants would be, and complainant's answer to such defense . . . .

* * *

The application of this rule to the case at bar is decisive against the jurisdiction of the circuit court.

It is ordered that the judgment be reversed and the case remitted to the circuit court with instructions to dismiss the suit for want of jurisdiction.

DIRECTED READING QUESTIONS

45. According to *Osborn Bank*, when does a case "arise under" the Constitution or laws of the United States such that subject matter jurisdiction exists?

46. As we established earlier, in order for subject matter jurisdiction, there must be both a constitutional and a statutory grant of jurisdiction. Identify the constitutional and statutory grants of subject matter jurisdiction in the *Osborn Bank* case and in the *Mottley* case.

47. What are the facts of *Mottley*? What precisely is the plaintiff's cause of action?

48. Please explain whether federal law is an ingredient in the *Mottley* case and, if federal law is an ingredient in the cause of action, then explain why there is no subject matter jurisdiction in *Mottley*.

49. When does a case "arise under" the Constitution or laws of the United States according to *Mottley* and § 1331 such that subject matter jurisdiction exists? *Hint: This is sometimes referred to as the well-pleaded complaint rule.*

50. Draw a Venn diagram showing the relationship of the meaning of "arising under" in the Constitution and in 28 U.S.C. § 1331.

51. Reconcile the rule of *Mottley* with the rule of *Osborn Bank*.

52. After the *Mottley* opinion you just read, the case was remanded and reinstituted in Kentucky state court because the Supreme Court concluded there was no original jurisdiction. The plaintiffs prevailed in the state trial, appellate, and supreme courts. The defendant railroad then appealed to the United States Supreme Court which issued an opinion containing the following language.

> It is said, however, that, as the contract of Mottley and wife with the railroad company was originally valid, it cannot be supposed that Congress intended by the act of 1906 to annul or prevent its enforcement. But the purpose of Congress was to cut up by the roots every form of discrimination, favoritism, and inequality, except in the cases of certain excepted classes to which Mottley and his wife did not belong, and which exceptions rested upon peculiar grounds. Manifestly, from the face of the commerce act itself, Congress, before taking final action, considered the question as to what exceptions, if any, should be made in respect of the prohibition of free tickets, free passes, and free transportation. It solved the question when, without making any exceptions of *existing contracts*, it forbade by broad, explicit words *any* carrier to charge, demand, collect, or receive a 'greater or less *or different* compensation' for *any* services in connection with the transportation of passengers or property than was specified in its published schedules of rates. The court cannot add an exception based on equitable grounds when Congress forbore to make such an exception.

Despite the lack of original jurisdiction, when the Supreme Court heard the appeal from the state supreme court, it ruled on the merits of the case, holding that the only dispositive matter in the *Mottley* case was whether the federal statute invalidated the contract that the railroad had with Mottley that required the railroad to give Mottley free passes. If there was no original federal subject matter jurisdiction, how could the United States Supreme Court rule on the case the second time?

53. How is the difference between appellate and original jurisdiction significant in terms of the recognition of the states as independent sovereigns or in terms of the principle of federalism?

54. Pat sued Tracie in federal district court alleging Tracie violated a federal statute causing harm to Pat. Pat and Tracie are from the same state and Pat alleges that the amount in controversy is <$75,000.

    a.   Is there subject matter jurisdiction?

    b.   Could Pat have brough this lawsuit in state court instead of federal court?

55. A law student rented a furnished apartment. His landlord began to solicit his advice about her legal affairs, but he refused to provide it. The landlord then demanded that he vacate the apartment immediately. The landlord also engaged in a pattern of harassment, calling the student at home every evening and entering his apartment without his consent during times when he was at school. During these visits she removed the handles from the bathroom and kitchen sinks but did not touch anything belonging to the student. The student sues the landlord for trespass pursuant to state law in federal court. During pre-suit discussions, the landlord pointed out that under a federal statute, the Landlords' Entry Always Permitted Act ("LEAP"), she could enter the premises whenever she wanted and terminate the lease at will. If LEAP applies, then it is a complete defense to the trespass claim, and the plaintiff mentions this in his complaint. The landlord moves for dismissal pursuant to Rule 12(b)(1). In her motion, the landlord absolutely confirms that if the suit is not dismissed, she will raise LEAP as a defense. Should the action be dismissed if the basis of subject matter jurisdiction alleged in the complaint is 28 U.S.C. § 1331?

    a.   No. Federal law is an issue in the case and therefore federal jurisdiction exists.

    b.   No. Because an issue of federal law is an ingredient in the action.

    c.   Yes. Because LEAP is a defense.

    d.   No. Because the tenant recognized the applicability and inevitability of considering LEAP and mentioned this in his complaint.

56. An employee at a state college sues the administrator of the employee benefit plan (a self-funded health insurance plan) on a matter related to the plan, for breach of state contract law in federal court. Self-funded plans are plans in which health insurance claims are paid strictly from employer contributions and employee premiums. Self-funded health plans were created by a federal statute in 1974 known as the Employee Retirement and Income Security Act (ERISA). ERISA provides in part,

    > *Except as provided in subsection (b) of this section, the provisions of this subchapter and subchapter III of this chapter shall supersede any and all State laws insofar as they may now or hereafter relate to any employee benefit plan described in section 1003(a) of this title and not exempt under section 1003(b) of this title.*

    The defendant argues that despite the fact that this type of self-funded plan was created by a federal statute, there is no arising under jurisdiction because the actual cause of action is breach of state contract law. Is the defendant correct?

57. Does the Act of 1875 (which today is 28 U.S.C. § 1331), prevent Congress from enacting legislation giving more of the "arising under" jurisdiction than is conferred in 28 U.S.C. § 1331?

B. STATE LAW CLAIMS THAT ARISE UNDER FEDERAL LAW

GRABLE & SONS METAL PRODUCTS, INC. V. DARUE ENGINEERING & MFG. (2005)
Supreme Court of the United States
545 U.S. 308

JUSTICE SOUTER delivered the opinion of the Court.

The question is whether want of a federal cause of action to try claims of title to land obtained at a federal tax sale precludes removal to federal court of a state action with nondiverse parties raising a disputed issue of federal title law. We answer no, and hold that the national interest in providing a federal forum for federal tax litigation is sufficiently substantial to support the exercise of federal-question jurisdiction over the disputed issue on removal, which would not distort any division of labor between the state and federal courts, provided or assumed by Congress.

I

In 1994, the Internal Revenue Service seized Michigan real property belonging to petitioner Grable & Sons Metal Products, Inc., to satisfy Grable's federal tax delinquency. Title 26 U.S.C. § 6335 required the IRS to give notice of the seizure, and there is no dispute that Grable received actual notice by certified mail before the IRS sold the property to respondent Darue Engineering & Manufacturing. Although Grable also received notice of the sale itself, it did not exercise its statutory right to redeem the property within the [mandatory] period of 180 days of the sale, and after that period had passed, the Government gave Darue a quitclaim deed.

Five years later, Grable brought a quiet title action in state court, claiming that Darue's record title was invalid because the IRS had failed to notify Grable of its seizure of the property in the exact manner required by § 6335(a), which provides that written notice must be "given by the Secretary to the owner of the property [or] left at his usual place of abode or business." Grable said that the statute required personal service, not service by certified mail.

Darue removed the case to Federal District Court as presenting a federal question, because the claim of title depended on the interpretation of the notice statute in the federal tax law. The District Court declined to remand the case at Grable's behest after finding that the "claim does pose a 'significant question of federal law,' " and ruling that Grable's lack of a federal right of action to enforce its claim against Darue did not bar the exercise of federal jurisdiction. On the merits, the court granted summary judgment to Darue, holding that although § 6335 by its terms required personal service, substantial compliance with the statute was enough.

The Court of Appeals for the Sixth Circuit affirmed. On the jurisdictional question, the panel thought it sufficed that the title claim raised an issue of federal law that had to be resolved, and implicated a substantial federal interest (in construing federal tax law). The court went on to affirm the District Court's judgment on the merits. We granted certiorari on the jurisdictional question alone, to resolve a split within the Courts of Appeals on whether a federal cause of action [is always a necessary condition] for exercising federal-question jurisdiction. We now affirm.

II

Darue was entitled to remove the quiet title action if Grable could have brought it in federal district court originally, 28 U.S.C. § 1441(a), as a civil action "arising under the Constitution, laws, or treaties of the United States," § 1331. This provision for federal-question jurisdiction is invoked by and large by plaintiffs pleading a cause of action created by federal law (*See e.g.*, The Well Pleaded Complaint Rule). There is, however, another longstanding, if less frequently encountered, variety of federal "arising under" jurisdiction, this Court having recognized for nearly 100 years that in certain cases federal-question jurisdiction will lie over state-law claims that implicate significant federal issues.

* * *

But even when the state action discloses a contested and substantial federal question, the exercise of federal jurisdiction is subject to a possible veto. For the federal issue will ultimately qualify for a federal forum only if federal jurisdiction is consistent with congressional judgment about the sound division of labor between state and federal courts governing the application of § 1331.

* * *

Because arising-under jurisdiction to hear a state-law claim always raises the possibility of upsetting the state-federal line drawn (or at least assumed) by Congress, the presence of a disputed federal issue and the ostensible importance of a federal forum are never necessarily dispositive; there must always be an assessment of any disruptive portent in exercising federal jurisdiction.

These considerations have kept us from stating a "single, precise, all-embracing" test for jurisdiction over federal issues embedded in state-law claims between nondiverse parties. We have not kept them out simply because they appeared in state raiment . . . but neither have we treated "federal issue" as a password opening federal courts to any state action embracing a point of federal law. Instead, the question is, does a state-law claim necessarily raise a stated federal issue, actually disputed and substantial, which a federal forum may entertain without disturbing any congressionally approved balance of federal and state judicial responsibilities.

III

A

This case warrants federal jurisdiction. Grable's state complaint must specify "the facts establishing the superiority of [its] claim," and Grable has premised its superior title claim on a failure by the IRS to give it adequate notice, as defined by federal law. Whether Grable was given notice within the meaning of the federal statute is thus an essential element of its quiet title claim, and the meaning of the federal statute is actually in dispute; it appears to be the only legal or factual issue contested in the case. The meaning of the federal tax provision is an important issue of federal law that sensibly belongs in a federal court. The Government has a strong interest in the "prompt and certain collection of delinquent taxes and the ability of the IRS to satisfy its claims from the property of delinquents requires clear terms of notice to allow buyers like Darue to satisfy themselves that the Service has touched the bases necessary for good title. The Government thus has a direct interest in the availability of a federal forum to vindicate its own administrative action, and buyers (as well as tax delinquents) may find it valuable to come before judges used to federal tax matters. Finally, because it will be the rare state title case that raises a contested matter of federal law, federal jurisdiction to resolve genuine disagreement over federal tax title provisions will portend only a microscopic effect on the federal-state division of labor.

* * *

B

* * *

[I]t is the rare state quiet title action that involves contested issues of federal law. Consequently, jurisdiction over actions like Grable's would not materially affect, or threaten to affect, the normal currents of litigation. Given the absence of threatening structural consequences and the clear interest the Government, its buyers, and its delinquents have in the availability of a federal forum, there is no good reason to shirk from federal jurisdiction over the dispositive and contested federal issue at the heart of the state-law title claim.

IV

The judgment of the Court of Appeals, upholding federal jurisdiction over Grable's quiet title action, is affirmed.

It is so ordered.

DIRECTED READING QUESTIONS

58. List the two basic requirements that we have studied for federal jurisdiction and identify how each is met in *Grable*.

59. Discuss whether the typical test for satisfying statutory "arising under" jurisdiction that we have studied thus far is satisfied in *Grable*.

60. What are the operative facts of this case?

61. Please carefully describe the procedural aspects of the case from the time it was filed to the time it came before the Supreme Court.

62. Why precisely did the appellate court affirm the district court?

63. Why precisely did the Supreme Court grant certiorari?

64. What is the two-pronged test that the Supreme Court articulates for determining whether a state law claim arises under federal law for the purposes of 28 U.S.C. § 1331?

65. Apply the two-pronged test to the *Grable* case.

66. Apply the two-pronged test to the *Mottley* case.

67. Now redraw a Venn diagram showing the relationship of the meaning of arising under in the Constitution and in 28 U.S.C. § 1331, which includes the *Grable* opinion.

CHAPTER 12

SUPPLEMENTAL JURISDICTION

■ ■ ■

I. CONTEXTUALIZING SUPPLEMENTAL JURISDICTION

DIRECTED READING QUESTIONS

1. What does the word "supplemental" mean to you? If said I were going to supplement your income, what would that mean?

2. A client walks into your office and tells you a story which indicates that the client may have a claim against his employer for violation of a federal antidiscrimination statute based on the employer's failure to promote the client.

    a. May this suit be brought in state court? Why or why not?

    b. May this suit be brought in federal court? Why or why not?

    c. Assuming the suit was brought in federal court, what would be the alleged basis of subject matter jurisdiction in accordance with Rule 8(a)(1)?

3. After doing some more research on the client's case, you discover that the same facts which support the suit against the employer for violation of a federal antidiscrimination statute also support a claim for violation of a state antidiscrimination statute. Assume that you elected to sue the employer based solely on the employer's violation of state law because the federal statute required a high burden of proof.

    a. May this suit be brought in state court? Why or why not?

    b. May this suit be brought in federal court? Why or why not?

4. Assume the same facts as question 3, but instead you want to combine the violation of state law and the violation of federal law claims in one lawsuit. Read § 1367(a) BUT NOT ANY OTHER PART OF THE STATUTE YET carefully and answer the following questions.

    a. May this combined suit be brought in state court? Why or why not?

    b. May this combined suit be brought in federal court? Why or why not?

    c. Assuming the combined suit was brought in federal court, what would be the alleged basis of subject matter jurisdiction in accordance with Rule 8(a)(1)?

5. The test for how related a claim for which there is no original jurisdiction must be to a claim for which there is original jurisdiction, such that both claims form part of the same Article III case or controversy, pursuant to § 1367(a), resulting in original jurisdiction over both claims, was articulated in the *Gibbs* case. "[In order for a federal court to have jurisdiction over a state law claim with no independent basis of subject matter jurisdiction] [t]he state and federal claims must derive from a common nucleus of operative fact." *United Mine Workers v. Gibbs*, 383 U.S. 715 (1966).

a.   Explain supplemental jurisdiction in terms of an ice cream cone and sprinkles.

b.   Revisit Rules 13(a) and 20. Observe that relationships between claims are relevant to both rules. Draw a Venn diagram comparing "relationships between claims" in these two rules and in 28 U.S.C. § 1367(a).

6.   STOP WHATEVER YOU ARE DOING NOW AND THINK ABOUT THE FOLLOWING SLOWLY AND CAREFULLY. Article III indicates that the Constitution provides subject matter jurisdiction over "cases" or "controversies." Therefore if a state law claim which does not have its own basis of subject matter jurisdiction is part of the same Article III "case" or "controversy" as a claim for which there is federal subject matter jurisdiction, then according to Article III, there is supplemental jurisdiction over the entire "case" or "controversy" comprised of the different claims.

7.   AND ALSO THINK ABOUT THIS SLOWLY AND CAREFULLY. Section 1367(a) requires a "civil action of which the district courts have original jurisdiction" to operate. For the purposes of § 1367(a), we have a "civil action of which the district court has original jurisdiction" if there is one claim over which the federal court has original jurisdiction.

8.   Does 28 U.S.C. § 1367(a) operate differently depending on whether the basis of federal subject matter jurisdiction over the "ice cream cone" claim is arising under or diversity jurisdiction?

9.   Read § 1367(a) and (b). Make sure you understand the following and can explain why it is correct.

Section 1367(a) provides jurisdiction for a claim (sprinkle) that standing alone would not have a jurisdictional basis when that claim is "so related" to a claim for which "original jurisdiction" exists (ice cream cone). If both claims are "so related" or they share "a common nucleus of operative fact," then they "form part of the same case or controversy under Article III" and there is jurisdiction over the entire case or controversy.

Section 1367(b) is a "takeaway" of the jurisdiction provided in § 1367(a) that operates only in "certain situations" when the sole basis of original jurisdiction over the ice cream cone is diversity jurisdiction.

10.   What are the "certain situations" described in the previous question?

11. Examine 28 U.S.C. § 1367 carefully and find in the statute where the following language from the *Gibbs* opinion is reflected.

> [Supplemental jurisdiction] need not be exercised in every case in which it is found to exist. It has consistently been recognized that pendent jurisdiction is a doctrine of discretion, not of plaintiff's right. Its justification lies in considerations of judicial economy, convenience and fairness to litigants; if these are not present a federal court should hesitate to exercise jurisdiction over state claims . . . .

Explain how this statutory section reflects the language found in the *Gibbs* opinion.

12. What three things are necessary for supplemental jurisdiction to operate?

II. THE MECHANICS OF SUPPLEMENTAL JURISDICTION AND RELEVANCE OF THE JOINDER RULES

DIRECTED READING QUESTIONS

For the following questions, assume that 28 U.S.C. § 1367(c) does not apply.

13. Robert sues Glen for violation of a federal statute. Robert is a citizen of Alabama, and Glen is a citizen of Ohio. As per Rule 14, Glen impleads Susan (a citizen of Alabama) on a state law contribution claim. Is there supplemental jurisdiction for Glen's claim against Susan? *I have drawn the first diagram for you. You should draw similar diagrams for all the problems.*

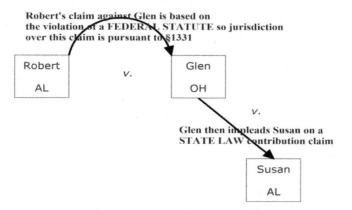

14. Assume the same facts as above, but Susan asserts a state law claim against Robert pursuant to Rule 14(a)(2)(C). Is there supplemental jurisdiction over Susan's claim against Robert?

15. Assume the same facts as question 13, but assume that jurisdiction for Robert's claim against Glen is based solely on diversity of citizenship and not on a federal statute. Is there supplemental jurisdiction for Glen's claim against Susan?

16. If the basis of jurisdiction is as described in question 15, is there supplemental jurisdiction over a state law claim by Susan against Robert as permitted by Rule 14(a)(2)(C)?

17. Assume the orientation of the parties and the bases of jurisdiction is the same as in question 16. Would there be supplemental jurisdiction over a state law claim by Robert against Susan brought pursuant to Rule 14(a)(3)?

18. Assume the orientation of the parties and the bases of jurisdiction are the same as in question 17, but Robert's claim against Susan is based on Susan's violation of a federal statute. Would there be supplemental jurisdiction over Robert's claim against Susan?

19. This question is one that we originally considered in the joinder section.

    A sues B for violation of a federal statute in federal court. A decides to join a state law claim that A has against B for conversion because B stole A's bicycle. Assume Rule 18 allowed the joinder of the conversion claim and the federal statutory claims. Does it make any difference in terms of the federal court's ability to hear the conversion claim if the conversion claim and the statutory claim are derived from a common nucleus of operative fact or if they are unrelated?

III. COMPLEXITIES INVOLVING THE INTERACTION OF DIVERSITY JURISDICTION AND 28 U.S.C. § 1367

EXXON MOBIL CORP. V. ALLAPATAH SERVICES INC. (2005)
Supreme Court of the United States
545 U.S. 546

These consolidated cases present the question whether a federal court in a diversity action may exercise supplemental jurisdiction over additional plaintiffs whose claims do not satisfy the minimum amount-in-controversy requirement, provided the claims are part of the same case or controversy as the claims of plaintiffs who do allege a sufficient amount in controversy. Our decision turns on the correct interpretation of 28 U.S.C. § 1367. The question has divided the Courts of Appeals, and we granted certiorari to resolve the conflict.

We hold that, where the other elements of jurisdiction are present and at least one named plaintiff in the action satisfies the amount-in-controversy requirement, § 1367 does authorize supplemental jurisdiction over the claims of other plaintiffs in the same Article III case or controversy, even if those claims are for less than the jurisdictional amount specified in the statute setting forth the requirements for diversity jurisdiction. We affirm the judgment of the Court of Appeals for the Eleventh Circuit and we reverse the judgment of the Court of Appeals for the First Circuit.

[The facts of the First Circuit case are], a 9-year-old girl sued Star-Kist in a diversity action in the United States District Court for the District of Puerto Rico, seeking damages for unusually severe injuries she received when she sliced her finger on a tuna can. Her family joined in the suit, seeking damages for emotional distress and certain medical expenses. The District Court granted summary judgment to Star-Kist, finding that none of the plaintiffs met the minimum amount-in-controversy requirement. The Court of Appeals for the First Circuit, however, ruled that the injured girl, but not her family members, had made allegations of damages in the requisite amount.

The Court of Appeals then addressed whether, in light of the fact that one plaintiff met the requirements for original jurisdiction, supplemental jurisdiction over the remaining plaintiffs' claims was proper under § 1367. The court held that § 1367 authorizes supplemental jurisdiction only when the district court has original jurisdiction over the action, and that in a diversity case original jurisdiction is lacking if one plaintiff fails to satisfy the amount-in-controversy requirement. Although the Court of Appeals claimed to "express no view" on whether the result would be the same in a class action, its analysis is inconsistent with that of the [*Exxon* case consolidated here from the] Court of Appeals for the Eleventh Circuit. The Court of Appeals for the First Circuit's view of § 1367 is, however, shared by the Courts of Appeals for the Third, Eighth, and Tenth Circuits, and the latter two Courts of Appeals have expressly applied this rule to class actions.

* * *

Section 1367(a) is a broad grant of supplemental jurisdiction over other claims within the same case or controversy, as long as the action is one in which the district courts would have original jurisdiction. The last sentence of § 1367(a) makes it clear that the grant of supplemental jurisdiction extends to claims involving joinder or intervention of additional parties. The single question before us, therefore, is whether a diversity case in which the claims of some plaintiffs satisfy the amount-in-controversy requirement, but the claims of other plaintiffs do not, presents a "civil action of which the district courts have original jurisdiction." If the answer is yes, § 1367(a) confers supplemental jurisdiction over all claims, including those that do not independently satisfy the amount-in-controversy requirement, if the claims are part of the same Article III case or controversy. If the answer is no, § 1367(a) is inapplicable and . . . the district court has no statutory basis for exercising supplemental jurisdiction over the additional claims.

We now conclude the answer must be yes. When the well-pleaded complaint contains at least one claim that satisfies the amount-in-controversy requirement, and there are no other relevant jurisdictional defects, the district court, beyond all question, has original jurisdiction over that claim. The presence of other claims in the complaint, over which the district court may lack original jurisdiction, is of no moment. If the court has original jurisdiction over a single claim in the complaint, it has original jurisdiction over a "civil action" within the meaning of § 1367(a), even if the civil action over which it has jurisdiction comprises fewer claims than were included in the complaint. Once the court determines it has original jurisdiction over the civil action, it can turn to the question whether it has a constitutional and statutory basis for exercising supplemental jurisdiction over the other claims in the action.

Section 1367(a) commences with the direction that §§ 1367(b) and (c), or other relevant statutes, may provide specific exceptions, but otherwise § 1367(a) is a broad jurisdictional grant, with no distinction drawn between [original jurisdiction based on 1331 and original jurisdiction based on 1332]. In fact, the last sentence of § 1367(a) makes clear that the provision grants supplemental jurisdiction over claims involving joinder or intervention of additional parties.

* * *

If § 1367(a) were the sum total of the relevant statutory language, our holding would rest on that language alone. The statute, of course, instructs us to examine § 1367(b) to determine if any of its exceptions apply [when, as here, the sole basis of jurisdiction is

§ 1332], so we proceed to that section. While § 1367(b) qualifies the broad rule of § 1367(a), it does not withdraw supplemental jurisdiction over the claims of the additional parties at issue here. The specific exceptions to § 1367(a) contained in § 1367(b), moreover, provide additional support for our conclusion that § 1367(a) confers supplemental jurisdiction over these claims. Section 1367(b), which applies only to diversity cases, withholds supplemental jurisdiction over the claims of plaintiffs proposed to be joined as indispensable parties under Federal Rule of Civil Procedure 19, or who seek to intervene pursuant to Rule 24. Nothing in the text of § 1367(b), however, withholds supplemental jurisdiction over the claims of plaintiffs permissively joined under Rule 20 . . . The natural, indeed the necessary, inference is that § 1367 confers supplemental jurisdiction over claims by Rule 20 and Rule 23 plaintiffs. This inference, at least with respect to Rule 20 plaintiffs, is strengthened by the fact that § 1367(b) explicitly excludes supplemental jurisdiction over claims against defendants joined under Rule 20.

We cannot accept the view, urged by some of the parties, commentators, and Courts of Appeals, that a district court lacks original jurisdiction over a civil action unless the court has original jurisdiction over every claim in the complaint. As we understand this position, it requires assuming either that all claims in the complaint must stand or fall as a single, indivisible "civil action" as a matter of definitional necessity—what we will refer to as the "indivisibility theory"—or else that the inclusion of a claim or party falling outside the district court's original jurisdiction somehow contaminates every other claim in the complaint, depriving the court of original jurisdiction over any of these claims— what we will refer to as the "contamination theory."

The indivisibility theory is easily dismissed, as it is inconsistent with the whole notion of supplemental jurisdiction. If a district court must have original jurisdiction over every claim in the complaint in order to have "original jurisdiction" over a "civil action," then in *Gibbs* there was no civil action of which the district court could assume original jurisdiction under § 1331, and so no basis for exercising supplemental jurisdiction over any of the claims.

* * *

We also find it unconvincing to say that the definitional indivisibility theory applies in the context of diversity cases but not in the context of federal-question cases. The broad and general language of the statute does not permit this result. The contention is premised on the notion that the phrase "original jurisdiction of all civil actions" means different things in §§ 1331 and 1332. It is implausible, however, to say that the identical phrase means one thing (original jurisdiction in all actions where at least one claim in the complaint meets the following requirements) in § 1331 and something else (original jurisdiction in all actions where every claim in the complaint meets the following requirements) in § 1332.

The contamination theory, as we have noted, can make some sense in the special context of the complete diversity requirement because the presence of nondiverse parties on both sides of a lawsuit eliminates the justification for providing a federal forum. The theory, however, makes little sense with respect to the amount-in-controversy requirement, which is meant to ensure that a dispute is sufficiently important to warrant federal-court attention. The presence of a single nondiverse party may eliminate the fear of bias with respect to all claims, but the presence of a claim that falls short of the minimum amount in controversy does nothing to reduce the importance of the claims that do meet this requirement.

It is fallacious to suppose, simply from the proposition that § 1332 imposes both the diversity requirement and the amount-in-controversy requirement, that the contamination theory germane to the former is also relevant to the latter. There is no inherent logical connection between the amount-in-controversy requirement and § 1332 diversity jurisdiction. After all, federal-question jurisdiction once had an amount-in-controversy requirement as well. If such a requirement were revived under § 1331, it is clear beyond peradventure that § 1367(a) provides supplemental jurisdiction over federal-question cases where some, but not all, of the federal-law claims involve a sufficient amount in controversy.

* * *

And so we circle back to the original question. When the well-pleaded complaint in district court includes multiple claims, all part of the same case or controversy, and some, but not all, of the claims are within the court's original jurisdiction, does the court have before it "any civil action of which the district courts have original jurisdiction"? It does. Under § 1367, the court has original jurisdiction over the civil action comprising the claims for which there is no jurisdictional defect. No other reading of § 1367 is plausible in light of the text and structure of the jurisdictional statute. Though the special nature and purpose of the diversity requirement mean that a single nondiverse party can contaminate every other claim in the lawsuit, the contamination does not occur with respect to jurisdictional defects that go only to the substantive importance of individual claims.

It follows from this conclusion that the threshold requirement of § 1367(a) is satisfied in cases, like those now before us, where some, but not all, of the plaintiffs in a diversity action allege a sufficient amount in controversy.

* * *

The judgment of the Court of Appeals for the Eleventh Circuit is affirmed. The judgment of the Court of Appeals for the First Circuit is reversed, and the case is remanded for proceedings consistent with this opinion.

It is so ordered.

DIRECTED READING QUESTIONS

20. Which of the following represents the jurisdictional deficiency present in the *Exxon* case?

   I. $A_{[AL]} + B_{[AK]} + C_{[CA]} + D_{[DE]}$ v. $E_{[KS]}$

        a.   The amount in controversy is more than \$75,000 exclusive of interests and costs for A's claim, but B, C, and D's amount in controversy is less than \$75,000.

OR

II.   A$_{[AL]}$ + B$_{[AK]}$ + C$_{[CA]}$ + D$_{[DE]}$ **v.** E$_{[AL]}$

     b.   The amount in controversy for each plaintiff is more than $75,000 exclusive of interests and costs.

21. Confirm that you appreciate that supplemental jurisdiction results in original jurisdiction which would not exist without the supplemental jurisdiction statute, or in other words, if jurisdiction was based solely on § 1331 and § 1332 and not on § 1367.

22. What joinder rule is at work in I and II above? If the plaintiffs are properly joined pursuant to this joinder rule, what does this mean regarding the satisfaction of the relationship test in § 1367(a)?

23. Once you have identified the relevant joinder rule (Rule ___) from the previous question, consider whether the following is true:

     a.   In an action where subject matter jurisdiction is founded on arising under jurisdiction there is supplemental jurisdiction over a party joined pursuant to Rule ___.

     b.   In an action where subject matter jurisdiction is founded on diversity jurisdiction, the relationship test of § 1367(a) is satisfied for a party joined pursuant to Rule ___, but we need to check if § 1367(b) strips the court of jurisdiction granted in § 1367(a) before we can conclude supplemental jurisdiction exists.

24. Identify the jurisdictional "defect" in in I and II above in question 20 if subject matter jurisdiction is premised only on 28 U.S.C. § 1332.

25. In light of the following language from the opinion please explain why the indivisibility theory is "inconsistent with the whole notion of supplemental jurisdiction."

> If the court has original jurisdiction over a single claim in the complaint, it has original jurisdiction over a "civil action" within the meaning of § 1367(a), even if the civil action over which it has jurisdiction comprises fewer claims than were included in the complaint. Once the court determines it has original jurisdiction over the civil action, it can turn to the question whether it has a constitutional and statutory basis for exercising supplemental jurisdiction over the other claims in the action.

* * *

> We cannot accept the view, urged by some of the parties, commentators, and Courts of Appeals, that a district court lacks original jurisdiction over a civil action unless the court has original jurisdiction over every claim in the complaint. As we understand this position, it requires assuming either that all claims in the complaint must stand or fall as a single, indivisible "civil action" as a matter of definitional necessity—what we will refer to as the "indivisibility theory"—or else that the inclusion of a claim or party falling outside the district court's original jurisdiction somehow contaminates every other claim in the complaint, depriving the court of original jurisdiction over any of these claims— what we will refer to as the "contamination theory."

> The indivisibility theory is easily dismissed, as it is inconsistent with the whole notion of supplemental jurisdiction.

26. Can you explain, after reading the *Exxon* decision, why the supplemental jurisdiction statute can "cure" the jurisdictional defect in I but not II above in question 20?

CHAPTER 13

REMOVAL

■ ■ ■

DIRECTED READING QUESTIONS

1. A sues B in state court on a federal cause of action. A then decides that he no longer wants to be in state court. May A remove the civil action to federal court? *Read 28 U.S.C. § 1441(a) carefully.*

2. Look at the map of the Florida Judicial Districts. There are three districts in Florida: the southern, middle and northern districts. May a defendant remove a case from a state court in Miami, Florida to the United States District Court for the Northern District of Florida? Why or why not? *Read 28 U.S.C. § 1441(a) carefully.*

3. Is it true that any action pending in a state court over which the federal courts have original jurisdiction may be removed to the appropriate federal court? *Read 1441(b) carefully.*

4. For the following civil action, KS v. AK + AZ + MO, where plaintiff's claim is based on violation of KS negligence law and where the amount in controversy is > $75,000 exclusive of interests and costs, please explain, after reading 1441(b)(2) carefully, whether;

   a. Federal subject matter jurisdiction exists;

   b. The action is removable if the plaintiff elects to bring the action in

      i. KS state court

      ii. MO state court

      iii. AK state court

      iv. AZ state court

5. Alan from Alaska sues Frank from Florida, in state court in Florida for violation of federal statute. In the same action Alan also joins a claim he has against Frank for an unrelated violation of state law. Frank removes the civil action to the appropriate federal court pursuant to a notice of removal.

   a. Does 28 U.S.C. § 1441(b) mandate remand?

   b. Does 28 U.S.C. § 1367 permit the court to retain jurisdiction over both the federal and state claims?

6. Alan from Alaska sues Frank from Florida, in state court in Florida for violation of federal statute. In the same action Alan also joins a state law claim he has against Frank based on Frank's actions which violated the federal statute. Frank removes the civil action to the appropriate federal court pursuant to a notice of removal.

   a. Does 1441(b) mandate remand?

   b. Does 28 U.S.C. § 1367 permit the court to retain jurisdiction over both claims?

7. Alan sues Greg and Michael in state court seeking damages based on Greg's and Michael's violation of a federal statute. Greg files a notice of removal within the time specified by Rule 1446(b). Is remand appropriate merely because Michael did not join the notice of removal or consent to it? *Read 1446(b)(2)(A) carefully.*

8. Alan sues Greg in state court seeking damages based on Greg's violation of a federal statute. Greg impleads Michael. Greg files a notice of removal. Is remand appropriate merely because Michael did not join the notice of removal or consent to it?

9. Alan from Alabama commences his action against Tony from Alabama and Brett from Mississippi in Alabama state court by filing a complaint alleging a violation of Alabama law. The claim against each defendant is based on the same transaction and occurrence and each claim is worth more than $75.000 exclusive of interests and costs. 6 months after commencement Tony is voluntarily dismissed. Brett then files a notice of removal. Alan files a motion for remand stating that Brett's notice of removal is violative of the thirty-day requirement in 1446(b). What result? *Read 1446(b)(3) carefully.*

10. Same facts as question 9 but Tony's voluntary dismissal occurred 13 months after Alan commenced the action. *Read 1446(c) carefully.*

11. What are examples of a "defect other than lack of subject matter jurisdiction" as a basis for remand which are waived as per 1447(c) if not brought in a motion to remand within thirty days after the filing of the notice of removal?

12. Lisa commences an action against Grace in state court and serves Grace on the same day. The action is based on Grace's violation of a state statute. Lisa and Grace are from different states but Grace is not from the state where the action is commenced. Lisa is seeking $80,000 in damages exclusive of interest and costs from Grace. The state court's rules of procedure require the defendant to answer the complaint within 20 days after service. 21 days after being served Grace files a timely notice of removal based on diversity of citizenship. The next day the state court issues a default judgment against Grace. Is the default judgment enforceable? *Read 1446(a), (b)(1) and (d) carefully.*

13. A case is removed to federal court and the federal court decides that even though federal subject matter jurisdiction exists because the action involves a federal constitutional issue, they should refrain from hearing the case, or abstain, because the state court may be able to resolve the issue by resolving only the state law claims without touching on the federal constitutional claims. The case is remanded to state court. Is the decision to remand appealable? *Read 1447(d) carefully.*

14. An action filed in state court is removed to federal court pursuant to 1441(a) because one of the claims in the action involved a federal question. The other claims in the action are state law claims which are so related to the federal question claim that they form part of the same Article III case as the federal question claim. After a careful statement based on 1367(c), the federal court elects not to exercise supplemental jurisdiction over the state law claims and remands those claims. Does 1447(d) prohibit the appeal of this decision to remand?

CHAPTER 14

CLASS ACTION

■ ■ ■

I. REQUIREMENTS FOR CERTIFICATION

DIRECTED READING QUESTIONS

1. The following is an example of the first page of style of a typical class action lawsuit complaint that I worked on. Rule 23(a)(3), (4) mention the "representative parties." Representative parties are also called class representatives or known parties. Rule 23(a) also mentions "the class." Identify the "representative parties" and the class in the style below.

UNITED STATES DISTRICT COURT
SOUTHERN DISTRICT OF FLORIDA
MIAMI DIVISION
CASE NO.:

HUGOLINO APARICIO, AMANDA MORALES, &
RICARDO NOLA
Individually and on behalf of all others similarly situated:
Plaintiff,

–vs–

PRINCESS CRUISE LINES, LTD. CORP.
Defendants,

2. Read the class action rule and the following text boxes and label each box with a letter (a–h) based on what section of Rule 23 is relevant to the content of each box.

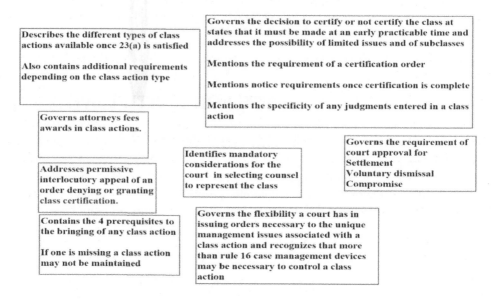

Describes the different types of class actions available once 23(a) is satisfied

Also contains additional requirements depending on the class action type

Governs the decision to certify or not certify the class at states that it must be made at an early practicable time and addresses the possibility of limited issues and of subclasses

Mentions the requirement of a certification order

Mentions notice requirements once certification is complete

Mentions the specificity of any judgments entered in a class action

Governs attorneys fees awards in class actions.

Addresses permissive interlocutory appeal of an order denying or granting class certification.

Identifies mandatory considerations for the court in selecting counsel to represent the class

Governs the requirement of court approval for Settlement Voluntary dismissal Compromise

Contains the 4 prerequisites to the bringing of any class action

If one is missing a class action may not be maintained

Governs the flexibility a court has in issuing orders necessary to the unique management issues associated with a class action and recognizes that more than rule 16 case management devices may be necessary to control a class action

IN RE AMERICAN MEDICAL SYSTEMS, INC. (1996)

United States Court of Appeal, Sixth Circuit
75 F.3d 1069

SUHRHEINRICH, CIRCUIT JUDGE.

Petitioners American Medical Systems ("AMS") and Pfizer, Inc., defendants below, both seek a writ of mandamus directing the district court to vacate orders conditionally certifying a class in a products liability suit involving penile prostheses.

I.

Since 1973, AMS, a wholly-owned subsidiary of Pfizer, has manufactured and marketed penile prostheses, which are used to treat impotence. The plaintiffs, respondents in this proceeding, all use or have used AMS' products.

Plaintiff Paul Vorhis was implanted with an AMS penile prosthesis on April 25, 1989. It failed to function in January of 1993, and Vorhis had the prosthesis replaced with an AMS 700 Ultrex prosthesis in May 1993. This second prosthesis caused him pain and discomfort, and plaintiff had it removed in August of 1993 and replaced with a third AMS prosthesis, with which he is presently satisfied. Vorhis filed this action against defendant AMS in the Southern District of Ohio on December 5, 1994, individually and on behalf of others similarly situated who suffered damages as a result of the implantation of penile prostheses manufactured by AMS. The complaint alleges strict product liability, negligence, breach of implied and express warranties, fraud and punitive damages, and seeks a declaratory judgment for medical monitoring.

On December 29, 1994, Vorhis filed a motion for class certification. On January 5, 1995, the district judge entered an order setting a hearing for January 27, 1995, later extended to February 24, 1995.

* * *

After expedited discovery, AMS submitted a brief in opposition to the class certification motion on February 17, 1995. Plaintiff filed his reply brief on February 23, 1995.

At the class certification hearing, the district judge indicated that he was concerned principally with the question of whether Vorhis was an appropriate class representative, and directed AMS to proceed first. AMS challenged Vorhis' suitability as a class representative on several grounds. First, AMS pointed out that Vorhis had a history of psychiatric problems, for which he received total and permanent disability benefits from the State of Ohio. AMS introduced reports prepared by Vorhis' psychiatrist and psychologist showing that Vorhis suffered from memory loss, impaired concentration, and a lack of common sense, all factors which AMS maintained would interfere with plaintiff's ability to make rational decisions on behalf of other members of the purported class. AMS also contended that Vorhis was an unsuitable representative because his need for the prosthesis stemmed from a unique condition, Peyronie's disease, or curvature of the penis. Third, AMS argued that because Vorhis had a problem with only one of the ten types of prostheses AMS manufactured, he could not represent those who had problems with the other kinds of devices.

In response to AMS' first argument, plaintiff offered the deposition testimony of his treating psychiatrist, Dr. Edelstein, who opined that Vorhis was competent to withstand the rigors of trial. As to defendant's third argument, plaintiff countered that the basic design of all ten devices was the same. Plaintiff pointed to a section 510(k) notice document for the AMS 700 Ultrex Penile Prosthesis (the second AMS prostheses used by Vorhis) stating that all but one of the device's components were indistinguishable to those previously marketed. Vorhis did not directly respond to AMS' second argument.

The judge made no factual findings but took the matter under advisement. However, at the conclusion of oral argument, the district judge queried:

THE COURT: "Do you agree that if [plaintiff's counsel] adds class plaintiffs, that argument's [regarding Vorhis' psychological fragility] moot?"

[AMS' COUNSEL]: "If those class plaintiffs are appropriate, absolutely."

On February 28, 1995, the district judge issued a two-page order stating, "based upon the information currently available to it, that class certification appears to be the most efficient and appropriate manner in which to handle this matter," and promised a "further order outlining the reasoning supporting that conclusion" to follow. The order was conditional, subject to decertification at any time, and conditioned further "upon class counsel acting to amend the complaint within thirty (30) days . . . in order to add additional plaintiffs who qualify as appropriate class representatives and who are free of the alleged infirmities on which Defendant's objections to the suitability of the current Plaintiff/class representative are premised."

On March 10, 1995, Vorhis filed an amended complaint, adding three additional plaintiffs as class representatives and Pfizer as an additional defendant.[6] AMS and Pfizer were both served with the amended complaint on March 13, 1995. . . .

Without any further discovery, briefing, or argument, the district judge issued an amended order of class certification on March 16, 1995. The judge found that all the prerequisites of Fed.R.Civ.P. 23(a) had been met, and that the class was maintainable under Fed.R.Civ.P. 23(b)(3) because common questions of law or fact predominated. As to "numerosity," the court held:

> It is asserted that the class to be certified consists of 15,000 to 120,000 persons. The United States Court of Appeals for the Sixth Circuit has previously held that a class of 35 was sufficient to meet the numerosity requirement.

Regarding "commonality," the judge stated:

> As persons who have undergone implantation of Defendants' inflatable penile prostheses [Plaintiffs] appear to have a common right to assert a claim against Defendants.

For the third requirement of subsection (a), "typicality," the judge held:

> The proposed representatives of the class assert claims that are typical of the class in that all plaintiffs allege injury from the American Medical Systems, Inc./Pfizer, Inc. inflatable penile prostheses manufactured and distributed by Defendants. These claims are similar enough to those of the class that the representatives will adequately represent such class.

> For purposes of the determination of liability at least, the claims of the representatives are the claims of the class.

---

[6]   The first amended complaint states in relevant part:

2.   Plaintiff Paul Vorhis is a resident of Middletown, Ohio and has resided in Middletown, Ohio at all times relevant to this litigation. On or about April 25, 1989, Mr. Vorhis was implanted with a American Medical Systems, Inc. 700 CX penile prosthesis. During January of 1993, the prosthesis ceased to function properly. Mr. Vorhis had the prosthesis explanted in February of 1993 and replaced with a American Medical Systems, Inc. 700 Ultrex prosthesis in May of 1993. During August of 1993, Mr. Vorhis had his second American Medical Systems, Inc. prosthesis removed and replaced with another prosthesis manufactured by Defendant American Medical Systems, Inc.

3.   Plaintiff Robert York is a resident of Cincinnati, Ohio. Plaintiff Robert York was implanted with a American Medical Systems, Inc. 700 inflatable penile prosetheis [sic] in January 1990 while a patient at Cincinnati Bethesda Oak Hospital. During the time that he has possessed the American Medical Systems, Inc. prosthesis, the prosthesis has malfunctioned. Currently the posthesis [sic] fails to fully inflate.

4.   Plaintiff James Kennedy is a resident of Garden City, Georgia. Plaintiff James Kennedy was implanted with a American Medical Systems, Inc. Ultrex inflatable penile prosthesis. On June 6, 1993, the prosthesis malfunctioned because the cylinders and pump leaked. On June 16, 1993, the defective components were explanted and replaced with new components from a American Medical Systems, Inc. 700 Ultrex Plus prosthesis.

5.   Plaintiff John W. Gordy is a resident of Rockville, Maryland. Mr. Gordy was implanted with a American Medical Systems, Inc. Hydroflex penile prosthesis on or about August 9, 1985. In 1993, the Hydroflex prosthesis failed and was explanted. On February 1, 1993, Mr. Gordy received a American Medical Systems, Inc. Dynaflex penile prosthesis. As of March 1, 1995, the Dynaflex prosthesis is not functioning because only one side inflates.

On the question of "adequate representation," the judge opined that

> This Court has considered the qualifications of Plaintiffs' counsel and considers that they have sufficient experience and ability to fairly and adequately protect the interests of the class.

Finally, the judge found the class maintainable under Rule 23(b)(3), stating:

> There is an assertion here that there may be thousands of persons who are in the same position as Plaintiffs. Plaintiffs have asserted causes of action in fraudulent and negligent misrepresentation, failure to warn, negligence, strict liability and breach of warranty, both expressed and implied. Without determining the merits of Plaintiffs' claims, it is clear that a class action is far superior to numerous individual determinations of the same rights.

The district judge therefore certified the class as:

> All persons residing in the United States, who have had inflatable penile prostheses developed, manufactured and/or sold by Defendant American Medical Systems, Inc. and/or Defendant Pfizer, Inc. implanted in their bodies.

In the notice attached to the class, the district judge named Vorhis as one of the parties that was bringing the class action lawsuit on behalf of all members of the class.

* * *

Meanwhile, defendants sought a stay of the March 16 amended order of class certification in the district court, which was denied on March 24, 1995. This court also granted a stay of the March 16 order, to the extent that it directed notice to the members of the class.

* * *

The Supreme Court has required district courts to conduct a "rigorous analysis" into whether the prerequisites of Rule 23 are met before certifying a class. The trial court has broad discretion in deciding whether to certify a class, but that discretion must be exercised within the framework of Rule 23.

A class is not maintainable as a class action by virtue of its designation as such in the pleadings. Although a hearing prior to the class determination is not always required, "it may be necessary for the court to probe behind the pleadings before coming to rest on the certification question." This court has stated that:

> Mere repetition of the language of Rule 23(a) is not sufficient. There must be an adequate statement of the basic facts to indicate that each requirement of the rule is fulfilled. Maintainability may be determined by the court on the basis of the pleadings, if sufficient facts are set forth, but ordinarily the determination should be predicated on more information than the pleadings will provide. . . . The parties should be afforded an opportunity to present evidence on the maintainability of the class action.

The party seeking the class certification bears the burden of proof. Subsection (a) of Rule 23 contains four prerequisites which must *all* be met before a class can be certified.

Once those conditions are satisfied, the party seeking certification must also demonstrate that it falls within at least *one* of the subcategories of Rule 23(b). We shall examine each of these factors individually.

1.

The first subdivision of Rule 23(a)(1) requires that the class be "so numerous that joinder of all members is impracticable." "The reason for [the impracticability] requirement is obvious. Only when joinder is impracticable is there a need for a class action device." There is no strict numerical test for determining impracticability of joinder. Rather, "[t]he numerosity requirement requires examination of the specific facts of each case and imposes no absolute limitations." When class size reaches substantial proportions, however, the impracticability requirement is usually satisfied by the numbers alone.

In the original complaint, Vorhis alleged that although he was unable to state the exact size of the class, "members of the class number at least in the thousands." The first amended complaint modified that estimate to "over 150,000." The district judge's finding of a class of 15,000 to 120,000 persons may not be unreasonable, especially since AMS has been producing penile prostheses for over twenty years, and has the largest share of the penile implant market. Defendant, moreover, does not contest this factor. Although the district judge made no findings but merely rubberstamped the plaintiffs' assertions that such potential class members truly exist, we do not hold that this factor is not established because petitioners do not contest it.

2.

Rule 23(a)(2) requires that for certification there must be "questions of law or fact common to the class." The commonality requirement is interdependent with the impracticability of joinder requirement, and the "tests together form the underlying conceptual basis supporting class actions." As the Supreme Court [has] described [ ]:

> The class-action was designed as "an exception to the usual rule that litigation is conducted by and on behalf of the individual named parties only." Class relief "is 'peculiarly appropriate' when the 'issues involved are common to the class as a whole' and when they 'turn on questions of law applicable in the same manner to each member of the class." For in such cases, "the class-action device saves the resources of both the courts and the parties by permitting an issue potentially affecting every [class member] to be litigated in an economical fashion under Rule 23."

The commonality test "is qualitative rather than quantitative, that is, there need be only a single issue common to all members of the class." But, as we shall see, there is an important check on this requirement under Rule 23(b)(3).

Plaintiffs' complaint and class certification motion simply allege in general terms that there are common issues without identifying any particular defect common to all plaintiffs. Yet AMS introduced uncontradicted evidence that since 1973 AMS has produced at least ten different models, and that these models have been modified over the years. Plaintiffs' claims of strict liability, fraudulent misrepresentation to both the FDA and the medical community, negligent testing, design and manufacture, and failure to warn will differ depending upon the model and the year it was issued.

Proofs as to strict liability, negligence, failure to warn, breach of express and implied warranties will also vary from plaintiff to plaintiff because complications with an AMS device may be due to a variety of factors, including surgical error, improper use of the device, anatomical incompatibility, infection, device malfunction, or psychological problems. Furthermore, each plaintiff's urologist would also be required to testify to determine what oral and written statements were made to the physician, and what he in turn told the patient, as well as to issues of reliance, causation and damages.

The amended complaint reflects that the plaintiffs received different models and have different complaints regarding each of those models. In the absence of more specific allegations and/or proof of commonality of any factual or legal claims, plaintiffs have failed to meet their burden of proof on Rule 23(a)(2).

This failure of proof highlights the error of the district judge. Despite evidence in the record presented by the nonmoving party that at least ten different models existed, testimony from a urologist that there is no "common cause" of prostheses malfunction, and conclusory allegations by the party with the burden of proof on certification, we find not even the hint of any serious consideration by the judge of commonality.

3.

Rule 23(a)(3) requires that "claims or defenses of the representative parties [be] typical of the claims or defenses of the class."

Typicality determines whether a sufficient relationship exists between the injury to the named plaintiff and the conduct affecting the class, so that the court may properly attribute a collective nature to the challenged conduct. In other words, when such a relationship is shown, a plaintiff's injury arises from or is directly related to a wrong to a class, and that wrong includes the wrong to the plaintiff. Thus, a plaintiff's claim is typical if it arises from the same event or practice or course of conduct that gives rise to the claims of other class members, and if his or her claims are based on the same legal theory.

A necessary consequence of the typicality requirement is that the representative's interests will be aligned with those of the represented group, and in pursuing his own claims, the named plaintiff will also advance the interests of the class members.

Vorhis' claim relates to a previous AMS penile prosthesis which, several years after insertion, allegedly could not be inflated due to a possible leak in the input tube of a CX device. This in turn may have been caused by rear-tip extender surgery Vorhis had in 1990, in an attempt to increase penile length that was lost through surgery to correct a curvature of his penis. Based on what little we have to go on, it is hard to imagine that Vorhis' claim is typical of the class certified in this case.

Because the district judge issued its amended order of certification before discovery of the plaintiffs other than Vorhis, we have less information about them. However, we know from the amended complaint that each plaintiff used a different model, and each experienced a distinct difficulty. York claims that his 700 inflatable penile prosthesis fails to fully inflate. Kennedy alleges that his Ultrex inflatable penile prosthesis malfunctioned because the cylinders and pump leaked. Finally, Gordy maintains that his Hyrdoflex failed, and that his current implant, the Dynaflex prosthesis, inflates on one side only. These allegations fail to establish a claim typical to each other, let alone a class.

Once again, it should have been obvious to the district judge that it needed to "probe behind the pleadings" before concluding that the typicality requirement was met. Instead, the district judge gave no serious consideration to this factor, but simply mimicked the language of the rule. This was error.

4.

Rule 23(a)(4) allows certification only if "the representative parties will fairly and adequately protect the interests of the class." Fed.R.Civ.P. 23(a). This prerequisite is essential to due process, because a final judgment in a class action is binding on all class members.

[The] two criteria for determining adequacy of representation [are]: "1) the representative must have common interests with unnamed members of the class, and 2) it must appear that the representatives will vigorously prosecute the interests of the class through qualified counsel." The adequate representation requirement overlaps with the typicality requirement because in the absence of typical claims, the class representative has no incentives to pursue the claims of the other class members.

Although the district judge considered the qualifications of plaintiff's counsel, he made no finding on the first criterion, and did not consider whether Vorhis or the other plaintiffs would "vigorously prosecute the interests of the class." AMS raised a serious question as to Vorhis' suitability to serve as a class representative given his history of psychological problems. At the hearing, the judge made no finding regarding plaintiff, but remarked that:

> I don't think he is going to control anything. I don't think a client in a class action ever controls anything. And if you want my feeling on it, he is a name. He's a symbol. I just want to make sure there aren't defenses against that symbol that would then be transmitted against the class.

* * *

As amply illustrated, plaintiffs' complaint and class certification motion simply allege the elements of Rule 23(a) in conclusory terms without submitting any persuasive evidence to show that these factors are met. Because the plaintiffs did not create a factual record, and petitioners have demonstrated that the products at issue are very different and that each plaintiff's claim is unique, class certification was inappropriate.

5.

The district judge certified the class under Rule 23(b)(3), which requires the court to find "that the questions of law or fact common to the members of the class predominate over any questions affecting only individual members, and that a class action is superior to other available methods for the fair and efficient adjudication of the controversy." Fed.R.Civ.P. 23(b)(3). Subdivision (b)(3) parallels subdivision (a)(2) in that both require that common questions exist, but subdivision (b)(3) contains the more stringent requirement that common issues "predominate" over individual issues.

* * *

As this case illustrates, the products are different, each plaintiff has a unique complaint, and each receives different information and assurances from his treating physician. Given the absence of evidence that common issues predominate, certification was improper.

* * *

Thus, even assuming common questions of law or fact, it cannot be said that these issues predominate, and that class treatment would be superior to other methods of litigation.

The superiority aspect of Rule 23(b)(3) also has not been established. A single litigation addressing every complication in every model of prosthesis, including changes in design, manufacturing, and representation over the course of twenty-two years, as well as the unique problems of each plaintiff, would present a nearly insurmountable burden on the district court. By contrast, an individual case of this type is relatively simple to litigate if narrowly focused on a claim regarding a specific model, a specific component, or specific statements made to a particular urologist during a particular period of time. Again, the district judge ignored the JPML finding that consolidated treatment of such claims would not "promote the just and efficient conduct of the entire litigation" and was not necessary because no judicial management crisis exits.

The district judge also failed to consider how the law of negligence differs from jurisdiction to jurisdiction, [given that] a federal court sitting in diversity must apply common law of the state in which case would normally be tried rather than a general federal common law.

"The law of negligence, including subsidiary concepts such as duty of care, foreseeability, and proximate cause, may . . . differ among the states only in nuance, . . . [b]ut nuance can be important, and its significance is suggested by a comparison of differing state pattern instructions on negligence and differing judicial formulations of the meaning of negligence and the subordinate concepts." The judge certified a nationwide class in this case. If more than a few of the laws of the fifty states differ, the district judge would face an impossible task of instructing a jury on the relevant law, yet another reason why class certification would not be the appropriate course of action.

Plaintiffs failed to meet their burden of demonstrating predominance of common issues. The district judge failed to "question the appropriateness of a class action" of "[a]ll persons residing in the United States, who have had inflatable penile prostheses developed, manufactured and/or sold by . . . [AMS or Pfizer] implanted in their bodies." The amended order does not identify allegedly common issues, does not explain why they predominate over individual issues and makes no finding of superiority. Certification was therefore improper.

6.

* * *

IV.

Under the various formulations of the writ, we conclude that petitioners have met their heavy burden. For all the foregoing reasons, the petitions for writ of mandamus are GRANTED, and the district judge is directed to decertify the plaintiff class.

3. What happened on the following dates: December 5, 1994 and December 29, 1994?

4. At the class certification hearing, the defendant argued that class certification should not be granted because the plaintiff should not be allowed to represent the class. Discuss the arguments made in this regard and the finding of the court.

5. At the class certification hearing, the judge orders Vorhis to add more plaintiffs as named representatives. Describe all the named representatives on the amended complaint and their particular issues with penile implants.

6. Examine the judge's March 16, 1995 certification order carefully. What, in addition to satisfying the requirements of Rule 23(a), does a party need to do in order for class certification to be appropriate?

7. How does the trial court conclude that the numerosity requirement of Rule 23(a)(1) is met?

8. How does the trial court conclude that the commonality requirement of Rule 23(a)(2) has been met?

9. How does the trial court conclude that the typicality requirement of Rule 23(a)(3) has been met? What about the court's finding indicates that typicality in Rule 23(a)(3) is not a completely separate consideration than adequacy in Rule 23(a)(4)?

10. How does the trial court conclude that the adequacy requirement of Rule 23(a)(4) has been met?

11. Once the court determined that the requirements of Rule 23(a) were satisfied, it had to do one more thing before class certification could occur. What was that one more thing?

12. What are the appellate court's findings regarding certification?

13. Does the granting or denying of class certification provide a right of appeal?

II. UNIQUE CONSIDERATIONS FOR CLASS ACTIONS

14. Assuming that all Rule 23(a) requirements are met, what "type[ ] of class action" could the following fact patterns be certified as and why?

  a. The sum of all the defendant's assets and any applicable insurance coverage are insufficient to satisfy all the plaintiffs' claims, and the total recovery allowed is based on a limited fund.

  b. Property owners in the city of Manhattan, New York want to get a factory on Staten Island declared a nuisance, when some of the property owners have owned property in Manhattan before the factory was established and others have owned property after the factory was established.

  c. A civil rights suit seeking to have a municipality's action banning a certain ethnic minority from engaging in a certain type of business declared unconstitutional.

  d. Heart attack deaths suffered by users of a pain medication when no warning regarding the heart attack risk was mentioned on the label of the medication.

15. According to Rule 23(c), what are some significant differences between the Rule 23(b)(3) class actions and the other types of class actions available under Rule 23(b)?

16. Motor Sellers Inc. ("MSI") is a New York corporation with its principal place of business in California. For the last decade, it has sold millions of automobiles directly to purchasers in every state. Five purchasers, Alpha, Beta, Charlie, Delta, and Epsilon, initiate a class action lawsuit in federal court against MSI, alleging that MSI was negligent because it failed to inspect their vehicles adequately, and as a result, defects which a reasonable seller would have detected caused harm to at least 35,000 individuals. The basis of jurisdiction is diversity jurisdiction, and they sue on behalf of all others similarly situated. Alpha is from Alabama, Beta is from Massachusetts, Charlie is from Florida, Delta is from Delaware, and Epsilon is from North Carolina. Many of the purchasers who are members of the class are from New York, California, and many other states. The total damage amount for all plaintiffs is $4.9 million. The amount in controversy exclusive of costs and interests for the claims of the named plaintiffs is as follows: Alpha $76,000, Beta $3000, Charlie $1500, Delta $1200, and Epsilon $1500. Which of the following statements, if any, is correct and why?

     a.   The federal court lacks subject matter jurisdiction over the action because the diversity requirement is not met.

     b.   The federal court must dismiss the action because the claims of four of the representatives do not meet the amount in controversy requirement.

17. Assume the same facts as question 16, but Alpha's claim is for $35,000, Beta is from New York, Charlie is from California, and the aggregate amount in controversy for all plaintiffs is $5.5 million. Read 28 U.S.C. § 1332(d)(1), (d)(2) carefully and explain how these facts change the subject matter jurisdiction analysis.

CHAPTER 15

THE *ERIE* DOCTRINE

∎ ∎ ∎

I. FORUM SHOPPING CONCERNS

28 U.S.C. § 1652—STATE LAWS AS RULES OF DECISION (1789)

The laws of the several states, except where the Constitution or treaties of the United States or Acts of Congress otherwise require or provide, shall be regarded as rules of decision in civil actions in the courts of the United States, in cases where they apply.

DIRECTED READING QUESTIONS

1. What is the practical effect of the above statute?

SWIFT V. TYSON (1842)
Supreme Court of the United States
41 U.S. 1

[The phrase "laws of the several states" in 28 U.S.C. § 1652 does not include state common law, but includes only state Constitutions, state statutes and state local rules or rules] "relating to rights and titles to things having a permanent locality, such as the rights and titles to real estate, and other matters immovable and intra-territorial in their nature and character." [Where the state law on point is state common law, federal courts should apply general federal common law principles.]

DIRECTED READING QUESTIONS

2. In 1843, A sues B for breach of contract pursuant to Illinois law in Illinois Federal Court. A is from Missouri and B is from Illinois. The amount in controversy is greater than the jurisdictional amount required under the then existing version of 28 U.S.C. § 1332.

    a. Explain what law governs the amount of damages recoverable if Illinois has a statute on point?

    b. Explain what law governs the amount of damages recoverable if Illinois has no statute on point but there are many Illinois court opinions on point?

3. Explain how the answer to question 2(b) could be interpreted as an encroachment on state sovereignty.

4. What significant event relating to procedure in the federal courts occurred in 1938? **Please read 28 U.S.C. §§ 2071–2074 CAREFULLY before proceeding.**

ERIE RR. CO. V. TOMPKINS (1938)

Supreme Court of the United States
304 U.S. 64

MR. JUSTICE BRANDEIS delivered the opinion of the Court.

The question for decision is whether the oft-challenged doctrine of Swift v. Tyson shall now be disapproved.

Tompkins, a citizen of Pennsylvania, was injured on a dark night by a passing freight train of the Erie Railroad Company while walking along its right of way at Hughestown in that state. He claimed that the accident occurred through negligence in the operation, or maintenance, of the train; that he was rightfully on the premises as licensee because on a commonly used beaten footpath which ran for a short distance alongside the tracks; and that he was struck by something which looked like a door projecting from one of the moving cars. To enforce that claim he brought an action in the federal court for Southern New York, which had jurisdiction because the company is a corporation of that state. It denied liability; and the case was tried by a jury.

The Erie insisted that its duty to Tompkins was no greater than that owed to a trespasser. It contended, among other things, that its duty to Tompkins, and hence its liability, should be determined in accordance with the Pennsylvania law; that under the law of Pennsylvania, as declared by its highest court, persons who use pathways along the railroad right of way—that is, a longitudinal pathway as distinguished from a crossing—are to be deemed trespassers; and that the railroad is not liable for injuries to undiscovered trespassers resulting from its negligence, unless it be wanton or willful. Tompkins denied that any such rule had been established by the decisions of the Pennsylvania courts; and contended that, since there was no statute of the state on the subject, the railroad's duty and liability is to be determined in federal courts as a matter of general law.

The trial judge refused to rule that the applicable law precluded recovery. The jury brought in a verdict of $30,000; and the judgment entered thereon was affirmed by the Circuit Court of Appeals, which held that it was unnecessary to consider whether the law of Pennsylvania was as contended, because the question was one not of local, but of general, law, and that 'upon questions of general law the federal courts are free, in absence of a local statute, to exercise their independent judgment as to what the law is; and it is well settled that the question of the responsibility of a railroad for injuries caused by its servants is one of general law. * * * Where the public has made open and notorious use of a railroad right of way for a long period of time and without objection, the company owes to persons on such permissive pathway a duty of care in the operation of its trains. * * * It is likewise generally recognized law that a jury may find that negligence exists toward a pedestrian using a permissive path on the railroad right of way if he is hit by some object projecting from the side of the train.'

The Erie had contended that application of the Pennsylvania rule was required, among other things, by [28 U.S.C. § 1652], which provides: 'The laws of the several States, except where the Constitution, treaties, or statutes of the United States otherwise require or provide, shall be regarded as rules of decision in trials at common law, in the courts of the United States, in cases where they apply.' Because of the importance of the question whether the federal court was free to disregard the alleged rule of the Pennsylvania common law, we granted certiorari.

[First] doubt [has repeatedly been] expressed as to the correctness of the construction given [28 U.S.C. § 1652 in *Swift v. Tyson*] and as to the soundness of the rule which it introduced. But it was the more recent research of a competent scholar, who examined the original document, which established that the construction given to it by the [*Swift*] Court was erroneous; and that the purpose of the section was merely to make certain that, in all matters except those in which some federal law is controlling, the federal courts exercising jurisdiction in diversity of citizenship cases would apply as their rules of decision the law of the state, unwritten as well as written.

Criticism of the doctrine became widespread after the decision of Black & White Taxicab & Transfer Co. v. Brown & Yellow Taxicab & Transfer Co. There, Brown &Yellow, a Kentucky corporation owned by Kentuckians, and the Louisville & Nashville Railroad, also a Kentucky corporation, wished that the former should have the exclusive privilege of soliciting passenger and baggage transportation at the Bowling Green, Ky., Railroad station; and that the Black & White, a competing Kentucky corporation, should be prevented from interfering with that privilege. Knowing that such a contract would be void under the common law of Kentucky, it was arranged that the Brown & Yellow reincorporate under the law of Tennessee, and that the contract with the railroad should be executed there. The suit was then brought by the Tennessee corporation in the federal court for Western Kentucky to enjoin competition by the Black & White; an injunction issued by the District Court was sustained by the Court of Appeals; and this Court, citing many decisions in which the doctrine of Swift & Tyson had been applied, affirmed the decree.

Second. Experience in applying the doctrine of *Swift v. Tyson*, had revealed its defects, political and social; and the benefits expected to flow from the rule did not accrue. Persistence of state courts in their own opinions on questions of common law prevented uniformity; and the impossibility of discovering a satisfactory line of demarcation between the province of general law and that of local law developed a new well of uncertainties.

On the other hand, the mischievous results of the doctrine had become apparent. Diversity of citizenship jurisdiction was conferred in order to prevent apprehended discrimination in state courts against those not citizens of the state. *Swift v. Tyson* introduced grave discrimination by noncitizens against citizens. It made rights enjoyed under the unwritten 'general law' vary according to whether enforcement was sought in the state or in the federal court; and the privilege of selecting the court in which the right should be determined was conferred upon the noncitizen. Thus, the doctrine rendered impossible equal protection of the law. In attempting to promote uniformity of law throughout the United States, the doctrine had prevented uniformity in the administration of the law of the state.

The discrimination resulting became in practice far-reaching. This resulted in part from the broad province accorded to the so-called 'general law' as to which federal courts exercised an independent judgment. In addition to questions of purely commercial law, 'general law' was held to include the obligations under contracts entered into and to be performed within the state, the extent to which a carrier operating within a state may stipulate for exemption from liability for his own negligence or that of his employee; the liability for torts committed within the state upon persons resident or property located there, even where the question of liability depended upon the scope of a property right conferred by the state; and the right to exemplary or punitive damages. Furthermore, state decisions construing local deeds, mineral conveyances, and even devises of real estate, were disregarded.

In part the discrimination resulted from the wide range of persons held entitled to avail themselves of the federal rule by resort to the diversity of citizenship jurisdiction. Through this jurisdiction individual citizens willing to remove from their own state and become citizens of another might avail themselves of the federal rule. And, without even change of residence, a corporate citizen of the state could avail itself of the federal rule by reincorporating under the laws of another state, as was done in the *Taxicab* Case.

The injustice and confusion incident to the doctrine of *Swift v. Tyson* have been repeatedly urged as reasons for abolishing or limiting diversity of citizenship jurisdiction. Other legislative relief has been proposed. If only a question of statutory construction were involved, we should not be prepared to abandon a doctrine so widely applied throughout nearly a century. But the unconstitutionality of the course pursued has now been made clear and compels us to do so.

Third. Except in matters governed by the Federal Constitution or by acts of Congress, the law to be applied in any case is the law of the state. And whether the law of the state shall be declared by its Legislature in a statute or by its highest court in a decision is not a matter of federal concern. There is no federal general common law. Congress has no power to declare substantive rules of common law applicable in a state whether they be local in their nature or 'general,' be they commercial law or a part of the law of torts. And no clause in the Constitution purports to confer such a power upon the federal courts. As stated by Mr. Justice Field when protesting in *Baltimore & Ohio R.R. Co. v. Baugh*, against ignoring the Ohio common law of fellow-servant liability: I am aware that what has been termed the general law of the country—which is often little less than what the judge advancing the doctrine thinks at the time should be the general law on a particular subject—has been often advanced in judicial opinions of this court to control a conflicting law of a state. I admit that learned judges have fallen into the habit of repeating this doctrine as a convenient mode of brushing aside the law of a state in conflict with their views. And I confess that, moved and governed by the authority of the great names of those judges, I have, myself, in many instances, unhesitatingly and confidently, but I think now erroneously, repeated the same doctrine. But, notwithstanding the great names which may be cited in favor of the doctrine, and notwithstanding the frequency with which the doctrine has been reiterated, there stands, as a perpetual protest against its repetition, the constitution of the United States, which recognizes and preserves the autonomy and independence of the states,—independence in their legislative and independence in their judicial departments. Supervision over either the legislative or the judicial action of the states is in no case permissible except as to matters by the constitution specifically authorized or delegated to the United States. Any interference with either, except as thus permitted, is an invasion of the authority of the state, and, to that extent, a denial of its independence.'

The fallacy underlying the rule declared in *Swift v. Tyson* is made clear by Mr. Justice Holmes. The doctrine rests upon the assumption that there is 'a transcendental body of law outside of any particular State but obligatory within it unless and until changed by statute,' that federal courts have the power to use their judgment as to what the rules of common law are; and that in the federal courts 'the parties are entitled to an independent judgment on matters of general law':

> 'But law in the sense in which courts speak of it today does not exist without some definite authority behind it. The common law so far as it is enforced in a State, whether called common law or not, is not the common law generally but the law of that State existing by the authority of that State without regard to what it may have been in England or anywhere else. * * *

> 'The authority and only authority is the State, and if that be so, the voice adopted by the State as its own (whether it be of its Legislature or of its Supreme Court) should utter the last word.'

Thus, the doctrine of *Swift v. Tyson* is, as Mr. Justice Holmes said, 'an unconstitutional assumption of powers by the Courts of the United States which no lapse of time or respectable array of opinion should make us hesitate to correct.' In disapproving that doctrine we do not hold unconstitutional 28 U.S.C. § 1652 or any other act of Congress. We merely declare that in applying the doctrine this Court and the lower courts have invaded rights which in our opinion are reserved by the Constitution to the several states.

Fourth. The defendant contended that by the common law of Pennsylvania as declared by its highest court [is that] the only duty owed to the plaintiff was to refrain from willful or wanton injury. The plaintiff denied that such is the Pennsylvania law. In support of their respective contentions the parties discussed and cited many decisions of the Supreme Court of the state. The Circuit Court of Appeals ruled that the question of liability is one of general law; and on that ground declined to decide the issue of state law. As we hold this was error, the judgment is reversed, and the case remanded to it for further proceedings in conformity with our opinion.

Reversed.

MR. JUSTICE REED (concurring in part).

The line between procedural and substantive law is hazy, but no one doubts federal power over procedure.

DIRECTED READING QUESTIONS

5. What state is the plaintiff a citizen of?

6. What state is the railroad defendant a citizen of?

7. How was the plaintiff harmed, and where did the harm occur?

8. What is the cause of action? Is it a federal or state law cause of action?

9. What is the basis of federal court jurisdiction?

10. What law does the railroad want the federal court to use in determining the duty that the railroad owed to the plaintiff? How does the railroad argue this law should apply

given *Swift v. Tyson*'s interpretation of the "laws of the several states" in 28 U.S.C. § 1652?

11. What law does the plaintiff want the federal court to use in determining the duty that the railroad owed to the plaintiff? How does the plaintiff argue this law should apply given *Swift v. Tyson*'s interpretation of the "laws of the several states" in 28 U.S.C. § 1652?

12. How do you know that the trial court did not apply Pennsylvania law?

13. Did the appellate court apply the *Swift* doctrine, and how do you know?

14. The Supreme Court uses a case involving two taxicab companies in Kentucky and/or Tennessee to illustrate the problems caused by the *Swift* doctrine, which allowed federal courts to ignore the common law of the state when the federal court was adjudicating state law causes of action pursuant to the federal court's diversity jurisdiction. How does this case illustrate the problems caused by the *Swift* doctrine?

15. Explain how *Swift* (1) created forum shopping and (2) rendered equal protection of the law impossible, and how these effects are inconsistent with the general principles of diversity jurisdiction.

16. What does the Supreme Court identify as the main goal of *Swift*, and what prevented that goal from being realized?

17. Explain the relationship of federalism to the Supreme Court's statement that "[t]here is no federal general common law."

18. How does legal positivism factor into the Supreme Court's decision about federal general common law?

19. Justice Reed's concurrence mentions that it is difficult to distinguish between substantive and procedural law. Why would Justice Reed mention this, even though the *Erie* majority decision is devoid of any reference to substance or procedure? In what way does this frame the *Erie* doctrine as a tension between the Rules Enabling Act and the Rules of Decision Act?

II. OUTCOME DETERMINATIVENESS AND CONSTITUTIONAL IMPEDIMENTS TO ACHIEVING *ERIE*'S TWIN AIMS

DIRECTED READING QUESTIONS

20. What were the twin aims of *Erie* previously discussed?

GUARANTY TRUST CO. OF N.Y. v. YORK (1945)

Supreme Court of the United States
326 U.S. 99

MR. JUSTICE FRANKFURTER delivered the opinion of the Court.

In *Russell v. Todd*, we had 'no occasion to consider the extent to which federal courts, in the exercise of the authority conferred upon them by Congress to administer equitable remedies, are bound to follow state statutes and decisions affecting those remedies.' The question thus carefully left open in *Russell v. Todd* is now before us. It arises under the following circumstances.

In May 1930, Van Sweringen Corporation issued notes to the amount of $30,000,000. Under an indenture of the same date, petitioner, Guaranty Trust Co., was named trustee with power and obligations to enforce the rights of the noteholders in the assets of the Corporation and of the Van Sweringen brothers. In October 1930, petitioner, with other banks, made large advances to companies affiliated with the Corporation and wholly controlled by the Van Sweringens. In October, 1931, when it was apparent that the Corporation could not meet its obligations, Guaranty co-operated in a plan for the purchase of the outstanding notes on the basis of cash for 50% of the face value of the notes and twenty shares of Van Sweringen Corporation's stock for each $1,000 note. This exchange offer remained open until December 15, 1931.

Respondent York received $6,000 of the notes as a gift in 1934, her donor not having accepted the offer of exchange. In April 1940, three accepting noteholders began suit against petitioner, charging fraud and misrepresentation. Respondent's application to intervene in that suit was denied and summary judgment in favor of Guaranty was affirmed. After [that dismissal], respondent, on January 22, 1942, began the present proceedings.

The suit, instituted as a class action on behalf of non-accepting noteholders and brought in a federal court solely because of diversity of citizenship, is based on an alleged breach of trust by Guaranty in that it failed to protect the interests of the noteholders in assenting to the exchange offer and failed to disclose its self-interest when sponsoring the offer. Petitioner moved for summary judgment, which was granted [based on the 1940] case. On appeal, the Circuit Court of Appeals, one Judge dissenting, found that the [1940] decision did not foreclose this suit, and held that in a suit brought on the equity side of a federal district court that court is not required to apply the State statute of limitations that would govern like suits in the courts of a State where the federal court is sitting even though the exclusive basis of federal jurisdiction is diversity of citizenship. The importance of the question for the disposition of litigation in the federal courts led us to bring the case here.

In view of the basis of the decision below, it is not for us to consider whether the New York statute would actually bar this suit were it brought in a State court. Our only concern is with the holding that the federal courts in a suit like this are not bound by local law.

We put to one side the considerations relevant in disposing of questions that arise when a federal court is adjudicating a claim based on a federal law. Our problem only touches transactions for which rights and obligations are created by one of the States, and for the assertion of which, in case of diversity of the citizenship of the parties, Congress has made a federal court another available forum.

Our starting point must be the policy of federal jurisdiction which *Erie R. Co. v. Tompkins* embodies. In overruling *Swift v. Tyson*, *Erie R. Co. v. Tompkins* did not merely overrule a venerable case. It overruled a particular way of looking at law which dominated the judicial process long after its inadequacies had been laid bare.

Law was conceived as a 'brooding omnipresence' of Reason, of which decisions were merely evidence and not themselves the controlling formulations. Accordingly, federal courts deemed themselves free to ascertain what Reason, and therefore Law, required wholly independent of authoritatively declared State law, even in cases where a legal right as the basis for relief was created by State authority and could not be created by federal authority and the case got into a federal court merely because it was 'between Citizens of different States' under Art. III, s of the Constitution of the United States.

This impulse to freedom from the rules that controlled State courts regarding State-created rights was so strongly rooted in the prevailing views concerning the nature of law, that the federal courts almost imperceptibly were led to mutilating construction even of the explicit command given to them by Congress to apply State law in cases purporting to enforce the law of a State. See [28 U.S.C. § 1652]. The matter was fairly summarized by the statement that 'During the period when *Swift v. Tyson* (1842–1938) ruled the decisions of the federal courts, its theory of their freedom in matters of general law from the authority of state courts pervaded opinions of this Court involving even state statutes or local law.

In relation to the problem now here, the real significance of *Swift v. Tyson* lies in the fact that it did not enunciate novel doctrine. Nor was it restricted to its particular situation. It summed up prior attitudes and expressions in cases that had come before this Court and lower federal courts for at least thirty years, at law as well as in equity. The short of it is that the doctrine was congenial to the jurisprudential climate of the time. Once established, judicial momentum kept it going. Since it was conceived that there was 'a transcendental body of law outside of any particular State but obligatory within it unless and until changed by statute', State court decisions were not 'the law' but merely someone's opinion—to be sure an opinion to be respected—concerning the content of this all-pervading law. Not unnaturally, the federal courts assumed power to find for themselves the content of such a body of law. The notion was stimulated by the attractive vision of a uniform body of federal law. To such sentiments for uniformity of decision and freedom from diversity in State law the federal courts gave currency, particularly in cases where equitable remedies were sought, because equitable doctrines are so often cast in terms of universal applicability when close analysis of the source of legal enforceability is not demanded.

In exercising their jurisdiction on the ground of diversity of citizenship, the federal courts, in the long course of their history, have not differentiated in their regard for State law between actions at law and suits in equity. Although [28 U.S.C. § 1652] directed that the 'laws of the several States * * * shall be regarded as rules of decision in trials of common law * * *', this was deemed, consistently for over a hundred years, to be merely declaratory of what would in any event have governed the federal courts and therefore was equally applicable to equity suits. Indeed, it may fairly be said that the federal courts gave greater respect to State-created 'substantive rights' in equity than they gave them on the law side, because rights at law were usually declared by State courts and as such increasingly flouted by extension of the doctrine of *Swift v. Tyson*, while rights in equity were frequently defined by legislative enactment and as such known and respected by the federal courts.

* * *

Whatever contradiction or confusion may be produced by a medley of judicial phrases severed from their environment, the body of adjudications concerning equitable relief in diversity cases leaves no doubt that the federal courts enforced State-created substantive rights if the mode of proceeding and remedy were consonant with the traditional body of equitable remedies, practice and procedure, and in so doing they were enforcing rights created by the States and not arising under any inherent or statutory federal law.

Inevitably, therefore, the principle of *Erie R. Co. v. Tompkins*, an action at law, was promptly applied to a suit in equity.

And so this case reduces itself to the narrow question whether, when no recovery could be had in a State court because the action is barred by the statute of limitations, a federal court in equity can take cognizance of the suit because there is diversity of citizenship between the parties. Is the outlawry, according to State law, of a claim created by the States a matter of 'substantive rights' to be respected by a federal court of equity when that court's jurisdiction is dependent on the fact that there is a State-created right, or is such statute of 'a mere remedial character,' which a federal court may disregard?

Matters of 'substance' and matters of 'procedure' are much talked about in the books as though they defined a great divide cutting across the whole domain of law. But, of course, 'substance' and 'procedure' are the same key-words to very different problems. Neither 'substance' nor 'procedure' represents the same invariants. Each implies different variables depending upon the particular problem for which it is used. And the different problems are only distantly related at best, for the terms are in common use in connection with situations turning on such different considerations as those that are relevant to questions pertaining to ex post facto legislation, the impairment of the obligations of contract, the enforcement of federal rights in the State courts and the multitudinous phases of the conflict of laws.

Here we are dealing with a right to recover derived not from the United States but from one of the States. When, because the plaintiff happens to be a nonresident, such a right is enforceable in a federal as well as in a State court, the forms and mode of enforcing the right may at times, naturally enough, vary because the two judicial systems are not identic. But since a federal court adjudicating a state-created right solely because of the diversity of citizenship of the parties is for that purpose, in effect, only another court of the State, it cannot afford recovery if the right to recover is made unavailable by the State nor can it substantially affect the enforcement of the right as given by the State.

And so the question is not whether a statute of limitations is deemed a matter of 'procedure' in some sense. The question is whether such a statute concerns merely the manner and the means by which a right to recover, as recognized by the State, is enforced, or whether such statutory limitation is a matter of substance in the aspect that alone is relevant to our problem, namely, does it significantly affect the result of a litigation for a federal court to disregard a law of a State that would be controlling in an action upon the same claim by the same parties in a State court?

It is therefore immaterial whether statutes of limitation are characterized either as 'substantive' or 'procedural' in State court opinions in any use of those terms unrelated to the specific issue before us. *Erie R. Co. v. Tompkins* was not an endeavor to formulate scientific legal terminology. It expressed a policy that touches vitally the proper distribution of judicial power between State and federal courts. In essence, the intent of that decision was to insure that, in all cases where a federal court is exercising jurisdiction solely because of the diversity of citizenship of the parties, the outcome of the litigation in the federal court should be substantially the same, so far as legal rules determine the outcome of a litigation, as it would be if tried in a State court. The nub of the policy that underlies *Erie R. Co. v. Tompkins* is that for the same transaction the accident of a suit by a non-resident litigant in a federal court instead of in a State court a block away, should not lead to a substantially different result. And so, putting to one side abstractions regarding' substance' and 'procedure', we have held that in diversity cases the federal courts must follow the law of the State as to burden of proof, as to conflict of laws, as to contributory negligence. *Erie R. Co. v. Tompkins* has been applied with an eye alert to essentials in avoiding disregard of State law in diversity cases in the federal courts. A policy so important to our federalism must be kept free from entanglements with analytical or terminological niceties.

Plainly enough, a statute that would completely bar recovery in a suit if brought in a State court bears on a State created right vitally and not merely formally or negligibly. As to consequences that so intimately affect recovery or non-recovery a federal court in a diversity case should follow State law. The fact that under New York law a statute of limitations might be lengthened or shortened, that a security may be foreclosed though the debt be barred, that a barred debt may be used as a set-off, are all matters of local law properly to be respected by federal courts sitting in New York when their incidence comes into play there. Such particular rules of local law, however, do not in the slightest change the crucial consideration that if a plea of the statute of limitations would bar recovery in a State court, a federal court ought not to afford recovery.

Prior to *Erie R. Co. v. Tompkins* it was not necessary, as we have indicated, to make the critical analysis required by the doctrine of that case of the nature of jurisdiction of the federal courts in diversity cases. But even before *Erie R. Co. v. Tompkins*, federal courts relied on statutes of limitations of the States in which they sat. In suits at law State limitations statutes were held to be 'rules of decision' within [28 U.S.C. § 1652] and as such applied in 'trials at common law'. While there was talk of freedom of equity from such State statutes of limitations, the cases generally refused recovery where suit was barred in a like situation in the State courts, even if only by way of analogy.

To make an exception to *Erie R. Co. v. Tompkins* on the equity side of a federal court is to reject the considerations of policy which, after long travail, led to that decision. Judge Augustus N. Hand thus summarized below the fatal objection to such inroad upon *Erie R. Co. v. Tompkins*: 'In my opinion it would be a mischievous practice to disregard state statutes of limitation whenever federal courts think that the result of adopting them may be inequitable. Such procedure would promote the choice of United States rather than of state courts in order to gain the advantage of different laws. The main foundation for the criticism of *Swift v. Tyson* was that a litigant in cases where federal jurisdiction is based only on diverse citizenship may obtain a more favorable decision by suing in the United States courts.'

Diversity jurisdiction is founded on assurance to non-resident litigants of courts free from susceptibility to potential local bias. The Framers of the Constitution, according to Marshall, entertained 'apprehensions' lest distant suitors be subjected to local bias in

State courts, or, at least, viewed with 'indulgence the possible fears and apprehensions' of such suitors. And so Congress afforded out-of-State litigants another tribunal, not another body of law. The operation of a double system of conflicting laws in the same State is plainly hostile to the reign of law. Certainly, the fortuitous circumstance of residence out of a State of one of the parties to a litigation ought not to give rise to a discrimination against others equally concerned but locally resident. The source of substantive rights enforced by a federal court under diversity jurisdiction, it cannot be said too often, is the law of the States. Whenever that law is authoritatively declared by a State, whether its voice be the legislature or its highest court, such law ought to govern in litigation founded on that law, whether the forum of application is a State or a federal court and whether the remedies be sought at law or may be had in equity.

Dicta may be cited characterizing equity as an independent body of law. To the extent that we have indicated, it is. But insofar as these general observations go beyond that, they merely reflect notions that have been replaced by a sharper analysis of what federal courts do when they enforce rights that have no federal origin. And so, before the true source of law that is applied by the federal courts under diversity jurisdiction was fully explored, some things were said that would not now be said. But nothing that was decided, unless it be the Kirby case, needs to be rejected.

The judgment is reversed and the case is remanded for proceedings not inconsistent with this opinion.

DIRECTED READING QUESTIONS

21. What is the sole basis of subject matter jurisdiction?

22. What does *Guaranty Trust* remind us about the relevance of the *Erie* doctrine when a federal court is adjudicating a claim based on federal law?

23. Explain the *Guaranty Trust* court's statement that *Erie* overruled more than a case, rather, it overruled an entire jurisprudential approach.

24. Does *Guaranty Trust* "remind" you of Federal Rule of Civil Procedure 2?

25. Is there any language in *Guaranty Trust*, which if read literally, suggests that a federal court should be a "mirror" of the state court when it is adjudicating claims with a state law origin?

26. What were the twin aims of the *Erie* opinion? How is the viewpoint that a federal court should be a "mirror" of the state court when it is adjudicating claims with a state law origin consistent with the twin aims of the *Erie* opinion?

27. Why is *Guaranty Trust*, decided only 8 years after the *Erie* opinion, discussing the *Erie* opinion as though it created a substantive/procedural dichotomy, even though the majority opinion in *Erie* makes no reference to substantive or procedural law?

28. Explain, in your own words, the meaning of the language in *Guaranty Trust* which describes diversity jurisdiction as Congress, affording "out-of-State litigants another tribunal, not another body of law."

29. Does *Guaranty Trust* reaffirm that consistent outcomes in adjudicating state law claims, regardless of whether the adjudication is in state or federal court, is a mandate derived from the U.S. Constitution?

30. What is the outcome determinative test that the *Guaranty Trust* opinion announces?

31. Before *Guaranty Trust*, in deciding whether state or federal law should apply when a federal court was adjudicating a state law claim, the general rule was that the law governing procedural matters would be federal and the substantive law to be applied in such a case would be state law. How does the outcome determinative test operate in relation to the substantive/procedural dichotomy?

BYRD V. BLUE RIDGE RURAL ELECTRIC COOPERATIVE (1958)
Supreme Court of the United States
356 U.S. 525

MR. JUSTICE BRENNAN delivered the opinion of the Court.

This case was brought in the District Court for the Western District of South Carolina. Jurisdiction was based on diversity of citizenship. The [plaintiff][/]petitioner, a resident of North Carolina, sued [defendant/]respondent, a South Carolina corporation, for damages for injuries allegedly caused by the respondent's negligence. He had judgment on a jury verdict. The Court of Appeals for the Fourth Circuit reversed and directed the entry of judgment for the respondent. We granted certiorari, and subsequently ordered reargument.

[The plaintiff was a construction worker injured while building powerlines for the defendant corporation. During the jury trial the contractor raised an affirmative defense that under S. Carolina Law the plaintiff was a statutory employee. This meant that he had to seek worker's compensation remedies and could maintain the current suit.

The District Court applied the test it thought South Carolina law required ("Test 1") to determine whether he was or wasn't a statutory employee under South Carolina Law. The District Court concluded he was not a statutory employee and struck the defendant's affirmative defense and the plaintiff prevailed and obtained a jury verdict in his favor. The Defendant appealed the judgment entered on the verdict.

The Appellate Court concluded that Test 1 was not the correct test to determine whether he was a statutory employee under South Carolina law. The Appellate Court then applied what it concluded thought was the correct test under South Carolina law was to determine statutory employee status. The test applied by the Appellate Court ("Test 2") was different than Test 1 and under this test the Appellate Court concluded that the plaintiff was a statutory employee. The Appellate Court reversed the District Court and further entered judgment as a matter of law for the Defendant rather than remanding the issue of Statutory employment status to the District Court.]

While the matter is not adverted to in the [Appellate] Court's opinion, implicit in the direction of verdict is the holding that the petitioner, although having no occasion to do so under the District Court's erroneous use of Test 1, was not entitled to an opportunity to meet the respondent's case under Test 2 . . . . '(T)he direction to enter judgment for the defendant instead of a direction to grant a new trial denies plaintiff his right to introduce evidence in contradiction to that of the defendant on the issue of defendant's affirmative defense, a right which he would have exercised if the District Judge had ruled adversely to him on his motion to dismiss, and thus deprives him of his constitutional right to a jury trial on a factual issue.'

* * *

A question is also presented as to whether on remand the factual issue is to be decided by the judge or by the jury. The respondent argues on the basis of the decision of the Supreme Court of South Carolina in *Adams v. Davison-Paxon Co.*, that the issue of immunity should be decided by the judge and not by the jury. [In that case] the South Carolina Supreme Court [held] that it was for the judge and not the jury to decide on the evidence whether [the statutory employee defense applied]. The court rested its holding on decisions, [ ] involving judicial review of the Industrial Commission and said:

> 'Thus the trial court should have in this case resolved the conflicts in the evidence and determined the fact of whether (the independent contractor) was performing a part of the 'trade, business or occupation' of the department store-appellant and, therefore, whether (the employee's) remedy is exclusively under the Workmen's Compensation Law.'

The respondent argues that this state-court decision governs the present diversity case and 'divests the jury of its normal function' to decide the disputed fact question of the respondent's immunity [ ]. This is to contend that the federal court is bound under *Erie R. Co. v. Tompkins*, to follow the state court's holding to secure uniform enforcement of the immunity created by the State.

First. It was decided in *Erie R. Co. v. Tompkins* that the federal courts in diversity cases must respect the definition of state-created rights and obligations by the state courts. We must, therefore, first examine the rule in *Adams v. Davison-Paxon Co.* to determine whether it is bound up with these rights and obligations in such a way that its application in the federal court is required.

The Workmen's Compensation Act is administered in South Carolina by its Industrial Commission. The South Carolina courts hold that, on judicial review of actions of the Commission, the question whether the claim of an injured workman is within the Commission's jurisdiction is a matter of law for decision by the court, which makes its own findings of fact relating to that jurisdiction. The South Carolina Supreme Court states no reasons in *Adams v. Davison-Paxon Co.* why, although the jury decides all other factual issues raised by the cause of action and defenses, the jury is displaced as to the factual issue raised by the affirmative defense. The decisions cited to support the holding are those [ ] which are concerned solely with defining the scope and method of judicial review of the Industrial Commission. A State may, of course, distribute the functions of its judicial machinery as it sees fit. The decisions relied upon, however, furnish no reason for selecting the judge rather than the jury to decide this single affirmative defense in the negligence action. [ ] The conclusion is inescapable that the *Adams* holding is grounded in the practical consideration that the question had theretofore come before the South Carolina courts from the Industrial Commission and the courts had become accustomed to deciding the factual issue of immunity without the aid of juries. We find nothing to suggest that this rule was announced as an integral part of the special relationship created by the statute. Thus, the requirement appears to be merely a form and mode of enforcing the immunity, *Guaranty Trust Co. of New York v. York*, and not a rule intended to be bound up with the definition of the rights and obligations of the parties.

* * *

Second. But cases following *Erie* have evinced a broader policy to the effect that the federal courts should conform as near as may be—in the absence of other considerations—to state rules even of form and mode where the state rules may bear substantially on the question whether the litigation would come out one way in the federal court and another way in the state court if the federal court failed to apply a particular local rule. *E.g., Guaranty Trust Co. of New York v. York* .... Concededly the nature of the tribunal which tries issues may be important in the enforcement of the parcel of rights making up a cause of action or defense [ ] and bear significantly upon achievement of uniform enforcement of the right. It may well be that in the instant personal-injury case the outcome would be substantially affected by whether the issue of immunity is decided by a judge or a jury. Therefore, were 'outcome' the only consideration, a strong case might appear for saying that the federal court should follow the state practice.

But there are affirmative countervailing considerations at work here. The federal system is an independent system for administering justice to litigants who properly invoke its jurisdiction. An essential characteristic of that system is the manner in which, in civil common-law actions, it distributes trial functions between judge and jury and, under the influence—if not the command—of the Seventh Amendment, assigns the decisions of disputed questions of fact to the jury. The policy of uniform enforcement of state-created rights and obligations, *see, e.g., Guaranty Trust Co. of New York v. York, supra,* cannot in every case exact compliance with a state rule—not bound up with rights and obligations—which disrupts the federal system of allocating functions between judge and jury. Thus the inquiry here is whether the federal policy favoring jury decisions of disputed fact questions should yield to the state rule in the interest of furthering the objective that the litigation should not come out one way in the federal court and another way in the state court.

We think that in the circumstances of this case the federal court should not follow the state rule. It cannot be gainsaid that there is a strong federal policy against allowing state rules to disrupt the judge-jury relationship in the federal courts. In *Herron v. Southern Pacific Co., supra,* the trial judge in a personal-injury negligence action brought in the District Court for Arizona on diversity grounds directed a verdict for the defendant when it appeared as a matter of law that the plaintiff was guilty of contributory negligence. The federal judge refused to be bound by a provision of the Arizona Constitution which made the jury the sole arbiter of the question of contributory negligence. This Court sustained the action of the trial judge, holding that 'state laws cannot alter the essential character or function of a federal court' because that function 'is not in any sense a local matter, and state statutes which would interfere with the appropriate performance of that function are not binding upon the federal court under either the Conformity Act or the 'Rules of Decision' Act.' Perhaps even more clearly in light of the influence of the Seventh Amendment, the function assigned to the jury 'is an essential factor in the process for which the Federal Constitution provides.' Concededly the *Herron* case was decided before *Erie R. Co. v. Tompkins,* but even when *Swift v. Tyson* was governing law and allowed federal courts sitting in diversity cases to disregard state decisional law, it was never thought that state statutes or constitutions were similarly to be disregarded. Yet Herron held that state statutes and constitutional provisions could not disrupt or alter the essential character or function of a federal court.

* * *

Reversed and remanded.

DIRECTED READING QUESTIONS

32. What precisely is the effect of applying federal law to the dispute in *Byrd*?

33. What precisely is the effect of applying state law to the dispute in *Byrd*?

34. Does the Supreme Court analyze the case as if these different effects are outcome determinative?

35. What precisely is the source of the federal law in *Byrd*?

36. In the *Byrd* opinion, what precisely is the source of the state law? Do you think that if the source of the state law was the state constitution or a state legislative enactment, it would have made any difference to the result reached in *Byrd*?

37. How does the analysis and holding in *Byrd* as demonstrate that federalism is not an absolute principle?

38. Create a hypothetical unrelated to law, illustrating the *Byrd* opinion as a limit rather than a contradiction of the outcome determinative test from *Guaranty Trust*.

39. Combine all the cases we have covered so far and come up with a test for determining which law to apply when a federal court is adjudicating a state law claim.

III. CONFLICT BETWEEN STATE LAW AND THE FEDERAL RULES OF CIVIL PROCEDURE

HANNA V. PLUMER (1965)
Supreme Court of the United States
380 U.S. 460

MR. CHIEF JUSTICE WARREN delivered the opinion of the Court.

The question to be decided is whether, in a civil action where the jurisdiction of the United States district court is based upon diversity of citizenship between the parties, service of process shall be made in the manner prescribed by state law or that set forth in Rule 4(d)(1) of the Federal Rules of Civil Procedure.

On February 6, 1963, petitioner, a citizen of Ohio, filed her complaint in the District Court for the District of Massachusetts, claiming damages in excess of $10,000 for personal injuries resulting from an automobile accident in South Carolina, allegedly caused by the negligence of one Louise Plumer Osgood, a Massachusetts citizen deceased at the time of the filing of the complaint. Respondent, Mrs. Osgood's executor and also a Massachusetts citizen, was named as defendant. On February 8, service was made by leaving copies of the summons and the complaint with respondent's wife at his residence, concededly in compliance with Rule 4(d)(1), which provides:

'The summons and complaint shall be served together. The plaintiff shall furnish the person making service with such copies as are necessary. Service shall be made as follows:

> '(1) Upon an individual other than an infant or an incompetent person, by delivering a copy of the summons and of the complaint to him personally or by leaving copies thereof at his dwelling house or usual place of abode with some person of suitable age and discretion then residing therein * * *.'

Respondent filed his answer on February 26, alleging, inter alia, that the action could not be maintained because it had been brought 'contrary to and in violation of the provisions of Massachusetts General Laws Chapter 197, § 9.' That section provides:

> 'Except as provided in this chapter, an executor or administrator shall not be held to answer to an action by a creditor of the deceased which is not commenced within one year from the time of his giving bond for the performance of his trust, or to such an action which is commenced within said year unless before the expiration thereof the writ in such action has been served by delivery in hand upon such executor or administrator or service thereof accepted by him or a notice stating the name of the estate, the name and address of the creditor, the amount of the claim and the court in which the action has been brought has been filed in the proper registry of probate. * * *'

On October 17, 1963, the District Court granted respondent's motion for summary judgment, citing *Ragan v. Merchants Transfer & Warehouse Co.*, and *Guaranty Trust Co. of New York v. York*, in support of its conclusion that the adequacy of the service was to be measured by § 9, with which, the court held, petitioner had not complied. On appeal, petitioner admitted noncompliance with § 9, but argued that Rule 4(d)(1) defines the method by which service of process is to be effected in diversity actions. The Court of Appeals for the First Circuit, finding that '(r)elatively recent amendments (to § 9) evince a clear legislative purpose to require personal notification within the year,' concluded that the conflict of state and federal rules was over 'a substantive rather than a procedural matter,' and unanimously affirmed. Because of the threat to the goal of uniformity of federal procedure posed by the decision below, we granted certiorari.

We conclude that the adoption of Rule 4(d)(1), designed to control service of process in diversity actions, neither exceeded the congressional mandate embodied in the Rules Enabling Act nor transgressed constitutional bounds, and that the Rule is therefore the standard against which the District Court should have measured the adequacy of the service. Accordingly, we reverse the decision of the Court of Appeals.

The Rules Enabling Act, 28 U.S.C. § 2072 provides, in pertinent part:

> 'The Supreme Court shall have the power to prescribe, by general rules, the forms of process, writs, pleadings, and motions, and the practice and procedure of the district courts of the United States in civil actions.

> 'Such rules shall not abridge, enlarge or modify any substantive right and shall preserve the right of trial by jury * * *.'

Under the cases construing the scope of the Enabling Act, Rule 4(d)(1) clearly passes muster. Prescribing the manner in which a defendant is to be notified that a suit has been instituted against him, it relates to the 'practice and procedure of the district courts.'

'The test must be whether a rule really regulates procedure,—the judicial process for enforcing rights and duties recognized by substantive law and for justly administering remedy and redress for disregard or infraction of them.'

* * *

Thus were there no conflicting state procedure, Rule 4(d)(1) would clearly control. However, respondent, focusing on the contrary Massachusetts rule, calls to the Court's attention another line of cases, a line which—like the Federal Rules—had its birth in 1938. *Erie R. Co. v. Tompkins*, overruling *Swift v. Tyson*, held that federal courts sitting in diversity cases, when deciding questions of 'substantive' law, are bound by state court decisions as well as state statutes. The broad command of *Erie* was therefore identical to that of the Enabling Act: federal courts are to apply state substantive law and federal procedural law. However, as subsequent cases sharpened the distinction between substance and procedure, the line of cases following Erie diverged markedly from the line construing the Enabling Act. *Guaranty Trust Co. of New York v. York*, made it clear that *Erie*-type problems were not to be solved by reference to any traditional or common-sense substance-procedure distinction:

'And so the question is not whether a statute of limitations is deemed a matter of 'procedure' in some sense. The question is * * * does it significantly affect the result of a litigation for a federal court to disregard a law of a State that would be controlling in an action upon the same claim by the same parties in a State court?

Respondent, by placing primary reliance on *York* and *Ragan*, suggests that the *Erie* doctrine acts as a check on the Federal Rules of Civil Procedure, that despite the clear command of Rule 4(d)(1), Erie and its progeny demand the application of the Massachusetts rule. Reduced to essentials, the argument is: (1) Erie, as refined in *York*, demands that federal courts apply state law whenever application of federal law in its stead will alter the outcome of the case. (2) In this case, a determination that the Massachusetts service requirements obtain will result in immediate victory for respondent. If, on the other hand, it should be held that Rule 4(d)(1) is applicable, the litigation will continue, with possible victory for petitioner. (3) Therefore, *Erie* demands application of the Massachusetts rule. The syllogism possesses an appealing simplicity but is for several reasons invalid.

In the first place, it is doubtful that, even if there were no Federal Rule making it clear that in-hand service is not required in diversity actions, the *Erie* rule would have obligated the District Court to follow the Massachusetts procedure. 'Outcome-determination' analysis was never intended to serve as a talisman. *Byrd v. Blue Ridge Rural Elec. Cooperative*. Indeed, the message of *York* itself is that choices between state and federal law are to be made not by application of any automatic, 'litmus paper' criterion, but rather by reference to the policies underlying the *Erie* rule. *Guaranty Trust Co. of New York v. York*.

The *Erie* rule is rooted in part in a realization that it would be unfair for the character of result of a litigation materially to differ because the suit had been brought in a federal court.

'Diversity of citizenship jurisdiction was conferred in order to prevent apprehended discrimination in state courts against those not citizens of the state. *Swift v. Tyson* introduced grave discrimination by noncitizens against citizens. It made rights enjoyed under the unwritten 'general law' vary according to whether enforcement was sought in the state or in the federal court; and the privilege of selecting the court in which the right should be determined was conferred upon the noncitizen. Thus, the doctrine rendered impossible equal protection of the law.' *Erie R. Co. v. Tompkins.*

The decision was also in part a reaction to the practice of 'forum-shopping' which had grown up in response to the rule of *Swift v. Tyson.* That the *York* test was an attempt to effectuate these policies is demonstrated by the fact that the opinion framed the inquiry in terms of 'substantial' variations between state and federal litigation. Not only are nonsubstantial, or trivial, variations not likely to raise the sort of equal protection problems which troubled the Court in Erie; they are also unlikely to influence the choice of a forum. The 'outcome-determination' test therefore cannot be read without reference to the twin aims of the *Erie* rule: discouragement of forum-shopping and avoidance of inequitable administration of the laws.[9]

The difference between the conclusion that the Massachusetts rule is applicable, and the conclusion that it is not, is of course at this point 'outcome-determinative' in the sense that if we hold the state rule to apply, respondent prevails, whereas if we hold that Rule 4(d)(1) governs, the litigation will continue. But in this sense every procedural variation is 'outcome-determinative.' For example, having brought suit in a federal court, a plaintiff cannot then insist on the right to file subsequent pleadings in accord with the time limits applicable in state courts, even though enforcement of the federal timetable will, if he continues to insist that he must meet only the state time limit, result in determination of the controversy against him. So it is here. Though choice of the federal or state rule will at this point have a marked effect upon the outcome of the litigation, the difference between the two rules would be of scant, if any, relevance to the choice of a forum. Petitioner, in choosing her forum, was not presented with a situation where application of the state rule would wholly bar recovery; rather, adherence to the state rule would have resulted only in altering the way in which process was served. Moreover, it is difficult to argue that permitting service of defendant's wife to take the place of inhand service of defendant himself alters the mode of enforcement of state-created rights in a fashion sufficiently 'substantial' to raise the sort of equal protection problems to which the *Erie* opinion alluded.

There is, however, a more fundamental flaw in respondent's syllogism: the incorrect assumption that the rule of *Erie R. Co. v. Tompkins* constitutes the appropriate test of the validity and therefore the applicability of a Federal Rule of Civil Procedure. The *Erie*

---

[9] Erie and its progeny make clear that when a federal court sitting in a diversity case is faced with a question of whether or not to apply state law, the importance of a state rule is indeed relevant, but only in the context of asking whether application of the rule would make so important a difference to the character or result of the litigation that failure to enforce it would unfairly discriminate against citizens of the forum State, or whether application of the rule would have so important an effect upon the fortunes of one or both of the litigants that failure to enforce it would be likely to cause a plaintiff to choose the federal court.

rule has never been invoked to void a Federal Rule. It is true that there have been cases where this Court has held applicable a state rule in the face of an argument that the situation was governed by one of the Federal Rules. But the holding of each such case was not that *Erie* commanded displacement of a Federal Rule by an inconsistent state rule, but rather that the scope of the Federal Rule was not as broad as the losing party urged, and therefore, there being no Federal Rule which covered the point in dispute, Erie commanded the enforcement of state law.

'Respondent contends in the first place that the charge was correct because of the fact that Rule 8(c) of the Rules of Civil Procedure makes contributory negligence an affirmative defense. We do not agree. Rule 8(c) covers only the manner of pleading. The question of the burden of establishing contributory negligence is a question of local law which federal courts in diversity of citizenship cases must apply.

(Here, of course, the clash is unavoidable; Rule 4(d)(1) says—implicitly, but with unmistakable clarity—that inhand service is not required in federal courts.) At the same time, in cases adjudicating the validity of Federal Rules, we have not applied the *York* rule or other refinements of *Erie*, but have to this day continued to decide questions concerning the scope of the Enabling Act and the constitutionality of specific Federal Rules in light of the distinction set forth in *Sibbach*.

Nor has the development of two separate lines of cases been inadvertent. The line between 'substance' and 'procedure' shifts as the legal context changes. 'Each implies different variables depending upon the particular problem for which it is used.' *Guaranty Trust Co. of New York v. York*. It is true that both the Enabling Act and the *Erie* rule say, roughly, that federal courts are to apply state 'substantive' law and federal 'procedural' law, but from that it need not follow that the tests are identical. For they were designed to control very different sorts of decisions. When a situation is covered by one of the Federal Rules, the question facing the court is a far cry from the typical, relatively unguided Erie Choice: the court has been instructed to apply the Federal Rule, and can refuse to do so only if the Advisory Committee, this Court, and Congress erred in their prima facie judgment that the Rule in question transgresses neither the terms of the Enabling Act nor constitutional restrictions.

We are reminded by the *Erie* opinion that neither Congress nor the federal courts can, under the guise of formulating rules of decision for federal courts, fashion rules which are not supported by a grant of federal authority contained in Article I or some other section of the Constitution; in such areas state law must govern because there can be no other law. But the opinion in *Erie*, which involved no Federal Rule and dealt with a question which was 'substantive' in every traditional sense (whether the railroad owed a duty of care to Tompkins as a trespasser or a licensee), surely neither said nor implied that measures like Rule 4(d)(1) are unconstitutional. For the constitutional provision for a federal court system (augmented by the Necessary and Proper Clause) carries with it congressional power to make rules governing the practice and pleading in those courts, which in turn includes a power to regulate matters which, though falling within the uncertain area between substance and procedure, are rationally capable of classification as either. Neither *York* nor the cases following it ever suggested that the rule there laid down for coping with situations where no Federal Rule applies is coextensive with the limitation on Congress to which *Erie* had adverted. Although this Court has never before been confronted with a case where the applicable Federal Rule is in direct collision with the law of the relevant State, courts of appeals faced with such clashes have rightly discerned the implications of our decisions.

'One of the shaping purposes of the Federal Rules is to bring about uniformity in the federal courts by getting away from local rules. This is especially true of matters which relate to the administration of legal proceedings, an area in which federal courts have traditionally exerted strong inherent power, completely aside from the powers Congress expressly conferred in the Rules. The purpose of the *Erie* doctrine, even as extended in *York* and *Ragan*, was never to bottle up federal courts with 'outcome-determinative' and 'integral-relations' stoppers—when there are 'affirmative countervailing (federal) considerations' and when there is a Congressional mandate (the Rules) supported by constitutional authority.'

Erie and its offspring cast no doubt on the long-recognized power of Congress to prescribe housekeeping rules for federal courts even though some of those rules will inevitably differ from comparable state rules. 'When, because the plaintiff happens to be a non-resident, such a right is enforceable in a federal as well as in a State court, the forms and mode of enforcing the right may at times, naturally enough, vary because the two judicial systems are not identic.' *Guaranty Trust Co. of New York v. York*. Thus, though a court, in measuring a Federal Rule against the standards contained in the Enabling Act and the Constitution, need not wholly blind itself to the degree to which the Rule makes the character and result of the federal litigation stray from the course it would follow in state courts, it cannot be forgotten that the *Erie* rule, and the guidelines suggested in *York*, were created to serve another purpose altogether. To hold that a Federal Rule of Civil Procedure must cease to function whenever it alters the mode of enforcing state-created rights would be to disembowel either the Constitution's grant of power over federal procedure or Congress' attempt to exercise that power in the Enabling Act. Rule 4(d)(1) is valid and controls the instant case.

Reversed.

MR. JUSTICE HARLAN, concurring.

It is unquestionably true that up to now Erie and the cases following it have not succeeded in articulating a workable doctrine governing choice of law in diversity actions. I respect the Court's effort to clarify the situation in today's opinion. However, in doing so I think it has misconceived the constitutional premises of Erie and has failed to deal adequately with those past decisions upon which the courts below relied.

Erie was something more than an opinion which worried about 'forum-shopping and avoidance of inequitable administration of the laws,' although to be sure these were important elements of the decision. I have always regarded that decision as one of the modern cornerstones of our federalism, expressing policies that profoundly touch the allocation of judicial power between the state and federal systems. Erie recognized that there should not be two conflicting systems of law controlling the primary activity of citizens, for such alternative governing authority must necessarily give rise to a debilitating uncertainty in the planning of everyday affairs. And it recognized that the scheme of our Constitution envisions an allocation of law-making functions between state and federal legislative processes which is undercut if the federal judiciary can make substantive law affecting state affairs beyond the bounds of congressional legislative powers in this regard. Thus, in diversity cases Erie commands that it be the state law governing primary private activity which prevails.

* * *

To my mind the proper line of approach in determining whether to apply a state or a federal rule, whether 'substantive' or 'procedural,' is to stay close to basic principles by inquiring if the choice of rule would substantially affect those primary decisions respecting human conduct which our constitutional system leaves to state regulation. If so, Erie and the Constitution require that the state rule prevail, even in the face of a conflicting federal rule.

* * *

The courts below relied upon this Court's decisions in *Ragan v. Merchants Transfer & Warehouse Co.* [That case] deserve[s] more attention than this Court has given it. [ ] Ragan, if still good law, would in my opinion call for affirmance of the result reached by the Court of Appeals.

In Ragan a Kansas statute of limitations provided that an action was deemed commenced when service was made on the defendant. Despite Federal Rule 3 which provides that an action commences with the filing of the complaint, the Court held that for purposes of the Kansas statute of limitations a diversity tort action commenced only when service was made upon the defendant. The effect of this holding was that although the plaintiff had filed his federal complaint within the state period of limitations, his action was barred because the federal marshal did not serve a summons on the defendant until after the limitations period had run. I think that the decision was wrong. At most, application of the Federal Rule would have meant that potential Kansas tort defendants would have to defer for a few days the satisfaction of knowing that they had not been sued within the limitations period. The choice of the Federal Rule would have had no effect on the primary stages of private activity from which torts arise, and only the most minimal effect on behavior following the commission of the tort. In such circumstances the interest of the federal system in proceeding under its own rules should have prevailed.

* * *

It remains to apply what has been said to the present case. The Massachusetts rule provides that an executor need not answer suits unless in-hand service was made upon him or notice of the action was filed in the proper registry of probate within one year of his giving bond. The evident intent of this statute is to permit an executor to distribute the estate which he is administering without fear that further liabilities may be outstanding for which he could be held personally liable. If the Federal District Court in Massachusetts applies Rule 4(d)(1) of the Federal Rules of Civil Procedure instead of the Massachusetts service rule, what effect would that have on the speed and assurance with which estates are distributed? As I see it, the effect would not be substantial. It would mean simply that an executor would have to check at his own house or the federal courthouse as well as the registry of probate before he could distribute the estate with impunity. As this does not seem enough to give rise to any real impingement on the vitality of the state policy which the Massachusetts rule is intended to serve, I concur in the judgment of the Court.

U.S. CONST. ART. III § 1

The judicial power of the United States, shall be vested in one Supreme Court, and in such inferior courts as the Congress may from time to time ordain and establish.

DIRECTED READING QUESTIONS

40. What two conditions must be satisfied before an *Erie* choice of law issue can arise? How are these two conditions satisfied in *Hanna*?

41. Why precisely does the trial court grant summary judgment for the defendant in this case? In answering this question, you will need to examine the *Ragan* case which the concurrence discusses.

42. Why does the appellate court affirm the trial court?

43. Explain precisely the defendant's argument to the Supreme Court, and how that argument places "primary reliance on *York* and *Ragan*."

44. Why does the Supreme Court conclude *that the argument you described in the previous question* is "invalid"? In answering this question, you should pay close attention to the Supreme Court's use of the *Byrd* case to conclude that "Outcome-determinative analysis was never intended to serve as a talisman."

45. How does the *Hanna* opinion modify the outcome determinative test initially described in *Guaranty Trust*? Consider the following excerpt from the opinion in formulating your answer,

> So it is here. Though choice of the federal or state rule will at this point have a marked effect upon the outcome of the litigation, the difference between the two rules would be of scant, if any, relevance to the choice of a forum. Petitioner, in choosing her forum, was not presented with a situation where application of the state rule would wholly bar recovery; rather, adherence to the state rule would have resulted only in altering the way in which process was served. Moreover, it is difficult to argue that permitting service of defendant's wife to take the place of inhand service of defendant himself alters the mode of enforcement of state-created rights in a fashion sufficiently 'substantial' to raise the sort of equal protection problems to which the *Erie* opinion alluded.

46. Is the Supreme Court's modification of the outcome determinative test in *Hanna* dispositive of the result reached in the case?

47. In addition to modifying the outcome determinative test, does the *Hanna* opinion create an entirely separate test to decide whether state or federal law should apply when a federal court is adjudicating a state law claim and the federal law conflicting with state law is a Federal Rule of Civil Procedure?

48. What is the "relatively unguided *Erie* Choice" that the Supreme Court refers to?

49. Explain why the *Hanna* Court concludes, "When a situation is covered by one of the Federal Rules, the question facing the Court is a far cry from the typical, relatively unguided, *Erie* Choice"? It is worth focusing on the following excerpt from the opinion in answering this question.

There is, however, a more fundamental flaw in respondent's syllogism: the incorrect assumption that the rule of *Erie R. Co. v. Tompkins* constitutes the appropriate test of the validity and therefore the applicability of a Federal Rule of Civil Procedure.

* * *

For the constitutional provision for a federal court system (augmented by the Necessary and Proper Clause) carries with it congressional power to make rules governing the practice and pleading in those courts, which in turn includes a power to regulate matters which, though falling within the uncertain area between substance and procedure, are rationally capable of classification as either.

* * *

To hold that a Federal Rule of Civil Procedure must cease to function whenever it alters the mode of enforcing state-created rights would be to disembowel either the Constitution's grant of power over federal procedure or Congress' attempt to exercise that power in the Enabling Act.

IV. DISTINGUISHING DIRECT AND INDIRECT CONFLICT BETWEEN STATE LAW AND FEDERAL RULES

A. INDIRECT CONFLICT

WALKER V. ARMCO STEEL CORP. (1980)
Supreme Court of the United States
446 U.S. 740

MR. JUSTICE MARSHALL delivered the opinion of the Court.

This case presents the issue whether in a diversity action the federal court should follow state law or, alternatively, Rule 3 of the Federal Rules of Civil Procedure in determining when an action is commenced for the purpose of tolling the state statute of limitations.

I

According to the allegations of the complaint, petitioner, a carpenter, was injured on August 22, 1975, in Oklahoma City, Okla., while pounding a Sheffield nail into a cement wall. Respondent was the manufacturer of the nail. Petitioner claimed that the nail contained a defect which caused its head to shatter and strike him in the right eye, resulting in permanent injuries. The defect was allegedly caused by respondent's negligence in manufacture and design.

Petitioner is a resident of Oklahoma, and respondent is a foreign corporation having its principal place of business in a State other than Oklahoma. Since there was diversity of citizenship, petitioner brought suit in the United States District Court for the Western District of Oklahoma. The complaint was filed on August 19, 1977. Although summons was issued that same day, service of process was not made on respondent's authorized service agent until December 1, 1977.[2] On January 5, 1978, respondent filed a motion to dismiss the complaint on the ground that the action was barred by the applicable Oklahoma statute of limitations. Although the complaint had been filed within the 2-year statute of limitations, Okla.Stat., Tit. 12, § 95 (1971),[3] state law does not deem the action "commenced" for purposes of the statute of limitations until service of the summons on the defendant, Okla.Stat., Tit. 12, § 97 (1971) . . . .[4] Petitioner in his reply brief to the motion to dismiss admitted that his case would be foreclosed in state court, but he argued that Rule 3 of the Federal Rules of Civil Procedure governs the manner in which an action is commenced in federal court for all purposes, including the tolling of the state statute of limitations.

The District Court dismissed the complaint as barred by the Oklahoma statute of limitations. The court concluded that Okla.Stat., Tit. 12, § 97 (1971) was "an integral part of the Oklahoma statute of limitations," and therefore, under *Ragan* state law applied. The court rejected the argument that *Ragan* had been implicitly overruled in *Hanna.*

The United States Court of Appeals for the Tenth Circuit affirmed. That court concluded that Okla.Stat., Tit. 12, § 97 (1971), was in "direct conflict" with Rule 3. However, the Oklahoma statute was "indistinguishable" from the statute involved in *Ragan,* and the court felt itself "constrained" to follow *Ragan.*

We granted certiorari because of a conflict among the Courts of Appeals. We now affirm.

The question whether state or federal law should apply on various issues arising in an action based on state law which has been brought in federal court under diversity of citizenship jurisdiction has troubled this Court for many years.

* * *

Ragan was not our last pronouncement in this difficult area, however. In 1965 we decided *Hanna v. Plumer.*

The Court in *Hanna* . . . concluded that the *Erie* doctrine was simply not the appropriate test of the validity and applicability of one of the Federal Rules of Civil Procedure:

> The *Erie* rule has never been invoked to void a Federal Rule. It is true that there have been cases where this Court had held applicable a state rule in the face of an argument that the situation was governed by one of the Federal Rules. But

---

[2]   The record does not indicate why this delay occurred. The face of the process record shows that the United States Marshal acknowledged receipt of the summons on December 1, 1977, and that service was effectuated that same day. At oral argument counsel for petitioner stated that the summons was found "in an unmarked folder in the filing cabinet" in counsel's office some 90 days after the complaint had been filed. Counsel conceded that the summons was not delivered to the Marshal until December 1. It is unclear why the summons was placed in the filing cabinet.

[3]   Under Oklahoma law, a suit for products liability, whether based on a negligence theory or a breach of implied warranty theory, is governed by the 2-year statute of limitations period of Okla.Stat., Tit. 12, § 95 (1971).

[4]   Oklahoma Stat., Tit. 12, § 97 (1971), provides in pertinent part: "An action shall be deemed commenced, within the meaning of this article [the statute of limitations], as to each defendant, at the date of the summons which is served on him, or on a codefendant, who is a joint contractor or otherwise united in interest with him. . . . An attempt to commence an action shall be deemed equivalent to the commencement thereof, within the meaning of this article, when the party faithfully, properly and diligently endeavors to procure a service; but such attempt must be followed by the first publication or service of the summons, . . . within sixty (60) days."

the holding of each such case was not that *Erie* commanded displacement of a Federal Rule by an inconsistent state rule, but rather that the scope of the Federal Rule was not as broad as the losing party urged, and therefore, there being no Federal Rule which covered the point in dispute, *Erie* commanded the enforcement of state law.

The Court cited *Ragan* as one of the examples of this proposition.[7] The Court explained that where the Federal Rule was clearly applicable, as in *Hanna*, the test was whether the Rule was within the scope of the Rules Enabling Act, 28 U.S.C. § 2072, and if so, within a constitutional grant of power such as the Necessary and Proper Clause of Art. I.

III

The present case is indistinguishable from *Ragan*. The statutes in both cases require service of process to toll the statute of limitations, and in fact the predecessor to the Oklahoma statute in this case was derived from the predecessor to the Kansas statute in *Ragan*. Here, as in *Ragan*, the complaint was filed in federal court under diversity jurisdiction within the 2-year statute of limitations, but service of process did not occur until after the 2-year period . . . had run. In both cases the suit would concededly have been barred in the applicable state court, and in both instances the state service statute was held to be an integral part of the statute of limitations by the lower court more familiar than we with state law. Accordingly, as the Court of Appeals held below, the instant action is barred by the statute of limitations unless *Ragan* is no longer good law.

* * *

This Court in *Hanna* distinguished *Ragan* rather than overruled it, and for good reason. Application of the *Hanna* analysis is premised on a "direct collision" between the Federal Rule and the state law. In *Hanna* itself the "clash" between Rule 4(d)(1) and the state in-hand service requirement was "unavoidable." The first question must therefore be whether the scope of the Federal Rule in fact is sufficiently broad to control the issue before the Court. It is only if that question is answered affirmatively that the *Hanna* analysis applies.

As has already been noted, we recognized in *Hanna* that the present case is an instance where "the scope of the Federal Rule [is] not as broad as the losing party urge[s], and therefore, there being no Federal Rule which cover[s] the point in dispute, *Erie* command[s] the enforcement of state law." Rule 3 simply states that "[a] civil action is commenced by filing a complaint with the court." There is no indication that the Rule was intended to toll a state statute of limitations,[10] much less that it purported to

---

[7]   The Court in *Hanna* noted that "this Court has never before been confronted with a case where the applicable Federal Rule is in direct collision with the law of the relevant State."

[10]   "Rule 3 simply provides that an action is commenced by filing the complaint and has as its primary purpose the measuring of time periods that begin running from the date of commencement; the rule does not state that filing tolls the statute of limitations." 4 C. Wright & A. Miller, Federal Practice and Procedure § 1057, p. 191 (1969) (footnote omitted).

The Note of the Advisory Committee on the Rules states:

"When a Federal or State statute of limitations is pleaded as a defense, a question may arise under this rule whether the mere filing of the complaint stops the running of the statute, or whether any further step is required, such as, service of the summons and complaint or their delivery to the marshal for service. The answer to this question may depend on whether it is competent for the Supreme Court, exercising the power

displace state tolling rules for purposes of state statutes of limitations. In our view, in diversity actions Rule 3 governs the date from which various timing requirements of the Federal Rules begin to run, but does not affect state statutes of limitations.

In contrast to Rule 3, the Oklahoma statute is a statement of a substantive decision by that State that actual service on, and accordingly actual notice by, the defendant is an integral part of the several policies served by the statute of limitations. The statute of limitations establishes a deadline after which the defendant may legitimately have peace of mind; it also recognizes that after a certain period of time it is unfair to require the defendant to attempt to piece together his defense to an old claim. A requirement of actual service promotes both of those functions of the statute. It is these policy aspects which make the service requirement an "integral" part of the statute of limitations both in this case and in *Ragan*. As such, the service rule must be considered part and parcel of the statute of limitations.[13] Rule 3 does not replace such policy determinations found in state law. Rule 3 and Okla.Stat., Tit. 12, § 97 (1971), can exist side by side, therefore, each controlling its own intended sphere of coverage without conflict.

Since there is no direct conflict between the Federal Rule and the state law, the *Hanna* analysis does not apply. Instead, the policies behind *Erie* and *Ragan* control the issue whether, in the absence of a federal rule directly on point, state service requirements which are an integral part of the state statute of limitations should control in an action based on state law which is filed in federal court under diversity jurisdiction. The reasons for the application of such a state service requirement in a diversity action in the absence of a conflicting federal rule are well explained in *Erie* and *Ragan*. It is sufficient to note that although in this case failure to apply the state service law might not create any problem of forum shopping,[15] the result would be an "inequitable administration" of the law. There is simply no reason why, in the absence of a controlling federal rule, an action based on state law which concededly would be barred in the state courts by the state statute of limitations should proceed through litigation to judgment in federal court solely because of the fortuity that there is diversity of citizenship between the litigants. The policies underlying diversity jurisdiction do not support such a distinction between state and federal plaintiffs, and *Erie* and its progeny do not permit it.

The judgment of the Court of Appeals is

Affirmed.

---

to make rules of procedure without affecting substantive rights, to vary the operation of statutes of limitations. The requirement of Rule 4(a) that the clerk shall forthwith issue the summons and deliver it to the marshal for service will reduce the chances of such a question arising."

This Note establishes that the Advisory Committee predicted the problem which arose in *Ragan* and arises again in the instant case. It does not indicate, however, that Rule 3 was *intended* to serve as a tolling provision for statute of limitations purposes; it only suggests that the Advisory Committee thought the Rule *might* have that effect.

[13] The substantive link of § 97 to the statute of limitations is made clear as well by another provision of Oklahoma law. Under Okla.Stat., Tit. 12, § 151 (1971), "[a] civil action is deemed commenced by filing in the office of the court clerk of the proper court a petition and by the clerk's issuance of summons thereon." This is the state-law corollary to Rule 3. However, § 97, not § 151, controls the commencement of the lawsuit for statute of limitations purposes. Just as § 97 and § 151 can both apply in state court for their separate purposes, so too § 97 and Rule 3 may both apply in federal court in a diversity action.

[15] There is no indication that when petitioner filed his suit in federal court he had any reason to believe that he would be unable to comply with the service requirements of Oklahoma law or that he chose to sue in federal court in an attempt to avoid those service requirements.

DIRECTED READING QUESTIONS

50. Are the two necessary conditions for an *Erie* choice of law issue satisfied in *Walker*?

51. What is the conflict between federal and state law, and how does that conflict materialize in this case?

52. What is meant by an indirect conflict between a federal rule of civil procedure and state law, and how does the *Walker* court find that there is no direct conflict between Federal Rule of Civil Procedure 3 and Oklahoma statute § 97? In answering the question, pay close attention to the difference between the *Hanna* court's description of the conflict in that case, "Here, of course, the clash is *unavoidable*; Rule 4(d)(1) says—implicitly, but with unmistakable clarity—that inhand service is not required in federal courts" and footnote 13 of the *Walker* opinion which describes the conflict in that case. The following language in *Walker*, distinguishing *Ragan* and *Walker* on the one hand from *Hanna*, is also important to understanding the difference between a direct and an indirect conflict,

    As has already been noted, we recognized in *Hanna* that the present case is an instance where "the scope of the Federal Rule [is] not as broad as the losing party urge[s], and therefore, there being no Federal Rule which cover[s] the point in dispute, *Erie* command[s] the enforcement of state law."

53. When a court finds that there is no direct conflict between a Federal Rule of Civil Procedure and state law, what test is used to determine which law to apply?

54. How is that test applied here to find that state law should apply? In answering this question, be sure to remember that *Erie* identified two problems with the *Swift* doctrine and the presence of only one of those is enough to invoke outcome determinativeness.

55. As you read the next case, *Burlington Northern*, and struggle to distinguish it from the *Walker* case, pay particular attention to this language found in *Walker*, explaining why the conflict is indirect in *Walker*: "Rule 3 and Okla.Stat., Tit. 12, § 97 (1971), can exist side by side, therefore, each controlling its own intended sphere of coverage *without conflict*."

B. DIRECT CONFLICT

BURLINGTON NORTHERN R. CO. v. WOODS (1987)

Supreme Court of the United States
480 U.S. 1

JUSTICE MARSHALL delivered the opinion of the Court.

This case presents the issue whether, in diversity actions, federal courts must apply a state statute that imposes a fixed penalty on appellants who obtain stays of judgment pending unsuccessful appeals.

I

Respondents brought this tort action in Alabama state court to recover damages for injuries sustained in a motorcycle accident. Petitioner removed the case to a Federal District Court having diversity jurisdiction. A jury trial resulted in a judgment of $300,000 for respondent Alan Woods and $5,000 for respondent Cara Woods. Petitioner posted bond to stay the judgment pending appeal, and the Court of Appeals affirmed without modification.

Respondents then moved in the Court of Appeals, pursuant to Ala.Code § 12–22–72 for imposition of that State's mandatory affirmance penalty of 10% of the amount of judgment. Petitioner challenged the application of this statute as a . . . "a procedural rule . . . inapplicable in federal court under the doctrine of *Erie Railroad Company v. Tompkins* and its progeny." The Court of Appeals summarily granted respondents' motion to assess the penalty and subsequently denied a petition for rehearing. The parties have stipulated that the final judgment has been paid, except for the $30,500 statutory affirmance penalty, which petitioner has withheld pending proceedings in this Court.

We granted certiorari to consider . . . the *Erie* claim. [W]e conclude that the Alabama statute imposing a mandatory affirmance penalty has no application in federal diversity actions . . . .

II

Alabama statute [§ 12–22–72] provides in relevant part:

> "When a judgment or decree is entered or rendered for money, whether debt or damages, and the same has been stayed on appeal by the execution of bond, with surety, if the appellate court affirms the judgment of the court below, it must also enter judgment against all or any of the obligors on the bond for the amount of the affirmed judgment, 10 percent damages thereon and the costs of the appellate court. . . ."

As set forth in the statute, then, a combination of three conditions will automatically trigger the 10% penalty: (1) the trial court must enter a money judgment or decree, (2) the judgment or decree must be stayed by the requisite bond,[2] and (3) the judgment or decree must be affirmed without substantial modification. The purposes of the mandatory affirmance penalty are to penalize frivolous appeals and appeals interposed for delay, and to provide "additional damages" as compensation to the appellees for having to suffer the ordeal of defending the judgments on appeal.

Petitioner contends that the statute's underlying purposes and mandatory mode of operation conflict with the purposes and operation of Rule 38 of the Federal Rules of Appellate Procedure, and therefore that the statute should not be applied by federal courts sitting in diversity. Entitled "Damages for delay," Rule 38 provides: "If the court of appeals shall determine that an appeal is frivolous, it may award just damages and single or double costs to the appellee." Under this Rule, "damages are awarded by the court in its discretion in the case of a frivolous appeal as a matter of justice to the appellee and as a penalty against the appellant."

In *Hanna v. Plumer,* we set forth the appropriate test for resolving conflicts between state law and the Federal Rules. The initial step is to determine whether, when fairly construed, the scope of Federal Rule 38 is "sufficiently broad" to cause a "direct collision" with the state law or, implicitly, to "control the issue" before the court, thereby leaving

---

[2]   Under Alabama law, an appellant may obtain a stay of judgment pending appeal by providing an acceptable surety bond of a set amount, which in this case would have been 125% of the trial court's judgment had the case been tried in state court.

no room for the operation of that law. *Walker v. Armco Steel Corp., Hanna, supra.* The Rule must then be applied if it represents a valid exercise of Congress' rulemaking authority, which originates in the Constitution and has been bestowed on this Court by the Rules Enabling Act, *Hanna,* 380 U.S., at 471–474, 85 S.Ct., at 1143–45.

The constitutional constraints on the exercise of this rulemaking authority define a test of reasonableness. Rules regulating matters indisputably procedural are *a priori* constitutional. Rules regulating matters "which, though falling within the uncertain area between substance and procedure, are rationally capable of classification as either," also satisfy this constitutional standard. The Rules Enabling Act, however, contains an additional requirement. The Federal Rule must not "abridge, enlarge or modify any substantive right. . . ." 28 U.S.C. § 2072. The cardinal purpose of Congress in authorizing the development of a uniform and consistent system of rules governing federal practice and procedure suggests that Rules which incidentally affect litigants' substantive rights do not violate this provision if reasonably necessary to maintain the integrity of that system of rules.

Moreover, the study and approval given each proposed Rule by the Advisory Committee, the Judicial Conference, and this Court, and the statutory requirement that the Rule be reported to Congress for a period of review before taking effect, see 28 U.S.C. § 2072, give the Rules presumptive validity under both the constitutional and statutory constraints. See *Hanna.*

Applying the *Hanna* analysis to an analogous Mississippi statute which provides for a mandatory affirmance penalty, the United States Court of Appeals for the Fifth Circuit concluded that the statute conflicted with Rule 38 and thus was not applicable in federal diversity actions. The Fifth Circuit discussed two aspects of the conflict: (1) the discretionary mode of operation of the Federal Rule, compared to the mandatory operation of the Mississippi statute, and (2) the limited effect of the Rule in penalizing only frivolous appeals or appeals interposed for purposes of delay, compared to the effect of the Mississippi statute in penalizing every unsuccessful appeal regardless of merit.

We find the Fifth Circuit's analysis persuasive. Rule 38 affords a court of appeals plenary discretion to assess "just damages" in order to penalize an appellant who takes a frivolous appeal and to compensate the injured appellee for the delay and added expense of defending the district court's judgment. Thus, the Rule's discretionary mode of operation unmistakably conflicts with the mandatory provision of Alabama's affirmance penalty statute.

* * *

Respondents argue that, because Alabama has a similar Appellate Rule which may be applied in state court alongside the affirmance penalty statute, see Ala.Rule App.Proc. 38; a federal court sitting in diversity could impose the mandatory penalty and likewise remain free to exercise its discretionary authority under Federal Rule 38. This argument, however, ignores the significant possibility that a court of appeals may, in any given case, find a limited justification for imposing penalties in an amount *less than* 10% of the lower court's judgment. Federal Rule 38 adopts a case-by-case approach to identifying and deterring frivolous appeals; the Alabama statute precludes any exercise of discretion within its scope of operation. Whatever circumscriptive effect the mandatory affirmance penalty statute may have on the state court's exercise of discretion under Alabama's Rule 38, that Rule provides no authority for defining the scope of discretion allowed under Federal Rule 38.

Federal Rule 38 regulates matters which can reasonably be classified as procedural, thereby satisfying the constitutional standard for validity. Its displacement of the Alabama statute also satisfies the statutory constraints of the Rules Enabling Act. The choice made by the drafters of the Federal Rules in favor of a discretionary procedure affects only the process of enforcing litigants' rights and not the rights themselves.

III

We therefore hold that the Alabama mandatory affirmance penalty statute has no application to judgments entered by federal courts sitting in diversity.

Reversed.

DIRECTED READING QUESTIONS

56. Just like in *Walker*, there are three statutes/rules involved (2 state and one federal). The statutes/rules that the court mentions are Federal Rule of Appellate Procedure 38, State Rule of Appellate Procedure 38 and state statute § 12–22–72. Please explain precisely what each statute provides.

57. Both *Walker and Burlington* involve situations where one state law is identical to a federal rule, but another state law is different to the federal rule. In *Walker*, the court concludes that this means the federal and state laws can coexist, and therefore the conflict is indirect. Why, then, does the *Burlington* court conclude that there is a direct conflict between federal and state law?

V. MULTIPLE CONFLICTS

GASPERINI V. CENTER FOR HUMANITIES, INC. (1996)
Supreme Court of the United States
518 U.S. 415

JUSTICE GINSBURG delivered the opinion of the Court.

Under the law of New York, appellate courts are empowered to review the size of jury verdicts and to order new trials when the jury's award "deviates materially from what would be reasonable compensation." N.Y. Civ. Prac. Law and Rules (CPLR) § 5501(c) (McKinney 1995). Under the Seventh Amendment, which governs proceedings in federal court, but not in state court, "the right of trial by jury shall be preserved, and no fact tried by a jury, shall be otherwise re-examined in any Court of the United States, than according to the rules of the common law." The compatibility of these provisions, in an action based on New York law but tried in federal court by reason of the parties' diverse citizenship, is the issue we confront in this case. We hold that New York's law controlling compensation awards for excessiveness or inadequacy can be given effect, without detriment to the Seventh Amendment, if the review standard set out in CPLR § 5501(c) is applied by the federal trial court judge, with appellate control of the trial court's ruling limited to review for "abuse of discretion."

I

Petitioner William Gasperini, a journalist for CBS News and the Christian Science Monitor, began reporting on events in Central America in 1984. He earned his living primarily in radio and print media and only occasionally sold his photographic work. During the course of his seven-year stint in Central America, Gasperini took over 5,000 slide transparencies, depicting active war zones, political leaders, and scenes from daily life. In 1990, Gasperini agreed to supply his original color transparencies to The Center for Humanities, Inc. (Center) for use in an educational videotape, Conflict in Central America. Gasperini selected 300 of his slides for the Center; its videotape included 110 of them. The Center agreed to return the original transparencies, but upon the completion of the project, it could not find them.

Gasperini commenced suit in the United States District Court for the Southern District of New York, invoking the court's diversity jurisdiction pursuant to 28 U.S.C. § 1332. He alleged several state-law claims for relief, including breach of contract, conversion, and negligence. The Center conceded liability for the lost transparencies and the issue of damages was tried before a jury.

At trial, Gasperini's expert witness testified that the "industry standard" within the photographic publishing community valued a lost transparency at $1,500. This industry standard, the expert explained, represented the average license fee a commercial photograph could earn over the full course of the photographer's copyright, i.e., in Gasperini's case, his lifetime plus 50 years. Gasperini estimated that his earnings from photography totaled just over $10,000 for the period from 1984 through 1993. He also testified that he intended to produce a book containing his best photographs from Central America.

After a three-day trial, the jury awarded Gasperini $450,000 in compensatory damages. This sum, the jury foreperson announced, "is [$]1500 each, for 300 slides." Id., at 313. Moving for a new trial under Federal Rule of Civil Procedure 59, the Center attacked the verdict on various grounds, including excessiveness. Without comment, the District Court denied the motion.

The Court of Appeals for the Second Circuit vacated the judgment entered on the jury's verdict. Mindful that New York law governed the controversy, the Court of Appeals endeavored to apply CPLR § 5501(c), which instructs that, when a jury returns an itemized verdict, as the jury did in this case, the New York Appellate Division "shall determine that an award is excessive or inadequate if it deviates materially from what would be reasonable compensation." The Second Circuit's application of § 5501(c) as a check on the size of the jury's verdict followed Circuit precedent elaborated two weeks earlier in Consorti v. Armstrong World Industries, Inc. Surveying Appellate Division decisions that reviewed damage awards for lost transparencies, the Second Circuit concluded that testimony on industry standard alone was insufficient to justify a verdict; prime among other factors warranting consideration were the uniqueness of the slides' subject matter and the photographer's earning level.

Guided by Appellate Division rulings, the Second Circuit held that the $450,000 verdict "materially deviates from what is reasonable compensation." Some of Gasperini's transparencies, the Second Circuit recognized, were unique, notably those capturing combat situations in which Gasperini was the only photographer present. But others "depicted either generic scenes or events at which other professional photojournalists were present." No more than 50 slides merited a $1,500 award, the court concluded, after "[g]iving Gasperini every benefit of the doubt." Absent evidence showing significant earnings from photographic endeavors or concrete plans to publish a book, the court further determined, any damage award above $100 each for the remaining slides would be excessive. Remittiturs "presen[t] difficult problems for appellate courts," the Second Circuit acknowledged, for court of appeals judges review the evidence from "a cold paper record." Nevertheless, the Second Circuit set aside the $450,000 verdict and ordered a new trial, unless Gasperini agreed to an award of $100,000.

This case presents an important question regarding the standard a federal court uses to measure the alleged excessiveness of a jury's verdict in an action for damages based on state law. We therefore granted certiorari.

II

Before 1986, state and federal courts in New York generally invoked the same judge-made formulation in responding to excessiveness attacks on jury verdicts: courts would not disturb an award unless the amount was so exorbitant that it "shocked the conscience of the court." As described by the Second Circuit:

> The standard for determining excessiveness and the appropriateness of remittitur in New York is somewhat ambiguous. Prior to 1986, New York law employed the same standard as the federal courts, which authorized remittitur only if the jury's verdict was so excessive that it 'shocked the conscience of the court.

In both state and federal courts, trial judges made the excessiveness assessment in the first instance, and appellate judges ordinarily deferred to the trial court's judgment.

> The trial court's determination as to the adequacy of the jury verdict will only be disturbed by an appellate court where it can be said that the trial court's exercise of discretion was not reasonably grounded [or stated another way] [t]he trial court's refusal to set aside or reduce a jury award will be overturned only for abuse of discretion.

In 1986, as part of a series of tort reform measures, [to curtail medical and dental malpractice, and to contain "already high malpractice premiums. . ."] New York codified a standard for judicial review of the size of jury awards. Placed in CPLR § 5501(c), the prescription reads:

> [The appellate division shall review questions of law and questions of fact on an appeal from a judgment or order of a court of original instance and on an appeal from an order of the supreme court, a county court or an appellate term determining an appeal. In reviewing a money judgment in an action in which an itemized verdict is required by rule forty-one hundred eleven of this chapter in which it is contended that the award is excessive or inadequate and that a new trial should have been granted unless a stipulation is entered to a different award, the appellate division shall determine that an award is excessive or inadequate if it deviates materially from what would be reasonable compensation.]

As stated in Legislative Findings and Declarations accompanying New York's adoption of the "deviates materially" formulation, the lawmakers found the "shock the conscience"* test an insufficient check on damage awards; the legislature therefore installed a standard "invit[ing] more careful appellate scrutiny." At the same time, the legislature instructed the Appellate Division, in amended § 5522, to state the reasons for the court's rulings on the size of verdicts, and the factors the court considered in complying with § 5501(c).[5] In his signing statement, then-Governor Mario Cuomo emphasized that the CPLR amendments were meant to rachet up the review standard: "This will assure greater scrutiny of the amount of verdicts and promote greater stability in the tort system and greater fairness for similarly situated defendants throughout the State and "was intended to . . . encourage Appellate Division modification of excessive awards."

New York state-court opinions confirm that § 5501(c)'s "deviates materially" standard calls for closer surveillance than "shock the conscience" oversight. See, *e.g., O'Connor v. Graziosi* ("apparent intent" of 1986 legislation was "to facilitate appellate changes in verdicts"); *Harvey v. Mazal American Partners* (instructing Appellate Division to use, in setting remittitur, only the "deviates materially" standard, and not the "shock the conscience" test); see also *Consorti* ("Material deviation from reasonableness is less than that deviation required to find an award so excessive as to 'shock the conscience.' "); 7 J. Weinstein, H. Korn, & A. Miller, New York Civil Practice ¶ 5501.21, p. 55–64 (1995) ("Under [§ 5501(c)'s] new standard, the reviewing court is given greater power to review the size of a jury award than had heretofore been afforded. . . .").

Although phrased as a direction to New York's intermediate appellate courts, § 5501(c)'s "deviates materially" standard, as construed by New York's courts, instructs state trial judges as well. See, *e.g., Inya v. Ide Hyundai, Inc.* (error for trial court to apply "shock the conscience" test to motion to set aside damages; proper standard is whether award "materially deviates from what would be reasonable compensation"); *Cochetti v. Gralow* ("settled law" that trial courts conduct "materially deviates" inquiry); *Shurgan v. Tedesco,* (approving trial court's application of "materially deviates" standard); see also *Lightfoot v. Union Carbide Corp.* (CPLR 5501(c)'s "materially deviates" standard "is pretty well established as applicable to [state] trial and appellate courts."). Application of § 5501(c) at the trial level is key to this case.

To determine whether an award "deviates materially from what would be reasonable compensation," New York state courts look to awards approved in similar cases. * * * The "deviates materially" standard, however, in design and operation, influences outcomes by tightening the range of tolerable awards.

---

* In New York the state trial court is called the Supreme Court, the intermediate appellate court is called The Appellate Division and the state's highest court is called the Court of Appeals.

[5] CPLR § 5522(b) provides:

In an appeal from a money judgment in an action . . . in which it is contended that the award is excessive or inadequate, the appellate division shall set forth in its decision the reasons therefor, including the factors it considered in complying with subdivision (c) of section fifty-five hundred one of this chapter.

III

In cases like Gasperini's, in which New York law governs the claims for relief, does New York law also supply the test for federal-court review of the size of the verdict? The Center answers yes. The "deviates materially" standard, it argues, is a substantive standard that must be applied by federal appellate courts in diversity cases. The Second Circuit agreed. [that] ("[CPLR § 5501(c)] is the substantive rule provided by New York law."). Gasperini, emphasizing that § 5501(c) trains on the New York Appellate Division, characterizes the provision as procedural, an allocation of decision-making authority regarding damages, not a hard cap on the amount recoverable. Correctly comprehended, Gasperini urges, § 5501(c)'s direction to the Appellate Division cannot be given effect by federal appellate courts without violating the Seventh Amendment's Re-examination Clause.

As the parties' arguments suggest, CPLR § 5501(c), appraised under *Erie R. Co. v. Tompkins,* and decisions in *Erie* 's path, is both "substantive" and "procedural": "substantive" in that § 5501(c)'s "deviates materially" standard controls how much a plaintiff can be awarded; "procedural" in that § 5501(c) assigns decision making authority to New York's Appellate Division. Parallel application of § 5501(c) at the federal appellate level would be out of sync with the federal system's division of trial and appellate court functions, an allocation weighted by the Seventh Amendment. The dispositive question, therefore, is whether federal courts can give effect to the substantive thrust of § 5501(c) without untoward alteration of the federal scheme for the trial and decision of civil cases.

A

Federal diversity jurisdiction provides an alternative forum for the adjudication of state-created rights, but it does not carry with it generation of rules of substantive law. As *Erie* read the Rules of Decision Act: "Except in matters governed by the Federal Constitution or by Acts of Congress, the law to be applied in any case is the law of the State." Under the *Erie* doctrine, federal courts sitting in diversity apply state substantive law and federal procedural law.

Classification of a law as "substantive" or "procedural" for *Erie* purposes is sometimes a challenging endeavor. *Guaranty Trust Co. v. York,* an early interpretation of *Erie,* propounded an "outcome-determination" test: "[D]oes it significantly affect the result of a litigation for a federal court to disregard a law of a State that would be controlling in an action upon the same claim by the same parties in a State court?" Ordering application of a state statute of limitations to an equity proceeding in federal court, the Court said in *Guaranty Trust*: "[W]here a federal court is exercising jurisdiction solely because of the diversity of citizenship of the parties, the outcome of the litigation in the federal court should be substantially the same, so far as legal rules determine the outcome of a litigation, as it would be if tried in a State court." * * * A later pathmarking case, qualifying *Guaranty Trust,* explained that the "outcome-determination" test must not be applied mechanically to sweep in all manner of variations; instead, its application must be guided by "the twin aims of the *Erie* rule: discouragement of forum-shopping and avoidance of inequitable administration of the laws." *Hanna v. Plumer.*

Informed by these decisions, we address the question whether New York's "deviates materially" standard, codified in CPLR § 5501(c), is outcome affective in this sense: Would "application of the [standard] . . . have so important an effect upon the fortunes of one or both of the litigants that failure to [apply] it would [unfairly discriminate against citizens of the forum State, or] be likely to cause a plaintiff to choose the federal court"?

We start from a point the parties do not debate. *Gasperini* acknowledges that a statutory cap on damages would supply substantive law for *Erie* purposes. See Reply Brief for Petitioner 2 ("[T]he state as a matter of its substantive law may, among other things, eliminate the availability of damages for a particular claim entirely, limit the factors a jury may consider in determining damages, or place an absolute cap on the amount of damages available, and such substantive law would be applicable in a federal court sitting in diversity.") Although CPLR § 5501(c) is less readily classified, it was designed to provide an analogous control.

New York's Legislature codified in § 5501(c) a new standard, one that requires closer court review than the common-law "shock the conscience" test. More rigorous comparative evaluations attend application of § 5501(c)'s "deviates materially" standard. To foster predictability, the legislature required the reviewing court, when overturning a verdict under § 5501(c), to state its reasons, including the factors it considered relevant. We think it a fair conclusion that CPLR § 5501(c) differs from a statutory cap principally "in that the maximum amount recoverable is not set forth by statute, but rather is determined by case law." In sum, § 5501(c) contains a procedural instruction, but the State's objective is manifestly substantive.

It thus appears that if federal courts ignore the change in the New York standard and persist in applying the "shock the conscience" test to damage awards on claims governed by New York law, " substantial' variations between state and federal [money judgments]" may be expected. We therefore agree with the Second Circuit that New York's check on excessive damages implicates what we have called *Erie* 's "twin aims." Just as the *Erie* principle precludes a federal court from giving a state-created claim "longer life . . . than [the claim] would have had in the state court," *Ragan,* so *Erie* precludes a recovery in federal court significantly larger than the recovery that would have been tolerated in state court.

B

CPLR § 5501(c), as earlier noted, is phrased as a direction to the New York Appellate Division. Acting essentially as a surrogate for a New York appellate forum, the Court of Appeals reviewed Gasperini's award to determine if it "deviate[d] materially" from damage awards the Appellate Division permitted in similar circumstances. The Court of Appeals performed this task without benefit of an opinion from the District Court, which had denied "without comment" the Center's Rule 59 motion. Concentrating on the authority § 5501(c) gives to the Appellate Division, Gasperini urges that the provision shifts fact-finding responsibility from the jury and the trial judge to the appellate court. Assigning such responsibility to an appellate court, he maintains, is incompatible with the Seventh Amendment's Reexamination Clause, and therefore, Gasperini concludes, § 5501(c) cannot be given effect in federal court. Although we reach a different conclusion than Gasperini, we agree that the Second Circuit did not attend to "[a]n essential characteristic of [the federal court] system," *Byrd v. Blue Ridge Rural Elec. Cooperative, Inc.*, when it used § 5501(c) as "the standard for [federal] appellate review."

That "essential characteristic" was described in *Byrd,* a diversity suit for negligence in which a pivotal issue of fact would have been tried by a judge were the case in state court. The *Byrd* Court held that, despite the state practice, the plaintiff was entitled to a jury trial in federal court. In so ruling, the Court said that the *Guaranty Trust* "outcome-determination" test was an insufficient guide in cases presenting countervailing federal interests. See *Byrd.* The Court described the countervailing federal interests present in *Byrd* this way:

> The federal system is an independent system for administering justice to litigants who properly invoke its jurisdiction. An essential characteristic of that system is the manner in which, in civil common-law actions, it distributes trial functions between judge and jury and, under the influence—if not the command—of the Seventh Amendment, assigns the decisions of disputed questions of fact to the jury.

The Seventh Amendment, which governs proceedings in federal court, but not in state court, bears not only on the allocation of trial functions between judge and jury, the issue in *Byrd;* it also controls the allocation of authority to review verdicts, the issue of concern here. The Amendment reads:

> "In Suits at common law, where the value in controversy shall exceed twenty dollars, the right of trial by jury shall be preserved, and no fact tried by a jury, shall be otherwise re-examined in any Court of the United States, than according to the rules of the common law."

Byrd involved the first Clause of the Amendment, the "trial by jury" Clause. This case involves the second, the "Reexamination" Clause. In keeping with the historic understanding, the Reexamination Clause does not inhibit the authority of trial judges to grant new trials "for any of the reasons for which new trials have heretofore been granted in actions at law in the courts of the United States." Fed. Rule Civ. Proc. 59(a). That authority is large. See 6A Moore's Federal Practice ¶ 59.05[2], pp. 59–44 to 59–46 (2d ed. 1996) ("The power of the English common law trial courts to grant a new trial for a variety of reasons with a view to the attainment of justice was well established prior to the establishment of our Government."); see also *Aetna Casualty & Surety Co. v. Yeatts* ("The exercise of [the trial court's power to set aside the jury's verdict and grant a new trial] is not in derogation of the right of trial by jury but is one of the historic safeguards of that right."); *Blunt v. Little* ("[I]f it should clearly appear that the jury have committed a gross error, or have acted from improper motives, or have given damages excessive in relation to the person or the injury, it is as much the duty of the court to interfere, to prevent the wrong, as in any other case."). "The trial judge in the federal system," we have reaffirmed, "has . . . discretion to grant a new trial if the verdict appears to [the judge] to be against the weight of the evidence." This discretion includes overturning verdicts for excessiveness and ordering a new trial without qualification, or conditioned on the verdict winner's refusal to agree to a reduction (remittitur).

In contrast, appellate review of a federal trial court's denial of a motion to set aside a jury's verdict as excessive is a relatively late, and less secure, development. Such review was once deemed inconsonant with the Seventh Amendment's Reexamination Clause.

Before today, we have not "expressly [held] that the Seventh Amendment allows appellate review of a district court's denial of a motion to set aside an award as excessive. But in successive reminders that the question was worthy of this Court's attention, we noted, without disapproval, that courts of appeals engage in review of district court excessiveness determinations applying "abuse of discretion" as their standard. [I]n *Browning-Ferris,* we again referred to appellate court abuse-of-discretion review:

> "[T]he role of the district court is to determine whether the jury's verdict is within the confines set by state law, and to determine, by reference to federal standards developed under Rule 59, whether a new trial or remittitur should be ordered. The court of appeals should then review the district court's determination under an abuse-of-discretion standard."

As the Second Circuit explained, appellate review for abuse of discretion is reconcilable with the Seventh Amendment as a control necessary and proper to the fair administration of justice: "We must give the benefit of every doubt to the judgment of the trial judge; but surely there must be an upper limit, and whether that has been surpassed is not a question of fact with respect to which reasonable men may differ, but a question of law." We now approve this line of decisions, and thus make explicit what Justice Stewart thought implicit, "[N]othing in the Seventh Amendment . . . precludes appellate review of the trial judge's denial of a motion to set aside [a jury verdict] as excessive."

C

In *Byrd,* the Court faced a one-or-the-other choice: trial by judge as in state court, or trial by jury according to the federal practice. In the case before us, a choice of that order is not required, for the principal state and federal interests can be accommodated. The Second Circuit correctly recognized that when New York substantive law governs a claim for relief, New York law and decisions guide the allowable damages. But that court did not take into account the characteristic of the federal court system that caused us to reaffirm: The proper role of the trial and appellate courts in the federal system in reviewing the size of jury verdicts is . . . a matter of federal law. [T]he role of the district court is to determine whether the jury's verdict is within the confines set by state law. . . . The court of appeals should then review the district court's determination under an abuse-of-discretion standard.

New York's dominant interest can be respected, without disrupting the federal system, once it is recognized that the federal district court is capable of performing the checking function, *i.e.,* that court can apply the State's "deviates materially" standard in line with New York case law evolving under CPLR § 5501(c).[22] We recall, in this regard,

---

[22] Justice SCALIA finds in Federal Rule of Civil Procedure 59 a "federal standard" for new trial motions in " 'direct collision' " with, and " 'leaving no room for the operation of,' " a state law like CPLR § 5501(c). The relevant prescription, Rule 59(a), has remained unchanged since the adoption of the Federal Rules by this Court in 1937. Rule 59(a) is as encompassing as it is uncontroversial. It is indeed "Hornbook" law that a most usual ground for a Rule 59 motion is that "the damages are excessive." Whether damages are excessive for the claim-in-suit must be governed by *some law.* And there is no candidate for that governance other than the law that gives rise to the claim for relief—here, the law of New York. See 28 U.S.C. §§ 2072(a) and (b) ("Supreme Court shall have the power to prescribe general rules of . . . procedure"; "[s]uch rules shall not abridge, enlarge or modify any substantive right"); *Browning-Ferris,* 492 U.S., at 279, 109 S.Ct., at 2922 ("standard of excessiveness" is a "matte[r] of state, and not federal, common law"); see also R. Fallon, D. Meltzer, & D. Shapiro, Hart and Wechsler's The Federal Courts and the Federal System 729–730 (4th ed.1996) (observing that Court "has continued since [*Hanna v. Plumer,* 380 U.S. 460, 85 S.Ct. 1136, 14 L.Ed.2d 8 (1965),] to interpret the federal rules to avoid conflict with important state regulatory policies," citing *Walker v. Armco Steel Corp.*

that the "deviates materially" standard serves as the guide to be applied in trial as well as appellate courts in New York.

Within the federal system, practical reasons combine with Seventh Amendment constraints to lodge in the district court, not the court of appeals, primary responsibility for application of § 5501(c)'s "deviates materially" check. Trial judges have the "unique opportunity to consider the evidence in the living courtroom context," while appellate judges see only the "cold paper record."

District court applications of the "deviates materially" standard would be subject to appellate review under the standard the Circuits now employ when inadequacy or excessiveness is asserted on appeal: abuse of discretion. In light of *Erie* 's doctrine, the federal appeals court must be guided by the damage-control standard state law supplies, but as the Second Circuit itself has said: "If we reverse, it must be because of an abuse of discretion. . . . The very nature of the problem counsels restraint. . . . We must give the benefit of every doubt to the judgment of the trial judge."

IV

It does not appear that the District Court checked the jury's verdict against the relevant New York decisions demanding more than "industry standard" testimony to support an award of the size the jury returned in this case. As the Court of Appeals recognized, the uniqueness of the photographs and the plaintiff's earnings as photographer—past and reasonably projected—are factors relevant to appraisal of the award. Accordingly, we vacate the judgment of the Court of Appeals and instruct that court to remand the case to the District Court so that the trial judge, revisiting his ruling on the new trial motion, may test the jury's verdict against CPLR § 5501(c)'s "deviates materially" standard.

It is so ordered.

JUSTICE SCALIA, with whom THE CHIEF JUSTICE and JUSTICE THOMAS join, dissenting.

[I]n my view, one does not even reach the Erie question in this case. The standard to be applied by a district court in ruling on a motion for a new trial is set forth in Rule 59 of the Federal Rules of Civil Procedure, which provides that "[a] new trial may be granted . . . for any of the reasons for which new trials have heretofore been granted in actions at law in the courts of the United States." (Emphasis added.) That is undeniably a federal standard.[12] Federal District Courts in the Second Circuit have interpreted that standard to permit the granting of new trials where " 'it is quite clear that the jury has reached a seriously erroneous result' " and letting the verdict stand would result in a " 'miscarriage of justice.' " Assuming (as we have no reason to question) that this is a correct interpretation of what Rule 59 requires, it is undeniable that the Federal Rule is " 'sufficiently broad' to cause a 'direct collision' with the state law or, implicitly, to 'control the issue' before the court, thereby leaving no room for the operation of that law." Burlington Northern R. Co. v. Woods. It is simply not possible to give controlling effect both to the federal standard and the state standard in reviewing the jury's award. That

---

[12] I agree with the Court's entire progression of reasoning in its footnote 22 leading to the conclusion that *state* law must determine "[w]hether damages are excessive." But the question whether damages are excessive is quite separate from the question of when a jury award may be set aside for excessiveness. It is the latter that is governed by Rule 59; as *Browning-Ferris* said, district courts are "to determine, by reference to *federal standards developed under Rule 59,* whether a new trial or remittitur should be ordered."

being so, the court has no choice but to apply the Federal Rule, which is an exercise of what we have called Congress's "power to regulate matters which, though falling within the uncertain area between substance and procedure, are rationally capable of classification as either," *Hanna*.

* * *

I respectfully dissent.

DIRECTED READING QUESTIONS

58. Please recap precisely what happened in the trial court.

59. The appellate court reversed the trial court because the appellate court held that the verdict "deviates materially from what would be reasonable compensation." What is the source of law for the "deviates materially" standard that the appellate court applies?

60. Identify the three conflicts between § 5501(c) and federal law in the *Gasperini* majority opinion.

61. How does the difference between the dissent's and the majority's conclusions about the source of the federal "shocks the conscience" standard impact their different analyses of the conflict?

62. What is the first thing the majority does to determine whether state law (deviates materially) or federal law (shocks the conscience) should apply to determine whether the verdict is excessive?

63. After determining that the state law is both substantive and procedural, what does the majority do next to determine whether federal or state law should apply to determine if the verdict is excessive?

64. How do you know that the majority is applying the outcome determinative test as modified by *Hanna*, rather than the pre-*Hanna* outcome determinative test?

65. What does the majority conclude about whether the law is outcome determinative, and how does it arrive at that conclusion?

66. Why does the Supreme Court conclude that the aspect of the state law, which makes the appellate court rather than the trial court the primary arbiter of whether the verdict was excessive, should not apply in this case?

67. The answer to the previous question invokes the Seventh Amendment. Is this argument identical to the Seventh Amendment argument that was used in the *Byrd* case?

68. The Supreme Court also concludes that state law, which mandates that appellate courts review a district court's denial of a motion for a new trial based on excessiveness of the verdict *de novo*, is inapplicable in federal court. Explain how the Court reaches this conclusion.

69. What does the *Gasperini* case ultimately teach?

VI. BIG PICTURE REVIEW

1. What is the mandate of the Rules of Decision Act?

2. What is the Rules Enabling Act?

3. What is/are the holding(s) of the *Erie* case?

4. What is the relevance of the *Erie* case to the Rules of Decision Act?

5. Describe the *Erie* doctrine as the result of tension between the Rules of Decision Act and the Rules Enabling Act?

6. What are the twin aims of the *Erie* case?

7. What does *Guaranty Trust* add to the analysis of whether state law or federal law should apply when federal courts are adjudicating state law claims?

8. Explain how the Reed concurrence in *Erie* makes the need for *Guaranty Trust*'s formulation unsurprising.

9. How does the *Hanna* case modify the outcome determinative test?

10. Explain *Byrd*'s restriction on the outcome determinative test.

11. What test for whether federal or state law should apply when a federal court is adjudicating a state law claim is first articulated in *Hanna*?

12. What is the "relatively unguided *Erie* Choice," mentioned in *Hanna*?

13. Explain why the *Hanna* test applies in *Burlington* but not in *Walker*.

14. Why does the court in *Gasperini* apply the relatively unguided *Erie* choice to determine whether state or federal law should apply to determine if a jury verdict was excessive?

15. Both *Gasperini* and *Byrd* found that essential characteristics of the federal court system or countervailing federal interests, based on the Seventh Amendment, prevented the application of state law. Please identify the specific federal characteristics/interests discussed in each case, and explain how they impacted the outcome of both cases.

CHAPTER 16

PERSONAL JURISDICTION

∎ ∎ ∎

Francine was a college student in Wichita, Kansas. She was born in Kansas and had never left the state, except for a brief road trip to Oklahoma City, Oklahoma. One day, Francine got a call from a strange number on her phone, but she answered it anyway. The person on the other end told Francine that he was a representative of a small company in Florida that needed a small part from a factory located in Wichita, Kansas but they were having trouble getting it shipped.

Francine and the representative chatted for a while, and Francine agreed to help them get the part because the factory was located was very close to her house. A few days after the conversation, Francine walked over to the factory and picked up the tiny part. She put the part in a prepaid, stamped envelope provided by the Florida company and mailed the part to the company in Florida.

One year later, Francine won free tickets to Disney World in Orlando, Florida. She left for Orlando with a friend immediately after winning the tickets. As soon she landed and disembarked the airplane in Orlando, she was confronted by two representatives from the Florida company. They gave her a piece of paper. The paper indicated that a federal court in Florida had entered a default judgment against her in the conversion action, *Florida Company vs. Francine*.

After she caught her breath, Francine realized that the company never received the part she mailed. The company assumed she kept the part. A week after they failed to receive the part, they initiated an action against her in the United States District Court for the Random District of Florida. Because Francine never even knew about this lawsuit, she failed to respond to the conversion claim. The trial court then entered a default judgment against Francine, which requires her to pay a significant amount of money to the company.

Explain, without using any legal terminology, rules or knowledge you have gained since entering law school, why Francine might think the result is unjust.

DIRECTED READING QUESTIONS

1. Explain, without using any of the legal terminology, rules or knowledge that you have gained since entering law school, why Francine might think that the result is unjust.

2. Explain how Federal Rule of Civil Procedure 4(a)–(c), (e) ameliorates some of the unjustness of the result above.

3. Plaintiff is a citizen of Iowa, and Defendant is a citizen of Nebraska. Plaintiff sues Defendant in the United States District Court for the District of Hawaii. The claim is a state law claim, related to an auto accident which occurred in Nebraska, and the amount in controversy is $74,000, exclusive of interests and costs. Neither Plaintiff nor Defendant has ever been to Hawaii, nor have they had any prior contact with that state.

Plaintiff's 8(a)(1) statement alleges that diversity of citizenship is the basis of subject matter jurisdiction.

a. May the Plaintiff, Defendant, or the court waive the requirement that the amount in controversy be in excess of $75,000 exclusive of costs and fees in order for subject matter jurisdiction to exist?

b. Assume that the claim satisfied the requirements of diversity subject matter jurisdiction. May the Plaintiff and Defendant agree that, because Hawaii is a relaxing location, they will just let the federal court in Hawaii adjudicate the claim, even though neither the parties nor the claim have any relationship to the state of Hawaii?

c. Do the answers to (a) and (b) explain what is meant by, "personal jurisdiction but not subject matter jurisdiction is waivable," and why the existence of personal jurisdiction over a plaintiff is usually a nonissue?

4. Does personal jurisdiction in a federal court over a defendant sometimes depend on whether a state court in the state where the federal court is located would have personal jurisdiction over the defendant? Read Rule 4(k)(1)(A) carefully to answer this question.

5. Rule 4(k)(1)(A) demonstrates that service of process alone is not enough to establish personal jurisdiction over a defendant, but rather it is service of process over a defendant who is "subject to the jurisdiction" of the court. What, apart from a lack of notice, might render Francine not "subject to the jurisdiction" of the federal court in Florida?

FED. R. CIV. P. 4

(k) TERRITORIAL LIMITS OF EFFECTIVE SERVICE.

(1) *In General.* **Serving a summons or filing a waiver of service establishes personal jurisdiction over a defendant:**

(A) who is subject to the jurisdiction of a court of general jurisdiction in the state where the district court is located;

(B) who is a party joined under Rule 14 or 19 and is served within a judicial district of the United States and not more than 100 miles from where the summons was issued; or

(C) when authorized by a federal statute.

(2) *Federal Claim Outside State-Court Jurisdiction.* For a claim that arises under federal law, serving a summons or filing a waiver of service establishes personal jurisdiction over a defendant if:

(A) the defendant is not subject to jurisdiction in any state's courts of general jurisdiction; and

(B) exercising jurisdiction is consistent with the United States Constitution and laws.

I. THE STATE POWER THEORY

PENNOYER V. NEFF (1877)
Supreme Court of the United States
95 U.S. 714

[There are] two well-established principles of public law respecting the jurisdiction of an independent State over persons and property. The several States of the Union are not, it is true, in every respect independent, many of the right and powers which originally belonged to them being now vested in the government created by the Constitution. But, except as restrained and limited by that instrument, they possess and exercise the authority of independent States, and the principles of public law to which we have referred are applicable to them. One of these principles is, that every State possesses exclusive jurisdiction and sovereignty over persons and property within its territory. As a consequence, every State has the power to determine for itself the civil *status* and capacities of its inhabitants; to prescribe the subjects upon which they may contract, the forms and solemnities with which their contracts shall be executed, the rights and obligations arising from them, and the mode in which their validity shall be determined and their obligations enforced; and also the regulate the manner and conditions upon which property situated within such territory, both personal and real, may be acquired, enjoyed, and transferred.

The other principle of public law referred to follows from the one mentioned; that is, that no State can exercise direct jurisdiction and authority over persons or property without its territory. The several States are of equal dignity and authority, and the independence of one implies the exclusion of power from all others. And so it is laid down by jurists, as an elementary principle, that the laws of one State have no operation outside of its territory, except so far as is allowed by comity; and that no tribunal established by it can extend its process beyond that territory so as to subject either persons or property to its decisions. 'Any exertion of authority of this sort beyond this limit,' says Story, 'is a mere nullity, and incapable of binding such persons or property in any other tribunals.'

But as contracts made in one State may be enforceable only in another State, and property may be held by non-residents, the exercise of the jurisdiction which every State is admitted to possess over persons and property within its own territory will often affect persons and property without it. To any influence exerted in this way by a State affecting persons resident or property situated elsewhere, no objection can be justly taken; whilst any direct exertion of authority upon them, in an attempt to give ex-territorial operation to its laws, or to enforce an ex-territorial jurisdiction by its tribunals, would be deemed an encroachment upon the independence of the State in which the persons are domiciled or the property is situated, and be resisted as usurpation.

Thus the State, through its tribunals, may compel persons domiciled within its limits to execute, in pursuance of their contracts respecting property elsewhere situated, instruments in such form and with such solemnities as to transfer the title, so far as such formalities can be complied with; and the exercise of this jurisdiction in no manner interferes with the supreme control over the property by the State within which it is situated.

So the State, through its tribunals, may subject property situated within its limits owned by non-residents to the payment of the demand of its own citizens against them; and the exercise of this jurisdiction in no respect infringes upon the sovereignty of the State where the owners are domiciled. Every State owes protection to its own citizens; and, when non-residents deal with them, it is a legitimate and just exercise of authority to hold and appropriate any property owned by such non-residents to satisfy the claims of its citizens. It is in virtue of the State's jurisdiction over the property of the non-resident situated within its limits that its tribunals can inquire into that non-resident's obligations to its own citizens, and the inquiry can then be carried only to the extent necessary to control the disposition of the property. If the non-resident have no property in the State, there is nothing upon which the tribunals can adjudicate.

These views are not new. They have been frequently expressed, with more or less distinctness, in opinions of eminent judges, and have been carried into adjudications in numerous cases. Thus, in *Picquet* v. *Swan*, Mr. Justice Story said:—

'Where a party is within a territory, he may justly be subjected to its process, and bound personally by the judgment pronounced on such process against him. Where he is not within such territory, and is not personally subject to its laws, if, on account of his supposed or actual property being within the territory, process by the local laws may, by attachment, go to compel his appearance, and for his default to appear judgment may be pronounced against him, such a judgment must, upon general principles, be deemed only to bind him to the extent of such property, and cannot have the effect of a conclusive judgment *in personam*, for the plain reason, that, except so far as the property is concerned, it is a judgment *coram non judice*.'

And in *Boswell's Lessee* v. *Otis*, where the title of the plaintiff in ejectment was acquired on a sheriff's sale, under a money decree rendered upon publication of notice against non-residents, in a suit brought to enforce a contract relating to land, Mr. Justice McLean said:—

'Jurisdiction is acquired in one of two modes: first, as against the person of the defendant by the service of process; or, secondly, by a procedure against the property of the defendant within the jurisdiction of the court. In the latter case, the defendant is not personally bound by the judgment beyond the property in question. And it is immaterial whether the proceeding against the property be by an attachment or bill in chancery. It must be substantially a proceeding *in rem*.'

DIRECTED READING QUESTIONS

6.   What are the two principles of public law that the *Pennoyer* case articulates?

7.   How do these two principles reflect limits on the power of the states, relative to each other?

8.   When, according to *Pennoyer*, may a state exercise personal jurisdiction over persons and property outside of its borders?

9.   The *Pennoyer* case recognizes that, "Jurisdiction is acquired in one of two modes . . . ." Explain what these modes are.

10. *Pennoyer* was a case decided in 1877. The next case, *International Shoe*, was decided in 1945. Explain what changed between 1877 and 1945, prompting the *International Shoe* court to state:

> Historically the jurisdiction of courts to render judgment *in personam* is grounded on their de facto power over the defendant's person. Hence his presence within the territorial jurisdiction of court was prerequisite to its rendition of a judgment personally binding him. *Pennoyer v. Neff*. But now . . . due process requires only that in order to subject a defendant to a judgment *in personam*, if he be not present within the territory of the forum, he have certain minimum contacts with it such that the maintenance of the suit does not offend 'traditional notions of fair play and substantial justice.'

II. MINIMUM CONTACTS AND PURPOSEFUL AVAILMENT

A. THE ORIGIN OF MINIMUM CONTACTS

INTERNATIONAL SHOE CO. v. WASHINGTON (1945)
Supreme Court of the United States
326 U.S. 310

MR. CHIEF JUSTICE STONE delivered the opinion of the Court.

The question[ ] for decision [is] whether, within the limitations of the due process clause of the Fourteenth Amendment, appellant, a Delaware corporation, has by its activities in the State of Washington rendered itself amenable to proceedings in the courts of that state to recover unpaid contributions to the state unemployment compensation fund exacted by state statutes.

The statutes in question set up a comprehensive scheme of unemployment compensation, the costs of which are defrayed by contributions required to be made by employers to a state unemployment compensation fund. The contributions are a specified percentage of the wages payable annually by each employer for his employees' services in the state. The assessment and collection of the contributions and the fund are administered by respondents. [The statutes], authorize[ ] respondent Commissioner to issue an order and notice of assessment of delinquent contributions upon prescribed personal service of the notice upon the employer if found within the state, or, if not so found, by mailing the notice to the employer by registered mail at his last known address.

* * *

In this case notice of assessment for the years in question was personally served upon a sales solicitor employed by appellant in the State of Washington, and a copy of the notice was mailed by registered mail to appellant at its address in St. Louis, Missouri. Appellant appeared specially before the office of unemployment and moved to set aside the order and notice of assessment on the ground that the service upon appellant's salesman was not proper service upon appellant; [and] that appellant was not a corporation of the State of Washington and was not doing business within the state[.]

The motion was heard on evidence and a stipulation of facts by the appeal tribunal which denied the motion and ruled that respondent Commissioner was entitled to recover the unpaid contributions. That action was affirmed by the Commissioner; both the Superior Court and the Supreme Court affirmed. Appellant in each of these courts assailed the statute as applied, as a violation of the due process clause of the Fourteenth Amendment[.] The cause comes here on appeal [with] appellant assigning as error that the challenged statutes as applied infringe the due process clause of the Fourteenth Amendment[.]

The facts as found by the appeal tribunal and accepted by the state Superior Court and Supreme Court, are not in dispute. Appellant is a Delaware corporation, having its principal place of business in St. Louis, Missouri, and is engaged in the manufacture and sale of shoes and other footwear. It maintains places of business in several states, other than Washington, at which its manufacturing is carried on and from which its merchandise is distributed interstate through several sales units or branches located outside the State of Washington.

Appellant has no office in Washington and makes no contracts either for sale or purchase of merchandise there. It maintains no stock of merchandise in that state and makes there no deliveries of goods in intrastate commerce. During the years from 1937 to 1940, now in question, appellant employed eleven to thirteen salesmen under direct supervision and control of sales managers located in St. Louis. These salesmen resided in Washington; their principal activities were confined to that state; and they were compensated by commissions based upon the amount of their sales. The commissions for each year totaled more than $31,000. Appellant supplies its salesmen with a line of samples, each consisting of one shoe of a pair, which they display to prospective purchasers. On occasion they rent permanent sample rooms, for exhibiting samples, in business buildings, or rent rooms in hotels or business buildings temporarily for that purpose. The cost of such rentals is reimbursed by appellant.

The authority of the salesmen is limited to exhibiting their samples and soliciting orders from prospective buyers, at prices and on terms fixed by appellant. The salesmen transmit the orders to appellant's office in St. Louis for acceptance or rejection, and when accepted the merchandise for filling the orders is shipped f.o.b. from points outside Washington to the purchasers within the state. All the merchandise shipped into Washington is invoiced at the place of shipment from which collections are made. No salesman has authority to enter into contracts or to make collections.

The Supreme Court of Washington was of opinion that the regular and systematic solicitation of orders in the state by appellant's salesmen, resulting in a continuous flow of appellant's product into the state, was sufficient to constitute doing business in the state so as to make appellant amenable to suit in its courts. But it was also of opinion that there were sufficient additional activities shown to bring the case within the rule frequently stated, that solicitation within a state by the agents of a foreign corporation plus some additional activities there are sufficient to render the corporation amenable to suit brought in the courts of the state to enforce an obligation arising out of its activities there. The court found such additional activities in the salesmen's display of samples sometimes in permanent display rooms, and the salesmen's residence within the state, continued over a period of years, all resulting in a substantial volume of merchandise regularly shipped by appellant to purchasers within the state.

* * *

Appellant [ ] insists that its activities within the state were not sufficient to manifest its 'presence' there and that in its absence the state courts were without jurisdiction, that consequently it was a denial of due process for the state to subject appellant to suit. It refers to those cases in which it was said that the mere solicitation of orders for the purchase of goods within a state, to be accepted without the state and filled by shipment of the purchased goods interstate, does not render the corporation seller amenable to suit within the state. And appellant further argues that since it was not present within the state, it is a denial of due process to subject it to taxation or other money exaction. It thus denies the power of the state to lay the tax or to subject appellant to a suit for its collection.

Historically the jurisdiction of courts to render judgment *in personam* is grounded on their de facto power over the defendant's person. Hence his presence within the territorial jurisdiction of court was prerequisite to its rendition of a judgment personally binding him. Pennoyer v. Neff. But now that the capias ad respondendum has given way to personal service of summons or other form of notice, due process requires only that in order to subject a defendant to a judgment *in personam,* if he be not present within the territory of the forum, he have certain minimum contacts with it such that the maintenance of the suit does not offend 'traditional notions of fair play and substantial justice.'

Since the corporate personality is a fiction, although a fiction intended to be acted upon as though it were a fact, it is clear that unlike an individual its 'presence' without, as well as within, the state of its origin can be manifested only by activities carried on in its behalf by those who are authorized to act for it. To say that the corporation is so far 'present' there as to satisfy due process requirements, for purposes of taxation or the maintenance of suits against it in the courts of the state, is to beg the question to be decided. For the terms 'present' or 'presence' are used merely to symbolize those activities of the corporation's agent within the state which courts will deem to be sufficient to satisfy the demands of due process. Those demands may be met by such contacts of the corporation with the state of the forum as make it reasonable, in the context of our federal system of government, to require the corporation to defend the particular suit which is brought there. An 'estimate of the inconveniences' which would result to the corporation from a trial away from its 'home' or principal place of business is relevant in this connection.

'Presence' in the state in this sense has never been doubted when the activities of the corporation there have not only been continuous and systematic, but also give rise to the liabilities sued on, even though no consent to be sued or authorization to an agent to accept service of process has been given. Conversely it has been generally recognized that the casual presence of the corporate agent or even his conduct of single or isolated items of activities in a state in the corporation's behalf are not enough to subject it to suit on causes of action unconnected with the activities there. To require the corporation in such circumstances to defend the suit away from its home or other jurisdiction where it carries on more substantial activities has been thought to lay too great and unreasonable a burden on the corporation to comport with due process.

Finally, although the commission of some single or occasional acts of the corporate agent in a state sufficient to impose an obligation or liability on the corporation has not been thought to confer upon the state authority to enforce it, other such acts, because of their nature and quality and the circumstances of their commission, may be deemed sufficient to render the corporation liable to suit. True, some of the decisions holding the corporation amenable to suit have been supported by resort to the legal fiction that it has given its consent to service and suit, consent being implied from its presence in the state through the acts of its authorized agents. But more realistically it may be said that those authorized acts were of such a nature as to justify the fiction.

It is evident that the criteria by which we mark the boundary line between those activities which justify the subjection of a corporation to suit, and those which do not, cannot be simply mechanical or quantitative. The test is not merely, as has sometimes been suggested, whether the activity, which the corporation has seen fit to procure through its agents in another state, is a little more or a little less. Whether due process is satisfied must depend rather upon the quality and nature of the activity in relation to the fair and orderly administration of the laws which it was the purpose of the due process clause to insure. That clause does not contemplate that a state may make binding a judgment *in personam* against an individual or corporate defendant with which the state has no contacts, ties, or relations.

But to the extent that a corporation exercises the privilege of conducting activities within a state, it enjoys the benefits and protection of the laws of that state. The exercise of that privilege may give rise to obligations; and, so far as those obligations arise out of or are connected with the activities within the state, a procedure which requires the corporation to respond to a suit brought to enforce them can, in most instances, hardly be said to be undue.

Applying these standards, the activities carried on in behalf of appellant in the State of Washington were neither irregular nor casual. They were systematic and continuous throughout the years in question. They resulted in a large volume of interstate business, in the course of which appellant received the benefits and protection of the laws of the state, including the right to resort to the courts for the enforcement of its rights. The obligation which is here sued upon arose out of those very activities. It is evident that these operations establish sufficient contacts or ties with the state of the forum to make it reasonable and just according to our traditional conception of fair play and substantial justice to permit the state to enforce the obligations which appellant has incurred there. Hence we cannot say that the maintenance of the present suit in the State of Washington involves an unreasonable or undue procedure.

We are likewise unable to conclude that the service of the process within the state upon an agent whose activities establish appellant's 'presence' there was not sufficient notice of the suit, or that the suit was so unrelated to those activities as to make the agent an inappropriate vehicle for communicating the notice. It is enough that appellant has established such contacts with the state that the particular form of substituted service adopted there gives reasonable assurance that the notice will be actual. Nor can we say that the mailing of the notice of suit to appellant by registered mail at its home office was not reasonably calculated to apprise appellant of the suit.

* * *

Appellant having rendered itself amenable to suit upon obligations arising out of the activities of its salesmen in Washington, the state may maintain the present suit *in personam* to collect the tax laid upon the exercise of the privilege of employing appellant's salesmen within the state. For Washington has made one of those activities, which taken together establish appellant's 'presence' there for purposes of suit, the taxable event by which the state brings appellant within the reach of its taxing power. The state thus has constitutional power to lay the tax and to subject appellant to a suit to recover it. The activities which establish its 'presence' subject it alike to taxation by the state and to suit to recover the tax.

MR. JUSTICE BLACK delivered the following opinion.

I believe that the Federal Constitution leaves to each State, without any 'ifs' or 'buts', a power to tax and to open the doors of its courts for its citizens to sue corporations whose agents do business in those States. Believing that the Constitution gave the States that power, I think it a judicial deprivation to condition its exercise upon this Court's notion of 'fairplay', however appealing that term may be. Nor can I stretch the meaning of due process so far as to authorize this Court to deprive a State of the right to afford judicial protection to its citizens on the ground that it would be more 'convenient' for the corporation to be sued somewhere else.

There is a strong emotional appeal in the words 'fair play', 'justice', and 'reasonableness.' But they were not chosen by those who wrote the original Constitution or the Fourteenth Amendment as a measuring rod for this Court to use in invalidating State or Federal laws passed by elected legislative representatives. No one, not even those who most feared a democratic government, ever formally proposed that courts should be given power to invalidate legislation under any such elastic standards. Express prohibitions against certain types of legislation are found in the Constitution, and under the long-settled practice, courts invalidate laws found to conflict with them. This requires interpretation, and interpretation, it is true, may result in extension of the Constitution's purpose. But that is no reason for reading the due process clause so as to restrict a State's power to tax and sue those whose activities affect persons and businesses within the State, provided proper service can be had. Superimposing the natural justice concept on the Constitution's specific prohibitions could operate as a drastic abridgment of democratic safeguards they embody, such as freedom of speech, press and religion, and the right to counsel.

For application of this natural law concept, whether under the terms 'reasonableness', 'justice', or 'fair play', makes judges the supreme arbiters of the country's laws and practices. This result, I believe, alters the form of government our Constitution provides. I cannot agree.

DIRECTED READING QUESTIONS

11. Describe International Shoe the corporation.

12. Describe the corporation's contacts with Washington state.

13. Why is the state of Washington suing International Shoe? In what court are they suing the corporation?

14. Notice and fairness are the two basic issues in personal jurisdiction cases. How is notice satisfied in this case?

15. The opinion mentions that the defendant "appeared specially." What is a special appearance?

16. What does capias ad **respondendum** mean?

17. Explain the essence of the corporation's argument that it is unfair (or in other words, violates the Due Process clause of the 14th Amendment) to permit a court in Washington state to adjudicate this claim and issue a valid judgment.

18. How does the Supreme Court negate the corporation's argument that it is not present in Washington state?

19. What is the minimum contacts test?

20. According to *International Shoe,* can a single activity in a state ever rise to the level of minimum contacts?

21. The following language from *International Shoe* creates an important restriction on personal jurisdiction when minimum contacts is asserted as the basis of personal jurisdiction,

> Appellant having rendered itself amenable to suit upon obligations arising out of the activities of its salesmen in Washington, the state may maintain the present suit *in personam* to collect the tax laid upon the exercise of the privilege of employing appellant's salesmen within the state. For Washington has made one of those activities, which taken together establish appellant's 'presence' there for purposes of suit, the taxable event by which the state brings appellant within the reach of its taxing power. The state thus has constitutional power to lay the tax and to subject appellant to a suit to recover it. The activities which establish its 'presence' subject it alike to taxation by the state and to suit to recover the tax.

What is the restriction created by the above language? Why might this restriction result in personal jurisdiction based on minimum contacts being described as specific jurisdiction?

22. How is Justice Black's concurrence similar to the majority decision in *Erie*?

B. PURPOSEFUL AVAILMENT AND INTENTIONAL ACTS

McGee v. International Life Ins. Co. (1957)
Supreme Court of the United States
355 U.S. 220

Opinion of the Court by MR. JUSTICE BLACK, announced by MR. JUSTICE DOUGLAS.

Petitioner, Lulu B. McGee, recovered a judgment in a California state court against respondent, International Life Insurance Company, on a contract of insurance. Respondent was not served with process in California but by registered mail at its principal place of business in Texas. The California court based its jurisdiction on a state statute which subjects foreign corporations to suit in California on insurance contracts with residents of that State even though such corporations cannot be served with process within its borders.

Unable to collect the judgment in California petitioner went to Texas where she filed suit on the judgment in a Texas court. But the Texas courts refused to enforce her judgment holding it was void under the Fourteenth Amendment because service of process outside California could not give the courts of that State jurisdiction over respondent. Since the case raised important questions, not only to California but to other States which have similar laws, we granted certiorari. It is not controverted that if the California court properly exercised jurisdiction over respondent the Texas courts erred in refusing to give its judgment full faith and credit.

The material facts are relatively simple. In 1944, Lowell Franklin, a resident of California, purchased a life insurance policy from the Empire Mutual Insurance Company, an Arizona corporation. In 1948 the respondent agreed with Empire Mutual to assume its insurance obligations. Respondent then mailed a reinsurance certificate to Franklin in California offering to insure him in accordance with the terms of the policy he held with Empire Mutual. He accepted this offer and from that time until his death in 1950 paid premiums by mail from his California home to respondent's Texas office. Petitioner Franklin's mother, was the beneficiary under the policy. She sent proofs of his death to the respondent but it refused to pay claiming that he had committed suicide. It appears that neither Empire Mutual nor respondent has ever had any office or agent in California. And so far as the record before us shows, respondent has never solicited or done any insurance business in California apart from the policy involved here.

Since *Pennoyer v. Neff* this Court has held that the Due Process Clause of the Fourteenth Amendment places some limit on the power of state courts to enter binding judgments against persons not served with process within their boundaries. But just where this line of limitation falls has been the subject of prolific controversy, particularly with respect to foreign corporations. In a continuing process of evolution this Court accepted and then abandoned 'consent,' 'doing business,' and 'presence' as the standard for measuring the extent of state judicial power over such corporations. See Henderson, The Position of Foreign Corporations in American Constitutional Law, c. V. More recently in *International Shoe Co. v. State of Washington*, the Court decided that 'due process requires only that in order to subject a defendant to a judgment *in personam*, if he be not present within the territory of the forum, he have certain minimum contacts with it such that the maintenance of the suit does not offend 'traditional notions of fair play and substantial justice.

Looking back over this long history of litigation a trend is clearly discernible toward expanding the permissible scope of state jurisdiction over foreign corporations and other nonresidents. In part this is attributable to the fundamental transformation of our national economy over the years. Today many commercial transactions touch two or more States and may involve parties separated by the full continent. With this increasing nationalization of commerce has come a great increase in the amount of business conducted by mail across state lines. At the same time modern transportation and communication have made it much less burdensome for a party sued to defend himself in a State where he engages in economic activity.

Turning to this case we think it apparent that the Due Process Clause did not preclude the California court from entering a judgment binding on respondent. It is sufficient for purposes of due process that the suit was based on a contract which had substantial connection with that State. The contract was delivered in California, the premiums were mailed from there and the insured was a resident of that State when he died. It cannot be denied that California has a manifest interest in providing effective means of redress for its residents when their insurers refuse to pay claims. These residents would be at a severe disadvantage if they were forced to follow the insurance company to a distant State in order to hold it legally accountable. When claims were small or moderate individual claimants frequently could not afford the cost of bringing an action in a foreign forum—thus in effect making the company judgment proof. Often the crucial witnesses—as here on the company's defense of suicide—will be found in the insured's locality. Of course there may be inconvenience to the insurer if it is held amenable to suit in California where it had this contract but certainly nothing which amounts to a denial of due process. There is no contention that respondent did not have adequate notice of the suit or sufficient time to prepare its defenses and appear.

* * *

The judgment is reversed and the cause is remanded to the Court of Civil Appeals of the State of Texas, First Supreme Judicial District, for further proceedings not inconsistent with this opinion.

It is so ordered.

HANSON V. DENCKLA (1958)

Supreme Court of the United States
357 U.S. 235

[A woman from Pennsylvania set up a trust with a trustee in Delaware. She subsequently moved to Florida and died there. While in Florida she made a number of important decisions regarding the trust. The Florida courts found the trust invalid under Florida law because she retained too much power over the trust. In making this determination the Florida court exercised jurisdiction over the trustee residing in Delaware. "A copy of the pleadings and a 'Notice to Appear and Defend' were sent to each of these defendants by ordinary mail, and notice was published locally as required by the Florida statutes dealing with constructive service."]

Prior to the Fourteenth Amendment an exercise of jurisdiction over persons or property outside the forum State was thought to be an absolute nullity, but the matter remained a question of state law over which this Court exercised no authority. With the adoption of that Amendment, any judgment purporting to bind the person of a defendant over whom the court had not acquired *in personam* jurisdiction was void within the State as well as without. *Pennoyer v. Neff.*

* * *

Appellees' stronger argument is for *in personam* jurisdiction over the Delaware trustee. They urge that the circumstances of this case amount to sufficient affiliation with the State of Florida to empower its courts to exercise personal jurisdiction over this nonresident defendant. Principal reliance is placed upon *McGee v. International Life Ins. Co.* In *McGee* the Court noted the trend of expanding personal jurisdiction over nonresidents. As technological progress has increased the flow of commerce between States, the need for jurisdiction over nonresidents has undergone a similar increase. At the same time, progress in communications and transportation has made the defense of a suit in a foreign tribunal less burdensome. In response to these changes, the requirements for personal jurisdiction over nonresidents have evolved from the rigid rule of *Pennoyer v. Neff* to the flexible standard of *International Shoe.*

But it is a mistake to assume that this trend heralds the eventual demise of all restrictions on the personal jurisdiction of state courts. Those restrictions are more than a guarantee of immunity from inconvenient or distant litigation. They are a consequence of territorial limitations on the power of the respective States. However minimal the burden of defending in a foreign tribunal, a defendant may not be called upon to do so unless he has had the 'minimal contacts' with that State that are a prerequisite to its exercise of power over him. *See International Shoe Co. v. State of Washington.*

We fail to find such contacts in the circumstances of this case. The defendant trust company has no office in Florida and transacts no business there. None of the trust assets has ever been held or administered in Florida, and the record discloses no solicitation of business in that State either in person or by mail.

The cause of action in this case is not one that arises out of an act done or transaction consummated in the forum State. In that respect, it differs from *McGee*, and the cases there cited. In *McGee*, the nonresident defendant solicited a reinsurance agreement with a resident of California. The offer was accepted in that State, and the insurance premiums were mailed from there until the insured's death. Noting the interest California has in providing effective redress for its residents when nonresident insurers refuse to pay claims on insurance they have solicited in that State, the Court upheld jurisdiction because the suit 'was based on a contract which had substantial connection with that State.' In contrast, this action involves the validity of an agreement that was entered without any connection with the forum State. The agreement was executed in Delaware by a trust company incorporated in that State and a settlor domiciled in Pennsylvania. The first relationship Florida had to the agreement was years later when the settlor became domiciled there, and the trustee remitted the trust income to her in that State. From Florida Mrs. Donner carried on several bits of trust administration that may be compared to the mailing of premiums in *McGee*. But the record discloses no instance in which the trustee performed any acts in Florida that bear the same relationship to the agreement as the solicitation in McGee. Consequently, this suit cannot be said to be one to enforce an obligation that arose from a privilege the defendant exercised in Florida.

* * *

The execution in Florida of the powers of appointment under which the beneficiaries and appointees claim does not give Florida a substantial connection with the contract on which this suit is based. It is the validity of the trust agreement, not the appointment, that is at issue here.

* * *

The unilateral activity of those who claim some relationship with a nonresident defendant cannot satisfy the requirement of contact with the forum State. The application of that rule will vary with the quality and nature of the defendant's activity, but it is essential in each case that there be some act by which the defendant purposefully avails itself of the privilege of conducting activities within the forum State, thus invoking the benefits and protections of its laws. *International Shoe Co. v. State of Washington*. The settlor's execution in Florida of her power of appointment cannot remedy the absence of such an act in this case.

* * *

The judgment of the Delaware Supreme Court is affirmed, and the judgment of the Florida Supreme Court is reversed and the cause is remanded for proceedings not inconsistent with this opinion.

It is so ordered.

CALDER V. JONES (1984)
Supreme Court of the United States
465 U.S. 783

Petitioners' analogy does not wash. [P]etitioners are not charged with mere untargeted negligence. Rather, their intentional, and allegedly tortious, actions were expressly aimed at California. Petitioner South wrote and petitioner Calder edited an article that they knew would have a potentially devastating impact upon respondent. And they knew that the brunt of that injury would be felt by respondent in the State in which she lives and works and in which the *National Enquirer* has its largest circulation. Under the circumstances, petitioners must "reasonably anticipate being haled into court there" to answer for the truth of the statements made in their article.

An individual injured in California need not go to Florida to seek redress from persons who, though remaining in Florida, knowingly cause the injury in California.

We hold that jurisdiction over petitioners in California is proper because of their intentional conduct in Florida calculated to cause injury to respondent in California.

DIRECTED READING QUESTIONS

23. Where was the suit in *McGee* filed, and how was notice satisfied?

24. In *McGee*, why does the insurance beneficiary travel to Texas, and why does the Texas court refuse to enforce the judgment?

25. What does the *McGee* court identify as "sufficient" for establishing personal jurisdiction over the insurer?

26. Is *McGee* an example of a single act being enough to satisfy minimum contacts?

27. What does *McGee* identify as the justification for expanding personal jurisdiction?

28. Explain the existence of personal jurisdiction in *McGee* but not in *Hanson*, even though the contract in *Hanson* also had a "substantial connection" with the state of Florida?

C. TENSIONS BETWEEN FAIRNESS AND FEDERALISM

WORLD-WIDE VOLKSWAGEN CORP. V. WOODSON (1980)
Supreme Court of the United States
444 U.S. 286

MR. JUSTICE WHITE delivered the opinion of the Court.

The issue before us is whether, consistently with the Due Process Clause of the Fourteenth Amendment, an Oklahoma court may exercise *in personam* jurisdiction over a nonresident automobile retailer and its wholesale distributor in a products-liability action, when the defendants' only connection with Oklahoma is the fact that an automobile sold in New York to New York residents became involved in an accident in Oklahoma.

I

Respondents Harry and Kay Robinson purchased a new Audi automobile from petitioner Seaway Volkswagen, Inc. (Seaway), in Massena, N. Y., in 1976. The following year the Robinson family, who resided in New York, left that State for a new home in Arizona. As they passed through the State of Oklahoma, another car struck their Audi in the rear, causing a fire which severely burned Kay Robinson and her two children.[1]

The Robinsons subsequently brought a products-liability action in the District Court for Creek County, Okla., claiming that their injuries resulted from defective design and placement of the Audi's gas tank and fuel system. They joined as defendants the automobile's manufacturer, Audi NSU Auto Union Aktiengesellschaft (Audi); its importer Volkswagen of America, Inc. (Volkswagen); its regional distributor, petitioner World-Wide Volkswagen Corp. (World-Wide); and its retail dealer, petitioner Seaway. Seaway and World-Wide entered special appearances,[3] claiming that Oklahoma's exercise of jurisdiction over them would offend the limitations on the State's jurisdiction imposed by the Due Process Clause of the Fourteenth Amendment.

The facts presented to the District Court showed that World-Wide is incorporated and has its business office in New York. It distributes vehicles, parts, and accessories, under contract with Volkswagen, to retail dealers in New York, New Jersey, and Connecticut. Seaway, one of these retail dealers, is incorporated and has its place of business in New York. Insofar as the record reveals, Seaway and World-Wide are fully independent corporations whose relations with each other and with Volkswagen and Audi are contractual only. Respondents adduced no evidence that either World-Wide or Seaway does any business in Oklahoma, ships or sells any products to or in that State, has an agent to receive process there, or purchases advertisements in any media calculated to reach Oklahoma. In fact, as respondents' counsel conceded at oral argument, there was no showing that any automobile sold by World-Wide or Seaway has ever entered Oklahoma with the single exception of the vehicle involved in the present case.

---

[1] The driver of the other automobile does not figure in the present litigation.

[3] Volkswagen also entered a special appearance in the District Court, but unlike World-Wide and Seaway did not seek review in the Supreme Court of Oklahoma and is not a petitioner here. Both Volkswagen and Audi remain as defendants in the litigation pending before the District Court in Oklahoma.

Despite the apparent paucity of contacts between petitioners and Oklahoma, the District Court rejected their constitutional claim and reaffirmed that ruling in denying petitioners' motion for reconsideration. Petitioners then sought a writ of prohibition in the Supreme Court of Oklahoma to restrain the District Judge, respondent Charles S. Woodson, from exercising *in personam* jurisdiction over them. They renewed their contention that, because they had no "minimal contacts," with the State of Oklahoma, the actions of the District Judge were in violation of their rights under the Due Process Clause.

The Supreme Court of Oklahoma denied the writ, holding that personal jurisdiction over petitioners was authorized by Oklahoma's "long-arm" statute Okla.Stat., Tit. 12, § 1701.03(a)(4) (1971).[7] Although the court noted that the proper approach was to test jurisdiction against both statutory and constitutional standards, its analysis did not distinguish these questions, probably because § 1701.03(a)(4) has been interpreted as conferring jurisdiction to the limits permitted by the United States Constitution. The court's rationale was contained in the following paragraph,

> In the case before us, the product being sold and distributed by the petitioners is by its very design and purpose so mobile that petitioners can foresee its possible use in Oklahoma. This is especially true of the distributor, who has the exclusive right to distribute such automobile in New York, New Jersey and Connecticut. The evidence presented below demonstrated that goods sold and distributed by the petitioners were used in the State of Oklahoma, and under the facts we believe it reasonable to infer, given the retail value of the automobile, that the petitioners derive substantial income from automobiles which from time to time are used in the State of Oklahoma. This being the case, we hold that under the facts presented, the trial court was justified in concluding that the petitioners derive substantial revenue from goods used or consumed in this State.

We granted certiorari, to consider an important constitutional question with respect to state-court jurisdiction and to resolve a conflict between the Supreme Court of Oklahoma and the highest courts of at least four other States. We reverse.

II

The Due Process Clause of the Fourteenth Amendment limits the power of a state court to render a valid personal judgment against a nonresident defendant. A judgment rendered in violation of due process is void in the rendering State and is not entitled to full faith and credit elsewhere. Due process requires that the defendant be given adequate notice of the suit, and be subject to the personal jurisdiction of the court, *International Shoe Co.* In the present case, it is not contended that notice was

---

[7] This subsection provides:

A court may exercise personal jurisdiction over a person, who acts directly or by an agent, as to a cause of action or claim for relief arising from the person's . . . causing tortious injury in this state by an act or omission outside this state if he regularly does or solicits business or engages in any other persistent course of conduct, or derives substantial revenue from goods used or consumed or services rendered, in this state
. . . .

The State Supreme Court rejected jurisdiction based on § 1701.03(a)(3), which authorizes jurisdiction over any person "causing tortious injury in this state by an act or omission in this state." Something in addition to the infliction of tortious injury was required.

inadequate; the only question is whether these particular petitioners were subject to the jurisdiction of the Oklahoma courts.

As has long been settled, and as we reaffirm today, a state court may exercise personal jurisdiction over a nonresident defendant only so long as there exist "minimum contacts" between the defendant and the forum State. *International Shoe Co.* The concept of minimum contacts, in turn, can be seen to perform two related, but distinguishable, functions. It protects the defendant against the burdens of litigating in a distant or inconvenient forum. And it acts to ensure that the States through their courts, do not reach out beyond the limits imposed on them by their status as coequal sovereigns in a federal system.

The protection against inconvenient litigation is typically described in terms of "reasonableness" or "fairness." We have said that the defendant's contacts with the forum State must be such that maintenance of the suit "does not offend 'traditional notions of fair play and substantial justice.' " *International Shoe Co.* The relationship between the defendant and the forum must be such that it is "reasonable . . . to require the corporation to defend the particular suit which is brought there." Implicit in this emphasis on reasonableness is the understanding that the burden on the defendant, while always a primary concern, will in an appropriate case be considered in light of other relevant factors, including the forum State's interest in adjudicating the dispute, the plaintiff's interest in obtaining convenient and effective relief, at least when that interest is not adequately protected by the plaintiff's power to choose the forum; the interstate judicial system's interest in obtaining the most efficient resolution of controversies; and the shared interest of the several States in furthering fundamental substantive social policies.

The limits imposed on state jurisdiction by the Due Process Clause, in its role as a guarantor against inconvenient litigation, have been substantially relaxed over the years. As we noted in *McGee,* this trend is largely attributable to a fundamental transformation in the American economy:

> Today many commercial transactions touch two or more States and may involve parties separated by the full continent. With this increasing nationalization of commerce has come a great increase in the amount of business conducted by mail across state lines. At the same time modern transportation and communication have made it much less burdensome for a party sued to defend himself in a State where he engages in economic activity.

The historical developments noted in *McGee,* of course, have only accelerated in the generation since that case was decided.

Nevertheless, we have never accepted the proposition that state lines are irrelevant for jurisdictional purposes, nor could we, and remain faithful to the principles of interstate federalism embodied in the Constitution. The economic interdependence of the States was foreseen and desired by the Framers. In the Commerce Clause, they provided that the Nation was to be a common market, a "free trade unit" in which the States are debarred from acting as separable economic entities. But the Framers also intended that the States retain many essential attributes of sovereignty, including, in particular, the sovereign power to try causes in their courts. The sovereignty of each State, in turn, implied a limitation on the sovereignty of all of its sister States—a limitation express or implicit in both the original scheme of the Constitution and the Fourteenth Amendment.

Hence, even while abandoning the shibboleth that "[t]he authority of every tribunal is necessarily restricted by the territorial limits of the State in which it is established," *Pennoyer v. Neff,* we emphasized that the reasonableness of asserting jurisdiction over the defendant must be assessed "in the context of our federal system of government," *International Shoe Co. v. Washington,* and stressed that the Due Process Clause ensures not only fairness, but also the "orderly administration of the laws. As we noted in *Hanson v. Denckla:*

> As technological progress has increased the flow of commerce between the States, the need for jurisdiction over nonresidents has undergone a similar increase. At the same time, progress in communications and transportation has made the defense of a suit in a foreign tribunal less burdensome. In response to these changes, the requirements for personal jurisdiction over nonresidents have evolved from the rigid rule of *Pennoyer v. Neff,* to the flexible standard of *International Shoe* But it is a mistake to assume that this trend heralds the eventual demise of all restrictions on the personal jurisdiction of state courts. [Citation omitted.] Those restrictions are more than a guarantee of immunity from inconvenient or distant litigation. They are a consequence of territorial limitations on the power of the respective States.

Thus, the Due Process Clause "does not contemplate that a state may make binding a judgment *in personam* against an individual or corporate defendant with which the state has no contacts, ties, or relations." *International Shoe Co.* Even if the defendant would suffer minimal or no inconvenience from being forced to litigate before the tribunals of another State; even if the forum State has a strong interest in applying its law to the controversy; even if the forum State is the most convenient location for litigation, the Due Process Clause, acting as an instrument of interstate federalism, may sometimes act to divest the State of its power to render a valid judgment. *Hanson v. Denckla.*

III

Applying these principles to the case at hand, we find in the record before us a total absence of those affiliating circumstances that are a necessary predicate to any exercise of state-court jurisdiction. Petitioners carry on no activity whatsoever in Oklahoma. They close no sales and perform no services there. They avail themselves of none of the privileges and benefits of Oklahoma law. They solicit no business there either through salespersons or through advertising reasonably calculated to reach the State. Nor does the record show that they regularly sell cars at wholesale or retail to Oklahoma customers or residents or that they indirectly, through others, serve or seek to serve the Oklahoma market. In short, respondents seek to base jurisdiction on one, isolated occurrence and whatever inferences can be drawn therefrom: the fortuitous circumstance that a single Audi automobile, sold in New York to New York residents, happened to suffer an accident while passing through Oklahoma.

It is argued, however, that because an automobile is mobile by its very design and purpose it was "foreseeable" that the Robinsons' Audi would cause injury in Oklahoma. Yet "foreseeability" alone has never been a sufficient benchmark for personal jurisdiction under the Due Process Clause. In *Hanson v. Denckla* it was no doubt foreseeable that the settlor of a Delaware trust would subsequently move to Florida and seek to exercise a power of appointment there; yet we held that Florida courts could not constitutionally exercise jurisdiction over a Delaware trustee that had no other contacts with the forum State.

* * *

If foreseeability were the criterion, . . . [e]very seller of chattels would in effect appoint the chattel his agent for service of process. His amenability to suit would travel with the chattel.

* * *

This is not to say, of course, that foreseeability is wholly irrelevant. But the foreseeability that is critical to due process analysis is not the mere likelihood that a product will find its way into the forum State. Rather, it is that the defendant's conduct and connection with the forum State are such that he should reasonably anticipate being haled into court there. The Due Process Clause, by ensuring the "orderly administration of the laws," *International Shoe Co. v. Washington*, gives a degree of predictability to the legal system that allows potential defendants to structure their primary conduct with some minimum assurance as to where that conduct will and will not render them liable to suit.

When a corporation "purposefully avails itself of the privilege of conducting activities within the forum State," *Hanson v. Denckla*, it has clear notice that it is subject to suit there, and can act to alleviate the risk of burdensome litigation by procuring insurance, passing the expected costs on to customers, or, if the risks are too great, severing its connection with the State. Hence if the sale of a product of a manufacturer or distributor such as Audi or Volkswagen is not simply an isolated occurrence, but arises from the efforts of the manufacturer or distributor to serve directly or indirectly, the market for its product in other States, it is not unreasonable to subject it to suit in one of those States if its allegedly defective merchandise has there been the source of injury to its owner or to others. The forum State does not exceed its powers under the Due Process Clause if it asserts personal jurisdiction over a corporation that delivers its products into the stream of commerce with the expectation that they will be purchased by consumers in the forum State.

But there is no such or similar basis for Oklahoma jurisdiction over World-Wide or Seaway in this case. Seaway's sales are made in Massena, N. Y. World-Wide's market, although substantially larger, is limited to dealers in New York, New Jersey, and Connecticut. There is no evidence of record that any automobiles distributed by World-Wide are sold to retail customers outside this tristate area. It is foreseeable that the purchasers of automobiles sold by World-Wide and Seaway may take them to Oklahoma. But the mere "unilateral activity of those who claim some relationship with a nonresident defendant cannot satisfy the requirement of contact with the forum State." *Hanson v. Denckla*.

In a variant on the previous argument, it is contended that jurisdiction can be supported by the fact that petitioners earn substantial revenue from goods used in drawing the inference that because one automobile sold by petitioners had been used in

Oklahoma, others might have been used there also. While this inference seems less than compelling on the facts of the instant case, we need not question the court's factual findings in order to reject its reasoning.

This argument seems to make the point that the purchase of automobiles in New York, from which the petitioners earn substantial revenue, would not occur *but for* the fact that the automobiles are capable of use in distant States like Oklahoma. Respondents observe that the very purpose of an automobile is to travel, and that travel of automobiles sold by petitioners is facilitated by an extensive chain of Volkswagen service centers throughout the country, including some in Oklahoma.[12] However, financial benefits accruing to the defendant from a collateral relation to the forum State will not support jurisdiction if they do not stem from a constitutionally cognizable contact with that State. In our view, whatever marginal revenues petitioners may receive by virtue of the fact that their products are capable of use in Oklahoma is far too attenuated a contact to justify that State's exercise of *in personam* jurisdiction over them.

Because we find that petitioners have no "contacts, ties, or relations" with the State of Oklahoma, *International Shoe Co. v. Washington,* the judgment of the Supreme Court of Oklahoma is

Reversed.

MR. JUSTICE MARSHALL, with whom MR. JUSTICE BLACKMUN joins, dissenting.

* * *

This is a difficult case, and reasonable minds may differ as to whether respondents have alleged a sufficient "relationship among the defendant[s], the forum, and the litigation," to satisfy the requirements of *International Shoe.* I am concerned, however, that the majority has reached its result by taking an unnecessarily narrow view of petitioners' forum-related conduct. The majority asserts that "respondents seek to base jurisdiction on one, isolated occurrence and whatever inferences can be drawn therefrom: the fortuitous circumstance that a single Audi automobile, sold in New York to New York residents, happened to suffer an accident while passing through Oklahoma." If that were the case, I would readily agree that the minimum contacts necessary to sustain jurisdiction are not present. But the basis for the assertion of jurisdiction is not the happenstance that an individual over whom petitioner had no control made a unilateral decision to take a chattel with him to a distant State. Rather, jurisdiction is premised on the deliberate and purposeful actions of the defendants themselves in choosing to become part of a nationwide, indeed a global, network for marketing and servicing automobiles.

* * *

I sympathize with the majority's concern that the persons ought to be able to structure their conduct so as not to be subject to suit in distant forums. But that may not always be possible. Some activities by their very nature may foreclose the option of conducting them in such a way as to avoid subjecting oneself to jurisdiction in multiple forums. This is by no means to say that all sellers of automobiles should be subject to suit everywhere; but a distributor of automobiles to a multistate market and a local automobile dealer who makes himself part of a nationwide network of dealerships can

---

[12] As we have noted, petitioners earn no direct revenues from these service centers.

fairly expect that the cars they sell may cause injury in distant States and that they may be called on to defend a resulting lawsuit there.

* * *

MR. JUSTICE BLACKMUN, dissenting.

* * *

For me, a critical factor in the disposition of the litigation is the nature of the instrumentality under consideration. It has been said that we are a nation on wheels. What we are concerned with here is the automobile and its peripatetic character. One need only examine our national network of interstate highways, or make an appearance on one of them, or observe the variety of license plates present not only on those highways but in any metropolitan area, to realize that any automobile is likely to wander far from its place of licensure or from its place of distribution and retail sale. Miles per gallon on the highway (as well as in the city) and mileage per tankful are familiar allegations in manufacturers' advertisements today. To expect that any new automobile will remain in the vicinity of its retail sale—like the 1914 electric driven car by the proverbial "little old lady"—is to blink at reality. The automobile is intended for distance as well as for transportation within a limited area.

It therefore seems to me not unreasonable—and certainly not unconstitutional and beyond the reach of the principles laid down in *International Shoe Co. v. Washington,* and its progeny—to uphold Oklahoma jurisdiction over this New York distributor and this New York dealer when the accident happened in Oklahoma. I see nothing more unfair for them than for the manufacturer and the importer. All are in the business of providing vehicles that spread out over the highways of our several States. It is not too much to anticipate at the time of distribution and at the time of retail sale that this Audi would be in Oklahoma.

* * *

DIRECTED READING QUESTIONS

29. How do you know this case is not about the notice aspect of personal jurisdiction?

30. Who are the plaintiffs and defendants in this case? Who among the parties are citizens of New York, and in which court is the action brought?

31. Can you explain why only World-Wide and Seaway challenged Oklahoma's assertion of personal jurisdiction, as mentioned in footnote 3?

32. Explain, in terms of minimum contacts and purposeful availment, how the Oklahoma Supreme Court concluded that Oklahoma had personal jurisdiction over World-Wide and Seaway given the following language from the opinion:

> [W]orld-Wide is incorporated and has its business office in New York. It distributes vehicles, parts, and accessories, under contract with Volkswagen, to retail dealers in New York, New Jersey, and Connecticut. Seaway, one of these retail dealers, is incorporated and has its place of business in New York. Insofar as the record reveals, Seaway and World-Wide are fully independent corporations whose relations with each other and with Volkswagen and Audi are contractual only. Respondents adduced no evidence that either World-Wide

or Seaway does any business in Oklahoma, ships or sells any products to or in that State, has an agent to receive process there, or purchases advertisements in any media calculated to reach Oklahoma. In fact, as respondents' counsel conceded at oral argument, there was no showing that any automobile sold by World-Wide or Seaway has ever entered Oklahoma with the single exception of the vehicle involved in the present case.

33. Precisely explain why the United States Supreme Court reversed the Oklahoma Supreme Court, and the relevance of federalism and foreseeability to the reversal.

D. THE STREAM OF COMMERCE METAPHOR AND REASONABLENESS

ASAHI METAL INDUS. CO. V. SUPERIOR COURT (1987)
Supreme Court of the United States
480 U.S. 102

JUSTICE O'CONNOR announced the judgment of the Court and delivered the unanimous opinion of the Court with respect to Part I, the opinion of the Court with respect to Part II-B, in which THE CHIEF JUSTICE, JUSTICE BRENNAN, JUSTICE WHITE, JUSTICE MARSHALL, JUSTICE BLACKMUN, JUSTICE POWELL, and JUSTICE STEVENS join, and an opinion with respect to Parts II-A and III, in which THE CHIEF JUSTICE, JUSTICE POWELL, and JUSTICE SCALIA join.

This case presents the question whether the mere awareness on the part of a foreign defendant that the components it manufactured, sold, and delivered outside the United States would reach the forum State in the stream of commerce constitutes "minimum contacts" between the defendant and the forum State such that the exercise of jurisdiction "does not offend 'traditional notions of fair play and substantial justice.'"

I

On September 23, 1978, on Interstate Highway 80 in Solano County, California, Gary Zurcher lost control of his Honda motorcycle and collided with a tractor. Zurcher was severely injured, and his passenger and wife, Ruth Ann Moreno, was killed. In September 1979, Zurcher filed a product liability action in the Superior Court of the State of California in and for the County of Solano. Zurcher alleged that the 1978 accident was caused by a sudden loss of air and an explosion in the rear tire of the motorcycle, and alleged that the motorcycle tire, tube, and sealant were defective. Zurcher's complaint named, Honda [and] Cheng Shin Rubber Industrial Co., Ltd. (Cheng Shin), the Taiwanese manufacturer of the tube. Cheng Shin in turn filed a cross-complaint seeking indemnification from its codefendants and from petitioner, Asahi Metal Industry Co., Ltd. (Asahi), the manufacturer of the tube's valve assembly. Zurcher's claims against Cheng Shin and the other defendants were eventually settled and dismissed, leaving only Cheng Shin's indemnity action against Asahi.

The Supreme Court of the State of California . . . found the exercise of jurisdiction over Asahi to be consistent with the Due Process Clause. It concluded that Asahi knew that some of the valve assemblies sold to Cheng Shin would be incorporated into tire tubes sold in California, and that Asahi benefited indirectly from the sale in California of products incorporating its components. The court considered Asahi's intentional act of placing its components into the stream of commerce—that is, by delivering the components to Cheng Shin in Taiwan—coupled with Asahi's awareness that some of the components would eventually find their way into California, sufficient to form the basis for state court jurisdiction under the Due Process Clause.

II

A

[Justice O'Connor's opinion referred to the ruling in *World-Wide Volkswagen* requiring more than just foreseeability that a product placed in the stream of commerce by defendant will end up in the forum state to be sufficient for the defendant to be subject to the personal jurisdiction in the state.]

The "substantial connection" between the defendant and the forum State necessary for a finding of minimum contacts must come about by *an action of the defendant purposefully directed toward the forum State*. The placement of a product into the stream of commerce, without more, is not an act of the defendant purposefully directed toward the forum State. Additional conduct of the defendant may indicate an intent or purpose to serve the market in the forum State, for example, designing the product for the market in the forum State, advertising in the forum State, establishing channels for providing regular advice to customers in the forum State, or marketing the product through a distributor who has agreed to serve as the sales agent in the forum State. But a defendant's awareness that the stream of commerce may or will sweep the product into the forum State does not convert the mere act of placing the product into the stream into an act purposefully directed toward the forum State.

II

B

[She then went on to conclude that even if minimum contacts existed, the exercise of jurisdiction would be unreasonable in this particular case.]

We have previously explained that the determination of the reasonableness of the exercise of jurisdiction in each case will depend on an evaluation of several factors. A court must consider the burden on the defendant, the interests of the forum State, and the plaintiff's interest in obtaining relief. It must also weigh in its determination "the interstate judicial system's interest in obtaining the most efficient resolution of controversies; and the shared interest of the several States in furthering fundamental substantive social policies." *World-Wide Volkswagen.*

A consideration of these factors in the present case clearly reveals the unreasonableness of the assertion of jurisdiction over Asahi, even apart from the question of the placement of goods in the stream of commerce.

Certainly the burden on the defendant in this case is severe. Asahi has been commanded by the Supreme Court of California not only to traverse the distance between Asahi's headquarters in Japan and the Superior Court of California in and for the County of Solano, but also to submit its dispute with Cheng Shin to a foreign nation's judicial system. The unique burdens placed upon one who must defend oneself in a foreign legal system should have significant weight in assessing the reasonableness of stretching the long arm of personal jurisdiction over national borders.

When minimum contacts have been established, often the interests of the plaintiff and the forum in the exercise of jurisdiction will justify even the serious burdens placed on the alien defendant. In the present case, however, the interests of the plaintiff and the forum in California's assertion of jurisdiction over Asahi are slight. All that remains is a claim for indemnification asserted by Cheng Shin, a Taiwanese corporation, against Asahi. The transaction on which the indemnification claim is based took place in Taiwan; Asahi's components were shipped from Japan to Taiwan. Cheng Shin has not demonstrated that it is more convenient for it to litigate its indemnification claim against Asahi in California rather than in Taiwan or Japan.

Because the plaintiff is not a California resident, California's legitimate interests in the dispute have considerably diminished. The Supreme Court of California argued that the State had an interest in "protecting its consumers by ensuring that foreign manufacturers comply with the state's safety standards." The State Supreme Court's definition of California's interest, however, was overly broad. The dispute between Cheng Shin and Asahi is primarily about indemnification rather than safety standards. Moreover, it is not at all clear at this point that California law should govern the question whether a Japanese corporation should indemnify a Taiwanese corporation on the basis of a sale made in Taiwan and a shipment of goods from Japan to Taiwan. The possibility of being haled into a California court as a result of an accident involving Asahi's components undoubtedly creates an additional deterrent to the manufacture of unsafe components; however, similar pressures will be placed on Asahi by the purchasers of its components as long as those who use Asahi components in their final products, and sell those products in California, are subject to the application of California tort law.

World-Wide Volkswagen also admonished courts to take into consideration the interests of the "several States," in addition to the forum State, in the efficient judicial resolution of the dispute and the advancement of substantive policies. In the present case, this advice calls for a court to consider the procedural and substantive policies of other *nations* whose interests are affected by the assertion of jurisdiction by the California court. The procedural and substantive interests of other nations in a state court's assertion of jurisdiction over an alien defendant will differ from case to case. In every case, however, those interests, as well as the Federal interest in Government's foreign relations policies, will be best served by a careful inquiry into the reasonableness of the assertion of jurisdiction in the particular case, and an unwillingness to find the serious burdens on an alien defendant outweighed by minimal interests on the part of the plaintiff or the forum State. "Great care and reserve should be exercised when extending our notions of personal jurisdiction into the international field."

Considering the international context, the heavy burden on the alien defendant, and the slight interests of the plaintiff and the forum State, the exercise of personal jurisdiction by a California court over Asahi in this instance would be unreasonable and unfair.

III

Because the facts of this case do not establish minimum contacts such that the exercise of personal jurisdiction is consistent with fair play and substantial justice, the judgment of the Supreme Court of California is reversed, and the case is remanded for further proceedings not inconsistent with this opinion.

JUSTICE BRENNAN, with whom JUSTICE WHITE, JUSTICE MARSHALL, and JUSTICE BLACKMUN join, concurring in part and concurring in the judgment.

I do not agree with the interpretation in Part II-A of the stream-of-commerce theory, nor with the conclusion that Asahi did not "purposely avail itself of the California market." I do agree, however, with the Court's conclusion in Part II-B that the exercise of personal jurisdiction over Asahi in this case would not comport with "fair play and substantial justice." This is one of those rare cases in which "minimum requirements inherent in the concept of 'fair play and substantial justice' . . . defeat the reasonableness of jurisdiction even [though] the defendant has purposefully engaged in forum activities." I therefore join Parts I and II-B of the Court's opinion, and write separately to explain my disagreement with Part II-A.

The stream of commerce refers not to unpredictable currents or eddies, but to the regular and anticipated flow of products from manufacture to distribution to retail sale. As long as a participant in this process is aware that the final product is being marketed in the forum State, the possibility of a lawsuit there cannot come as a surprise. Nor will the litigation present a burden for which there is no corresponding benefit. A defendant who has placed goods in the stream of commerce benefits economically from the retail sale of the final product in the forum State, and indirectly benefits from the State's laws that regulate and facilitate commercial activity. These benefits accrue regardless of whether that participant directly conducts business in the forum State, or engages in additional conduct directed toward that State. Accordingly, most courts and commentators have found that jurisdiction premised on the placement of a product into the stream of commerce is consistent with the Due Process Clause, and have not required a showing of additional conduct.

* * *

The Court in World-Wide Volkswagen thus took great care to distinguish "between a case involving goods which reach a distant State through a chain of distribution and a case involving goods which reach the same State because a consumer . . . took them there." The California Supreme Court took note of this distinction, and correctly concluded that our holding in World-Wide Volkswagen preserved the stream-of-commerce theory.

In this case, the facts found by the California Supreme Court support its finding of minimum contacts. The court found that "[a]lthough Asahi did not design or control the system of distribution that carried its valve assemblies into California, Asahi was aware of the distribution system's operation, and it knew that it would benefit economically from the sale in California of products incorporating its components." Accordingly, I cannot join the determination in Part II-A that Asahi's regular and extensive sales of component parts to a manufacturer it knew was making regular sales of the final product in California is insufficient to establish minimum contacts with California.

DIRECTED READING QUESTIONS

34. Justice O'Connor and Justice Brennan both agree that conceptualizing commercial distribution systems as the "stream of commerce" is useful in determining whether a defendant "purposefully avails itself of the privilege of conducting activities within the forum State," thereby creating minimum contacts with the forum state. Describe the difference between the ways each uses the "stream of commerce" metaphor to establish minimum contacts of the defendant in a state where the defendant's product ends up and causes harm.

35. Explain how Justice O'Connor's stream of commerce test is similar to Justice White's opinion in World-Wide Volkswagen.

36. Explain how Justice Brennan's stream of commerce test is similar to the Oklahoma Supreme Court's test in World-Wide Volkswagen.

37. Justice O'Connor concludes that minimum contacts do not exist in this case, while Justice Brennan concludes that minimum contacts exist, but both agree that the exercise of personal jurisdiction by the California court here would be "unreasonable." What factors does the court analyze to conclude that jurisdiction is unreasonable?

38. Explain the Court's analysis of the factors you identified in determining whether the exercise of personal jurisdiction is unreasonable. In doing this, it will be helpful to do the following while paying attention to where each of the parties is from: (1) diagram the original law suit filed by the plaintiff against Honda and Cheng Shin; (2) diagram the lawsuit after Cheng Shin filed the cross claim seeking indemnification against Asahi; and (3) diagram the lawsuit after the plaintiff settled with Honda and Cheng Shin.

39. What is the role of the reasonableness analysis in determining whether personal jurisdiction exists?

J. MCINTYRE MACHINERY, LTD. V. NICASTRO (2011)
Supreme Court of the United States
564 U.S. 873

JUSTICE KENNEDY announced the judgment of the Court and delivered an opinion, in which THE CHIEF JUSTICE, JUSTICE SCALIA, and JUSTICE THOMAS join.

Whether a person or entity is subject to the jurisdiction of a state court despite not having been present in the State either at the time of suit or at the time of the alleged injury, and despite not having consented to the exercise of jurisdiction, is a question that arises with great frequency in the routine course of litigation. The rules and standards for determining when a State does or does not have jurisdiction over an absent party have been unclear because of decades-old questions left open in *Asahi Metal Industry Co. v. Superior Court of Cal., Solano Cty.*

Here, the Supreme Court of New Jersey, relying in part on *Asahi*, held that New Jersey's courts can exercise jurisdiction over a foreign manufacturer of a product so long as the manufacturer "knows or reasonably should know that its products are distributed through a nationwide distribution system that might lead to those products being sold in any of the fifty states." Applying that test, the court concluded that a British manufacturer of scrap metal machines was subject to jurisdiction in New Jersey, even though at no time had it advertised in, sent goods to, or in any relevant sense targeted the State.

That decision cannot be sustained. Although the New Jersey Supreme Court issued an extensive opinion with careful attention to this Court's cases and to its own precedent, the "stream of commerce" metaphor carried the decision far afield. Due process protects the defendant's right not to be coerced except by lawful judicial power. As a general rule, the exercise of judicial power is not lawful unless the defendant "purposefully avails itself of the privilege of conducting activities within the forum State, thus invoking the benefits and protections of its laws." *Hanson v. Denckla*. There may be exceptions, say, for instance, in cases involving an intentional tort. But the general rule is applicable in this products-liability case, and the so-called "stream-of-commerce" doctrine cannot displace it.

I

This case arises from a products-liability suit filed in New Jersey state court. Robert Nicastro seriously injured his hand while using a metal-shearing machine manufactured by J. McIntyre Machinery, Ltd. (J. McIntyre). The accident occurred in New Jersey, but the machine was manufactured in England, where J. McIntyre is incorporated and operates. The question here is whether the New Jersey courts have jurisdiction over J. McIntyre, notwithstanding the fact that the company at no time either marketed goods in the State or shipped them there. Nicastro was a plaintiff in the New Jersey trial court and is the respondent here; J. McIntyre was a defendant and is now the petitioner.

At oral argument in this Court, Nicastro's counsel stressed three primary facts in defense of New Jersey's assertion of jurisdiction over J. McIntyre. First, an independent company agreed to sell J. McIntyre's machines in the United States. J. McIntyre itself did not sell its machines to buyers in this country beyond the U.S. distributor, and there is no allegation that the distributor was under J. McIntyre's control. Second, J. McIntyre officials attended annual conventions for the scrap recycling industry to advertise J. McIntyre's machines alongside the distributor. The conventions took place in various States, but never in New Jersey. Third, no more than four machines (the record suggests only one) including the machine that caused the injuries that are the basis for this suit, ended up in New Jersey.

In addition to these facts emphasized by respondent, the New Jersey Supreme Court noted that J. McIntyre held both United States and European patents on its recycling technology. It also noted that the U.S. distributor "structured [its] advertising and sales efforts in accordance with" J. McIntyre's "direction and guidance whenever possible," and that "at least some of the machines were sold on consignment to" the distributor.

In light of these facts, the New Jersey Supreme Court concluded that New Jersey courts could exercise jurisdiction over petitioner without contravention of the Due Process Clause. Jurisdiction was proper, in that court's view, because the injury occurred in New Jersey; because petitioner knew or reasonably should have known "that its products are distributed through a nationwide distribution system that might lead to those products being sold in any of the fifty states"; and because petitioner failed to "take some reasonable step to prevent the distribution of its products in this State."

Both the New Jersey Supreme Court's holding and its account of what it called "[t]he stream-of-commerce doctrine of jurisdiction," were incorrect, however. This Court's *Asahi* decision may be responsible in part for that court's error regarding the stream of commerce, and this case presents an opportunity to provide greater clarity.

II

The Due Process Clause protects an individual's right to be deprived of life, liberty, or property only by the exercise of lawful power. This is no less true with respect to the power of a sovereign to resolve disputes through judicial process than with respect to the power of a sovereign to prescribe rules of conduct for those within its sphere. As a general rule, neither statute nor judicial decree may bind strangers to the State.

A court may subject a defendant to judgment only when the defendant has sufficient contacts with the sovereign "such that the maintenance of the suit does not offend 'traditional notions of fair play and substantial justice.'" *International Shoe Co. v. Washington*. Freeform notions of fundamental fairness divorced from traditional practice cannot transform a judgment rendered in the absence of authority into law.

As a general rule, the sovereign's exercise of power requires some act by which the defendant "purposefully avails itself of the privilege of conducting activities within the forum State, thus invoking the benefits and protections of its laws," *Hanson*, though in some cases, as with an intentional tort, the defendant might well fall within the State's authority by reason of his attempt to obstruct its laws. In products-liability cases like this one, it is the defendant's purposeful availment that makes jurisdiction consistent with "traditional notions of fair play and substantial justice."

A person may submit to a State's authority in a number of ways. There is, of course, explicit consent. Presence within a State at the time suit commences through service of process is another example. Citizenship or domicile—or, by analogy, incorporation or principal place of business for corporations—also indicates general submission to a State's powers. Each of these examples reveals circumstances, or a course of conduct, from which it is proper to infer an intention to benefit from and thus an intention to submit to the laws of the forum State. These examples support exercise of the general jurisdiction of the State's courts and allow the State to resolve both matters that originate within the State and those based on activities and events elsewhere. By contrast, those who live or operate primarily outside a State have a due process right not to be subjected to judgment in its courts as a general matter.

There is also a more limited form of submission to a State's authority for disputes that "arise out of or are connected with the activities within the state." *International Shoe Co.* Where a defendant "purposefully avails itself of the privilege of conducting activities within the forum State, thus invoking the benefits and protections of its laws," *Hanson*, it submits to the judicial power of an otherwise foreign sovereign to the extent that power is exercised in connection with the defendant's activities touching on the State. In other words, submission through contact with and activity directed at a sovereign may justify specific jurisdiction "in a suit arising out of or related to the defendant's contacts with the forum."

The imprecision arising from *Asahi,* for the most part, results from its statement of the relation between jurisdiction and the "stream of commerce." The stream of commerce, like other metaphors, has its deficiencies as well as its utility. It refers to the movement of goods from manufacturers through distributors to consumers, yet beyond that descriptive purpose its meaning is far from exact. This Court has stated that a defendant's placing goods into the stream of commerce "with the expectation that they will be purchased by consumers in the forum State" may indicate purposeful availment. *World-Wide Volkswagen Corp. v. Woodson* (finding that expectation lacking). But that statement does not amend the general rule of personal jurisdiction. It merely observes that a defendant may in an appropriate case be subject to jurisdiction without entering the forum—itself an unexceptional proposition—as where manufacturers or distributors "seek to serve" a given State's market. The principal inquiry in cases of this sort is whether the defendant's activities manifest an intention to submit to the power of a sovereign. In other words, the defendant must "purposefully avai[l] itself of the privilege of conducting activities within the forum State, thus invoking the benefits and protections of its laws." *Hanson.* Sometimes a defendant does so by sending its goods rather than its agents. The defendant's transmission of goods permits the exercise of jurisdiction only where the defendant can be said to have targeted the forum; as a general rule, it is not enough that the defendant might have predicted that its goods will reach the forum State.

In *Asahi,* an opinion by Justice Brennan for four Justices outlined a different approach. It discarded the central concept of sovereign authority in favor of considerations of fairness and foreseeability. As that concurrence contended, "jurisdiction premised on the placement of a product into the stream of commerce [without more] is consistent with the Due Process Clause," for "[a]s long as a participant in this process is aware that the final product is being marketed in the forum State, the possibility of a lawsuit there cannot come as a surprise." It was the premise of the concurring opinion that the defendant's ability to anticipate suit renders the assertion of jurisdiction fair. In this way, the opinion made foreseeability the touchstone of jurisdiction.

The standard set forth in Justice Brennan's concurrence was rejected in an opinion written by Justice O'Connor; but the relevant part of that opinion, too, commanded the assent of only four Justices, not a majority of the Court. That opinion stated: "The 'substantial connection' between the defendant and the forum State necessary for a finding of minimum contacts must come about by an action of the defendant purposefully directed toward the forum State. The placement of a product into the stream of commerce, without more, is not an act of the defendant purposefully directed toward the forum State."

Since *Asahi* was decided, the courts have sought to reconcile the competing opinions. But Justice Brennan's concurrence, advocating a rule based on general notions of fairness and foreseeability, is inconsistent with the premises of lawful judicial power. This Court's precedents make clear that it is the defendant's actions, not his expectations, that empower a State's courts to subject him to judgment.

The conclusion that jurisdiction is in the first instance a question of authority rather than fairness explains, for example, why the principal opinion in *Burnham* "conducted no independent inquiry into the desirability or fairness" of the rule that service of process within a State suffices to establish jurisdiction over an otherwise foreign defendant. As that opinion explained, "[t]he view developed early that each State had the power to hale before its courts any individual who could be found within its borders." Furthermore, were general fairness considerations the touchstone of jurisdiction, a lack of purposeful availment might be excused where carefully crafted judicial procedures could otherwise protect the defendant's interests, or where the plaintiff would suffer substantial hardship if forced to litigate in a foreign forum. That such considerations have not been deemed controlling is instructive. See, *e.g., World-Wide Volkswagen.*

Two principles are implicit in the foregoing. First, personal jurisdiction requires a forum-by-forum, or sovereign-by-sovereign, analysis. The question is whether a defendant has followed a course of conduct directed at the society or economy existing within the jurisdiction of a given sovereign, so that the sovereign has the power to subject the defendant to judgment concerning that conduct. Personal jurisdiction, of course, restricts "judicial power not as a matter of sovereignty, but as a matter of individual liberty," for due process protects the individual's right to be subject only to lawful power. But whether a judicial judgment is lawful depends on whether the sovereign has authority to render it.

The second principle is a corollary of the first. Because the United States is a distinct sovereign, a defendant may in principle be subject to the jurisdiction of the courts of the United States but not of any particular State. This is consistent with the premises and unique genius of our Constitution. Ours is "a legal system unprecedented in form and design, establishing two orders of government, each with its own direct relationship, its own privity, its own set of mutual rights and obligations to the people who sustain it and are governed by it." For jurisdiction, a litigant may have the requisite relationship with the United States Government but not with the government of any individual State. That would be an exceptional case, however. If the defendant is a domestic domiciliary, the courts of its home State are available and can exercise general jurisdiction. And if another State were to assert jurisdiction in an inappropriate case, it would upset the federal balance, which posits that each State has a sovereignty that is not subject to unlawful intrusion by other States. Furthermore, foreign corporations will often target or concentrate on particular States, subjecting them to specific jurisdiction in those forums.

It must be remembered, however, that although this case and *Asahi* both involve foreign manufacturers, the undesirable consequences of Justice Brennan's approach are no less significant for domestic producers. The owner of a small Florida farm might sell crops to a large nearby distributor, for example, who might then distribute them to grocers across the country. If foreseeability were the controlling criterion, the farmer could be sued in Alaska or any number of other States' courts without ever leaving town. And the issue of foreseeability may itself be contested so that significant expenses are incurred just on the preliminary issue of jurisdiction. Jurisdictional rules should avoid these costs whenever possible.

The conclusion that the authority to subject a defendant to judgment depends on purposeful availment, consistent with Justice O'Connor's opinion in *Asahi,* does not by itself resolve many difficult questions of jurisdiction that will arise in particular cases. The defendant's conduct and the economic realities of the market the defendant seeks to serve will differ across cases, and judicial exposition will, in common-law fashion, clarify the contours of that principle.

III

In this case, petitioner directed marketing and sales efforts at the United States.

* * *

Respondent has not established that J. McIntyre engaged in conduct purposefully directed at New Jersey. Recall that respondent's claim of jurisdiction centers on three facts: The distributor agreed to sell J. McIntyre's machines in the United States; J. McIntyre officials attended trade shows in several States but not in New Jersey; and up to four machines ended up in New Jersey. The British manufacturer had no office in New Jersey; it neither paid taxes nor owned property there; and it neither advertised in, nor sent any employees to, the State. Indeed, after discovery the trial court found that the "defendant does not have a single contact with New Jersey short of the machine in question ending up in this state." These facts may reveal an intent to serve the U.S. market, but they do not show that J. McIntyre purposefully availed itself of the New Jersey market.

It is notable that the New Jersey Supreme Court appears to agree, for it could "not find that J. McIntyre had a presence or minimum contacts in this State—in any jurisprudential sense—that would justify a New Jersey court to exercise jurisdiction in this case." The court nonetheless held that petitioner could be sued in New Jersey based on a "stream-of-commerce theory of jurisdiction." As discussed, however, the stream-of-commerce metaphor cannot supersede either the mandate of the Due Process Clause or the limits on judicial authority that Clause ensures. The New Jersey Supreme Court also cited "significant policy reasons" to justify its holding, including the State's "strong interest in protecting its citizens from defective products." That interest is doubtless strong, but the Constitution commands restraint before discarding liberty in the name of expediency.

* * *

Due process protects petitioner's right to be subject only to lawful authority. At no time did petitioner engage in any activities in New Jersey that reveal an intent to invoke or benefit from the protection of its laws. New Jersey is without power to adjudge the rights and liabilities of J. McIntyre, and its exercise of jurisdiction would violate due process. The contrary judgment of the New Jersey Supreme Court is

Reversed.

JUSTICE BREYER, with whom JUSTICE ALITO joins, concurring in the judgment.

[Justice Breyer felt that it was "unwise to announce a rule of broad applicability without full consideration of" the reality of modern day commerce which facilitates conducting business in all the states at the same time without actively targeting a particular state.]

In my view, the outcome of this case is determined by our precedents. Based on the facts found by the New Jersey courts, respondent Robert Nicastro failed to meet his burden to demonstrate that it was constitutionally proper to exercise jurisdiction over petitioner J. McIntyre Machinery, Ltd. (British Manufacturer), a British firm that manufactures scrap-metal machines in Great Britain and sells them through an independent distributor in the United States (American Distributor). On that basis, I agree with the plurality that the contrary judgment of the Supreme Court of New Jersey should be reversed.

* * *

None of our precedents finds that a single isolated sale, even if accompanied by the kind of sales effort indicated here, is sufficient. Rather, this Court's previous holdings suggest the contrary. The Court has held that a single sale to a customer who takes an accident-causing product to a different State (where the accident takes place) is not a sufficient basis for asserting jurisdiction. See World-Wide Volkswagen Corp. And the Court, in separate opinions, has strongly suggested that a single sale of a product in a State does not constitute an adequate basis for asserting jurisdiction over an out-of-state defendant, even if that defendant places his goods in the stream of commerce, fully aware (and hoping) that such a sale will take place. See Asahi (opinion of O'Connor, J.) (requiring "something more" than simply placing "a product into the stream of commerce," even if defendant is "awar[e]" that the stream "may or will sweep the product into the forum State"); (Brennan, J., concurring in part and concurring in judgment) (jurisdiction should lie where a sale in a State is part of "the regular and anticipated flow" of commerce into the State, but not where that sale is only an "edd[y]," i.e., an isolated occurrence); id., at (Stevens, J., concurring in part and concurring in judgment) (indicating that "the volume, the value, and the hazardous character" of a good may affect the jurisdictional inquiry and emphasizing Asahi's "regular course of dealing").

* * *

Accordingly, on the record present here, resolving this case requires no more than adhering to our precedents.

* * *

The plurality seems to state strict rules that limit jurisdiction where a defendant does not "inten[d] to submit to the power of a sovereign" and cannot "be said to have targeted the forum." But what do those standards mean when a company targets the world by selling products from its Web site? And does it matter if, instead of shipping the products directly, a company consigns the products through an intermediary (say, Amazon.com) who then receives and fulfills the orders? And what if the company markets its products through popup advertisements that it knows will be viewed in a forum? Those issues have serious commercial consequences but are totally absent in this case.

* * *

JUSTICE GINSBURG, with whom JUSTICE SOTOMAYOR and JUSTICE KAGAN join, dissenting.

A foreign industrialist seeks to develop a market in the United States for machines it manufactures. It hopes to derive substantial revenue from sales it makes to United States purchasers. Where in the United States buyers reside does not matter to this manufacturer. Its goal is simply to sell as much as it can, wherever it can. It excludes no region or State from the market it wishes to reach. But, all things considered, it prefers to avoid products liability litigation in the United States. To that end, it engages a U.S. distributor to ship its machines stateside. Has it succeeded in escaping personal jurisdiction in a State where one of its products is sold and causes injury or even death to a local user?

* * *

[Also] the constitutional limits on a state court's adjudicatory authority derive from considerations of due process, not state sovereignty. As the Court clarified in *Insurance Corp. of Ireland v. Compagnie des Bauxites de Guinee,* 456 U.S. 694 (1982).

"The restriction on state sovereign power described in World-Wide Volkswagen Corp. . . . must be seen as ultimately a function of the individual liberty interest preserved by the Due Process Clause. That Clause is the only source of the personal jurisdiction requirement and the Clause itself makes no mention of federalism concerns. Furthermore, if the federalism concept operated as an independent restriction on the sovereign power of the court, it would not be possible to waive the personal jurisdiction requirement: Individual actions cannot change the powers of sovereignty, although the individual can subject himself to powers from which he may otherwise be protected."

[Justice Ginsburg then proceeded to explain why neither World-Wide Volkswagen nor Asahi provided any support for the Kennedy plurality opinion.]

World-Wide Volkswagen concerned a New York car dealership that sold solely in the New York market, and a New York distributor who supplied retailers in three States only: New York, Connecticut, and New Jersey. New York residents had purchased an Audi from the New York dealer and were driving the new vehicle through Oklahoma en route to Arizona. On the road in Oklahoma, another car struck the Audi in the rear, causing a fire which severely burned the Audi's occupants. Rejecting the Oklahoma courts' assertion of jurisdiction over the New York dealer and distributor, this Court observed that the defendants had done nothing to serve the market for cars in Oklahoma. Jurisdiction, the Court held, could not be based on the customer's unilateral act of driving the vehicle to Oklahoma. World-Wide Volkswagen "rejected the assertion that a consumer's unilateral act of bringing the defendant's product into the forum State was a sufficient constitutional basis for personal jurisdiction over the defendant."

Notably, the foreign manufacturer of the Audi in World-Wide Volkswagen did not object to the jurisdiction of the Oklahoma courts and the U.S. importer abandoned its initially stated objection. And most relevant here, the Court's opinion indicates that an objection to jurisdiction by the manufacturer or national distributor would have been unavailing. To reiterate, the Court said in World-Wide Volkswagen that, when a manufacturer or distributor aims to sell its product to customers in several States, it is reasonable "to subject it to suit in [any] one of those States if its allegedly defective [product] has there been the source of injury."

Asahi arose out of a motorcycle accident in California. Plaintiff, a California resident injured in the accident, sued the Taiwanese manufacturer of the motorcycle's tire tubes, claiming that defects in its product caused the accident. The tube manufacturer cross-claimed against Asahi, the Japanese maker of the valve assembly, and Asahi contested the California courts' jurisdiction. By the time the case reached this Court, the injured plaintiff had settled his case and only the indemnity claim by the Taiwanese company against the Japanese valve-assembly manufacturer remained.

The decision was not a close call. The Court had before it a foreign plaintiff, the Taiwanese manufacturer, and a foreign defendant, the Japanese valve-assembly maker, and the indemnification dispute concerned a transaction between those parties that occurred abroad. All agreed on the bottom line: The Japanese valve-assembly manufacturer was not reasonably brought into the California courts to litigate a dispute with another foreign party over a transaction that took place outside the United States.

Given the confines of the controversy, the dueling opinions of Justice Brennan and Justice O'Connor were hardly necessary. How the Court would have "estimate[d] . . . the inconveniences," International Shoe, had the injured Californian originally sued Asahi is a debatable question. Would this Court have given the same weight to the burdens on the foreign defendant had those been counterbalanced by the burdens litigating in Japan imposed on the local California plaintiff?

In any event, Asahi, unlike McIntyre UK, did not itself seek out customers in the United States, it engaged no distributor to promote its wares here, it appeared at no trade shows in the United States, and, of course, it had no Web site advertising its products to the world. Moreover, Asahi was a component-part manufacturer with "little control over the final destination of its products once they were delivered into the stream of commerce." It was important to the Court in Asahi that "those who use Asahi components in their final products, and sell those products in California, [would be] subject to the application of California tort law." To hold that Asahi controls this case would, to put it bluntly, be dead wrong.[15]

DIRECTED READING QUESTIONS

40. Describe the corporation J. McIntyre Machinery Ltd. ("J. McIntyre") and its activities or contacts with the United States.

41. Explain in detail why the New Jersey Supreme Court concluded that New Jersey courts had personal jurisdiction over J. McIntyre.

42. Explain why Justice Kennedy's plurality opinion reverses the New Jersey Supreme Court, and briefly articulate how this opinion is consistent with Justice White's opinion in World-Wide Volkswagen and Justice O'Connor's opinion in Asahi.

43. Discuss how Justice Kennedy's plurality opinion can be empirically sustainable in light of the following language from Justice Ginsburg's dissent:

> The restriction on state sovereign power described in *World-Wide Volkswagen Corp.* . . . must be seen as ultimately a function of the individual liberty interest preserved by the Due Process Clause. That Clause is the only source of the personal jurisdiction requirement and the Clause itself makes no mention of federalism concerns. Furthermore, if the federalism concept operated as an independent restriction on the sovereign power of the court, it would not be

---

[15] The plurality notes the low volume of sales in New Jersey. A $24,900 shearing machine, however, is unlikely to sell in bulk worldwide, much less in any given State. By dollar value, the price of a single machine represents a significant sale. Had a manufacturer sold in New Jersey $24,900 worth of flannel shirts, cigarette lighters, *Oswalt v. Scripto, Inc.*, 616 F.2d 191 (C.A.5 1980), or wire-rope splices, see *Hedrick v. Daiko Shoji Co.*, 715 F.2d 1355 (C.A.9 1983), the Court would presumably find the defendant amenable to suit in that State.

possible to waive the personal jurisdiction requirement: Individual actions cannot change the powers of sovereignty, although the individual can subject himself to powers from which he may otherwise be protected.

44. Justice Kennedy's plurality opinion relies on World-Wide Volkswagen and Asahi as supportive of the rule it articulates. How does Justice Ginsburg argue those cases are inapposite?

45. How does this court reaffirm *Calder v. Jones*?

46. Please explain the distinction between general and specific personal jurisdiction that the Nicastro court makes and what conditions give rise to each form of personal jurisdiction.

47. What is the central justification for Justice Kennedy's absolute rule that a state cannot exercise personal jurisdiction over a nonconsenting/non-waiving defendant, unless the defendant targeted the state, and what example does Justice Kennedy employ to give context to his central justification?

48. Why does Justice Breyer's concurrence take issue with the absolute rule, based on state geographical borders, that the Kennedy plurality announces for personal jurisdiction?

49. Explain how Justice Breyer concludes that "the outcome of this case is determined by our precedents."

50. Is the rationale of Justice Breyer's concurrence, which distinguishes between a stream and an eddy of commerce, sustainable given Justice Ginsburg's statement in footnote 15 of the opinion?

51. Articulate precisely the different normative positions of Justice Ginsburg and Justice Kennedy in this case, and explain which if any you think the correct approach is.

III. DEFENDANT'S PROPERTY IN THE FORUM STATE

After *Pennoyer*, if a defendant possessed property in a state with which the defendant neither had minimum contacts nor was present in, personal jurisdiction could still be asserted by the forum state over the defendant, even if the lawsuit was unrelated to the property in the forum state.

Consider the following scenario:

- **A** is a resident of Oregon who owns property in Florida but otherwise has no contact with the state of Florida.

- **B**, a citizen of California, claims **A** breached a contract that **A** entered into with **B**.

- The contract was unconnected to the state of Florida. For example, **A** agreed to repair **B**'s home in California but failed to do so after **B** paid **A**.

- If **B** decided to sue **A** for breach of contract, he could attach **A**'s property in Florida and, as a result of the presence of **A**'s property, albeit property unrelated to the dispute between **B** and **A**, the Florida courts would have personal jurisdiction over A in the adjudication of the contract dispute.

- The restriction on this method of acquiring personal jurisdiction was that the value of the judgment entered by the Florida courts against **A** could not be higher than the value of **A**'s property in Florida.

This method of attaching property unrelated to the dispute to establish personal jurisdiction over the defendant in an *in personam* dispute is known as *quasi in rem type II* jurisdiction. The *Shaffer v. Heitner* case reexamined the validity of this method of obtaining personal jurisdiction.

SHAFFER V. HEITNER (1977)

Supreme Court of the United States
433 U.S. 186

MR. JUSTICE MARSHALL delivered the opinion of the Court.

The controversy in this case concerns the constitutionality of a Delaware statute that allows a court of that State to take jurisdiction of a lawsuit by sequestering any property of the defendant that happens to be located in Delaware. Appellants contend that the sequestration statute as applied in this case violates the Due Process Clause of the Fourteenth Amendment both because it permits the state courts to exercise jurisdiction despite the absence of sufficient contacts among the defendants, the litigation, and the State of Delaware and because it authorizes the deprivation of defendants' property without providing adequate procedural safeguards. We find it necessary to consider only the first of these contentions.

I

Appellee Heitner, a nonresident of Delaware, is the owner of one share of stock in the Greyhound Corp., a business incorporated under the laws of Delaware with its principal place of business in Phoenix, Ariz. On May 22, 1974, he filed a shareholder's derivative suit in the Court of Chancery for New Castle County, Del., in which he named as defendants Greyhound, its wholly owned subsidiary Greyhound Lines, Inc., and 28 present or former officers or directors of one or both of the corporations. In essence, Heitner alleged that the individual defendants had violated their duties to Greyhound by causing it and its subsidiary to engage in actions that resulted in the corporations being held liable for substantial damages in a private antitrust suit and a large fine in a criminal contempt action. The activities which led to these penalties took place in Oregon.

Simultaneously with his complaint, Heitner filed a motion for an order of sequestration of the Delaware property of the individual defendants pursuant to Del.Code Ann., Tit. 10, s 366 (1975).* This motion was accompanied by a supporting affidavit of counsel which stated that the individual defendants were nonresidents of Delaware. The affidavit identified the property to be sequestered as

> common stock, 3% Second Cumulative Preferred Stock and stock unit credits of the Defendant Greyhound Corporation, a Delaware corporation, as well as all options and all warrants to purchase said stock issued to said individual Defendants and all contractual (sic) obligations, all rights, debts or credits due or accrued to or for the benefit of any of the said Defendants under any type of

---

*   This Delaware Statute allowed the seizure or sequestration of property owned by non-residents of Delaware which was located in the State of Delaware. The sequestration or seizure of the property purported to create personal jurisdiction in Delaware courts over the Defendant even for matters unrelated to the property. Under Delaware law the share of a Corporation incorporated in Delaware is considered property located in Delaware. The other 49 states consider the share as property present wherever the certificate of ownership of the share is located.

written agreement, contract or other legal instrument of any kind whatever between any of the individual Defendants and said corporation.

The requested sequestration order was signed the day the motion was filed. Pursuant to that order, the sequestrator "seized" approximately 82,000 shares of Greyhound common stock belonging to 19 of the defendants, and options belonging to another 2 defendants.

* * *

"The primary purpose of 'sequestration' as authorized by 10 Del.C. s 366 is not to secure possession of property pending a trial between resident debtors and creditors on the issue of who has the right to retain it. On the contrary, as here employed, 'sequestration' is a process used to compel the personal appearance of a nonresident defendant to answer and defend a suit brought against him in a court of equity. It is accomplished by the appointment of a sequestrator by this Court to seize and hold property of the nonresident located in this State subject to further Court order. If the defendant enters a general appearance, the sequestered property is routinely released, unless the plaintiff makes special application to continue its seizure, in which event the plaintiff has the burden of proof and persuasion."

This limitation on the purpose and length of time for which sequestered property is held, the court concluded, rendered inapplicable the due process requirements. The court also found no state-law or federal constitutional barrier to the sequestrator's reliance on Del.Code Ann., Tit. 8, s 169 (1975). Finally, the court held that the statutory Delaware situs of the stock provided a sufficient basis for the exercise of *quasi in rem* jurisdiction by a Delaware court.

On appeal, the Delaware Supreme Court affirmed the judgment of the Court of Chancery.

* * *

Appellants' claim that the Delaware courts did not have jurisdiction to adjudicate this action received [ ] cursory treatment. The court's analysis of the jurisdictional issue is contained in two paragraphs:

There are significant constitutional questions at issue here but we say at once that we do not deem the rule of International Shoe to be one of them. . . . The reason of course, is that jurisdiction under s 366 remains . . . *quasi in rem* founded on the presence of capital stock here, not on prior contact by defendants with this forum. Under 8 Del.C. s 169 the 'situs of the ownership of the capital stock of all corporations existing under the laws of this State . . . (is) in this State,' and that provides the initial basis for jurisdiction. Delaware may constitutionally establish situs of such shares here, . . . it has done so and the presence thereof provides the foundation for s 366 in this case. . .

* * *

"We hold that seizure of the Greyhound shares is not invalid because plaintiff has failed to meet the prior contacts tests of International Shoe."

We noted probable jurisdiction. We reverse.

II

The Delaware courts rejected appellants' jurisdictional challenge by noting that this suit was brought as a *quasi in rem* proceeding. Since *quasi in rem* jurisdiction is traditionally based on attachment or seizure of property present in the jurisdiction, not on contacts between the defendant and the State, the courts considered appellants' claimed lack of contacts with Delaware to be unimportant. This categorical analysis assumes the continued soundness of the conceptual structure founded on the century-old case of *Pennoyer v. Neff.*

[After reviewing the *Pennoyer* case and the line of minimum contacts cases the court concluded that these cases did not specifically address the *in rem* or *quasi in rem* jurisdiction recognized in *Pennoyer* but addressed only *in personam* actions.]

No equally dramatic change has occurred in the law governing jurisdiction *in rem*. There have, however, been intimations that the collapse of the *in personam* wing of *Pennoyer* has not left that decision unweakened as a foundation for *in rem* jurisdiction. Well-reasoned lower court opinions have questioned the proposition that the presence of property in a State gives that State jurisdiction to adjudicate rights to the property regardless of the relationship of the underlying dispute and the property owner to the forum. The overwhelming majority of commentators have also rejected Pennoyer's premise that a proceeding "against" property is not a proceeding against the owners of that property. Accordingly, they urge that the "traditional notions of fair play and substantial justice" that govern a State's power to adjudicate *in personam* should also govern its power to adjudicate personal rights to property located in the State.

Although this Court has not addressed this argument directly, we have held that property cannot be subjected to a court's judgment unless reasonable and appropriate efforts have been made to give the property owners actual notice of the action. This conclusion recognizes, contrary to Pennoyer, that an adverse judgment *in rem* directly affects the property owner by divesting him of his rights in the property before the court. Moreover, in *Mullane* we hold that Fourteenth Amendment rights cannot depend on the classification of an action as *in rem* or *in personam*, since that is "a classification for which the standards are so elusive and confused generally and which, being primarily for state courts to define, may and do vary from state to state."

It is clear, therefore, that the law of state-court jurisdiction no longer stands securely on the foundation established in Pennoyer. We think that the time is ripe to consider whether the standard of fairness and substantial justice set forth in International Shoe should be held to govern actions *in rem* as well as *in personam*.

III

The case for applying to jurisdiction *in rem* the same test of "fair play and substantial justice" as governs assertions of jurisdiction *in personam* is simple and straightforward. It is premised on recognition that "(t)he phrase, 'judicial jurisdiction over a thing', is a customary elliptical way of referring to jurisdiction over the interests of persons in a thing." This recognition leads to the conclusion that in order to justify an exercise of jurisdiction *in rem*, the basis for jurisdiction must be sufficient to justify exercising "jurisdiction over the interests of persons in a thing."[23] The standard for determining whether an exercise of jurisdiction over the interests of persons is consistent with the Due Process Clause is the minimum-contacts standard elucidated in *International Shoe*.

This argument, of course, does not ignore the fact that the presence of property in a State may bear on the existence of jurisdiction by providing contacts among the forum State, the defendant, and the litigation. For example, when claims to the property itself are the source of the underlying controversy between the plaintiff and the defendant,[24] it would be unusual for the State where the property is located not to have jurisdiction. In such cases, the defendant's claim to property located in the State would normally indicate that he expected to benefit from the State's protection of his interest. The State's strong interests in assuring the marketability of property within its borders and in providing a procedure for peaceful resolution of disputes about the possession of that property would also support jurisdiction, as would the likelihood that important records and witnesses will be found in the State. The presence of property may also favor jurisdiction in cases such as suits for injury suffered on the land of an absentee owner, where the defendant's ownership of the property is conceded but the cause of action is otherwise related to rights and duties growing out of that ownership.[29]

It appears, therefore, that jurisdiction over many types of actions which now are or might be brought *in rem* would not be affected by a holding that any assertion of state-court jurisdiction must satisfy the *International Shoe* standard. For the type of *quasi in rem* action typified by . . . the present case, however, accepting the proposed analysis would result in significant change. These are cases where the property which now serves as the basis for state-court jurisdiction is completely unrelated to the plaintiff's cause of action. Thus, although the presence of the defendant's property in a State might suggest the existence of other ties among the defendant, the State, and the litigation, the presence of the property alone would not support the State's jurisdiction. If those other ties did not exist, cases over which the State is now thought to have jurisdiction could not be brought in that forum.

Since acceptance of the *International Shoe* test would most affect this class of cases, we examine the arguments against adopting that standard as they relate to this category of litigation.[31] Before doing so, however, we note that this type of case also presents the clearest illustration of the argument in favor of assessing assertions of jurisdiction by a single standard. For in cases such as . . . this one, the only role played by the property is to provide the basis for bringing the defendant into court.[32] [ ]In such cases, if a direct assertion of personal jurisdiction over the defendant would violate the Constitution, it

---

[23] It is true that the potential liability of a defendant in an *in rem* action is limited by the value of the property, but that limitation does not affect the argument. The fairness of subjecting a defendant to state-court jurisdiction does not depend on the size of the claim being litigated.

[24] This category includes true *in rem* actions and the first type of *quasi in rem* proceedings.

[29] If such an action were brought under the *in rem* jurisdiction rather than under a long-arm statute, it would be a *quasi in rem* action of the second type.

[31] Concentrating on this category of cases is also appropriate because in the other categories, to the extent that presence of property in the State indicates the existence of sufficient contacts under *International Shoe*, there is no need to rely on the property as justifying jurisdiction regardless of the existence of those contacts.

[32] The value of the property seized does serve to limit the extent of possible liability, but that limitation does not provide support for the assertion of jurisdiction. See n. 23, supra. In this case, appellants' potential liability under the *in rem* jurisdiction exceeds $1 million.

would seem that an indirect assertion of that jurisdiction should be equally impermissible.

* * *

It might also be suggested that allowing *in rem* jurisdiction avoids the uncertainty inherent in the *International Shoe* standard and assures a plaintiff of a forum.[37] We believe, however, that the fairness standard of *International Shoe* can be easily applied in the vast majority of cases. Moreover, when the existence of jurisdiction in a particular forum under *International Shoe* is unclear, the cost of simplifying the litigation by avoiding the jurisdictional question may be the sacrifice of "fair play and substantial justice." That cost is too high.

* * *

The fiction that an assertion of jurisdiction over property is anything but an assertion of jurisdiction over the owner of the property supports an ancient form without substantial modern justification. Its continued acceptance would serve only to allow state-court jurisdiction that is fundamentally unfair to the defendant.

We therefore conclude that all assertions of state-court jurisdiction must be evaluated according to the standards set forth in *International Shoe* and its progeny.[39]

IV

The Delaware courts based their assertion of jurisdiction in this case solely on the statutory presence of appellants' property in Delaware. Yet that property is not the subject matter of this litigation, nor is the underlying cause of action related to the property. Appellants' holdings in Greyhound do not, therefore, provide contacts with Delaware sufficient to support the jurisdiction of that State's courts over appellants. If it exists, that jurisdiction must have some other foundation.

Appellee Heitner did not allege and does not now claim that appellants have ever set foot in Delaware. Nor does he identify any act related to his cause of action as having taken place in Delaware.

* * *

Moreover, appellants had no reason to expect to be haled before a Delaware court. Delaware, unlike some States, has not enacted a statute that treats acceptance of a directorship as consent to jurisdiction in the State. And "(i)t strains reason . . . to suggest that anyone buying securities in a corporation formed in Delaware 'impliedly consents' to subject himself to Delaware's . . . jurisdiction on any cause of action."

* * *

The Due Process Clause "does not contemplate that a state may make binding a judgment . . . against an individual or corporate defendant with which the state has no contacts, ties, or relations." *International Shoe Co. v. Washington.*

---

[37] This case does not raise, and we therefore do not consider, the question whether the presence of a defendant's property in a State is a sufficient basis for jurisdiction when no other forum is available to the plaintiff.

[39] [ ]To the extent that prior decisions are inconsistent with this standard, they are overruled.

Delaware's assertion of jurisdiction over appellants in this case is inconsistent with that constitutional limitation on state power. The judgment of the Delaware Supreme Court must, therefore, be reversed.

It is so ordered.

MR. JUSTICE POWELL, concurring.

I agree that the principles of International Shoe Co., should be extended to govern assertions of in rem as well as in personam jurisdiction in a state court. I also agree that neither the statutory presence of appellants' stock in Delaware nor their positions as directors and officers of a Delaware corporation can provide sufficient contacts to support the Delaware courts' assertion of jurisdiction in this case.

I would explicitly reserve judgment, however, on whether the ownership of some forms of property whose situs is indisputably and permanently located within a State may, without more, provide the contacts necessary to subject a defendant to jurisdiction within the State to the extent of the value of the property. In the case of real property, in particular, preservation of the common-law concept of quasi in rem jurisdiction arguably would avoid the uncertainty of the general International Shoe standard without significant cost to " 'traditional notions of fair play and substantial justice.' " Subject to the foregoing reservation, I join the opinion of the Court.

DIRECTED READING QUESTIONS

52. What is a shareholder's derivative suit?

53. In what state did the activities of the defendant, giving rise to the suit filed in Delaware, occur?

54. What exactly is the property of the defendants which is located in Delaware?

55. Why does the plaintiff allege that personal jurisdiction is proper in Delaware, even though there is no relationship between the defendants' activities giving rise to the lawsuit and Delaware?

56. Please list the different categories of actions that the Supreme Court identifies as in rem, and give the examples that the Court uses to illustrate each category.

57. Please explain the impact of the Shaffer ruling on each of the categories identified above.

58. In Nicastro, Justice Kennedy's plurality opinion justifies the use of state borders as a factor in personal jurisdiction, because it is necessary to prevent the uncertainty of using foreseeability as the basis of determining whether purposeful availment exists. How does the plaintiff in Shaffer argue that avoiding uncertainty should prevent the injection of the in personam minimum contacts concept into personal jurisdiction questions in in rem actions? Is the plaintiff successful?

59. According to Justice Powell's concurrence, does the type of property make a difference?

IV. PRESENCE IN THE FORUM: GENERAL JURISDICTION

BURNHAM V. SUPERIOR COURT (1990)
Supreme Court of the United States
495 U.S. 604

JUSTICE SCALIA announced the judgment of the Court and delivered an opinion in which THE CHIEF JUSTICE and JUSTICE KENNEDY join, and in which JUSTICE WHITE joins with respect to Parts I, II-A, II-B, and II-C.

The question presented is whether the Due Process Clause of the Fourteenth Amendment denies California courts jurisdiction over a nonresident, who was personally served with process while temporarily in that State, in a suit unrelated to his activities in the State.

I

Petitioner Dennis Burnham married Francie Burnham in 1976 in West Virginia. In 1977 the couple moved to New Jersey, where their two children were born. In July 1987 the Burnhams decided to separate. They agreed that Mrs. Burnham, who intended to move to California, would take custody of the children. Shortly before Mrs. Burnham departed for California that same month, she and petitioner agreed that she would file for divorce on grounds of "irreconcilable differences."

In October 1987, petitioner filed for divorce in New Jersey state court on grounds of "desertion." Petitioner did not, however, obtain an issuance of summons against his wife and did not attempt to serve her with process. Mrs. Burnham, after unsuccessfully demanding that petitioner adhere to their prior agreement to submit to an "irreconcilable differences" divorce, brought suit for divorce in California state court in early January 1988.

In late January, petitioner visited southern California on business, after which he went north to visit his children in the San Francisco Bay area, where his wife resided. He took the older child to San Francisco for the weekend. Upon returning the child to Mrs. Burnham's home on January 24, 1988, petitioner was served with a California court summons and a copy of Mrs. Burnham's divorce petition. He then returned to New Jersey.

Later that year, petitioner made a special appearance in the California Superior Court, moving to quash the service of process on the ground that the court lacked personal jurisdiction over him because his only contacts with California were a few short visits to the State for the purposes of conducting business and visiting his children. The Superior Court denied the motion, and the California Court of Appeal denied mandamus relief, rejecting petitioner's contention that the Due Process Clause prohibited California courts from asserting jurisdiction over him because he lacked "minimum contacts" with the State. The court held it to be "a valid jurisdictional predicate for *in personam* jurisdiction" that the "defendant [was] present in the forum state and personally served with process." We granted certiorari.

II

A

* * *

B

Among the most firmly established principles of personal jurisdiction in American tradition is that the courts of a State have jurisdiction over nonresidents who are physically present in the State. The view developed early that each State had the power to hale before its courts any individual who could be found within its borders, and that once having acquired jurisdiction over such a person by properly serving him with process, the State could retain jurisdiction to enter judgment against him, no matter how fleeting his visit.

* * *

C

Despite this formidable body of precedent, petitioner contends, in reliance on our decisions applying the *International Shoe* standard, that in the absence of "continuous and systematic" contacts with the forum, a nonresident defendant can be subjected to judgment only as to matters that arise out of or relate to his contacts with the forum. This argument rests on a thorough misunderstanding of our cases.

* * *

Nothing in *International Shoe* or the cases that have followed it, however, offers support for the very different proposition petitioner seeks to establish today: that a defendant's presence in the forum is not only unnecessary to validate novel, nontraditional assertions of jurisdiction, but is itself no longer sufficient to establish jurisdiction. That proposition is unfaithful to both elementary logic and the foundations of our due process jurisprudence. The distinction between what is needed to support novel procedures and what is needed to sustain traditional ones is fundamental . . . .

* * *

The short of the matter is that jurisdiction based on physical presence alone constitutes due process because it is one of the continuing traditions of our legal system that define the due process standard of "traditional notions of fair play and substantial justice." That standard was developed by *analogy* to "physical presence," and it would be perverse to say it could now be turned against that touchstone of jurisdiction.

D

Petitioner's strongest argument, though we ultimately reject it, relies upon our decision in *Shaffer v. Heitner.* In that case, a Delaware court hearing a shareholder's derivative suit against a corporation's directors secured jurisdiction *quasi in rem* by sequestering the out-of-state defendants' stock in the company, the situs of which was Delaware under Delaware law.

Reasoning that Delaware's sequestration procedure was simply a mechanism to compel the absent defendants to appear in a suit to determine their personal rights and obligations, we concluded that the normal rules we had developed under *International*

Shoe for jurisdiction over suits against absent defendants should apply—viz., Delaware could not hear the suit because the defendants' sole contact with the State (ownership of property there) was unrelated to the lawsuit.

It goes too far to say, as petitioner contends, that *Shaffer* compels the conclusion that a State lacks jurisdiction over an individual unless the litigation arises out of his activities in the State. *Shaffer,* like *International Shoe,* involved jurisdiction over an *absent defendant,* and it stands for nothing more than the proposition that when the "minimum contact" that is a substitute for physical presence consists of property ownership it must, like other minimum contacts, be related to the litigation. Petitioner wrenches out of its context our statement in *Shaffer* that "all assertions of state-court jurisdiction must be evaluated according to the standards set forth in *International Shoe* and its progeny." When read together with the two sentences that preceded it, the meaning of this statement becomes clear:

> "The fiction that an assertion of jurisdiction over property is anything but an assertion of jurisdiction over the owner of the property supports an ancient form without substantial modern justification. Its continued acceptance would serve only to allow state-court jurisdiction that is fundamentally unfair to the defendant.

> "We *therefore conclude* that all assertions of state-court jurisdiction must be evaluated according to the standards set forth in *International Shoe* and its progeny." (emphasis added).

Shaffer was saying, in other words, not that all bases for the assertion of *in personam* jurisdiction (including, presumably, in-state service) must be treated alike and subjected to the "minimum contacts" analysis of *International Shoe;* but rather that *quasi in rem* jurisdiction, that fictional "ancient form," and *in personam* jurisdiction, are really one and the same and must be treated alike—leading to the conclusion that *quasi in rem* jurisdiction, *i.e.,* that form of *in personam* jurisdiction based upon a "property ownership" contact and by definition unaccompanied by personal, in-state service, must satisfy the litigation-relatedness requirement of *International Shoe.*

* * *

International Shoe confined its "minimum contacts" requirement to situations in which the defendant "be not present within the territory of the forum," and nothing in *Shaffer* expands that requirement beyond that.

* * *

Because the Due Process Clause does not prohibit the California courts from exercising jurisdiction over petitioner based on the fact of in-state service of process, the judgment is

Affirmed.

JUSTICE WHITE concurring in part.

The rule allowing jurisdiction to be obtained over a nonresident by personal service in the forum State, without more, has been and is so widely accepted throughout this country that I could not possibly strike it down, either on its face or as applied in this case, on the ground that it denies due process of law guaranteed by the Fourteenth Amendment.

* * *

At least this would be the case where presence in the forum State is intentional, which would almost always be the fact.

JUSTICE BRENNAN, with whom JUSTICE MARSHALL, JUSTICE BLACKMUN, and JUSTICE O'CONNOR join, concurring in the judgment.

I agree with Justice SCALIA that the Due Process Clause of the Fourteenth Amendment generally permits a state court to exercise jurisdiction over a defendant if he is served with process while voluntarily present in the forum State. I do not perceive the need, however, to decide that a jurisdictional rule that " 'has been immemorially the actual law of the land,' " automatically comports with due process simply by virtue of its "pedigree." Although I agree that history is an important factor in establishing whether a jurisdictional rule satisfies due process requirements, I cannot agree that it is the only factor such that all traditional rules of jurisdiction are, ipso facto, forever constitutional. Unlike Justice SCALIA, I would undertake an "independent inquiry into the . . . fairness of the prevailing in-state service rule."

* * *

By visiting the forum State, a transient defendant actually "avail[s]" himself, of significant benefits provided by the State. His health and safety are guaranteed by the State's police, fire, and emergency medical services; he is free to travel on the State's roads and waterways; he likely enjoys the fruits of the State's economy as well. Moreover, the Privileges and Immunities Clause of Article IV prevents a state government from discriminating against a transient defendant by denying him the protections of its law or the right of access to its courts. Subject only to the doctrine of forum non conveniens, an out-of-state plaintiff may use state courts in all circumstances in which those courts would be available to state citizens. Without transient jurisdiction, an asymmetry would arise: A transient would have the full benefit of the power of the forum State's courts as a plaintiff while retaining immunity from their authority as a defendant.

The potential burdens on a transient defendant are slight. " '[M]odern transportation and communications have made it much less burdensome for a party sued to defend himself' " in a State outside his place of residence. That the defendant has already journeyed at least once before to the forum—as evidenced by the fact that he was served with process there—is an indication that suit in the forum likely would not be prohibitively inconvenient. Finally, any burdens that do arise can be ameliorated by a variety of procedural devices. For these reasons, as a rule the exercise of personal jurisdiction over a defendant based on his voluntary presence in the forum will satisfy the requirements of due process.

In this case, it is undisputed that petitioner was served with process while voluntarily and knowingly in the State of California. I therefore concur in the judgment.

DIRECTED READING QUESTIONS

60. Why might the husband originally agree to a divorce based on irreconcilable differences, but then file for divorce in New Jersey based on desertion?

61. Why did the husband go to California in January of 1988?

62. After being served with the complaint, the husband objected to personal jurisdiction in California. Explain precisely his objection to jurisdiction in California.

63. Why did the husband's objection to personal jurisdiction in California fail?

64. How does Justice Scalia get around the statement in Shaffer that, "all assertions of state-court jurisdiction must be evaluated according to the standards set forth in International Shoe and its progeny"?

65. Consider, a resident of Wyoming is playing a game of Frisbee on a beach in Florida, a few feet south of the Georgia border. She briefly runs over the Florida-Georgia border to retrieve an errant toss. In the less than 30 second time she spends in Georgia to retrieve the frisbee, she is served personally by a process server. The cause of action in the complaint attached to the summons indicates that the forum is the United States District Court for the Southern District of Georgia. The cause of action alleges that she caused harm to a German tourist when she negligently ran down a street in Paris the year before. According to Justice Scalia, would personal jurisdiction in Georgia be appropriate? In answering, review the *Nicastro* decision to see its description of general jurisdiction based on presence.

66. What restriction on general jurisdiction based on presence would Justice White add to Justice Scalia's formulation? Create an example where there would be a different outcome under Justice Scalia's test and Justice White's test.

67. Justice Brennan does not attempt to limit the statement in *Shaffer* that, "all assertions of state-court jurisdiction must be evaluated according to the standards set forth in *International Shoe* and its progeny." Rather, he suggests that even assertions of jurisdiction based on presence must also satisfy the minimum contacts standard. Explain how, even though he suggests this formulation, he concurred in the judgment.

DAIMLER AG V. BAUMAN (2014)
Supreme Court of the United States
571 U.S. 117

JUSTICE GINSBURG delivered the opinion of the Court.

This case concerns the authority of a court in the United States to entertain a claim brought by foreign plaintiffs against a foreign defendant based on events occurring entirely outside the United States. The litigation commenced in 2004, when twenty-two Argentinian residents filed a complaint in the United States District Court for the Northern District of California against DaimlerChrysler Aktiengesellschaft (Daimler), a German public stock company, headquartered in Stuttgart, that manufactures Mercedes-Benz vehicles in Germany. The complaint alleged that during Argentina's 1976–1983 "Dirty War," Daimler's Argentinian subsidiary, Mercedes-Benz Argentina (MB Argentina) collaborated with state security forces to kidnap, detain, torture, and kill certain MB Argentina workers, among them, plaintiffs or persons closely related to plaintiffs. Damages for the alleged human-rights violations were sought from Daimler under the laws of the United States, California, and Argentina. Jurisdiction over the lawsuit was predicated on the California contacts of Mercedes-Benz USA, LLC (MBUSA), a subsidiary of Daimler incorporated in Delaware with its principal place of business in New Jersey. MBUSA distributes Daimler-manufactured vehicles to independent dealerships throughout the United States, including California.

The question presented is whether the Due Process Clause of the Fourteenth Amendment precludes the District Court from exercising jurisdiction over Daimler in this case, given the absence of any California connection to the atrocities, perpetrators, or victims described in the complaint. Plaintiffs invoked the court's general or all-purpose jurisdiction. California, they urge, is a place where Daimler may be sued on any and all claims against it, wherever in the world the claims may arise. For example, as plaintiffs' counsel affirmed, under the proffered jurisdictional theory, if a Daimler-manufactured vehicle overturned in Poland, injuring a Polish driver and passenger, the injured parties could maintain a design defect suit in California. Exercises of personal jurisdiction so exorbitant, we hold, are barred by due process constraints on the assertion of adjudicatory authority.

In *Goodyear Dunlop Tires Operations, S.A. v. Brown* (2011), we addressed the distinction between general or all-purpose jurisdiction, and specific or conduct-linked jurisdiction. As to the former, we held that a court may assert jurisdiction over a foreign corporation "to hear any and all claims against [it]" only when the corporation's affiliations with the State in which suit is brought are so constant and pervasive "as to render [it] essentially at home in the forum State." Instructed by *Goodyear*, we conclude Daimler is not "at home" in California, and cannot be sued there for injuries plaintiffs attribute to MB Argentina's conduct in Argentina.

I

In 2004, plaintiffs (respondents here) filed suit in the United States District Court for the Northern District of California, alleging that MB Argentina collaborated with Argentinian state security forces to kidnap, detain, torture, and kill plaintiffs and their relatives during the military dictatorship in place there from 1976 through 1983, a period known as Argentina's "Dirty War." Based on those allegations, plaintiffs asserted claims under the Alien Tort Statute, and the Torture Victim Protection Act of 1991, as well as claims for wrongful death and intentional infliction of emotional distress under the laws of California and Argentina. The incidents recounted in the complaint center on MB Argentina's plant in Gonzalez Catan, Argentina; no part of MB Argentina's alleged collaboration with Argentinian authorities took place in California or anywhere else in the United States.

Plaintiffs' operative complaint names only one corporate defendant: Daimler, the petitioner here. Plaintiffs seek to hold Daimler vicariously liable for MB Argentina's alleged malfeasance. Daimler is a German *Aktiengesellschaft* (public stock company) that manufactures Mercedes-Benz vehicles primarily in Germany and has its headquarters in Stuttgart. At times relevant to this case, MB Argentina was a subsidiary wholly owned by Daimler's predecessor in interest.

Daimler moved to dismiss the action for want of personal jurisdiction. Opposing the motion, plaintiffs submitted declarations and exhibits purporting to demonstrate the presence of Daimler itself in California. Alternatively, plaintiffs maintained that jurisdiction over Daimler could be founded on the California contacts of MBUSA, a distinct corporate entity that, according to plaintiffs, should be treated as Daimler's agent for jurisdictional purposes.

MBUSA, an indirect subsidiary of Daimler, is a Delaware limited liability corporation.[3] MBUSA serves as Daimler's exclusive importer and distributor in the United States, purchasing Mercedes-Benz automobiles from Daimler in Germany, then importing those vehicles, and ultimately distributing them to independent dealerships located throughout the Nation. Although MBUSA's principal place of business is in New Jersey, MBUSA has multiple California-based facilities, including a regional office in Costa Mesa, a Vehicle Preparation Center in Carson, and a Classic Center in Irvine. According to the record developed below, MBUSA is the largest supplier of luxury vehicles to the California market. In particular, over 10% of all sales of new vehicles in the United States take place in California, and MBUSA's California sales account for 2.4% of Daimler's worldwide sales.

The relationship between Daimler and MBUSA is delineated in a General Distributor Agreement, which sets forth requirements for MBUSA's distribution of Mercedes-Benz vehicles in the United States. That agreement established MBUSA as an "independent contracto[r]" that "buy[s] and sell[s] [vehicles] ... as an independent business for [its] own account." App. 179a. The agreement "does not make [MBUSA] ... a general or special agent, partner, joint venturer or employee of DAIMLERCHRYSLER or any DaimlerChrysler Group Company"; MBUSA "ha[s] no authority to make binding obligations for or act on behalf of DAIMLERCHRYSLER or any DaimlerChrysler Group Company."

After allowing jurisdictional discovery on plaintiffs' agency allegations, the District Court granted Daimler's motion to dismiss. Daimler's own affiliations with California, the court first determined, were insufficient to support the exercise of all-purpose jurisdiction over the corporation. Next, the court declined to attribute MBUSA's California contacts to Daimler on an agency theory, concluding that plaintiffs failed to demonstrate that MBUSA acted as Daimler's agent.

[The Ninth Circuit Court of Appeals reversed the District Court.]

We granted certiorari to decide whether, consistent with the Due Process Clause of the Fourteenth Amendment, Daimler is amenable to suit in California courts for claims involving only foreign plaintiffs and conduct occurring entirely abroad.

II

Federal courts ordinarily follow state law in determining the bounds of their jurisdiction over persons. See Fed. Rule Civ. Proc. 4(k)(1)(A) (service of process is effective to establish personal jurisdiction over a defendant "who is subject to the jurisdiction of a court of general jurisdiction in the state where the district court is located"). Under California's long-arm statute, California state courts may exercise personal jurisdiction "on any basis not inconsistent with the Constitution of this state or of the United States." California's long-arm statute allows the exercise of personal jurisdiction to the full extent permissible under the U.S. Constitution. We therefore

---

[3] At times relevant to this suit, MBUSA was wholly owned by DaimlerChrysler North America Holding Corporation, a Daimler subsidiary.

inquire whether the Ninth Circuit's holding comports with the limits imposed by federal due process.

* * *

IV

With this background, we turn directly to the question whether Daimler's affiliations with California are sufficient to subject it to the general (all-purpose) personal jurisdiction of that State's courts. In the proceedings below, the parties agreed on, or failed to contest, certain points we now take as given. Plaintiffs have never attempted to fit this case into the *specific* jurisdiction category. Nor did plaintiffs challenge on appeal the District Court's holding that Daimler's own contacts with California were, by themselves, too sporadic to justify the exercise of general jurisdiction. While plaintiffs ultimately persuaded the Ninth Circuit to impute MBUSA's California contacts to Daimler on an agency theory, at no point have they maintained that MBUSA is an alter ego of Daimler.

Daimler, on the other hand, failed to object below to plaintiffs' assertion that the California courts could exercise all-purpose jurisdiction over MBUSA.[12] We will assume then, for purposes of this decision only, that MBUSA qualifies as at home in California.

A

In sustaining the exercise of general jurisdiction over Daimler, the Ninth Circuit relied on an agency theory, determining that MBUSA acted as Daimler's agent for jurisdictional purposes and then attributing MBUSA's California contacts to Daimler. The Ninth Circuit's agency analysis derived from Circuit precedent considering principally whether the subsidiary "performs services that are sufficiently important to the foreign corporation that if it did not have a representative to perform them, the corporation's own officials would undertake to perform substantially similar services."

This Court has not yet addressed whether a foreign corporation may be subjected to a court's general jurisdiction based on the contacts of its in-state subsidiary. Daimler argues, and several Courts of Appeals have held, that a subsidiary's jurisdictional contacts can be imputed to its parent only when the former is so dominated by the latter as to be its alter ego. The Ninth Circuit adopted a less rigorous test based on what it described as an "agency" relationship. Agencies, we note, come in many sizes and shapes: "One may be an agent for some business purposes and not others so that the fact that one may be an agent for one purpose does not make him or her an agent for every purpose." A subsidiary, for example, might be its parent's agent for claims arising in the place where the subsidiary operates, yet not its agent regarding claims arising elsewhere. The Court of Appeals did not advert to that prospect. But we need not pass judgment on invocation of an agency theory in the context of general jurisdiction, for in no event can the appeals court's analysis be sustained.

The Ninth Circuit's agency finding rested primarily on its observation that MBUSA's services were "important" to Daimler, as gauged by Daimler's hypothetical readiness to perform those services itself if MBUSA did not exist. Formulated this way, the inquiry into importance stacks the deck, for it will always yield a pro-jurisdiction

---

[12]　MBUSA is not a defendant in this case.

answer: "Anything a corporation does through an independent contractor, subsidiary, or distributor is presumably something that the corporation would do 'by other means' if the independent contractor, subsidiary, or distributor did not exist." The Ninth Circuit's agency theory thus appears to subject foreign corporations to general jurisdiction whenever they have an in-state subsidiary or affiliate, an outcome that would sweep beyond even the "sprawling view of general jurisdiction" we rejected in *Goodyear*.

B

Even if we were to assume that MBUSA is at home in California, and further to assume MBUSA's contacts are imputable to Daimler, there would still be no basis to subject Daimler to general jurisdiction in California, for Daimler's slim contacts with the State hardly render it at home there.

Goodyear made clear that only a limited set of affiliations with a forum will render a defendant amenable to all-purpose jurisdiction there. "For an individual, the paradigm forum for the exercise of general jurisdiction is the individual's domicile; for a corporation, it is an equivalent place, one in which the corporation is fairly regarded as at home." With respect to a corporation, the place of incorporation and principal place of business are "paradig[m] . . . bases for general jurisdiction." Those affiliations have the virtue of being unique—that is, each ordinarily indicates only one place—as well as easily ascertainable. ("Simple jurisdictional rules . . . promote greater predictability.")

These bases afford plaintiffs recourse to at least one clear and certain forum in which a corporate defendant may be sued on any and all claims.

Goodyear did not hold that a corporation may be subject to general jurisdiction *only* in a forum where it is incorporated or has its principal place of business; it simply typed those places paradigm all-purpose forums. Plaintiffs would have us look beyond the exemplar bases *Goodyear* identified, and approve the exercise of general jurisdiction in every State in which a corporation "engages in a substantial, continuous, and systematic course of business." That formulation, we hold, is unacceptably grasping.

As noted, the words "continuous and systematic" were used in *International Shoe* to describe instances in which the exercise of *specific* jurisdiction would be appropriate. Turning to all-purpose jurisdiction, in contrast, *International Shoe* speaks of "instances in which the continuous corporate operations within a state [are] so substantial and of such a nature as to justify suit . . . *on causes of action arising from dealings entirely distinct from those activities.*" Accordingly, the inquiry under *Goodyear* is not whether a foreign corporation's in-forum contacts can be said to be in some sense "continuous and systematic," it is whether that corporation's "affiliations with the State are so 'continuous and systematic' as to render [it] essentially at home in the forum State."[19]

Here, neither Daimler nor MBUSA is incorporated in California, nor does either entity have its principal place of business there. If Daimler's California activities sufficed to allow adjudication of this Argentina-rooted case in California, the same global reach

---

[19] We do not foreclose the possibility that in an exceptional case, see, *e.g., Perkins*, a corporation's operations in a forum other than its formal place of incorporation or principal place of business may be so substantial and of such a nature as to render the corporation at home in that State. But this case presents no occasion to explore that question, because Daimler's activities in California plainly do not approach that level. It is one thing to hold a corporation answerable for operations in the forum State, quite another to expose it to suit on claims having no connection whatever to the forum State.

would presumably be available in every other State in which MBUSA's sales are sizable. Such exorbitant exercises of all-purpose jurisdiction would scarcely permit out-of-state defendants "to structure their primary conduct with some minimum assurance as to where that conduct will and will not render them liable to suit."

It was therefore error for the Ninth Circuit to conclude that Daimler, even with MBUSA's contacts attributed to it, was at home in California, and hence subject to suit there on claims by foreign plaintiffs having nothing to do with anything that occurred or had its principal impact in California.

* * *

For the reasons stated, the judgment of the United States Court of Appeals for the Ninth Circuit is

Reversed.

DIRECTED READING QUESTIONS

68. *Who* are the plaintiffs in this case? What are the events that form the basis of the allegation of wrongdoing by the defendant in this case?

69. Explain how the plaintiff argues that general jurisdiction in California is appropriate and the Supreme Court's response. Why doesn't the plaintiff argue for specific jurisdiction?

70. What are the three options for general jurisdiction over corporations after *Daimler*?

71. The Supreme Court concludes that Daimler, through its subsidiary, engages in a continuous and systematic course of business in California. Yet, the Court finds that general jurisdiction is unavailable in California. Carefully read the case and see if you can articulate the distinction I am hinting at by suggesting, that "systematic and continuous" is different from SYSTEMATIC AND CONTINUOUS.

72. What allegation must be made in order to establish minimum contacts that is not required to establish general jurisdiction?

73. What allegation must be made to establish general jurisdiction that is not required to establish minimum contacts?

V. FEDERAL JURISDICTION NOT CONDITIONED ON STATE COURT JURISDICTION

FED. R. CIV. P. 4

(k) TERRITORIAL LIMITS OF EFFECTIVE SERVICE.

(1) *In General.* Serving a summons or filing a waiver of service establishes personal jurisdiction over a defendant:

(A) who is subject to the jurisdiction of a court of general jurisdiction in the state where the district court is located;

    (B) who is a party joined under Rule 14 or 19 and is served within a judicial district of the United States and not more than 100 miles from where the summons was issued; or

    (C) when authorized by a federal statute.

    (2) *Federal Claim Outside State-Court Jurisdiction.* **For a claim that arises under federal law, serving a summons or filing a waiver of service establishes personal jurisdiction over a defendant if:**

    (A) the defendant is not subject to jurisdiction in any state's courts of general jurisdiction; and

    (B) exercising jurisdiction is consistent with the United States Constitution and laws.

DIRECTED READING QUESTIONS

74. Alpha sues Beta in Illinois Federal Court for negligence. Beta claims that Charlie, a resident of Missouri living within 100 miles of the federal court room where the action is pending, is liable to Beta if Beta is liable to Alpha, and therefore Beta impleads Charlie. Charlie does not have minimum contacts with Illinois. Is there personal jurisdiction over Charlie in the Illinois Federal Court?

75. Is there personal jurisdiction over Charlie if the facts are the same, except that the action is taking place in Illinois state court?

76. Alpha sues Beta in North Dakota Federal Court for negligence. The forum court is 30 miles from the Canadian border. Charlie lives 30 miles inside the Canadian border (60 miles away from the forum court) and does not have minimum contacts with North Dakota. Beta alleges that without Charlie's joinder, the court cannot accord complete relief among the existing parties. Is Beta correct that the North Dakota federal court has personal jurisdiction pursuant to Rule 4(k)(1)(B) over Charlie, if Beta joins Charlie pursuant to Rule 19?

77. Alpha sues Beta and Charlie in Illinois Federal Court for negligence. Alpha is a resident of Illinois, and Charlie is a resident of Missouri living within 100 miles of the federal court room where the action is pending. Charlie does not have minimum contacts with Illinois. If Beta files a cross-claim against Charlie seeking contribution from Charlie, does Rule 4(k)(1)(B) establish personal jurisdiction over Charlie?

78. In *Nicastro*, Justice Kennedy explains, "Because the United States is a distinct sovereign, a defendant may in principle be subject to the jurisdiction of the courts of the United States but not of any particular state. For jurisdiction, a litigant may have the requisite relationship with the United States Government but not with the government of any state." Was *Nicastro* an example of where nationwide personal jurisdiction pursuant to Rule 4(k)(1)(C) would be appropriate?

79. Was *Nicastro* an example of where nationwide personal jurisdiction pursuant to Rule 4(k)(2) would be appropriate?

VI. LONGARM STATUTES

DIRECTED READING QUESTIONS

80. What is the purpose of a long-arm statute?

81. The state of Sasnak has a long-arm statute which states, "Anyone driving a blue car is subject to the jurisdiction of the courts of this state." Alpha from Oregon is driving a blue car negligently and crashes into Beta from California while they are driving in Washington state. Beta sues Alpha in the United States District Court for the District of Sasnak for damages sustained in the accident and complies with the relevant service of process requirements. Does the United States District Court for the District of Sasnak have personal jurisdiction over Alpha, if Alpha does not consent to jurisdiction?

82. What difference does it make if a state has an enumerated long-arm statute or an unenumerated long-arm statute?

Kansas Enumerated Long Arm Statute	California Unenumerated Long Arm Statute
(b) Submitting to jurisdiction. (1) Any person, whether or not a citizen or resident of this state, who in person or through an agent or instrumentality does any of the following acts, thereby submits the person and, if an individual, the individual's representative, to the jurisdiction of the courts of this state for any claim for relief arising from the act: (A) Transacting any business in this state; (B) committing a tortious act in this state; (C) owning, using or possessing real estate located in this state; (D) contracting to insure any person, property or risk located in this state at the time of contracting; (E) entering into an express or implied contract, by mail or otherwise, with a resident of this state to be performed in whole or in part by either party in this state; (F) acting in this state as director, manager, trustee or other officer of any corporation organized under the laws of or having a place of business in this state or as executor or administrator of any estate in this state. . . .	A court of this state may exercise jurisdiction on any basis not inconsistent with the Constitution of this state or of the United States.

83. Why might a state, pursuant to an enumerated long-arm statute, give itself less power over out of state defendants than the Constitution allows?

CHAPTER 17

VENUE

■ ■ ■

I. STATUTORY VENUE (28 U.S.C. § 1391)

DIRECTED READING QUESTIONS

1. Personal jurisdiction is largely concerned with the geographical borders of a _____ whereas venue is concerned with the geographical boundaries of a _____ _____.

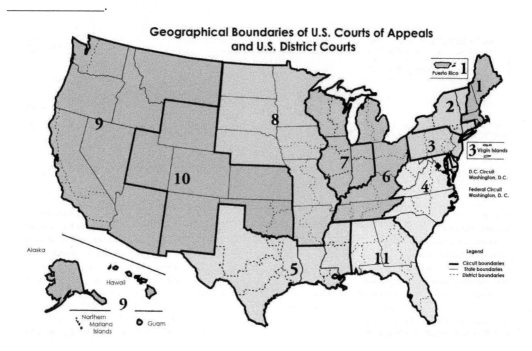

2. What do the numbers 1–11 represent on the map?*

---

*   Map taken from https://www.flmd.uscourts.gov/you-are-here.

3. The following image* is an expanded image of the state of Oklahoma, showing the federal judicial districts. In terms of their judicial districts, what is the difference between Kansas and Oklahoma?

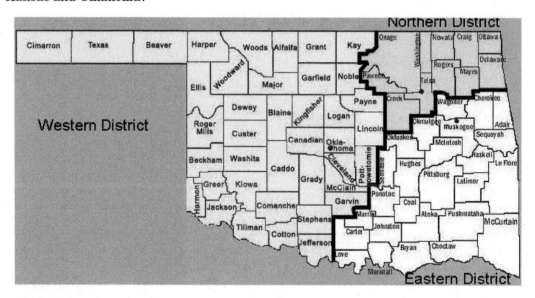

4. Is there an "or" between § 1391(b)(1) and (b)(2)? Is there an "or" between § 1391(b)(2) and (b)(3)?

5. What is the significance of the absence or presence of an "or" between the subsections of § 1391(b)?

6. Alpha lives in Texas County, Oklahoma, and Beta lives in Latimer County, Oklahoma. They decide to visit their friend Gamma in Miami, Florida. Florida has three federal judicial districts: the Southern, Middle and Northern districts. Miami is in the Southern District of Florida. While in Miami, Alpha and Beta get into an argument with a server at a beach bar over the correct placement of mini umbrellas in tropical drinks. The argument turns into an altercation, and now the server is suing Alpha and Beta for battery. Assuming there is subject matter jurisdiction, use the maps above to decide where venue is proper.

7. Susan, a resident of Kansas City, Missouri, and Johnny, a resident of Miami, are sued by Tough Guy, who is a resident of New York City, for breach of a contract that was negotiated in Orlando, Florida and supposed to be performed in Kansas City, Kansas. Susan and Johnny failed to perform as per the contract. Orlando is located in the middle district of Florida. Where is venue proper?

8. Susan is a resident of Miami, Florida, which is in the southern district of Florida, and Ralph is a resident of Kansas City, Kansas. While all three are in the Dominican Republic, Susan and Ralph get into a fight and batter Phillip, who is a resident of Boston, Massachusetts. Where is venue proper if Phillip sues Susan and Ralph?

9. Target is a national retailer incorporated in Delaware (which has only one judicial district) with its principal place of business in Montebello, California but has stores in every county in California, Florida, and New York. Montebello is located in the central

---

*   Image taken from https://www.okwb.uscourts.gov/service-area.

district of California. Reagan is a resident of Kansas City, Kansas who slips and falls due to negligently maintained floors in a Target store in Miami, Florida. Miami is in the Southern District of Florida. Reagan wants to sue Target for negligence. Is venue proper in the Southern District of Florida, Middle District of Florida, Northern District of Florida, Central District of California, Northern District of California, Eastern District of California, Southern District of California, or the District of Delaware?

II. COMMON LAW VENUE (*FORUM NON CONVENIENS*)

PIPER AIRCRAFT CO. V. REYNO (1981)
Supreme Court of the United States
454 U.S. 235

JUSTICE MARSHALL delivered the opinion of the Court.

These cases arise out of an air crash that took place in Scotland. Respondent, acting as representative of the estates of several Scottish citizens killed in the accident, brought wrongful-death actions against petitioners that were ultimately transferred to the United States District Court for the Middle District of Pennsylvania. Petitioners moved to dismiss on the ground of *forum non conveniens*. After noting that an alternative forum existed in Scotland, the District Court granted their motions. The United States Court of Appeals for the Third Circuit reversed. The Court of Appeals based its decision, at least in part, on the ground that dismissal is automatically barred where the law of the alternative forum is less favorable to the plaintiff than the law of the forum chosen by the plaintiff. Because we conclude that the possibility of an unfavorable change in law should not, by itself, bar dismissal, and because we conclude that the District Court did not otherwise abuse its discretion, we reverse.

I

A

In July 1976, a small commercial aircraft crashed in the Scottish highlands during the course of a charter flight from Blackpool to Perth. The pilot and five passengers were killed instantly. The decedents were all Scottish subjects and residents, as are their heirs and next of kin. There were no eyewitnesses to the accident. At the time of the crash the plane was subject to Scottish air traffic control.

The aircraft, a twin-engine Piper Aztec, was manufactured in Pennsylvania by petitioner Piper Aircraft Co. (Piper). The propellers were manufactured in Ohio by petitioner Hartzell Propeller, Inc. (Hartzell). At the time of the crash the aircraft was registered in Great Britain and was owned and maintained by Air Navigation and Trading Co., Ltd. (Air Navigation). It was operated by McDonald Aviation, Ltd. (McDonald), a Scottish air taxi service. Both Air Navigation and McDonald were organized in the United Kingdom. The wreckage of the plane is now in a hangar in Farnsborough, England.

The British Department of Trade investigated the accident shortly after it occurred. A preliminary report found that the plane crashed after developing a spin, and suggested that mechanical failure in the plane or the propeller was responsible. At Hartzell's request, this report was reviewed by a three-member Review Board, which held a 9-day adversary hearing attended by all interested parties. The Review Board found no evidence of defective equipment and indicated that pilot error may have contributed to the accident. The pilot, who had obtained his commercial pilot's license only three months earlier, was flying over high ground at an altitude considerably lower than the minimum height required by his company's operations manual.

In July 1977, a California probate court appointed respondent Gaynell Reyno administratrix of the estates of the five passengers. Reyno is not related to and does not know any of the decedents or their survivors; she was a legal secretary to the attorney who filed this lawsuit. Several days after her appointment, Reyno commenced separate wrongful-death actions against Piper and Hartzell in the Superior Court of California, claiming negligence and strict liability. Air Navigation, McDonald, and the estate of the pilot are not parties to this litigation. The survivors of the five passengers whose estates are represented by Reyno filed a separate action in the United Kingdom against Air Navigation, McDonald, and the pilot's estate. Reyno candidly admits that the action against Piper and Hartzell was filed in the United States because its laws regarding liability, capacity to sue, and damages are more favorable to her position than are those of Scotland. Scottish law does not recognize strict liability in tort. Moreover, it permits wrongful-death actions only when brought by a decedent's relatives. The relatives may sue only for "loss of support and society."

On petitioners' motion, the suit was removed to the United States District Court for the Central District of California. Piper then moved for transfer to the United States District Court for the Middle District of Pennsylvania, pursuant to 28 U.S.C. § 1404(a). [At the time the suit was filed Piper did business in California but Hartzell did not and neither Hartzell's nor Piper's principal place of business was in California. Additionally Piper was incorporated in Pennsylvania and Hartzell was incorporated in Ohio.*] Hartzell moved to dismiss for lack of personal jurisdiction, or in the alternative, to transfer.[5] In December 1977, the District Court quashed service on Hartzell and transferred the case to the Middle District of Pennsylvania. Respondent then properly served process on Hartzell.

B

In May 1978, after the suit had been transferred, both Hartzell and Piper moved to dismiss the action on the ground of *forum non conveniens*. The District Court granted these motions in October 1979. It relied on the balancing test set forth by this Court in *Gulf Oil Corp. v. Gilbert*, and its companion case, *Koster v. Lumbermens Mut. Cas. Co.* In those decisions, the Court stated that a plaintiff's choice of forum should rarely be disturbed. However, when an alternative forum has jurisdiction to hear the case, and when trial in the chosen forum would "establish . . . oppressiveness and vexation to a defendant . . . out of all proportion to plaintiff's convenience," or when the "chosen forum [is] inappropriate because of considerations affecting the court's own administrative and legal problems," the court may, in the exercise of its sound discretion, dismiss the case. To guide trial court discretion, the Court provided a list of "private interest factors"

---

   *   Author's addition.

   [5]   The District Court concluded that it could not assert personal jurisdiction over Hartzell consistent with due process. However, it decided not to dismiss Hartzell because the corporation would be amenable to process in Pennsylvania.

affecting the convenience of the litigants, and a list of "public interest factors" affecting the convenience of the forum. *Gilbert.*[6]

After describing our decisions in *Gilbert* and *Koster*, the District Court analyzed the facts of these cases. It began by observing that an alternative forum existed in Scotland; Piper and Hartzell had agreed to submit to the jurisdiction of the Scottish courts and to waive any statute of limitations defense that might be available. It then stated that plaintiff's choice of forum was entitled to little weight. The court recognized that a plaintiff's choice ordinarily deserves substantial deference. It noted, however, that Reyno "is a representative of foreign citizens and residents seeking a forum in the United States because of the more liberal rules concerning products liability law," and that "the courts have been less solicitous when the plaintiff is not an American citizen or resident, and particularly when the foreign citizens seek to benefit from the more liberal tort rules provided for the protection of citizens and residents of the United States."

The District Court next examined several factors relating to the private interests of the litigants, and determined that these factors strongly pointed towards Scotland as the appropriate forum. Although evidence concerning the design, manufacture, and testing of the plane and propeller is located in the United States, the connections with Scotland are otherwise "overwhelming." The real parties in interest are citizens of Scotland, as were all the decedents. Witnesses who could testify regarding the maintenance of the aircraft, the training of the pilot, and the investigation of the accident—all essential to the defense—are in Great Britain. Moreover, all witnesses to damages are located in Scotland. Trial would be aided by familiarity with Scottish topography, and by easy access to the wreckage.

The District Court reasoned that because crucial witnesses and evidence were beyond the reach of compulsory process, and because the defendants would not be able to implead potential Scottish third-party defendants, it would be "unfair to make Piper and Hartzell proceed to trial in this forum." The survivors had brought separate actions in Scotland against the pilot, McDonald, and Air Navigation. "[I]t would be fairer to all parties and less costly if the entire case was presented to one jury with available testimony from all relevant witnesses." *Ibid.* Although the court recognized that if trial were held in the United States, Piper and Hartzell could file indemnity or contribution actions against the Scottish defendants, it believed that there was a significant risk of inconsistent verdicts.

The District Court concluded that the relevant public interests also pointed strongly towards dismissal. The court determined that Pennsylvania law would apply to Piper and Scottish law to Hartzell if the case were tried in the Middle District of Pennsylvania.[8]

---

[6]   The factors pertaining to the private interests of the litigants included the "relative ease of access to sources of proof; availability of compulsory process for attendance of unwilling, and the cost of obtaining attendance of willing, witnesses; possibility of view of premises, if view would be appropriate to the action; and all other practical problems that make trial of a case easy, expeditious and inexpensive." *Gilbert,* 330 U.S., at 508, 67 S.Ct., at 843. The public factors bearing on the question included the administrative difficulties flowing from court congestion; the "local interest in having localized controversies decided at home"; the interest in having the trial of a diversity case in a forum that is at home with the law that must govern the action; the avoidance of unnecessary problems in conflict of laws, or in the application of foreign law; and the unfairness of burdening citizens in an unrelated forum with jury duty.

[8]   Under *Klaxon v. Stentor Electric Mfg. Co.,* 313 U.S. 487, 61 S.Ct. 1020, 85 L.Ed. 1477 (1941), a court ordinarily must apply the choice-of-law rules of the State in which it sits. However, where a case is transferred pursuant to 28 U.S.C. § 1404(a), it must apply the choice-of-law rules of the State from which the case was

As a result, "trial in this forum would be hopelessly complex and confusing for a jury." In addition, the court noted that it was unfamiliar with Scottish law and thus would have to rely upon experts from that country. The court also found that the trial would be enormously costly and time-consuming; that it would be unfair to burden citizens with jury duty when the Middle District of Pennsylvania has little connection with the controversy; and that Scotland has a substantial interest in the outcome of the litigation.

In opposing the motions to dismiss, respondent contended that dismissal would be unfair because Scottish law was less favorable. The District Court explicitly rejected this claim. It reasoned that the possibility that dismissal might lead to an unfavorable change in the law did not deserve significant weight; any deficiency in the foreign law was a "matter to be dealt with in the foreign forum."

C

On appeal, the United States Court of Appeals for the Third Circuit reversed and remanded for trial. The decision to reverse appears to be based on two alternative grounds. First, the Court held that the District Court abused its discretion in conducting the *Gilbert* analysis. Second, the Court held that dismissal is never appropriate where the law of the alternative forum is less favorable to the plaintiff.

The Court of Appeals began its review of the District Court's *Gilbert* analysis by noting that the plaintiff's choice of forum deserved substantial weight, even though the real parties in interest are nonresidents. It then rejected the District Court's balancing of the private interests. It found that Piper and Hartzell had failed adequately to support their claim that key witnesses would be unavailable if trial were held in the United States: they had never specified the witnesses they would call and the testimony these witnesses would provide. The Court of Appeals gave little weight to the fact that Piper and Hartzell would not be able to implead potential Scottish third-party defendants, reasoning that this difficulty would be "burdensome" but not "unfair". Finally, the court stated that resolution of the suit would not be significantly aided by familiarity with Scottish topography, or by viewing the wreckage.

The Court of Appeals also rejected the District Court's analysis of the public interest factors. It found that the District Court gave undue emphasis to the application of Scottish law: " 'the mere fact that the court is called upon to determine and apply foreign law does not present a legal problem of the sort which would justify the dismissal of a case otherwise properly before the court.' " In any event, it believed that Scottish law need not be applied. After conducting its own choice-of-law analysis, the Court of Appeals determined that American law would govern the actions against both Piper and Hartzell.[10] The same choice-of-law analysis apparently led it to conclude that

---

transferred. *Van Dusen v. Barrack*, 376 U.S. 612, 84 S.Ct. 805, 11 L.Ed.2d 945 (1946). Relying on these two cases, the District Court concluded that California choice-of-law rules would apply to Piper, and Pennsylvania choice-of-law rules would apply to Hartzell. It further concluded that California applied a "governmental interests" analysis in resolving choice-of-law problems, and that Pennsylvania employed a "significant contacts" analysis. The court used the "governmental interests" analysis to determine that Pennsylvania liability rules would apply to Piper, and the "significant contacts" analysis to determine that Scottish liability rules would apply to Hartzell.

[10] The Court of Appeals agreed with the District Court that California choice-of-law rules applied to Piper, and that Pennsylvania choice-of-law rules applied to Hartzell, see n. 8, *supra*. It did not agree, however, that California used a "governmental interests" analysis and that Pennsylvania used a "significant contacts" analysis. Rather, it believed that both jurisdictions employed the "false conflicts" test. Applying this test, it concluded that Ohio and

Pennsylvania and Ohio, rather than Scotland, are the jurisdictions with the greatest policy interests in the dispute, and that all other public interest factors favored trial in the United States.

In any event, it appears that the Court of Appeals would have reversed even if the District Court had properly balanced the public and private interests. The court stated:

> "[I]t is apparent that the dismissal would work a change in the applicable law so that the plaintiff's strict liability claim would be eliminated from the case. But ... a dismissal for forum non conveniens, like a statutory transfer, 'should not, despite its convenience, result in a change in the applicable law.' Only when American law is not applicable, or when the foreign jurisdiction would, as a matter of its own choice of law, give the plaintiff the benefit of the claim to which she is entitled here, would dismissal be justified."

In other words, the court decided that dismissal is automatically barred if it would lead to a change in the applicable law unfavorable to the plaintiff.

We granted certiorari in these cases to consider the questions they raise concerning the proper application of the doctrine of *forum non conveniens.*

II

The Court of Appeals erred in holding that plaintiffs may defeat a motion to dismiss on the ground of *forum non conveniens* merely by showing that the substantive law that would be applied in the alternative forum is less favorable to the plaintiffs than that of the present forum. The possibility of a change in substantive law should ordinarily not be given conclusive or even substantial weight in the *forum non conveniens* inquiry.

We expressly rejected the position adopted by the Court of Appeals in our decision in *Canada Malting Co. v. Paterson Steamships, Ltd.* That case arose out of a collision between two vessels in American waters. The Canadian owners of cargo lost in the accident sued the Canadian owners of one of the vessels in Federal District Court. The cargo owners chose an American court in large part because the relevant American liability rules were more favorable than the Canadian rules. The District Court dismissed on grounds of *forum non conveniens.* The plaintiffs argued that dismissal was inappropriate because Canadian laws were less favorable to them. This Court nonetheless affirmed:

> "We have no occasion to enquire by what law the rights of the parties are governed, as we are of the opinion that, under any view of that question, it lay within the discretion of the District Court to decline to assume jurisdiction over the controversy. ... '[T]he court will not take cognizance of the case if justice would be as well done by remitting the parties to their home forum.' "

The Court further stated that "[t]here was no basis for the contention that the District Court abused its discretion."

It is true that *Canada Malting* was decided before *Gilbert,* and that the doctrine of *forum non conveniens* was not fully crystallized until our decision in that case. However, *Gilbert* in no way affects the validity of *Canada Malting.* Indeed, by holding that the

---

Pennsylvania had a greater policy interest in the dispute than Scotland, and that American law would apply to both Piper and Hartzell.

central focus of the *forum non conveniens* inquiry is convenience, *Gilbert* implicitly recognized that dismissal may not be barred solely because of the possibility of an unfavorable change in law. Under *Gilbert*, dismissal will ordinarily be appropriate where trial in the plaintiff's chosen forum imposes a heavy burden on the defendant or the court, and where the plaintiff is unable to offer any specific reasons of convenience supporting his choice. If substantial weight were given to the possibility of an unfavorable change in law, however, dismissal might be barred even where trial in the chosen forum was plainly inconvenient.

The Court of Appeals' decision is inconsistent with this Court's earlier *forum non conveniens* decisions in another respect. Those decisions have repeatedly emphasized the need to retain flexibility. In *Gilbert*, the Court refused to identify specific circumstances "which will justify or require either grant or denial of remedy." Similarly, in *Koster*, the Court rejected the contention that where a trial would involve inquiry into the internal affairs of a foreign corporation, dismissal was always appropriate. "That is one, but only one, factor which may show convenience." And in *Williams v. Green Bay & Western R. Co.*, we stated that we would not lay down a rigid rule to govern discretion, and that "[e]ach case turns on its facts." If central emphasis were placed on any one factor, the *forum non conveniens* doctrine would lose much of the very flexibility that makes it so valuable.

In fact, if conclusive or substantial weight were given to the possibility of a change in law, the *forum non conveniens* doctrine would become virtually useless. Jurisdiction and venue requirements are often easily satisfied. As a result, many plaintiffs are able to choose from among several forums. Ordinarily, these plaintiffs will select that forum whose choice-of-law rules are most advantageous. Thus, if the possibility of an unfavorable change in substantive law is given substantial weight in the *forum non conveniens* inquiry, dismissal would rarely be proper.

Except for the court below, every Federal Court of Appeals that has considered this question after *Gilbert* has held that dismissal on grounds of *forum non conveniens* may be granted even though the law applicable in the alternative forum is less favorable to the plaintiff's chance of recovery. Several courts have relied expressly on *Canada Malting* to hold that the possibility of an unfavorable change of law should not, by itself, bar dismissal.

The Court of Appeals' approach is not only inconsistent with the purpose of the *forum non conveniens* doctrine, but also poses substantial practical problems. If the possibility of a change in law were given substantial weight, deciding motions to dismiss on the ground of *forum non conveniens* would become quite difficult. Choice-of-law analysis would become extremely important, and the courts would frequently be required to interpret the law of foreign jurisdictions. First, the trial court would have to determine what law would apply if the case were tried in the chosen forum, and what law would apply if the case were tried in the alternative forum. It would then have to compare the rights, remedies, and procedures available under the law that would be applied in each forum. Dismissal would be appropriate only if the court concluded that the law applied by the alternative forum is as favorable to the plaintiff as that of the chosen forum. The doctrine of *forum non conveniens*, however, is designed in part to help courts avoid conducting complex exercises in comparative law. As we stated in *Gilbert*, the public interest factors point towards dismissal where the court would be required to "untangle problems in conflict of laws, and in law foreign to itself."

Upholding the decision of the Court of Appeals would result in other practical problems. At least where the foreign plaintiff named an American manufacturer as defendant,[17] a court could not dismiss the case on grounds of *forum non conveniens* where dismissal might lead to an unfavorable change in law. The American courts, which are already extremely attractive to foreign plaintiffs, would become even more attractive. The flow of litigation into the United States would increase and further congest already crowded courts.

The Court of Appeals based its decision, at least in part, on an analogy between dismissals on grounds of *forum non conveniens* and transfers between federal courts pursuant to § 1404(a). In *Van Dusen v. Barrack*, this Court ruled that a § 1404(a) transfer should not result in a change in the applicable law. Relying on dictum in an earlier Third Circuit opinion interpreting *Van Dusen*, the court below held that that principle is also applicable to a dismissal on *forum non conveniens* grounds. However, § 1404(a) transfers are different than dismissals on the ground of *forum non conveniens*.

Congress enacted § 1404(a) to permit change of venue between federal courts. Although the statute was drafted in accordance with the doctrine of *forum non conveniens*, it was intended to be a revision rather than a codification of the common law. District courts were given more discretion to transfer under § 1404(a) than they had to dismiss on grounds of *forum non conveniens*.

The reasoning employed in *Van Dusen v. Barrack* is simply inapplicable to dismissals on grounds of *forum non conveniens*. That case did not discuss the common-law doctrine. Rather, it focused on "the construction and application" of § 1404(a). Emphasizing the remedial purpose of the statute, *Barrack* concluded that Congress could not have intended a transfer to be accompanied by a change in law. The statute was designed as a "federal housekeeping measure," allowing easy change of venue within a unified federal system. The Court feared that if a change in venue were accompanied by a change in law, forum-shopping parties would take unfair advantage of the relaxed standards for transfer. The rule was necessary to ensure the just and efficient operation of the statute.

We do not hold that the possibility of an unfavorable change in law should *never* be a relevant consideration in a *forum non conveniens* inquiry. Of course, if the remedy provided by the alternative forum is so clearly inadequate or unsatisfactory that it is no remedy at all, the unfavorable change in law may be given substantial weight; the district court may conclude that dismissal would not be in the interests of justice.[22] In

---

[17] In fact, the defendant might not even have to be American. A foreign plaintiff seeking damages for an accident that occurred abroad might be able to obtain service of process on a foreign defendant who does business in the United States. Under the Court of Appeals' holding, dismissal would be barred if the law in the alternative forum were less favorable to the plaintiff—even though none of the parties are American, and even though there is absolutely no nexus between the subject matter of the litigation and the United States.

[22] At the outset of any *forum non conveniens* inquiry, the court must determine whether there exists an alternative forum. Ordinarily, this requirement will be satisfied when the defendant is "amenable to process" in the other jurisdiction. *Gilbert*, 330 U.S., at 506–507, 67 S.Ct., at 842. In rare circumstances, however, where the remedy offered by the other forum is clearly unsatisfactory, the other forum may not be an adequate alternative, and the initial requirement may not be satisfied. Thus, for example, dismissal would not be appropriate where the alternative forum does not permit litigation of the subject matter of the dispute. Cf. *Phoenix Canada Oil Co. Ltd. v. Texaco, Inc.*,

these cases, however, the remedies that would be provided by the Scottish courts do not fall within this category. Although the relatives of the decedents may not be able to rely on a strict liability theory, and although their potential damages award may be smaller, there is no danger that they will be deprived of any remedy or treated unfairly.

III

The Court of Appeals also erred in rejecting the District Court's *Gilbert* analysis. The Court of Appeals stated that more weight should have been given to the plaintiff's choice of forum, and criticized the District Court's analysis of the private and public interests. However, the District Court's decision regarding the deference due plaintiff's choice of forum was appropriate. Furthermore, we do not believe that the District Court abused its discretion in weighing the private and public interests.

A

The District Court acknowledged that there is ordinarily a strong presumption in favor of the plaintiff's choice of forum, which may be overcome only when the private and public interest factors clearly point towards trial in the alternative forum. It held, however, that the presumption applies with less force when the plaintiff or real parties in interest are foreign.

The District Court's distinction between resident or citizen plaintiffs and foreign plaintiffs is fully justified. In *Koster*, the Court indicated that a plaintiff's choice of forum is entitled to greater deference when the plaintiff has chosen the home forum.[23] When the home forum has been chosen, it is reasonable to assume that this choice is convenient. When the plaintiff is foreign, however, this assumption is much less reasonable. Because the central purpose of any *forum non conveniens* inquiry is to ensure that the trial is convenient, a foreign plaintiff's choice deserves less deference.[24]

B

The *forum non conveniens* determination is committed to the sound discretion of the trial court. It may be reversed only when there has been a clear abuse of discretion; where the court has considered all relevant public and private interest factors, and where its balancing of these factors is reasonable, its decision deserves substantial deference. *Gilbert*. Here, the Court of Appeals expressly acknowledged that the standard of review was one of abuse of discretion. In examining the District Court's analysis of the public and private interests, however, the Court of Appeals seems to have lost sight of this rule, and substituted its own judgment for that of the District Court.

---

78 F.R.D. 445 (Del.1978) (court refuses to dismiss, where alternative forum is Ecuador, it is unclear whether Ecuadorean tribunal will hear the case, and there is no generally codified Ecuadorean legal remedy for the unjust enrichment and tort claims asserted).

   [23] Citizens or residents deserve somewhat more deference than foreign plaintiffs, but dismissal should not be automatically barred when a plaintiff has filed suit in his home forum. As always, if the balance of conveniences suggests that trial in the chosen forum would be unnecessarily burdensome for the defendant or the court, dismissal is proper.

   [24] Respondent argues that since plaintiffs will ordinarily file suit in the jurisdiction that offers the most favorable law, establishing a strong presumption in favor of both home and foreign plaintiffs will ensure that defendants will always be held to the highest possible standard of accountability for their purported wrongdoing. However, the deference accorded a plaintiff's choice of forum has never been intended to guarantee that the plaintiff will be able to select the law that will govern the case.

(1)

In analyzing the private interest factors, the District Court stated that the connections with Scotland are "overwhelming." This characterization may be somewhat exaggerated. Particularly with respect to the question of relative ease of access to sources of proof, the private interests point in both directions. As respondent emphasizes, records concerning the design, manufacture, and testing of the propeller and plane are located in the United States. She would have greater access to sources of proof relevant to her strict liability and negligence theories if trial were held here.[25] However, the District Court did not act unreasonably in concluding that fewer evidentiary problems would be posed if the trial were held in Scotland. A large proportion of the relevant evidence is located in Great Britain.

The Court of Appeals found that the problems of proof could not be given any weight because Piper and Hartzell failed to describe with specificity the evidence they would not be able to obtain if trial were held in the United States. It suggested that defendants seeking *forum non conveniens* dismissal must submit affidavits identifying the witnesses they would call and the testimony these witnesses would provide if the trial were held in the alternative forum. Such detail is not necessary. Piper and Hartzell have moved for dismissal precisely because many crucial witnesses are located beyond the reach of compulsory process, and thus are difficult to identify or interview. Requiring extensive investigation would defeat the purpose of their motion. Of course, defendants must provide enough information to enable the District Court to balance the parties' interests. Our examination of the record convinces us that sufficient information was provided here. Both Piper and Hartzell submitted affidavits describing the evidentiary problems they would face if the trial were held in the United States.[27]

The District Court correctly concluded that the problems posed by the inability to implead potential third-party defendants clearly supported holding the trial in Scotland. Joinder of the pilot's estate, Air Navigation, and McDonald is crucial to the presentation of petitioners' defense. If Piper and Hartzell can show that the accident was caused not by a design defect, but rather by the negligence of the pilot, the plane's owners, or the charter company, they will be relieved of all liability. It is true, of course, that if Hartzell and Piper were found liable after a trial in the United States, they could institute an action for indemnity or contribution against these parties in Scotland. It would be far more convenient, however, to resolve all claims in one trial. The Court of Appeals rejected this argument. Forcing petitioners to rely on actions for indemnity or contributions would be "burdensome" but not "unfair." Finding that trial in the plaintiff's chosen forum would be burdensome, however, is sufficient to support dismissal on grounds of *forum non conveniens*.

(2)

The District Court's review of the factors relating to the public interest was also reasonable. On the basis of its choice-of-law analysis, it concluded that if the case were

---

[25] In the future, where similar problems are presented, district courts might dismiss subject to the condition that defendant corporations agree to provide the records relevant to the plaintiff's claims.

[27] The affidavit provided to the District Court by Piper states that it would call the following witnesses: the relatives of the decedents; the owners and employees of McDonald; the persons responsible for the training and licensing of the pilot; the persons responsible for servicing and maintaining the aircraft; and two or three of its own employees involved in the design and manufacture of the aircraft.

tried in the Middle District of Pennsylvania, Pennsylvania law would apply to Piper and Scottish law to Hartzell. It stated that a trial involving two sets of laws would be confusing to the jury. It also noted its own lack of familiarity with Scottish law. Consideration of these problems was clearly appropriate under *Gilbert*; in that case we explicitly held that the need to apply foreign law pointed towards dismissal. The Court of Appeals found that the District Court's choice-of-law analysis was incorrect, and that American law would apply to both Hartzell and Piper. Thus, lack of familiarity with foreign law would not be a problem. Even if the Court of Appeals' conclusion is correct, however, all other public interest factors favored trial in Scotland.

Scotland has a very strong interest in this litigation. The accident occurred in its airspace. All of the decedents were Scottish. Apart from Piper and Hartzell, all potential plaintiffs and defendants are either Scottish or English. As we stated in *Gilbert*, there is "a local interest in having localized controversies decided at home." Respondent argues that American citizens have an interest in ensuring that American manufacturers are deterred from producing defective products, and that additional deterrence might be obtained if Piper and Hartzell were tried in the United States, where they could be sued on the basis of both negligence and strict liability. However, the incremental deterrence that would be gained if this trial were held in an American court is likely to be insignificant. The American interest in this accident is simply not sufficient to justify the enormous commitment of judicial time and resources that would inevitably be required if the case were to be tried here.

IV

The Court of Appeals erred in holding that the possibility of an unfavorable change in law bars dismissal on the ground of *forum non conveniens*. It also erred in rejecting the District Court's *Gilbert* analysis. The District Court properly decided that the presumption in favor of the respondent's forum choice applied with less than maximum force because the real parties in interest are foreign. It did not act unreasonably in deciding that the private interests pointed towards trial in Scotland. Nor did it act unreasonably in deciding that the public interests favored trial in Scotland. Thus, the judgment of the Court of Appeals is

Reversed.

DIRECTED READING QUESTIONS

10. What was the airplane's route, and where did the airplane crash?

11. Describe the corporation that manufactured the airplane.

12. Describe the corporation that manufactured the propellers.

13. Describe the corporation that owned and maintained the airplane.

14. Describe the corporation that operated the airplane.

15. Where was the plane's wreckage at the time of the Supreme Court opinion?

16. What is the nationality of the people (pilot and all passengers) killed in the airplane crash?

17. What are the conclusions regarding the cause of the crash, according to:

    a. The British Board of Trade investigation?

    b. The "three-member Review Board," which Hartzell asked to review the report of the British Board of Trade?

18. Describe the lawsuit filed in Scotland.

19. Describe the lawsuit filed in California.

20. Why was the wrongful death lawsuit filed in California?

21. How did the lawsuit filed in California end up in the United States District Court for the Central District of California?

22. According to 28 U.S.C. § 1391, how is venue proper in federal court in California for each of the defendants?

23. In footnote 8, "the District Court concluded [after the case was transferred to Pennsylvania] that California choice-of-law rules would apply to Piper, and Pennsylvania choice-of-law rules would apply to Hartzell." Similarly, in footnote 10, "The Court of Appeals agreed with the District Court that [after the case was transferred to Pennsylvania] California choice-of-law rules applied to Piper, and that Pennsylvania choice-of-law rules applied to Hartzell." What is a choice-of-law rule?

24. 28 U.S.C. § 1404(a) and 28 U.S.C. § 1406(a) are venue statutes which facilitate the transfer of civil actions from one venue to another. What initially appears to be the biggest difference between the two statutes?

25. It is unclear in the opinion that the transfer of the claim against Piper was pursuant to 28 U.S.C. § 1404(a) and the transfer of the claim against Hartzell was pursuant to 28 U.S.C. § 1406(a). If removal cures all venue defects, how is it possible that the claim against Hartzell was transferred to Pennsylvania, pursuant to 28 U.S.C. § 1406(a)?

26. How are venue and personal jurisdiction appropriate for each defendant in Pennsylvania?

27. Can you explain why it is consistent with the *Erie* doctrine for California choice-of-law rules to apply to the claim against Piper in Pennsylvania, but for Pennsylvania choice-of-law rules to apply to the claim against Hartzell in Pennsylvania?

28. If both the appellate and district courts agree that, in Pennsylvania, California choice-of-law rules apply to the claim against Piper, and Pennsylvania choice-of-law rules apply to the claim against Hartzell, why do they disagree on the substantive law that should be used to resolve the claims against each defendant?

29. How is the choice of law, referred to in footnote 8 and footnote 10, different from the choice of law involved in an *Erie* analysis?

30. What is the relationship between *forum non conveniens* analysis and whether venue is appropriate under 28 U.S.C. § 1391?

31. What is the most glaring difference between transfers pursuant to 28 U.S.C. § 1404(a) and § 1406(a) on the one hand and *forum non conveniens* on the other?

32. What erroneous rule does the appellate court rely on in denying *forum non conveniens*? According to the Supreme Court, what is the correct articulation of the purported rule?

33. What test from personal jurisdiction do the *forum non conveniens* factors remind you of, and why is the similarity unsurprising?

34. List the private and public interest factors that comprise the *Gilbert* balancing test for deciding if to dismiss on the basis of *forum non conveniens*.

35. Before performing the *Gilbert* analysis, the district court articulates two broad principles which are relevant to *forum non conveniens* analysis. What are these two broad principles?

36. How does the district court analyze the private and public interest factors?

37. List the two reasons why the appellate court reversed the district court.

38. How does the appellate court analyze the public and private interest factors?

39. How does the appellate court err in performing the *Gilbert* analysis? What about the Supreme Court's analysis reminds you of *Asahi*?

40. How much discretion does the Supreme Court give the district court in its *forum non conveniens* analysis?

41. How heavy is the defendant's burden of proof to show that the private interest factors warrant *forum non conveniens* dismissal?

42. In analyzing the public interest factors, what difference would it have made to the Supreme Court's decision if the appellate court was correct that Scottish law *did not* apply to the controversy?

CHAPTER 18

APPEALS

■ ■ ■

I. APPEALS GENERALLY

DIRECTED READING QUESTIONS

1. Why have appellate review?

2. Is an appeal a matter of right or discretion? In answering this question pay attention to the wording of 28 U.S.C. § 1291.

3. How often do parties in civil disputes typically succeed on appeal in the federal system? What do these rates indicate? Please Google this question.

4. According to Federal Rule of Appellate Procedure 4(a)(1)(a), generally, how much time does a party have to file a notice of appeal with the appellate court after the entry of final judgment in the trial court?

5. What is a final judgment?

6. Read Federal Rule of Appellate Procedure 4(a)(2) to answer the following question. In a suit *A vs. B*, the jury returns a verdict for A. Thirty days before the entry of judgment by the trial court, B files a notice of appeal. Does B have to refile the notice of appeal within thirty days of the entry of judgment?

7. In a suit *Alpha vs. Beta*, the jury returns a verdict for Alpha. Alpha is unhappy with the size of the verdict and believes the trial court erred as a matter of law in the method used to calculate the verdict. But Alpha does not appeal, as they are advised by counsel that they should accept the verdict rather than risk appealing and ending up with the same or a lower verdict. However, Beta files a notice of appeal 12 days after the jury verdict. Alpha, seeing that Beta has appealed, now decides they should also appeal. The judgment on the verdict is entered 10 days after Beta filed their notice of appeal. How many days after Beta filed their notice of appeal does Alpha have to file their notice of appeal? In answering this question, pay particular attention to Federal Rule of Appellate Procedure 4(a)(3).

8. Below is a table comparing various sections of Federal Rule of Civil Procedure 58 and Federal Rule of Appellate Procedure 4. Examine the sections carefully and answer the questions after the table.

FRCP 58	FRAP 4
(a) Separate Document. Every judgment and amended judgment must be set out in a separate document, but a separate document is not required for an order disposing of a motion:	**(a)(4)** *Effect of a Motion on a Notice of Appeal.* (A) If a party timely files in the district court any of the following motions under the Federal Rules of Civil Procedure, the time to file an appeal runs for all parties

(1) for judgment under Rule 50(b);

(2) to amend or make additional findings under Rule 52(b);

(3) for attorney's fees under Rule 54;

(4) for a new trial, or to alter or amend the judgment, under Rule 59; or

(5) for relief under Rule 60.

from the entry of the order disposing of the last such remaining motion:

(i) for judgment under Rule 50(b);

(ii) to amend or make additional factual findings under Rule 52(b), whether or not granting the motion would alter the judgment;

(iii) for attorney's fees under Rule 54 if the district court extends the time to appeal under Rule 58;

(iv) to alter or amend the judgment under Rule 59;

(v) for a new trial under Rule 59; or

(vi) for relief under Rule 60 if the motion is filed no later than 28 days after the judgment is entered.

(c) Time of Entry.

For purposes of these rules, judgment is entered at the following times:

(1) if a separate document is not required, when the judgment is entered in the civil docket under Rule 79(a); or

(2) if a separate document is required, when the judgment is entered in the civil docket under Rule 79(a) and the earlier of these events occurs:

(A) it is set out in a separate document; or

(B) 150 days have run from the entry in the civil docket.

(a)(7) *Entry Defined.*

(A) A judgment or order is entered for purposes of this Rule 4(a):

(i) if Federal Rule of Civil Procedure 58(a) does not require a separate document, when the judgment or order is entered in the civil docket under Federal Rule of Civil Procedure 79(a); or

(ii) if Federal Rule of Civil Procedure 58(a) requires a separate document, when the judgment or order is entered in the civil docket under Federal Rule of Civil Procedure 79(a) and when the earlier of these events occurs:

the judgment or order is set forth on a separate document, or

150 days have run from entry of the judgment or order in the civil docket under Federal Rule of Civil Procedure 79(a).

a. When does entry of judgment typically occur?

b. When are separate documents not required for entry of judgment?

c. What triggers the thirty-day period in Federal Rule of Appellate Procedure 4(a)(1)?

d. A sues B. B wins, and a judgment is entered on the verdict for B. A moves for a renewed motion for judgment as a matter of law. It takes 75 days from the filing of the renewed motion for the motion to be granted. How many days after the entry of the original judgment does B have to file his appeal?

9. Why is it important that the general rule provided for in 28 U.S.C. § 1291 is that only final decisions are appealable?

10. Can you now read 28 U.S.C. § 1292(a) and (b) as exceptions to the general rule that only final decisions are available?

II. INTERLOCUTORY APPEALS

DIRECTED READING QUESTIONS

11. From what acts by a district court does § 1292(a)(1) provide interlocutory appeals?

12. What must a party show in addition to the granting or refusing to grant an injunction by the district court in order to invoke § 1292(a)(1)?

13. What, in your own words, does 28 U.S.C. § 1292(b) permit?

14. Can you list some interesting points about certification?

III. THE COLLATERAL ORDER DOCTRINE

The Collateral Order Doctrine is a common law exception to the general rule that only final decisions are appealable. Remember, we have already addressed 28 U.S.C. § 1292 which was a statutory exception to the general rule that only final decisions are appealable.

In order for a trial court decision to fall under the collateral order exception to the rule that only final judgments are appealable:

    a.   The trial court decision must resolve an important issue that is completely separate or **collateral** from the merits of the action;

    b.   The trial court decision must **conclusively determine** the completely separate or collateral issue; and

    c.   The order must be **effectively unreviewable** on appeal.

COHEN V. BENEFICIAL INDUSTRIAL LOAN CORP. (1949)
Supreme Court of the United States
337 U.S. 541

[The owner of a small amount of shares in a corporation sued the corporation and managers alleging breach of fiduciary duty in federal court in New Jersey. The basis of subject matter jurisdiction was diversity of citizenship such that the federal court was adjudicating a claim arising under New Jersey Law.

New Jersey statutory law required that, when a shareholder held less than a certain percent of the shares (as this plaintiff did) in a corporation and was the plaintiff in a derivative action, the shareholder needed to post a bond before the suit could go forward. Pursuant to the *Erie* doctrine, there was a question about whether the New Jersey Statute applied in the federal diversity action. The District Court ruled the statute did not apply. The District Court ruled the statute did not apply, and the action was allowed to continue without the posting of the bond. The Defendants appealed.]

DIRECTED READING QUESTIONS

15. Please explain why the district court's decision about the inapplicability of the statute is not a final decision.

16. Why doesn't the district court's decision about the statute's applicability fall under 28 U.S.C. § 1292(a)?

17. Why doesn't the district court's decision about the statute's applicability fall under 28 U.S.C. § 1292(b)? How then is this appeal permitted?

18. Because the district court's decision about the statute's applicability is neither a final decision nor does it fall under a statutory exception to the rule that only final decisions are appealable, the appellate court uses the common law exception to the rule or the collateral order doctrine to hear the appeal of this non-final decision. Please attempt to analyze how each of the three elements of the collateral order doctrine is satisfied by the district court's decision that the statute does not apply. It is useful to begin the analysis by identifying the main issue or the merits of the trial and the other question which is collateral or separate from the merits.

19. In a subsequent case on the collateral order doctrine, the Supreme Court stated "we reiterate that the class of collaterally appealable orders must remain 'narrow and selective in membership.'" *Mohawk Industries Inc. v. Carpenter*, 558 U.S. 100 (2009). Why is it necessary that this exception to the rule that only final decisions are appealable remain "narrow and selective"?

20. Quite apart from the answer to the previous question, the Supreme Court in *Mohawk* found another reason which independently reinforced the idea that collaterally appealable orders are a very narrow class of orders. That reason is contained in the following excerpt from Mohawk,

> This admonition has acquired special force in recent years with the enactment of legislation designating rulemaking, "not expansion by court decision," as the preferred means for determining whether and when prejudgment orders should be immediately appealable. Specifically, Congress in 1990 amended the Rules Enabling Act to authorize this Court to adopt rules "defin[ing] when a ruling of a district court is final for the purposes of appeal under section 1291." § 2072(c). Shortly thereafter, and along similar lines, Congress empowered this Court to "prescribe rules, in accordance with [§ 2072], to provide for an appeal of an interlocutory decision to the courts of appeals that is not otherwise provided for under [§ 1292]." § 1292(e). These provisions, we have recognized, "warran[t] the Judiciary's full respect."
>
> Indeed, the rulemaking process has important virtues. It draws on the collective experience of bench and bar, see 28 U.S.C. § 2073, and it facilitates the adoption of measured, practical solutions. We expect that the combination of standard postjudgment appeals, § 1292(b) appeals, mandamus, and contempt appeals will continue to provide adequate protection to litigants ordered to disclose materials purportedly subject to the attorney-client privilege. Any further avenue for immediate appeal of such rulings should be

furnished, if at all, through rulemaking, with the opportunity for full airing it provides.

Mohawk, 558 U.S. 609.

Please explain what this language means in your own words.

21. Consider this: (1) *Mohawk* explains that the "virtues" of the rulemaking process limit the common law development of the collateral order doctrine; and (2) the Rules Enabling Act's impact in *Hanna* is such that a court can refuse to apply the federal rules, "only if the Advisory Committee, this Court, and Congress erred in their prima facie judgment that the Rule in question transgresses neither the terms of the Enabling Act nor constitutional restrictions." What about the rulemaking process is illustrated?

CHAPTER 19

CLAIM AND ISSUE PRECLUSION

■ ■ ■

I. INTRODUCTORY HYPOTHETICAL

Alpha sues Beta for negligence, or in other words, Alpha files a **CLAIM** for damages against Beta alleging that Beta's negligence while driving his (Beta's) car caused damage to Alpha's car when Beta's and Alpha's cars collided. In deciding whether Alpha should recover in her **CLAIM** against Beta, the court needs to decide, among others, the following **ISSUE**: whether Beta was driving negligently.

DIRECTED READING QUESTIONS

1. Assume Alpha won a judgment against Beta. After the judgment, Charlie, another driver who was also injured by Beta's driving which caused the collision with Alpha, files a claim against Beta for negligence exactly like Alpha did. Why is Charlie's claim against Beta a different claim than Alpha's claim against Beta?

2. Even though Charlie's claim against Beta is a different claim than Alpha's claim against Beta, is the same issue of whether Beta was driving negligently common to both claims?

3. Based on the above questions, please articulate a rough distinction between a claim and an issue.

II. PRELIMINARY CONSIDERATIONS

*   Claim and issue preclusion always require two judicial proceedings: an initial action where a judgment was entered and a subsequent action.

*   The doctrines *preclude* relitigation of claims or issues from the initial action in the subsequent action.

    o   If a party is attempting to preclude relitigation of certain *claims* in the subsequent action because that party asserts that these claims were addressed in the first action, the doctrine is called **claim preclusion or *res judicata***.

    o   If a party is attempting to preclude relitigation of certain *issues* in the subsequent action because that party asserts that these claims were addressed in the first action, then the doctrine is called **issue preclusion or *collateral estoppel***.

*   ELEMENTS:

	Claim Preclusion or *res judicata*	Issue Preclusion or *collateral estoppel*
1	Final judgment on the merits in the initial action	Final judgment on the merits in the initial action

2	Prevents relitigation of claims in a subsequent action that were brought or should have been brought in the initial action	Prevents relitigation of issues in a subsequent action: 1. which were actually litigated and decided in the initial action, and 2. the litigation of the issues were actually necessary to the judgment in the initial action
3	**Mutuality of parties always required** in first action and second action	**Mutuality of parties not always required** in first action and second action

Mutuality simply means that the parties in the first and second action are identical.

DIRECTED READING QUESTIONS

4. What again is the difference between a claim and an issue? How does this difference explain why mutuality is always required for claim preclusion but not necessarily for issue preclusion?

III. CLAIM PRECLUSION OR *RES JUDICATA*

A. APPLICATION AND RATIONALE FOR THE DOCTRINE

MANEGO V. ORLEANS BOARD OF TRADE (1985)
United States Court of Appeals, First Circuit
773 F.2d 1

BOWNES, CIRCUIT JUDGE.

In late 1978 and early 1979, Manego applied to the Orleans Board of Selectmen for entertainment and liquor licenses for a disco which he wanted to build on a vacant lot. The lot was located in a commercial district a few hundred feet from an ice skating rink. The rink at that time was primarily used by children for hockey and figure skating. During the winter there was also a "Disco on Ice" program for children under sixteen. As a result of a mortgage foreclosure, the Cape Cod Five Cents Savings Bank owned the rink from 1978 until July 1979. The vice-president of the bank, David Willard, served as general manager of the rink during this period. As owner of the rink, the bank was concerned about the close proximity of an establishment serving liquor to a recreational facility primarily patronized by children and the increased likelihood of automobile accidents involving inebriated drivers and children walking to and from the rink. The bank also had more general concerns about the presence of a disco in the area.

In January of 1979, there was a meeting of the Orleans Board of Trade, a private organization which functions as the chamber of commerce for the town. At that time, Willard was also the president of the Board of Trade. Membership in this organization is open to anyone who pays the $15.00 membership fee. Willard raised the issue of the proposed disco at the meeting and after some discussion the membership voted to oppose the disco.

On January 11, 1979, a public hearing on Manego's liquor license application was held by the Orleans Board of Selectmen. Two of the selectmen, Gaston Norgeot and Thomas Nickerson, were also members of the Board of Trade. Over 100 people attended the meeting and expressed concern over the increased traffic and noise which would result from the disco as well as the effect of an establishment serving liquor in close proximity to the skating rink and the general effect of a disco on the atmosphere of the Town of Orleans. The Board of Selectmen received a petition containing 369 signatures opposing the disco and eleven letters, only two of which favored Manego's proposal. At the hearing, Willard announced that the Board of Trade had voted to oppose granting a license for the disco.

On February 8, 1979, the Selectmen denied Manego's application for a liquor license and Manego appealed this decision to the Board of Appeals, which met on February 8 and 14. Willard wrote a letter to the Board of Appeals setting forth the bank's opposition to the disco and its concern for the safety of the youngsters using the skating rink. Local counsel for the bank attended the Board of Appeals hearings. In late February, the Board of Appeals denied Manego's appeal.

On February 13, 1979, the Orleans Board of Trade held its monthly meeting and, according to the minutes, mention was made of a hearing scheduled for the next day on Manego's amusement license application and of Manego's appeal of the denial of the liquor license application by the Selectmen. At the February 14 amusement license hearing, the Selectmen requested that the Town Traffic Safety Committee study the effects of the proposed disco. On February 22, 1979, the Selectmen turned down Manego's application for an amusement license.

In spite of these license denials, the Orleans Board of Appeals granted Manego a building permit in May of 1979. The bank then filed suit in Barnstable Superior Court challenging the issuance of this permit. In July of 1979, the bank sold the rink to Paul Thibert and sometime in August withdrew its superior court suit.

In March of 1979, the entertainment license of the rink expired; no renewal was sought until July of 1979, after Thibert purchased the rink. Because the license had lapsed, the application was treated as a new application and not a renewal and a public hearing was held. During that summer, a concrete floor had been poured at the rink to allow roller skating so the new application added roller skating to the proposed activities of the facility. In addition, the rink planned to offer a ballroom dancing program for adults featuring live music from the 1940's and refreshments in the nature of soft drinks. This, too, was an addition to the rink's activities. The rink's application was granted by the Selectmen. Among the reasons cited by the Selectmen for their approval were its unique status as the only skating facility on the Lower Cape, its use by young people as safe and "noncorrupting" entertainment and the lack of noise or traffic problems created by the facility.

* * *

Manego brought a [ ] lawsuit in federal district court (*Manego II[ ]*), naming the Board of Selectmen, the Cape Cod Five Cents Savings Bank and Willard as defendants and claiming that they had conspired to deny him the licenses because of his race in violation of 42 U.S.C. §§ [et. al.] of the Fair Housing Act, and Mass.Gen.Laws Ann. ch. 151B, § 4(3B). The claims under [ ] the Fair Housing Act, and the state law claims were all dismissed by the district court for failure to state a cause of action. As to the other claims, the Board of Selectmen moved for summary judgment on the grounds that these claims were barred by the doctrines of *res judicata* and collateral estoppel. The district court rejected this argument because "claims made here were neither fully argued or adjudicated in the state proceeding." As part of our appellate review of the district court's opinion in *Manego I[ ]*, we noted in passing that the "proper test for the applicability of *res judicata* is not whether the plaintiff in fact argued his constitutional claims in the state proceedings, but whether he could have." *Manego v. Cape Cod Five Cents Savings Bank,* 692 F.2d 174, 175 (1st Cir.1982). We did not decide this issue, however, because we based our affirmation of the district court's grant of summary judgment upon the district court's determination that Manego had not provided even a "promise of evidence" that defendants were involved in a conspiracy to deny him the licenses because of his race.

The district court in *Manego I[ ]* found that despite being given an extra ninety days to produce some concrete, factual basis for his allegation of conspiracy, which defendants had affirmatively denied in their affidavits, Manego produced only the following: two personal affidavits explaining his theory and suggesting that direct evidence of the conspiracy would emerge under cross-examination and a third affidavit of a local building contractor employed by Manego reporting that he had heard that a lumber company had been told by the Bank not to supply Manego with materials and vaguely suggesting that his own relationship with the bank had been adversely affected by his association with Manego. The district court found that since Manego had not taken advantage of an "ample opportunity" to take depositions or conduct any other form of discovery, his promise of evidence arising out of cross-examination was pure speculation, and that, furthermore, the affidavit of the building contractor could not be given any weight because it consisted primarily of hearsay.

In our opinion affirming the district court's grant of summary judgment on this ground, we said:

> In this case, plaintiff sought to infer the existence of an illegal conspiracy from the fact that the Selectmen granted a license to someone who was white but not to plaintiff, who was black. His inference is supported only by affidavit evidence of a general racial animus in the community. The fact that a group of private citizens, organized as the Orleans Board of Trade, voted unanimously to oppose his license and that members of the Board of Selectmen may have attended the meeting established nothing about the motivation of those individuals in opposing his license. The defendants countered his inference with an explanation of the difference between his disco and the skating rink which was granted a license. . . .

In the face of this explanation, plaintiffs' [*sic*] promise that circumstantial evidence would emerge at trial could not withstand the defendants' motions for summary judgment.

Despite the [ ] rebuff[ ], Manego filed yet another lawsuit, this time against the bank, Willard, and the Orleans Board of Trade and its members. The [second] lawsuit (*Manego II[ ]*), which is the subject of this appeal, differed from *Manego I[ ]* in two respects: it dropped the Board of Selectmen as a defendant and added the Board of Trade; and it alleged a new legal theory, antitrust violations under the Sherman Antitrust Act, 15 U.S.C. § 1. As evidence of a conspiracy between the bank and the Board of Trade to prevent the proposed disco from competing with the rink, Manego offered depositions, answers to interrogatories, affidavits, and other documents which showed: that Willard was simultaneously an officer of the bank, general manager of the rink, and President of the Board of Trade; that various members of the Board present at the January and February meetings were also Selectmen; that the Selectmen denied the licenses after the Board of Trade voted to oppose their issuance; that the Selectmen subsequently granted an entertainment license to the rink which included live music, dancing and roller disco; and that the bank brought a lawsuit challenging a construction permit granted to Manego by the Orleans Board of Appeal but dropped the lawsuit after it sold the rink. According to Manego, the Board of Trade's interest in preventing the competition between the proposed disco and the rink was derived from the interest of its president, David Willard, who managed the rink for the bank.

Willard and the Bank moved for summary judgment on the grounds that these new claims were barred by the doctrine of *res judicata*. The Board of Trade also moved for summary judgment under the doctrine of *res judicata* and additionally argued that there was no genuine issue of fact concerning the alleged conspiracy.

DEFENDANTS CAPE COD FIVE CENTS SAVINGS BANK AND DAVID WILLARD

As to Willard and the bank, the district court found that this [second] lawsuit was barred by the final judgment of the Court of Appeals in *Manego I[ ]* affirming the district court's grant of summary judgment to the Bank and Willard on civil rights claims. Applying a "transactional" approach to claim preclusion, the district court found that the facts forming the basis of Manego's claim of antitrust violations were the same as those which formed the basis of his earlier civil rights claims and that they were, therefore, barred by the final judgment against Manego on the civil rights claims. We agree.

* * *

Under the doctrine of *res judicata,* "a final judgment on the merits of an action precludes the parties or their privies from relitigating issues that were or could have been raised in that action." This bar is limited, however, to cases arising out of the same cause of action or claim. Our adoption of the Restatement (Second) approach commits us to a "transactional" definition of the underlying claim or cause of action:

(1) When a valid and final judgment rendered in an action extinguishes the plaintiff's claim pursuant to the rules of merger or bar ..., the claim extinguished includes all rights of the plaintiff to remedies against the defendant with respect to all or any part of the transaction, or series of connected transactions, out of which the action arose.

(2) What factual grouping constitutes a "transaction", and what groupings constitute a "series", are to be determined pragmatically, giving weight to such

considerations as whether the facts are related in time, space, origin, or motivation, whether they form a convenient trial unit, and whether their treatment as a unit conforms to the parties' expectations or business understanding or usage.

Restatement (Second) of Judgments § 24 (1982).

Manego has argued that *Manego II[ ]* does not involve the same transaction as that which formed the basis for *Manego I[ ]* for three reasons: the nature of the conspiracy alleged is different; the parties to the conspiracy are different, although they do share common members; and there was no allegation in *Manego I[ ]* that the rink and disco would be offering similar entertainment and thus competing for the same customers.

As the district court pointed out, however, the mere fact that different legal theories are presented in each case does not mean that the same transaction is not behind each. Thus, the fact that one suit alleges a conspiracy with a racial animus and the other alleges a conspiracy with anticompetitive animus does not demonstrate that separate transactions are involved. Nor does it matter in this case that the named defendants are not identical. Even though the Board of Trade was not a defendant in *Manego I[ ]*, the fact that it met under the leadership of Willard and voted to oppose the disco was brought out and no new facts concerning conduct of the bank and the Board of Trade have been alleged.

We next consider whether the absence from *Manego I[ ]* of the allegation that the bank had plans to offer live music and dancing at the rink was sufficient to prevent the application of *res judicata*. The focus of the argument below was on whether Manego reasonably could have alleged this at the time of the racial discrimination suit. Manego claimed that he did not allege the "similar entertainment" facts in *Manego I[ ]* because he did not know of them until too late—three days before summary judgment issued. While it is the law that, if information is not reasonably discoverable, *res judicata* will not apply, the district court found that this exception was not available here because the "entertainment" facts could have been uncovered if Manego had been diligent in his discovery efforts. The court then went on to reason that because the legal theory which rested upon the "entertainment" facts *could have been* asserted during the prior suit, *res judicata* applied to bar its assertion in a later suit. We believe, however, that, once the reasonable discovery issue is resolved, the focus of a "transactional" analysis is not on whether a second claim *could* have been brought in a prior suit, but whether the underlying facts of both transactions were the same or substantially similar.

There will be situations where the factual bases for separate causes of action are different but intertwined and joining them together is both possible and convenient. A failure to do so, however, will not justify the application of *res judicata*. A good illustration of this can be found in *Landrigan v. City of Warwick*, 628 F.2d 736 (1st Cir. 1980), where we held that a law suit charging the police with covering-up an alleged use of excessive force was not precluded by a prior lawsuit based on the actual use of excessive force. The plaintiff in *Landrigan* could have pursued both causes of action in the same lawsuit and it might have been very convenient to do so, since the alleged cover-up was intimately connected to the initial police misconduct. We found, however, that because the factual basis for the cover-up was distinct from the factual basis for the misconduct, the plaintiff was not required to do so. This is to be contrasted with a situation in which the factual basis for each claim is essentially the same, so that not only *could* both claims be joined in one lawsuit, but *must* be joined or be barred by *res judicata.* A good example is again provided by *Landrigan,* where we held that a prior state court suit for assault and battery precluded a later federal suit under § 1983 for excessive use of force.

The question, therefore, is whether the absence from *Manego I[ ]* of an allegation that the bank had plans to offer live music and dancing at the rink creates a transactional difference precluding the application of *res judicata.* Manego now argues that because an allegation that the rink and disco were competitors was essential to provide a motive for a conspiracy to restrain trade, the factual basis for such a conspiracy is distinctly different from that needed to show racial discrimination and that the antitrust action cannot be considered to arise from the same transaction or series of transactions. The answer to this question depends upon whether the underlying facts are the same regardless of the different motives, *i.e.,* racial discrimination and restraint of trade. Aside from motive, the conduct alleged is precisely the same, *i.e.,* the actions of the bank and Willard vis-a-viz the proposed disco. Each alleged conspiracy had the same practical end—keeping Manego from operating the disco—and each used essentially the same means—denial of the licenses, intimidation of building suppliers, and an ultimately withdrawn lawsuit challenging a building permit. This is not a case like *Landrigan* where, although the events in question are closely connected in time and space, two relatively distinct sets of facts can be separated out as the bases for separate legal wrongs. We conclude, therefore, that the difference in motive for the conspiracy does not create a separate transaction. This means that once Manego chose to allege a conspiracy involving particular specified conspiratorial acts he was required to allege all possible motives for such a conspiracy and all facts necessary to support these allegations or lose the right to do so. Whether he took that risk by failure to discover the facts which diligent effort would have unearthed or by deliberate choice, the result is the same: the antitrust claim is barred by *res judicata* as to the bank and Willard.

DEFENDANT ORLEANS BOARD OF TRADE

The Board of Trade moved for summary judgment on the grounds that the present suit was barred by the doctrine of *res judicata.* The district court found that *res judicata* did not apply, but [on unrelated grounds] granted summary judgment for the Board of Trade. [ ] We affirm the grant of summary judgment to the Board of Trade and its members on the basis of the district court's opinion.

Affirmed.

DIRECTED READING QUESTIONS

5.　*Res judicata* always requires an initial action and a subsequent action. In the opinion, these actions are conveniently referred to as "*Manego I*" and "*Manego II*" respectively.

　　a.　Please carefully identify the plaintiffs, defendants, claims, and the facts which Manego asserts in support the claim in *Manego I.*

　　b.　Please carefully identify the plaintiffs, defendants, claims, and the facts which Manego asserts in support the claim in *Manego II.*

6. Why did the court conclude that the doctrine of *res judicata* did not apply to defendant "Orleans Board of Trade?" In answering this question, please carefully examine Row 3 of the previous table listing the elements of *res judicata*.

7. Why did the court grant summary judgment for the defendants in *Manego I?*

8. Manego makes three arguments as to why the claims in *Manego II* are different from those in *Manego I* or could not have been brought in *Manego I*. Please list those arguments and explain the court's response to each argument.

9. Are the elements of *res judicata* satisfied here?

    a. Was there an initial action with a final judgment on the merits?

    b. Is there a subsequent action in which a party is attempting the relitigation of the same claims that were **brought or should have been brought** in the initial action?

    c. Is there mutuality of parties, or are the parties in the first action the same as the parties in the subsequent action?

10. The *Manego* opinion cites to *Landrigan v. City of Warwick*. How does *Landrigan* demonstrate that *res judicata* does not bar relitigation of claims which **could** have been brought in the initial action, but rather bars relitigation of claims which **should** have been brought in the initial action?

11. What are the rationales for the doctrine of *res judicata*? How do the liberal joinder rules support the doctrine?

12. Revisit the appellate review chapter and articulate the reason why generally only final decisions are reviewable. Explain how the same principle that generally limits appeals to only review of final decisions also justifies the doctrine of *res judicata*.

13. Practice Hypotheticals:

    a. Lionel Messi plays soccer for FC Barcelona. His foot was injured when another soccer player, Cristiano Ronaldo, stepped on his foot while Messi was wearing a Nike Mercurial Soccer Cleat. The shoe failed to perform as reasonably expected and that resulted in the injury. Messi sued Nike alleging negligent manufacture. Nike wins the case, and judgment is entered for Nike. Messi is really upset because he thinks the judge did not admit an affidavit that should have been admitted, which tended to show Nike negligently manufactured the shoe. He sues Nike again on the same theory, asking the judge to include the affidavit in the second trial. If Nike raises the defense of *res judicata* what result?

    b. Assume that Messi did not file a second product liability action, but after Nike won the negligent manufacture case, Messi found out that Mesut Ozil who plays soccer for Fenerbahce S.K. and also wears mercurial soccer cleats had sued Nike because the exact same thing happened to Ozil in a game. Ozil chose to sue on the theory of product liability design defect instead of negligent manufacture. Design defect unlike negligence, focuses on the risk of the product compared to its utility and does not include the negligence or conduct of the manufacturer. Ozil won his case against Nike. Messi, upon hearing this, sued Nike a second time alleging product liability design defect. Does *res judicata* bar the suit, even though the first suit was based on a claim of negligent manufacture and the second suit was on product liability design defect?

c.   Lionel Messi plays soccer for FC Barcelona. His foot was injured when another soccer player, Cristiano Ronaldo, stepped on his foot while Messi was wearing a Nike Mercurial Soccer Cleat. The shoe failed to perform as reasonably expected and that resulted in the injury. Messi sues Nike alleging negligent manufacture. Nike loses the case, and judgment is entered for Messi. About a year after the judgment was entered, Messi develops a painful bone spur on the foot that was stepped on. He now sues Nike for damages based on the development of the bone spur. Does *res judicata* prohibit the suit for the bone spur? In answering this question, consider that complaints typically contain "future damage" clauses, to wit:

> As a result, of his fall Plaintiff suffered harm, including, without limitation, bodily injury and resulting pain and suffering, disability, mental anguish, loss of the capacity for the enjoyment of life, expense of hospitalization, medical and nursing care and treatment, loss of earnings, loss of ability to earn money and/or aggravation of a previously existing condition. One or more of the losses are permanent and/or continuing, and **Plaintiff will suffer the loss(es) in the future**.

d.   Lionel Messi plays soccer for FC Barcelona. His foot was injured when another soccer player, Cristiano Ronaldo, stepped on his foot while Messi was wearing a Nike Mercurial Soccer Cleat. The shoe failed to perform as reasonably expected and that resulted in the injury. Messi sues Nike alleging negligent manufacture. Nike loses the case, and judgment is entered for Messi. After three years, Nike files an action seeking to have the judgment set aside because Nike discovers that the court did not have subject matter jurisdiction. Does *res judicata* bar Nike's action to challenge subject matter jurisdiction?

B. *RES JUDICATA* EFFECT OF STATE COURT JUDGMENTS ON SUBSEQUENT FEDERAL ACTIONS AND VICE VERSA

FULL FAITH AND CREDIT CLAUSE, U.S. CONST. ART. IV § 1

Full Faith and Credit shall be given in each State to the . . . judicial Proceedings of every other State.

FULL FAITH AND CREDIT STATUTE, 28 U.S.C. § 1738

The records and judicial proceedings of any court of any such State, Territory or Possession, or copies thereof, shall be proved or admitted in other courts within the United States and its Territories and Possessions by the attestation of the clerk and seal of the court annexed, if a seal exists, together with a certificate of a judge of the court that the said attestation is in proper form.

Such Acts, records and judicial proceedings or copies thereof, so authenticated, shall have the same full faith and credit in every court within the United States and its Territories and Possessions as they have by law or usage in the courts of such State, Territory or Possession from which they are taken.

MARRESE V. AMERICAN ACADEMY OF ORTHOPEDIC SURGEONS (1985)

Supreme Court of the United States
470 U.S. 373

The preclusive effect of a state court judgment in a subsequent federal lawsuit generally is determined by the full faith and credit statute, which provides that state judicial proceedings "shall have the same full faith and credit in every court within the United States . . . as they have by law or usage in the courts of such State . . . from which they are taken." 28 U.S.C. § 1738. This statute directs a federal court to refer to the preclusion law of the State in which judgment was rendered. "It has long been established that § 1738 does not allow federal courts to employ their own rules of res judicata in determining the effect of state judgments. Rather, it goes beyond the common law and commands a federal court to accept the rules chosen by the State from which the judgment is taken." Section 1738 embodies concerns of comity and federalism that allow the States to determine, subject to the requirements of the statute and the Due Process Clause, the preclusive effect of judgments in their own courts.

SEMTEK INTERNATIONAL INC. V. LOCKHEED MARTIN CORP. (2001)

Supreme Court of the United States
531 U.S. 497

It is also true, however, that no federal textual provision addresses the claim-preclusive effect of States cannot give those judgments merely whatever effect they would give their own judgments, but must accord them the effect that this Court prescribes.

[However, in a diversity case] state, rather than federal, substantive law is at issue there is no need for a uniform federal rule. And indeed, nationwide uniformity in the substance of the matter is better served by having the same claim-preclusive rule (the state rule) apply whether the dismissal has been ordered by a state or a federal court. This is, it seems to us, a classic case for adopting, as the federally prescribed rule of decision, the law that would be applied by state courts in the State in which the federal diversity court sits. As we have alluded to above, any other rule would produce the sort of "forum-shopping . . . and . . . inequitable administration of the laws" that *Erie* seeks to avoid, *Hanna,* 380 U.S., at 468, 85 S.Ct. 1136, since filing in, or removing to, federal court would be encouraged by the divergent effects that the litigants would anticipate from likely grounds of dismissal. See *Guaranty Trust Co. v. York,* 326 U.S., at 109–110, 65 S.Ct. 1464.

DIRECTED READING QUESTIONS

14. According to *Marrese*, how is the preclusive effect of an initial state court judgment on a subsequent federal action determined?

15. Examine carefully the Full Faith and Credit Clause and the Full Faith and Credit Statute. While they clearly provide that federal courts must give full faith and credit to state court judgments, they do not mandate state courts giving full faith and credit to federal court judgments. What then, according to *Semtek*, determines the *res judicata* effect of a final judgment in an action initially brought in federal court on a subsequent state court action?

C. FINAL JUDGMENTS ON THE MERITS

While some judgments are obviously final and on the merits, in some cases the answers are not so clear. Consider whether the following are final judgments on the merits.

DIRECTED READING QUESTIONS

16. Dismissal of all claims via summary judgment?

17. Entry of judgment after a full trial and jury verdict?

18. Dismissal for failure to prosecute under FRCP 41(b)?

19. A default judgment?

20. Dismissal for improper venue or failure to join a party under Rule 19? *See* FRCP 41(b).

21. A second dismissal of the same claim via a notice of dismissal? *See* FRCP 41(a).

22. Dismissal for failure to state a claim pursuant to FRCP 12(b)(6)?

D. PRIVITY, OR WHEN A DIFFERENT PARTY TO THE SUBSEQUENT ACTION WHO WAS NOT A PARTY TO THE INITIAL ACTION IS TREATED AS IF THEY WERE ONE OF THE PARTIES IN THE INITIAL ACTION

TAYLOR V. STURGELL (2008)
Supreme Court of the United States
553 U.S. 880

[The Initial Action

Plaintiff 1 files a Freedom of Information Act ("FOIA") request asking the Federal Aviation Administration ("FAA") for info and specs on an F-45 airplane he is restoring to help him restore the plane. The FAA denied the request explaining that the information fell within FOIA exceptions because it was considered "trade secrets and commercial or financial information obtained from a person and privileged and confidential."

Plaintiff 1 then brings an action in Wyoming Federal District Court against the FAA challenging the FAA's denial arguing that a 1995 letter issued by the manufacturer to the FAA allowed him access to the information. The letter authorized the FAA to "lend any documents in its files to the public . . . ."

The District Court, however granted summary judgment for the FAA, concluding that the letter did not deprive the information of trade secret status and further that even if the letter had waived trade secret status the manufacturer's subsequent objection to the release of the information to Plaintiff 1was a reversal of the waiver.

The Tenth Circuit Court of Appeals affirmed stating,]

[The Subsequent Action

A week after the appellate opinion Plaintiff 2 who was a friend and neighbor of Plaintiff 1, submitted the same FOIA request for documents from FAA that Plaintiff 1 had and the FAA failed to respond.

Plaintiff 2 then initiated suit in federal court against the FAA arguing that the original letter from the manufacturer. The FAA failed to respond.

Plaintiff 2 then sued in federal court arguing that the original letter from manufacturer in 1955 stripped the information of trade secret status.

The FAA argued that *res judicata* should apply to prevent the relitigation of the claims in the subsequent action, even though the plaintiff in the second action was not the same plaintiff in the first action. The Supreme Court disagreed and concluded that *res judicata* would apply only in six established situations where the relationship between the different parties in the initial and subsequent action is such that they are considered the same. When one of these six relationships exist the parties in the first action and the second action are said to be in privity.]

The preclusive effect of a judgment is defined by claim preclusion. . . . Under the doctrine of claim preclusion, a final judgment forecloses "successive litigation of the very same claim, whether or not relitigation of the claim raises the same issues as the earlier suit . . . . By "preclud[ing] parties from contesting matters that they have had a full and fair opportunity to litigate," [this doctrine] protect[s] against "the expense and vexation attending multiple lawsuits, conserv[e] judicial resources, and foste[r] reliance on judicial action by minimizing the possibility of inconsistent decisions."

A person who was not a party to a suit generally has not had a "full and fair opportunity to litigate" the claims and issues settled in that suit. The application of claim preclusion to nonparties thus runs up against the "deep-rooted historic tradition that everyone should have his own day in court." Indicating the strength of that tradition, we have often repeated the general rule that "one is not bound by a judgment *in personam* in a litigation in which he is not designated as a party or to which he has not been made a party by service of process."

B

Though hardly in doubt, the rule against nonparty preclusion is subject to exceptions. For present purposes, the recognized exceptions can be grouped into six categories.

First, "[a] person who agrees to be bound by the determination of issues in an action between others is bound in accordance with the terms of his agreement." For example, "if separate actions involving the same transaction are brought by different plaintiffs against the same defendant, all the parties to all the actions may agree that the question of the defendant's liability will be definitely determined, one way or the other, in a 'test case.'" D. Shapiro, Civil Procedure: Preclusion in Civil Actions 77–78 (2001) (hereinafter Shapiro). See also *California v. Texas,* 459 U.S. 1096, 1097, 103 S.Ct. 714, 74 L.Ed.2d 944 (1983) (dismissing certain defendants from a suit based on a stipulation "that each of said defendants . . . will be bound by a final judgment of this Court" on a specified issue).

Second, nonparty preclusion may be justified based on a variety of pre-existing "substantive legal relationship[s]" between the person to be bound and a party to the judgment. Qualifying relationships include, but are not limited to, preceding and succeeding owners of property, bailee and bailor, and assignee and assignor. These exceptions originated "as much from the needs of property law as from the values of preclusion by judgment."

Third, we have confirmed that, "in certain limited circumstances," a nonparty may be bound by a judgment because she was "adequately represented by someone with the same interests who [wa]s a party" to the suit. Representative suits with preclusive effect on nonparties include properly conducted class actions and suits brought by trustees, guardians, and other fiduciaries.

Fourth, a nonparty is bound by a judgment if she "assume[d] control" over the litigation in which that judgment was rendered. Because such a person has had "the opportunity to present proofs and argument," he has already "had his day in court" even though he was not a formal party to the litigation.

Fifth, a party bound by a judgment may not avoid its preclusive force by relitigating through a proxy. Preclusion is thus in order when a person who did not participate in a litigation later brings suit as the designated representative of a person who was a party to the prior adjudication. And although our decisions have not addressed the issue directly, it also seems clear that preclusion is appropriate when a nonparty later brings suit as an agent for a party who is bound by a judgment.

Sixth, in certain circumstances a special statutory scheme may "expressly foreclos[e] successive litigation by nonlitigants . . . if the scheme is otherwise consistent with due process." Examples of such schemes include bankruptcy and probate proceedings, and *quo warranto* actions or other suits that, "under [the governing] law, [may] be brought only on behalf of the public at large."

* * *

For the foregoing reasons, we disapprove [of broadly expanding the concept of privity to include less well defined relationships] . . . . The preclusive effects of a judgment in a federal-question case decided by a federal court should instead be determined according to the [six] established grounds for nonparty preclusion described in this opinion.

DIRECTED READING QUESTIONS

23. Diagram the initial action and the subsequent action in *Taylor*, indicating the parties in both actions.

24. What is the meaning of the term mutuality? Hint: Compare the *res judicata* effect of the judgment in *Manego I* on the Bank and Willard, on the one hand, and the Board of Trade on the other, in *Manego II*.

25. How does the existence of privity impact the doctrine of mutuality?

26. List and describe the six relationships which qualify as privity in *Taylor*.

IV. ISSUE PRECLUSION OR *COLLATERAL ESTOPPEL*

A. INTRODUCTORY HYPOTHETICAL

Batman sued Robin for negligence in federal court. Robin moved for dismissal via Rule 12(b)(6). The court found that Batman failed to artfully plead negligence and dismissed the complaint. Batman failed to amend the complaint within the allotted time, and the dismissal became a final judgment on the merits. Batman sued Robin again in federal court on the same negligence claim. What result if Robin raises the defense of *res judicata*? If Robin fails to raise the defense of *res judicata*, will the doctrine apply? Carefully review the elements of issue preclusion/collateral estoppel in the table at the beginning of this section and determine whether Robin may use this doctrine to successfully assert that the initial action conclusively establishes Robin owed Batman no duty.

B. DETERMINING WHETHER THE ISSUES ATTEMPTING TO BE ESTOPPED IN THE SUBSEQUENT ACTION WERE ACTUALLY LITIGATED AND DECIDED IN THE INITIAL ACTION

LITTLE V. BLUE GOOSE MOTOR COACH CO. (1931)
Supreme Court of Illinois
178 N.E. 496

[Robert Little collided with a bus owned by the Blue Goose Coach company. The collision happened in the state of Illinois, which was a contributory negligence jurisdiction at the time of the collision. As a result of that collision, Blue Goose sued Little in small claims court alleging, that as a result of Little's negligent driving one of Blue Goose's coaches was damaged.

The small claims court eventually entered judgment for $139.35 in favor of the plaintiff Blue Goose.]

During the pendency of the case before the [small claims court], Dr. Little filed a suit in the city court of East St. Louis to recover damages for personal injuries alleged to have been suffered by him in the collision. Some months later a trial was had. After the jury had retired to consider its ver[d]ict, but before its verdict was returned, Dr. Little died. His death was suggested on the record, and the jury was discharged. Plaintiff [Little's widow] was by leave of court substituted as plaintiff, and filed the declaration here under consideration. Defendant [ ] filed a special plea to this declaration, setting out the judgment in the [small claims] court against Dr. Little, alleging that the issue there tried was as to his negligence and that of the driver of the bus, and that that issue was by the judgment of the [small claims] court settled and could not be raised in the present suit [because Illinois is a contributory negligence jurisdiction]. A demurrer to that plea was sustained, and a judgment was procured on the trial of the case. On appeal to the Appellate Court for the Fourth district that judgment was reversed and the cause was remanded, with directions to overrule the demurrer to the special plea. On reinstatement of the cause in the city court, the demurrer was overruled accordingly, and plaintiff [ ] joined issue on the plea of estoppel by verdict. Another trial was had, in which defendant [ ] offered in evidence the docket of the [small claims court] in the case against Dr. Little, together with a transcript of the judgment, and the files in the appeal to the county court. Defendant [ ] also sought to show by the [small claims court], before whom the judgment was rendered, what issues were before him. On objection of plaintiff [ ] that the transcript of the evidence taken before the [small claims court] was the best evidence, defendant [ ] called the reporter who took the evidence. He testified that he took the evidence in shorthand and transcribed to same and turned the transcript over to counsel for plaintiff [ ]. One of counsel for plaintiff [ ] was then called to the stand and testified that his firm had the transcript of the evidence, that it was their private property, and that they would not produce it. The [small claims court judge] was then recalled, and was permitted to testify that he presided at the trial between defendant [ ] and Robert M. Little; that the issue was for damages on account of an automobile collision in the city of East St. Louis; and that four or five witnesses testified in the case. Defendant [ ] also showed the entries on the docket of the [small claims court], showing a summons against Robert M. Little, on complaint of the Blue Goose Motor Coach Company, for failure to pay it a certain demand for damages in an automobile collision. This docket also shows summons returned, personally served; that a trial was had and issues submitted to the [small claims court]; that the cause was taken under advisement; and that later the [small claims court] found the issues for defendant[ ]; and that Dr. Little was indebted to defendant [ ] in the sum of $139.35 for damages, and judgment was entered thereon. There was also received in evidence an affidavit filed in the county court by counsel for Dr. Little, who is of counsel for plaintiff [ ]. This affidavit, made in support of a motion to set aside the order of the county court dismissing Dr. Little's appeal, stated: 'Said defendant has a good defense to this suit for the reason that plaintiff's claim is for damages to the bus caused by and through the negligence of the plaintiff's servants.' No evidence was offered on the part of plaintiff [ ] touching the issues formed on the special plea. On appeal from this judgment to the Appellate Court, that court reversed the same with the following finding of fact: 'The court finds that appellant sued Dr. Robert M. Little, appellee's testate, [in small claims court] for damages to its bus in the collision which occurred on November 1, 1925, and recovered a judgment therefor in the sum of $139.35; that in the rendition of said judgment it was necessarily determined that the collision and damages occasioned to the bus was due to the negligence of Dr. Little, and that immediately prior to his death he could not have maintained an action for personal injuries growing out of the same collision.'

The first question arises on the ruling of the Appellate Court invoking against the claim of plaintiff [ ] the doctrine of estopped by verdict. It is argued on behalf of plaintiff [ ] that, where a former adjudication is relied on as a bar to a subsequent action, it is essential that there be identity both of the subject-matter and of the parties, and that, in the instant case, the subject-matter is not the same, as this is the action for death by wrongful act for the benefit of the widow and next of kin, while the former suit was a claim for damages for injury to personal property. The issue on which this case is bottomed was the issue of fact which lay at the base of the judgment recovered before the [small claims court]. The allegation of the special plea is that the issue there raised was one of negligence on the part of Dr. Little on one hand and the defendant [ ] on the other, and that issue having been determined against Dr. Little, the fact is forever settled between these parties or their privies. Estoppel by verdict arises when a material fact in any litigation has been determined in a former suit between the same parties or between parties with whom the parties to the subsequent suit are in privity, where the fact was also material to the issue. The Appellate Court found as a matter of fact that the issue tried before the [small claims court] was an issue of negligence and was the same issue, arising on the same facts as those relied upon in the action for the wrongful death of Dr. Little, and that the issue of negligence was necessarily determined in the suit by the defendant [ ] against Dr. Little. That question of fact was tried before the city court in this case, and on the evidence there adduced the Appellate Court made its finding of fact. That issue of fact therefore is not open here, and we are to proceed to further consideration of the cause under the established fact that the issue of negligence, at least under the first count of the declaration, is the same issue tried before the [small claims court].

While on appeal to the county court the trial, and there been one, would have been de novo; yet, when the appeal was dismissed and a procedendo was issued to the [small claims court], the judgment of the [small claims court] became a final determination of that issue between the parties, and is conclusive not only upon the immediate parties to that suit, but also upon all persons in privity with them, and cannot be litigated again between the parties to that case or their privies in any subsequent action in the same or other court where that question arises, whether upon the same or a different cause of action or whatever may have been the nature or purpose of the action in which the judgment was rendered or of that in which the estoppel is set up. It follows that Dr. Little could not during his lifetime maintain the action filed by him against the defendant [ ], and since plaintiff[ ]'s right to recover damages under the Injuries Act depends upon Dr. Little's right, during his lifetime, to recover damages for injuries arising out of the same collision, plaintiff [ ] cannot recover here. In a suit under the Injuries Act the cause of action is the wrongful act and not merely the death itself. Plaintiff [ ] therefore was not entitled to recover under the first count of her declaration, and the Appellate Court did not err in so holding.

It is contended, however, that as the second count of the declaration charges wanton and willful negligence on the part of defendant [ ], contributory negligence on the part of Dr. Little is not a defense, and that the judgment of the city court was therefore right. Contributory negligence is not a defense to willful and wanton conduct, but it does not follow that the judgment of the city court was right because of that fact. In all cases charging willful and wanton negligence, it is necessary to make proof of such negligence, and, where there is no such proof, no recovery under such charge can be had. The finding of the Appellate Court that the collision was caused by the negligence of Dr. Little necessarily was a finding of fact on the willful negligence count as well as the general negligence count. Thus the rule that contributory negligence on the part of the plaintiff is not a defense to a charge of willful negligence does not apply. Whether Dr. Little or the bus driver was responsible for the accident was, as we have seen, settled. The judgment for $139.35 necessarily decided that the bus driver was not guilty of willful negligence.

Plaintiff [ ]'s counsel refer to contentions made by them in the Appellate Court of which no notice was taken in the opinion of that court. This court reviews that judgment of the Appellate Court, and reasons given or not given by that court in its opinion do not prevent the affirmance of its judgment if right.

From what we have said, it is clear that the Appellate Court was right in reversing the judgment without remanding it, and its judgment will be affirmed.

Judgment affirmed.

DIRECTED READING QUESTIONS

27. Before considering the issue preclusion/collateral estoppel questions, it is important to consider why claim preclusion or *res judicata* does not apply to bar the subsequent suit. In that regard answer the following questions:

    a. *Res judicata* requires an identity of parties in the initial action and the subsequent action. Can you explain how the doctrine of privity precludes the application of *res judicata*, even though the widow [plaintiff in the subsequent action] was not a party to the initial action?

    b. If privity prevents the application of *res judicata* despite the fact that the parties in the initial and subsequent actions are not identical or mutual, what ultimately precludes the application of *res judicata* to the subsequent suit?

28. What two arguments are made against the application of issue preclusion in the second suit, and how does the court respond to each argument?

29. Should issue preclusion apply to bar the subsequent action in the following scenario? Alpha, a contractor, sues Beta, an architect, alleging that a state statute requires contractors to be paid a percentage of the architectural design fees for building projects they work on together. As part of the trial, the court determines that the statute does not require architects to pay contractors in the manner alleged by Alpha. Because the issue is resolved, Alpha and Beta subsequently proceed to profitably and cordially work on a number of successful building projects together. The statute is then amended, and Alpha believes that the amended statute entitles him to a percentage of the architectural fees from projects they work on together. Alpha sues Beta alleging that he is entitled to a percentage of the architectural fees earned by Beta on all projects they worked on together since the amended statute became effective.

C. EVEN IF THE ISSUE WAS ACTUALLY LITIGATED AND DETERMINED IN THE INITIAL ACTION, THE ADJUDICATION OF THAT ISSUE MUST HAVE BEEN ESSENTIAL TO THE JUDGMENT IN THE FIRST ACTION FOR ISSUE PRECLUSION TO APPLY IN THE SECOND ACTION

HALPERN V. SCHWARTZ (1931)
United States Court of Appeals, Second Circuit
426 F.2d. 102

[The Initial Action

Creditors bring an action in federal court seeking to have Evelyn Halpern declared involuntarily bankrupt. In order for a person to be declared involuntarily bankrupt they have to have committed an "act of bankruptcy." In support of the declaration of involuntary bankruptcy, the creditors argued that when Halpern transferred a bond and mortgage to her son, she committed three acts of bankruptcy, either of which standing alone, was sufficient for a finding of involuntary bankruptcy.

The trial court agreed holding that "the transfer of the bond was an act of bankruptcy on three statutory grounds:"

1.   it was a removal of property with intent to hinder and delay creditors;

2.   it was a transfer of property fraudulent as to creditors; and

3.   it was a preferential transfer of property.

The court declared Evelyn bankrupt as a result, and a bankruptcy trustee was appointed to ensure the fair distribution of her assets among her creditors. The appellate court affirmed the trial court without opinion.

The Subsequent Action

In a subsequent action, brought by Evelyn against the trustee, she sought to be discharged from bankruptcy.]

Section 14c(4) of the Act, 11 U.S.C. § 32(c)(4) provides that:

'The court shall grant the discharge unless satisfied that the bankrupt has [ ] transferred, removed, destroyed, or concealed * * * any of his property, with intent to hinder, delay, or defraud his creditors.

* * *

The trustee then moved, pursuant to Rule 56 of the Federal Rules of Civil Procedure, for summary judgment denying Evelyn a discharge on the ground there was no defense to specification number 3 because the issue had been concluded in the bankruptcy adjudication and was now [precluded from relitigation]. Evelyn made a cross-motion for summary judgment dismissing specification number 3 and granting her a discharge. Referee Rudin, in a considered opinion of June 11, 1968, granted summary judgment for the trustee denying a discharge to Evelyn, and denied her cross-motion for summary judgment.

In order to deny discharge to a bankrupt under section 14c(4) of the Act, 11 U.S.C. § 32(c)(4), the court must find that the transfer or removal of property in question was effected with actual intent to hinder, delay, or defraud creditors. Therefore, one prerequisite to sustaining the summary denial of Evelyn's discharge on the ground of collateral estoppel is that in the prior adjudication of bankruptcy Judge Rosling found actual intent to hinder, delay or defraud creditors.

Only one of Judge Rosling's three legal bases for finding an act of bankruptcy necessarily involved a finding of actual intent. Thus, his finding that the assignment was a preferential transfer under section 3a(2) of the Act as defined in section 60, required no inquiry into the bankrupt's intent since the effect of the transfer is the sole criterion of whether it is preferential. Nor did his finding that the assignment was a transfer of property 'fraudulent within the intent of § 3a(1) under the provisions of § 67' of the Act, 11 U.S.C. §§ 21(a)(1), 107, entail a finding of any actual fraudulent intent.

* * *

Therefore only one of Judge Rosling's three grounds for adjudication necessarily entailed a finding of actual intent, namely his conclusion that the assignment was 'a removal of a part of the property of the said assignors with intent to hinder and delay the creditors of the said bankrupt' within the meaning of section 3a(1) of the Act, 11 U.S.C. § 21(a)(1).

It was with great care that the court below affirmed the denial of a discharge to Evelyn on the ground that this one finding by Judge Rosling concluded the issue of actual intent alleged in the specification of objection number 3 under section 14c(4), 11 U.S.C. § 32(c)(4).

This case presents a unique issue in the law of collateral estoppel which has not been analyzed exhaustively by any court. When the prior judgment rested on several (here three) independent, alternative grounds, is that judgment conclusive as to the facts which were necessarily found in order to establish only one separate ground? We conclude that on the facts before us it is not.

It is well established that although an issue was fully litigated and a finding on the issue was made in the prior litigation, the prior judgment will not foreclose reconsideration of the same issue if that issue was not necessary to the rendering of the prior judgment, and hence was incidental, collateral, or immaterial to that judgment.

The reason for this rule is twofold. First, the decision on an issue not essential to the prior judgment may not have been afforded the careful deliberation and analysis normally applied to essential issues, since a different disposition of the inessential issue would not affect the judgment. Second, the decision on an inessential issue in the prior judgment was not subject to the important safeguard as to its correctness, to wit: a contested review on appeal. An appeal from the prior judgment by the losing litigant, asserting error in the determination of an issue not central to the judgment, probably would be deemed frivolous by the appellate court, which would affirm without considering the merits of the claim of alleged error.

* * *

The same two considerations are present in the case (as here) of the conclusiveness of a prior judgment which is based on more than one alternative, independent ground. First, if the court in the prior case were sure as to one of the alternative grounds and this ground by itself was sufficient to support the judgment, then it may not feel as constrained to give rigorous consideration to the alternative grounds. In the present case, a finding of a transfer while insolvent was sufficient without inquiry into Evelyn's intent [ ] to establish the act of bankruptcy which supported the adjudication. Also, the finding that the transfer had the effect of preferring creditors, was sufficient [ ] to establish the act of bankruptcy. Therefore Judge Rosling may have made the determination as to Evelyn's intent in connection with the alternative ground of removal of property with confidence that nothing turned on the decision.

Second, since there are alternative grounds which could independently support the prior judgment, vigorous review of an asserted error as to one ground probably would not occur. The losing litigant would have little motivation to appeal from an alleged erroneous finding in connection with one of several independent alternative grounds, since even if his claim of error were sustained, the judgment would be affirmed on one of the other grounds.

* * *

It would be unwise to require a losing litigant in bankruptcy to take an appeal from alleged errors in one alternative ground simply to ward off the conclusive effect of collateral estoppel on a later discharge proceeding, when on appeal the court could affirm on one of the other alternative grounds.

* * *

Second, the winning litigant would not vigorously oppose the merits of the appeal as to one ground since he would simply stress the existence of alternative grounds on which to affirm. So, if the appellate court were to consider the merits of the claim of error, it might not have the benefit of adversary argument on the merits.

* * *

We therefore hold that when a prior judgment [ ] rests on two or more independent alternative grounds, it is not conclusive as to issues in trial of objections to discharge which issues were necessarily found in order to establish only one of those grounds.

* * *

Since Judge Rosling's finding of Evelyn's actual intent to hinder and delay her creditors was necessarily found in connection with only one of the three independent grounds establishing an act of bankruptcy, this finding cannot be given conclusive effect in the present litigation as to her application for a discharge. Since we hold that Judge Rosling's finding is not conclusive as to Evelyn's actual intent, we need not consider Evelyn's other contentions that the trustee, Schwartz, lacks privity with the petitioning creditor, Chase, in the involuntary adjudication, and that the trustee should be barred by his allegedly inconsistent statements from asserting collateral estoppel against her.

Reversed and remanded . . . .

DIRECTED READING QUESTIONS

30. Why was summary judgment granted in the second action?

31. Why did the court of appeals reverse the grant of summary judgment in the second trial?

32. What is the precise holding of this case?

33. What is the rationale for the holding of this case?

34. Hypothetical: Alpha sues Beta in a contributory negligence jurisdiction for personal injuries allegedly caused by Beta's negligence. Beta pleads contributory negligence as a defense. After a full trial, the jury renders a general verdict for Beta. In a subsequent suit by Alpha against Beta, is the issue of Alpha's or Beta's negligence collaterally estopped? Is your answer any different if the jury found for Alpha?

D. NON-MUTUAL COLLATERAL ESTOPPEL

RECAP OF MUTUALITY

Mutuality is the requirement that the only people who can be bound by the initial judgment are the persons who were parties in the previous suit or in privity with one of the parties in the previous suit.

For example, if landlord Alpha sues tenant Beta for unpaid rents and the court determines in the suit that the lease that is the basis of Alpha's attempt to collect rent is unenforceable, then the mutuality requirement of the doctrine should result in the following:

I.   In a subsequent suit by Alpha v. another tenant Charlie to collect rent, Charlie should not be able to use collateral estoppel to establish the unenforceability of the lease; or

II.   In a subsequent suit by another tenant, Delta v. Alpha for a refund of rents paid to Alpha, Delta should not be able to establish the unenforceability of the lease by arguing that Alpha is collaterally estopped by the previous determination on the issue of unenforceability in the initial action.

Mutuality is ALWAYS required for claim preclusion but in some cases the requirement is waived for issue preclusion.

DIRECTED READING QUESTIONS

35. What do you think the justifications for the mutuality requirement are?

36. In the action Alpha v. Charlie above, if Charlie were allowed to preclude Alpha from relitigating the issue of the enforceability of the lease because that issue was determined in the initial action (Alpha v. Beta), would Charlie be using issue preclusion offensively (sword) or defensively (shield)?

37. In the action Delta v. Alpha above, if Delta were allowed to preclude Alpha from relitigating the issue of the enforceability of the lease because that issue was determined in the initial action (Alpha v. Beta), would Delta be using issue preclusion offensively (sword) or defensively (shield)?

BERNHARD V. BANK OF AMERICA (1942)

California Supreme Court
122 P.2d 892

[In the initial action a beneficiary of an estate sued the estate's executor alleging that the executor's removal of money from the deceased person's bank account estate was conversion. The executor claimed that the funds were a gift from the deceased and so there was no conversion. The Court agreed that the funds were a gift and as a result found that there was no conversion.

In the subsequent action the beneficiary sued the bank where the deceased account was located arguing the bank breached a duty by allowing the executor to withdraw the money because the executor had no right to the money.

The court ruled for the bank in the subsequent action because the issue of ownership of the money/whether the executor had a right to the money was litigated and determined in the initial action. In other words the beneficiary was precluded or estopped from relitigating the issue.]

DIRECTED READING QUESTIONS

38. *Bernhard* was one of the first cases to permit non-mutual collateral estoppel. Why is this considered non-mutual?

39. What do you think was the justification for allowing non-mutual collateral estoppel in *Bernhard*?

40. The United States Supreme Court also allowed non-mutual collateral estoppel in *Blonder Tongue Labs., Inc. v. University of Ill. Foundation*, 402 U.S. 313 (1971). In that case, University of Illinois sued a defendant for allegedly infringing on a patent and lost the suit on the ground that the patent was invalid. After the judgment, the university sued another defendant for infringement of the same patent. The second defendant was able to use collateral estoppel to prevent relitigation of the issue of the patent's validity, and the university lost. This case overruled a 1936 Supreme Court opinion which held that mutuality was always required for issue preclusion to apply. The Court held that mutuality was not required if the plaintiff in the first action had a full and fair opportunity to litigate the issue in question.

    a. Why is this non-mutual collateral estoppel?

    b. Explain why *Bernhard* and *Blonder* are examples of defensive non-mutual collateral estoppel.

    c. Are courts more comfortable with defensive or offensive non-mutual collateral estoppel? Consider the *Parklane Hosiery* case in this regard.

PARKLANE HOSIERY CO., INC. V. SHORE (1979)
Supreme Court of the United States
439 U.S. 322

MR. JUSTICE STEWART delivered the opinion of the Court.

This case presents the question whether a party who has had issues of fact adjudicated adversely to it in an equitable action may be collaterally estopped from relitigating the same issues before a jury in a subsequent legal action brought against it by a new party.

The respondent brought this stockholder's class action against the petitioners in a Federal District Court. The complaint alleged that the petitioners, Parklane Hosiery Co., Inc. (Parklane), and 13 of its officers, directors, and stockholders, had issued a materially false and misleading proxy statement in connection with a merger. The proxy statement, according to the complaint, had violated §§ 14(a), 10(b), and 20(a) of the Securities Exchange Act of 1934, 48 Stat. 895, 891, 899, as amended, 15 U.S.C. §§ 78n(a), 78j(b), and 78t(a), as well as various rules and regulations promulgated by the Securities and Exchange Commission (SEC). The complaint sought damages, rescission of the merger, and recovery of costs.

Before this action came to trial, the SEC filed suit against the same defendants in the Federal District Court, alleging that the proxy statement that had been issued by Parklane was materially false and misleading in essentially the same respects as those that had been alleged in the respondent's complaint. Injunctive relief was requested. After a 4-day trial, the District Court found that the proxy statement was materially false and misleading in the respects alleged, and entered a declaratory judgment to that effect. The Court of Appeals for the Second Circuit affirmed this judgment.

The respondent in the present case then moved for partial summary judgment against the petitioners, asserting that the petitioners were collaterally estopped from relitigating the issues that had been resolved against them in the action brought by the SEC.[2] The District Court denied the motion on the ground that such an application of collateral estoppel would deny the petitioners their Seventh Amendment right to a jury trial. The Court of Appeals for the Second Circuit reversed, holding that a party who has had issues of fact determined against him after a full and fair opportunity to litigate in a nonjury trial is collaterally estopped from obtaining a subsequent jury trial of these same issues of fact. The appellate court concluded that "the Seventh Amendment preserves the right to jury trial only with respect to issues of fact, [and] once those issues have been fully and fairly adjudicated in a prior proceeding, nothing remains for trial, either with or without a jury." Because of an inter-circuit conflict, we granted certiorari.

I

The threshold question to be considered is whether, quite apart from the right to a jury trial under the Seventh Amendment, the petitioners can be precluded from relitigating facts resolved adversely to them in a prior equitable proceeding with another party under the general law of collateral estoppel. Specifically, we must determine whether a litigant who was not a party to a prior judgment may nevertheless use that judgment "offensively" to prevent a defendant from relitigating issues resolved in the earlier proceeding.[4]

A

Collateral estoppel, like the related doctrine of res judicata, has the dual purpose of protecting litigants from the burden of relitigating an identical issue with the same party or his privy and of promoting judicial economy by preventing needless litigation. Until relatively recently, however, the scope of collateral estoppel was limited by the doctrine of mutuality of parties. Under this mutuality doctrine, neither party could use a prior judgment as an estoppel against the other unless both parties were bound by the judgment. Based on the premise that it is somehow unfair to allow a party to use a prior

---

[2] A private plaintiff in an action under the proxy rules is not entitled to relief simply by demonstrating that the proxy solicitation was materially false and misleading. The plaintiff must also show that he was injured and prove damages. Since the SEC action was limited to a determination of whether the proxy statement contained materially false and misleading information, the respondent conceded that he would still have to prove these other elements of his prima facie case in the private action. The petitioners' right to a jury trial on those remaining issues is not contested.

[4] In this context, offensive use of collateral estoppel occurs when the plaintiff seeks to foreclose the defendant from litigating an issue the defendant has previously litigated unsuccessfully in an action with another party. Defensive use occurs when a defendant seeks to prevent a plaintiff from asserting a claim the plaintiff has previously litigated and lost against another defendant.

judgment when he himself would not be so bound,[7] the mutuality requirement provided a party who had litigated and lost in a previous action an opportunity to relitigate identical issues with new parties.

By failing to recognize the obvious difference in position between a party who has never litigated an issue and one who has fully litigated and lost, the mutuality requirement was criticized almost from its inception. Recognizing the validity of this criticism, the Court in *Blonder-Tongue Laboratories, Inc. v. University of Illinois Foundation* abandoned the mutuality requirement, at least in cases where a patentee seeks to relitigate the validity of a patent after a federal court in a previous lawsuit has already declared it invalid. The "broader question" before the Court, however, was "whether it is any longer tenable to afford a litigant more than one full and fair opportunity for judicial resolution of the same issue." The Court strongly suggested a negative answer to that question:

"In any lawsuit where a defendant, because of the mutuality principle, is forced to present a complete defense on the merits to a claim which the plaintiff has fully litigated and lost in a prior action, there is an arguable misallocation of resources. To the extent the defendant in the second suit may not win by asserting, without contradiction, that the plaintiff had fully and fairly, but unsuccessfully, litigated the same claim in the prior suit, the defendant's time and money are diverted from alternative uses—productive or otherwise—to relitigation of a decided issue. And, still assuming that the issue was resolved correctly in the first suit, there is reason to be concerned about the plaintiff's allocation of resources. Permitting repeated litigation of the same issue as long as the supply of unrelated defendants holds out reflects either the aura of the gaming table or 'a lack of discipline and of disinterestedness on the part of the lower courts, hardly a worthy or wise basis for fashioning rules of procedure.' Although neither judges, the parties, nor the adversary system performs perfectly in all cases, the requirement of determining whether the party against whom an estoppel is asserted had a full and fair opportunity to litigate is a most significant safeguard."

B

The *Blonder-Tongue* case involved defensive use of collateral estoppel—a plaintiff was estopped from asserting a claim that the plaintiff had previously litigated and lost against another defendant. The present case, by contrast, involves offensive use of collateral estoppel—a plaintiff is seeking to estop a defendant from relitigating the issues which the defendant previously litigated and lost against another plaintiff. In both the offensive and defensive use situations, the party against whom estoppel is asserted has litigated and lost in an earlier action. Nevertheless, several reasons have been advanced why the two situations should be treated differently.

First, offensive use of collateral estoppel does not promote judicial economy in the same manner as defensive use does. Defensive use of collateral estoppel precludes a plaintiff from relitigating identical issues by merely "switching adversaries." Thus defensive collateral estoppel gives a plaintiff a strong incentive to join all potential defendants in the first action if possible. Offensive use of collateral estoppel, on the other hand, creates precisely the opposite incentive. Since a [potential] plaintiff [in a

---

[7]   It is a violation of due process for a judgment to be binding on a litigant who was not a party or a privy and therefore has never had an opportunity to be heard.

subsequent suit] will be able to rely on a previous judgment against a defendant but will not be bound by that judgment if the defendant wins, the plaintiff has every incentive to adopt a "wait and see" attitude, in the hope that the first action by another plaintiff will result in a favorable judgment. Thus offensive use of collateral estoppel will likely increase rather than decrease the total amount of litigation, since potential plaintiffs will have everything to gain and nothing to lose by not intervening in the first action.[13]

A second argument against offensive use of collateral estoppel is that it may be unfair to a defendant. If a defendant in the first action is sued for small or nominal damages, he may have little incentive to defend vigorously, particularly if future suits are not foreseeable. [For example courts have denied the application of offensive collateral estoppel where defendant did not appeal an adverse judgment awarding damages of $35,000 and defendant was later sued for over $7 million.] Allowing offensive collateral estoppel may also be unfair to a defendant if the judgment relied upon as a basis for the estoppel is itself inconsistent with one or more previous judgments in favor of the defendant.[14] Still another situation where it might be unfair to apply offensive estoppel is where the second action affords the defendant procedural opportunities unavailable in the first action that could readily cause a different result.[15]

C

We have concluded that the preferable approach for dealing with these problems in the federal courts is not to preclude the use of offensive collateral estoppel, but to grant trial courts broad discretion to determine when it should be applied. The general rule should be that in cases where a plaintiff could easily have joined in the earlier action or where, either for the reasons discussed above or for other reasons, the application of offensive estoppel would be unfair to a defendant, a trial judge should not allow the use of offensive collateral estoppel.

In the present case, however, none of the circumstances that might justify reluctance to allow the offensive use of collateral estoppel is present. The application of offensive collateral estoppel will not here reward a private plaintiff who could have joined in the previous action, since the respondent probably could not have joined in the injunctive action brought by the SEC even had he so desired. Similarly, there is no unfairness to the petitioners in applying offensive collateral estoppel in this case. First, in light of the serious allegations made in the SEC's complaint against the petitioners, as well as the foreseeability of subsequent private suits that typically follow a successful Government judgment, the petitioners had every incentive to litigate the SEC lawsuit fully and

---

[13] The Restatement (Second) of Judgments § 88(3) (Tent. Draft No. 2, Apr. 15, 1975) provides that application of collateral estoppel may be denied if the party asserting it "could have effected joinder in the first action between himself and his present adversary.

[14] In Professor Currie's familiar example, a railroad collision injures 50 passengers all of whom bring separate actions against the railroad. After the railroad wins the first 25 suits, a plaintiff wins in suit 26. Professor Currie argues that offensive use of collateral estoppel should not be applied so as to allow plaintiffs 27 through 50 automatically to recover. Currie, *supra*, 9 Stan.L.Rev., at 304. See Restatement (Second) of Judgments § 88(4), *supra*.

[15] If, for example, the defendant in the first action was forced to defend in an inconvenient forum and therefore was unable to engage in full scale discovery or call witnesses, application of offensive collateral estoppel may be unwarranted. Indeed, differences in available procedures may sometimes justify not allowing a prior judgment to have estoppel effect in a subsequent action even between the same parties, or where defensive estoppel is asserted against a plaintiff who has litigated and lost. The problem of unfairness is particularly acute in cases of offensive estoppel, however, because the defendant against whom estoppel is asserted typically will not have chosen the forum in the first action. See *id.*, § 88(2) and Comment *d.*

vigorously. Second, the judgment in the SEC action was not inconsistent with any previous decision. Finally, there will in the respondent's action be no procedural opportunities available to the petitioners that were unavailable in the first action of a kind that might be likely to cause a different result.[19]

We conclude, therefore, that none of the considerations that would justify a refusal to allow the use of offensive collateral estoppel is present in this case. Since the petitioners received a "full and fair" opportunity to litigate their claims in the SEC action, the contemporary law of collateral estoppel leads inescapably to the conclusion that the petitioners are collaterally estopped from relitigating the question of whether the proxy statement was materially false and misleading.

DIRECTED READING QUESTIONS

41. Carefully map out the actions discussed in the *Parklane* case in the order they were filed and decided and then identify which of the actions is the "initial" action and which is the "subsequent" action for preclusion purposes.

42. Why is *Parklane* considered an example of offensive rather than defensive non-mutual collateral estoppel?

43. List the four elements the *Parklane* court says are necessary for non-mutual offensive collateral estoppel.

44. *Parklane* suggests that offensive non-mutual collateral estoppel should be less readily available than defensive non-mutual collateral estoppel. Explain the Court's reasoning in this regard.

45. How are the four elements for the application of offensive non-mutual collateral estoppel met in *Parklane*?

46. Hypothetical: Hulk was crossing the street without looking and Batman collided with him while he was driving the Batmobile. The Batmobile suffered minor damage and Batman successfully sued Hulk in negligence to recover damage to the car. Assume Robin, who was a passenger in the Batmobile, was also severely injured and that Hulk's negligence was actually litigated and determined in the first action *Batman v. Hulk*. However, the damage to Batman's car was only minor and worth only $100. According to *Parklane*, may Robin use offensive non-mutual collateral estoppel to prevent Hulk from relitigating the issue of his negligence?

---

[19] It is true, of course, that the petitioners in the present action would be entitled to a jury trial of the issues bearing on whether the proxy statement was materially false and misleading had the SEC action never been brought—a matter to be discussed in Part II of this opinion. But the presence or absence of a jury as factfinder is basically neutral, quite unlike, for example, the necessity of defending the first lawsuit in an inconvenient forum.

CHAPTER 20

RIGHT TO JURY TRIAL

■ ■ ■

DIRECTED READING QUESTIONS

1. What is the text of the Seventh Amendment relative to this topic?

2. And if the Seventh Amendment was not clear enough, is there a Federal Rule of Civil Procedure that reiterates the importance of a jury trial in federal court?

3. If the right to jury trial is so clear, then why do we have all this confusion about whether litigants are entitled to a jury trial?

4. Can you think of anything we studied this semester that might be implicated by bringing equitable and legal claims based on the same transaction and occurrence in one action?

5. How does the Declaratory Judgment Act function? You need to understand this before reading *Beacon Theaters*. Think of this example: Patent holder is accusing seller of infringing on their patented device. Patent holder told others in the trade that unless they stopped buying the device from seller that he would sue seller and those that bought the device. May seller sue patent holder in federal court on a state law libel cause of action, assuming there is no diversity jurisdiction, if seller believes patent holder's statements are untrue?

BEACON THEATERS, INC. V. WESTOVER (1959)

Supreme Court of the United States
359 U.S. 500

MR. JUSTICE BLACK delivered the opinion of the Court.

[Beacon was allegedly accusing Fox of violating the federal antitrust laws by having contracts with movie studios that gave Fox the exclusive right to show first run films and which provided that no other theater shall be able to show those films for a specified time (clearance) after Fox showed them. Beacon allegedly threatened to sue Fox for a violation of federal antitrust law which provided treble damages for its violation.*

Fox, based on the existence of, but as yet unfiled, federal antitrust claim available to Beacon, seeks relief under the declaratory judgment act asks for:

a. A declaration that the notification and threats of suit gave rise to duress and coercion and deprived them of a valuable property right and sought

b. A declaration that Fox is not violating antitrust law

c. To *enjoin* Beacon from suing pursuant to federal antitrust law pending the outcome of this equitable suit seeking an injunction

---

* If the statute provides damages then it is clearly an action at law. Note therefore that Beacon appears to have an antitrust claim arising under the laws of the United States which is ripe and ready to go for the purposes of the Declaratory Judgment Act.

Beacon responded to the complaint with an answer containing a counterclaim alleging among other things, a claim for treble damages under the antitrust laws alleging that the exclusive right and clearance time violated antitrust law and they *demanded a jury trial on the counterclaim.*]

The District Court, however, viewed the issues raised by the 'Complaint for Declaratory Relief,' including the question of competition between the two theatres, as essentially equitable. [ ] It directed that these issues be tried to the court before jury determination of the validity of the charges of antitrust violations made in the counterclaim and cross-claim. A common issue of the 'Complaint for Declaratory Relief,' the counterclaim, and the cross-claim was the reasonableness of the clearances granted to Fox, which depended, in part, on the existence of competition between the two theatres. Thus the effect of the action of the District Court could be, as the Court of Appeals believed, 'to limit the petitioner's opportunity fully to try to a jury every issue which has a bearing upon its treble damage suit,' for determination of the issue of clearances by the judge might 'operate either by way of res judicata or collateral estoppel so as to conclude both parties with respect thereto at the subsequent trial of the treble damage claim.'

[The Appellate Court affirmed the District Court because it concluded that the existence of a defense at law should not affect the right of Fox to seek equitable relief.]

* * *

[T]he justification for equity's deciding legal issues once it obtains jurisdiction, and refusing to dismiss a case, merely because subsequently a legal remedy becomes available, must be re-evaluated in the light of the liberal joinder provisions of the Federal Rules which allow legal and equitable causes to be brought and resolved in one civil action. Similarly the need for, and therefore, the availability of such equitable remedies as Bills of Peace, Quia Timet and Injunction must be reconsidered in view of the existence of the Declaratory Judgment Act as well as the liberal joinder provision of the Rules. This is not only in accord with the spirit of the Rules and the Act but is required by the provision in the Rules that '(t)he right of trial by jury as declared by the Seventh Amendment to the Constitution or as given by a statute of the United States shall be preserved * * * inviolate.'

If there should be cases where the availability of declaratory judgment or joinder in one suit of legal and equitable causes would not in all respects protect the plaintiff seeking equitable relief from irreparable harm while affording a jury trial in the legal cause, the trial court will necessarily have to use its discretion in deciding whether the legal or equitable cause should be tried first. Since the right to jury trial is a constitutional one, however, while no similar requirement protects trials by the court, that discretion is very narrowly limited and must, wherever possible, be exercised to preserve jury trial . . . . 'In the Federal courts this (jury) right cannot be dispensed with, except by the assent of the parties entitled to it; nor can it be impaired by any blending with a claim, properly cognizable at law, of a demand for equitable relief in aid of the legal action, or during its pendency.' This long-standing principle of equity dictates that only under the most imperative circumstances, circumstances which in view of the flexible procedures of the Federal Rules we cannot now anticipate, can the right to a jury trial of legal issues be lost through prior determination of equitable claims. As we have shown, this is far from being such a case.

The judgment of the Court of Appeals is reversed.

DIRECTED READING QUESTIONS

6.   What did the Supreme Court hold and why did it so hold?

DAIRY QUEEN INC. V. WOOD (1962)
Supreme Court of the United States
369 U.S. 469

[Franchisor notifies Franchisee that franchisee is in breach of contract for failing to pay agreed upon money for use of franchise and demands franchisee cease and desist using the Franchisor's name etc.

Franchisee continued to use the name and Franchisor sued seeking:

a.   Injunction (equitable) to make franchisee stop using franchise and trademark

b.   An accounting (equitable) to determine the exact money owed and a judgment for that amount (legal)

c.   An injunction (equitable) to prevent the franchisee from collecting any money from franchise stores

Franchisee raises equitable defenses to these claims.]

* * *

The respondents' contention that this money claim is 'purely equitable' is based primarily upon the fact that their complaint is cast in terms of an 'accounting,' rather than in terms of an action for 'debt' or 'damages.' But the constitutional right to trial by jury cannot be made to depend upon the choice of words used in the pleadings. The necessary prerequisite to the right to maintain a suit for an equitable accounting, like all other equitable remedies, is, as we pointed out in *Beacon Theatres*, the absence of an adequate remedy at law. Consequently, in order to maintain such a suit on a cause of action cognizable at law, as this one is, the plaintiff must be able to show that the 'accounts between the parties' are of such a 'complicated nature' that only a court of equity can satisfactorily unravel them. In view of the powers given to District Courts by Federal Rule of Civil Procedure 53(b) to appoint masters to assist the jury in those exceptional cases where the legal issues are too complicated for the jury adequately to handle alone, the burden of such a showing is considerably increased and it will indeed be a rare case in which it can be met.[19] But be that as it may, this is certainly not such a case.

---

[19]   It was settled in Beacon Theatres that procedural changes which remove the inadequacy of a remedy at law may sharply diminish the scope of traditional equitable remedies by making them unnecessary in many cases. Thus, the justification for equity's deciding legal issues once it obtains jurisdiction, and refusing to dismiss a case, merely because subsequently a legal remedy becomes available, must be re-evaluated in the light of the liberal joinder provisions of the Federal Rules which allow legal and equitable causes to be brought and resolved in one civil action. Similarly the need for, and therefore, the availability of such equitable remedies as Bills of Peace, Quia Timet and

* * *

Since th[e legal] issues are common with those upon which respondents' claim to equitable relief is based, the legal claims involved in the action must be determined prior to any final court determination of respondents' equitable claims.

* * *

Reversed and remanded.

DIRECTED READING QUESTIONS

7. What is the main point of the franchisee's claim that there should be no jury trial here?

8. What does the Supreme Court hold?

9. What is the complication exception to the holding of this case that the Supreme Court hints at?

Injunction must be reconsidered in view of the existence of the Declaratory Judgment Act as well as the liberal joinder provision of the Rules.'

INDEX

References are to Pages